D0554268

Symbolic Play

THE DEVELOPMENT OF SOCIAL UNDERSTANDING

Symbolic Play

THE DEVELOPMENT
OF SOCIAL UNDERSTANDING

Edited by

INGE BRETHERTON

Department of Human Development and Family Studies
Colorado State University
Fort Collins, Colorado

1984

ACADEMIC PRESS, INC.

(*Harcourt Brace Jovanovich, Publishers*)
Orlando   San Diego   San Francisco   New York   London
Toronto   Montreal   Sydney   Tokyo   São Paulo

ACADEMIC PRESS, INC.
Orlando, Florida 32887

United Kingdom Edition published by
ACADEMIC PRESS, INC. (LONDON) LTD.
24/28 Oval Road, London NW1 7DX

Library of Congress Cataloging in Publication Data

Main entry under title:

Symbolic play.

   Includes bibliographies and index.
   1. Play. 2. Symbolism (Psychology) in children.
3. Cognition in children. 4. Social interaction in
children. I. Bretherton, Inge. [DNLM: 1. Play and
playthings. 2. Interpersonal relations--In infancy and
childhood. WS 105.5.I5 S986]
BF717.S95 1984   155.4'18   83-11958
ISBN 0-12-132680-2

PRINTED IN THE UNITED STATES OF AMERICA

84 85 86 87   9 8 7 6 5 4 3 2 1

Contents

III. Symbolic Play with Toys and Words

11. *Conceptual Organization in the Play of Preschool Children:*
Effects of Meaning, Context, and Mother–Child Interaction

MARIA KREYE

12. *Toddlers' Play, Alone and With Mother:*
The Role of Maternal Guidance

BARBARA O'CONNELL AND INGE BRETHERTON

Contributors

Numbers in parentheses indicate the pages on which the authors' contributions begin.

Jennifer Altshuler (195), Harvard School of Education, Project Zero, Cambridge, Massachusetts 02138

Elizabeth Bates (271), Department of Psychology, University of California at San Diego, La Jolla, California 92093

Inge Bretherton (1,271,337), Department of Human Development and Family Studies, Colorado State University, Fort Collins, Colorado 80523

Naomi Dale[1] (131), MRC Unit on the Development and Integration of Behaviour, Cambridge University, Madingley, Cambridge CB3 8AA, England

Judy Dunn (131), MRC Unit on the Development and Integration of Behaviour, Cambridge University, Madingley, Cambridge CB3 8AA, England

Larry Fenson (249), Department of Psychology, San Diego State University, San Diego, California 92182

Susan K. Stockinger Forys (159), Department of Psychology, Rutgers University, New Brunswick, New Jersey 08903

Catherine Garvey[2] (101), Department of Psychology, Johns Hopkins University, Baltimore, Maryland 21218

Holly Giffin (73), Department of Communication, University of Colorado, Boulder, Colorado 80309

Maria Kreye (299), Department of Psychiatry, University of Colorado Health Sciences Center, Denver, Colorado 80262

Lorraine McCune-Nicolich (159), Graduate School of Education and Department of Psychology, Rutgers University, New Brunswick, New Jersey 08903

---

[1] Present address: Kids Centre, 13 Pond Street, London NW3, England.
[2] Present address: Department of Psychology, University of Maine, Orono, Maine 04469.

Peggy Miller (101), Center for the Study of Youth Development, Catholic University, Washington, D.C. 20064

Katherine Nelson (45), Department of Psychology, City University of New York Graduate Center, New York, New York 10036

Barbara O'Connell (271, 337), Department of Psychology, University of California at San Diego, La Jolla, California 92093

Jayne Rygh (195), Harvard School of Education, Project Zero, Cambridge, Massachusetts 02138

Susan Seidman (45), Department of Psychology, City University of New York Graduate Center, New York, New York 10036

Cecilia Shore (271), Department of Psychology, Miami University, Oxford, Ohio 45056

Virginia Volterra (219), Instituto di Psicologia (CNR), Roma 00157, Italy

Dennis Palmer Wolf (195), Harvard School of Education, Project Zero, Cambridge, Massachusetts 02138

Preface

This book describes the development of symbolic play from infancy through the preschool years. Unlike much recent research in this area, it does not emphasize parallels between pretense and other representational capacities such as language. Instead, the focus is on make-believe as an activity within which young children spontaneously represent and practice their understanding of the social world. Clinicians have, of course, for many years thought of pretense as a window into the child's inner world, but they have studied it from the point of view of conflicts expressed and mastered, not from the point of view of a developing ability to represent complex role and action structures. We hope that the reader will be as amazed as we are at the tremendous skill with which young children manipulate their knowledge of the social world within the simulated reality of play.

The study of pretense from a social cognitive point of view has been facilitated by a new approach to representation, which emphasizes temporal–causal–spatial frameworks (event schemata, scripts, and stories), as opposed to disembedded symbols or taxonomic structures. The contributors to this volume have made use of these ideas in a number of ways. In addition we have drawn on Bateson's notion of metacommunication or the ability to mark off pretense from everyday reality by the message "This is play." Much symbolic play beyond the toddler years proceeds on two levels: planning outside the playframe and acting within the playframe. In play with small human and animal figures, children assume dual roles as narrators (who describe what the figures are doing) and vicarious actors (by activating and talking for the figures). In joint pretense, children play the dual roles of director (planning roles, themes, and settings) and actor. The research presented in this book shows that, in the context of familiar event schemata or scripts, social knowledge can be manipulated at several levels in complex and subtle ways.

The book has three parts. Part I is a general introduction, documenting what we know about the development of event schemata produced in symbolic play, about children's management of the playframe, and about the development of subjunctive, or "What if?" thought.

Part II (Chapters 2 through 6) concerns the development of joint pretending. Chapter 2 (by Nelson & Seidman) discusses the use of shared scripts in the organization of make-believe play, Chapter 3 (by Giffin) documents the subtleties of metacommunication, ranging from ulterior conversation seemingly within the playframe to out-of-frame messages ("Let's pretend that . . ."). In Chapters 4 through 6, early joint pretense between the child and others is considered in detail. Chapter 4 (Miller & Garvey) emphasizes the supporting role of the mother in early collaborative make-believe, comparing earlier mother–child with later child–peer play. Chapter 5 (Dunn & Dale) contrasts 2-year-olds' joint pretense with mother and with an older sibling. Chapter 6 (Forys & McCune-Nicolich) illustrates some of the strategies whereby unfamiliar 36-month-old dyads enter into make-believe, describing both solo pretense and joint role-play.

The focus of Part III is on social interaction through symbolic play with dolls, toy animals, object props, and language. Wolf, Rygh, and Altshuler's contribution (Chapter 7) examines the child's growing ability to represent the internal states of the inanimate figures whose doings he or she vicariously enacts. Volterra's study (Chapter 8) is an amazing documentary of a 2-year-old's verbal fantasies —collected serendipitously as part of a language study—during his mother's second pregnancy. Chapters 9 (Fenson) and 10 (Bretherton, O'Connell, Shore, & Bates) analyze the effect of contextual variation on toddler's symbolic play and play-related language. Both are short-term longitudinal studies. Kreye (Chapter 11) illustrates the use of the symbolic play format for facilitating various types of conceptual organization in preschoolers. Finally, O'Connell and Bretherton (Chapter 12) contrast a child's play alone and with the mother, documenting that maternal guidance can increase the diversity of play.

Overall, the two most striking findings are the remarkable complexity of social understanding and the importance of language in the conduct of pretend play, whether with replicas or with live partners. Chapters 9 and 10 independently noted a tremendous increase in the use of "pretend" language between the ages of 20 and 30 months. The complex forms of dual-level representation (narrator-vicarious actor, director–actor), which are so striking after the age of 3 years, rely heavily on communicative abilities. It is fascinating to speculate how joint pretending is managed by signing deaf children. No such studies have been conducted so far. In any event, the widespread tendency to consider language and symbolic acts as two separate and parallel aspects of symbolic play (Chapter 9 and discussion in 10) becomes detrimental in studies of symbolic play during the later preschool years. The fictive world of play is more fruitfully studied as a multimodal phenomenon with different symbol systems serving complementary, not necessarily parallel, functions.

We suggest that the approach taken in this book is useful not only to investigators who wish to learn more about the extent of a young child's understanding of the social world, but also to clinicians and educators. In the conduct of play therapy it seems important to know the upper limits of what a child can represent in terms of roles, action sequences, and object substitutions. Such knowledge could aid in the interpretation of the child's played-out conflicts. Insight into individual differences (see Chapter 7) will also be useful. The information presented here can also be helpful to educators who wish to assess and facilitate young children's make-believe play. My hope—one that I share with my collaborators—is that this book will offer some ideas and tools for diverse applications and for more research into the development of the fascinating capacity to create "what ifs."

PART I

Introduction

CHAPTER 1

Representing the
Social World
in Symbolic Play:
Reality and Fantasy

INGE BRETHERTON

INTRODUCTION: PIAGET AND EVENT REPRESENTATION

Research on symbolic play owes an enormous debt to Piaget. The delightful accounts of his own children's pretend activities, published in *Play, Dreams and Imitation in Childhood*, (1962), have inspired a host of subsequent studies. Yet his own analyses leave many striking aspects of these rich observations almost completely unexplored.

Piaget's theory of representation as interiorized action revolutionized ideas about cognition. Representation began to be seen as a dynamic process instead of a static collection of symbols. However, Piaget did not apply this kind of thinking to the study of pretend play. In addition he emphasized the incoherence of pretending in spite of observations that illustrated its structure and coherence. Further, the ability to represent "what ifs," to engage in subjunctive thought, was simply taken for granted. This ability, as Hofstadter (1979) pointed out, is one of the most intriguing aspects of human cognition. Yet Piaget viewed young children's ability to disregard reality "as it is" as a prime example of egocentric,

3

nonsocialized thought, which serves purely affective needs and demands no explanation in cognitive terms. Make-believe, he claimed, permits young children to assimilate the world to the ego without being hampered by the need for accommodation (adaptation to present reality).

> For the child assimilation of reality to the ego is a vital condition for continuity and development, precisely because of the lack of equilibrium in his thought, and symbolic play satisfies this condition both as regards signifier and signified. From the point of view of the signified, play enables the child to relive his past experiences and makes for the satisfaction of the ego rather than for its subordination to reality. From the point of view of the signifier, symbolism provides the child with the live, dynamic, individual language indispensable for the expression of his subjective feelings, for which collective language alone is inadequate [Piaget, 1962; pp. 166–167].

The figurative representation of social events, be they factual or counterfactual, was not what intrigued Piaget about interiorized action. His overriding preoccupation was with those interiorized actions that lead to logicomathematical thought. Because pretending is "assimilation of the world to the ego" and therefore not accommodated to present reality, it cannot, he claimed, play an essential part in the development of operations (seriation, classification, conservation) that alone make the coherent representation of reality possible. Hence, pretending only continues so long as the child cannot effectively accommodate to the real world.

> Symbolic games decline after the age of four, for reasons which it is very important to discover, since they also explain why these games are so numerous earlier. In a general way it can be said that the more the child adapts himself to the natural and social world the less he indulges in symbolic distortions and transpositions, because instead of assimilating the external world to the ego he progressively subordinates the ego to reality [Piaget, 1962, p. 145].

This insistence on the importance of pretense for cognitive development only insofar as it faithfully reconstructs but not as it transforms reality has been critically reviewed by Sutton-Smith (1966).

It would, of course, be untrue to say that Piaget attributed no cognitive significance to symbolic play. Whereas he denied it a significant creative role in representational development, he did regard it as a useful yardstick for its progress (Piaget, 1962). In their early make-believe play, Piaget noted, children demonstrate a growing ability to dissociate the symbol from what it symbolizes. At the onset of pretending, when infants reenact their own activities (sleeping, eating, drinking) outside the normal, everyday context, the two are still closely linked, in the sense that a scheme, enacted out of context, serves as a symbol for the same scheme imagined in context. The symbol and what it symbolizes achieve somewhat greater separation when infants feed a doll, instead of themselves, or pretend at behavior they have observed in others (e.g., "read" a newspaper). Doll-directed behavior now stands for the infant's self-directed everyday action, whereas self-directed reproduction of another person's behavior stands for the model's imagined action. The dissociation of the symbol and the symbolized increases even further when the child begins to assume another person's role or uses one object as if it were another. In playing a role (identifying with the other person) the child becomes the symbol for the other person. In "eating" from a stick or "telephoning" with a spoon, the action performed with the substitute object symbolizes actual eating and telephoning with realistic objects. Piaget's description of the increasing distance of the symbol from the symbolized carries within it, I sense, the seeds of a theory of event representation, perhaps even of a theory of subjunctive thought. Because figurative representation held little interest for him, Piaget paid no heed of these seeds, however.

The approach to symbolic play taken in this chapter is deeply influenced by Piaget, but at the same time incompatible with some of his views. Although the emphasis on figurative as opposed to operative knowledge is un-Piagetian, the focus on representation as internal or mental action is deeply rooted in Piagetian thinking. It would be foolish to belittle the importance of operative representation. I suggest, however, that Piaget unjustly disregarded the implications of figurative representation for cognitive development. Work in the area of artificial intelligence (e.g., Schank & Abelson, 1977) and cognitive psychology (e.g., Aebli, 1980; Mandler, 1979; Nelson, 1981) supports this claim.

Persuasive evidence now exists that, at the most basic level, representation may not be organized in terms of taxonomic structures or classification hierarchies but in terms of event schemata or scripts that are skeletal frameworks of everyday events (Schank & Abelson, 1977). These frameworks are figurative in that they represent spatio-temporo-causal links among agents, recipients, and objects and are in this sense isomorphic with reality. They are constructed and revised in the course of repeated experiences with similar events, but they in turn guide understanding of such events. In Piagetian language, event schemata interpret reality (assimilation) and are adapted in response to it (accommodation). In the terminology of cognitive science, event schemata serve as top-down, conceptually driven processing mechanisms, which give meaning to incoming information (Mandler, 1979). Mandler suggested that taxonomic knowledge appears to be a secondary kind of organization, built onto a schematically organized memory system wherein linkage is based on spatial, temporal, or causal relations, not class membership. Along the same lines, Nelson (1981) proposed that scripts or event schemata may constitute a first-order organization from which other cognitive structures–processes (such as taxonomic hierarchies, roles, and problem-solving strategies) are then derived (see also Kreye, Chapter 11, this volume). Such a view attributes great significance to figurative representation as a basis for the construction of operative thought, turning Piagetian notions on the relationship of figurative to operative knowledge upside down.

The script model is intuitively appealing because, unlike the static, traditional models of knowledge, it can account for the dynamic relationships between agents, recipients, objects, and actions that make up everyday social interaction (Nelson, 1981). Nelson and Gruendel (1981) defined a script as a cognitive model of an event. I prefer to describe it as a cognitive–affective model that has meaning in the sense described by Kreye (Chapter 11, this volume). If mental (affective–cognitive) models of the world are to serve in the interpretation of real-world events and in the planning of future action, they must reflect the spatio-temporo-causal structure of that world. The causal structure includes goals and motivations of the actors and recipients, as well as physical causality.

Although we are largely ignorant of the processes whereby events rather than single objects might be schematically represented in and by the human mind, there is now a fair amount of circumstantial evidence in support of the script model. For example, adults tend to rectify the order of events on retelling a scrambled story (Mandler & DeForest, 1979; Stein & Nezworski, 1978). Similarly, when stories or texts do not explicitly state certain types of information, adults tend to rely on event schemata to fill in the blanks (Kintsch, 1974).

If the basic representational schemata are meaningful events, not disembedded units, it ought to be possible to demonstrate that infants have the ability to represent an experience in terms of temporo-causal relations among actors, recipients, objects, and locations (Nelson, 1981; see also Aebli, 1980). So far, however, only the development of event representation in 3–5-year-olds has received detailed scrutiny. Both interviews and story-retelling tasks (Nelson & Gruendel, 1981; Stein, 1978) have yielded encouraging results. At an even earlier age, symbolic play may give some clues as to the organization of event representation (Nelson, 1981) but pretense has not as yet been extensively analyzed from this point of view. However, language acquisition studies suggesting that children encode semantic relations (events) into single-word utterances (e.g., Bloom, 1973; Brown, 1973; Greenfield & Smith, 1976) are compatible with the script approach to early cognitive development.

Before considering how the development of symbolic play might be interpreted with respect to the script model, I would like to review briefly findings concerning the development of event representation during the preschool years. In terms of story retelling, both Nelson and Stein noted that, like adults, young children tend to repair noncanonical event sequences during reproduction of a scrambled story. Nelson (1981) documented this effect as early as 3 years of age. Children tended to preserve input order especially well when links between story events were based on psychological or physical causality, not just temporal contiguity (Nelson & Gruendel, 1981; Stein, 1978). Thus it appears that script representation makes use of causal understanding where this is available and, at least at the ages so far studied, consists of more than a rigid framework of behavioral sequences.

As regards the production of event schemata from memory, Nelson and colleagues (see Nelson & Gruendel, 1981) discovered that children as young as 3 years can respond appropriately to questions ("what happens when ") about well-practiced routines such as having lunch at the daycare center, going to McDonald's, going to the store, and making cookies. Even 3-year-olds report aspects of routine events in the correct sequence; older children merely add more details. There tends, moreover, to be unanimity among children about the order in which certain events ought to take place, particularly if the relationships are causal. For example, when asked "What happens when you have a birthday party?" children report that the candles are blown out before the cake is eaten, although they may disagree as to whether presents are to be unwrapped before or after eating the cake. In addition, Nelson and Gruendel (1981) found that children use a special form of speech during their descriptions of "what happens when. . . ." In their answers to questions about scripts ("What happens when you go to McDonald's?") they employ the impersonal you and tenseless verbs (e.g., "You eat and then you go home"). When asked about specific remembered events, on the other hand, they are likely to use the past tense and the first person pronoun.

To trace the acquisition of event representation even further back than the studies on story understanding and script elicitation, I review, in the first part of this chapter, how one might interpret the development of symbolic play as development of event representation. Emphasis is not, for the most part, on the content of particular event schemata or scripts such as eating, sleeping, taking a bath (see Bates, Benigni, Bretherton, Camaioni, & Volterra, 1979; Volterra, Bates, Benigni, Bretherton, & Camaioni, 1979). Instead, I focus on the development of the structural aspects of such scripts: role-representation (which and how many interacting roles are represented), action-representation (coherence, complexity, order) and use of props (realistic, abstract, invented). Roles are discussed in terms of replica play (with dolls or toy animals) as well as collaborative play (with another person).

Because the symbolic medium of pretense (enactment) bears a strong resemblance to real-world action, care must be taken to mark the boundary between the two levels: here-and-now reality and make-believe (Bateson, 1955/1972). This is especially true in collective pretense with other actors, which requires the sharing and coordination of script knowledge (Forys & McCune-Nicolich, Chapter 6, this volume; Garvey & Berndt, 1977; Giffin, Chapter 3, this volume; Nelson & Seidman, Chapter 2, this volume). Joint make-believe constitutes, in my view, collaborative event representation on two levels, planning and acting; this is considered in the second part of the chapter.

The third and final issue addressed is the topic of subjunctive thought. In make-believe, children use event schemata as raw material to create a fictive reality that does not merely simulate but transforms their affective–cognitive map of the social world. These transformations are analyzed in terms of the emergence of a subjunctive capacity (Hofstadter, 1979). By changing various parameters of an event schema, children can create a variety of more- or less-fantastic alternatives to everyday reality. The major thesis of this chapter, then, is not that symbolic play faithfully reflects children's ability to represent the social world but that it constitutes play with that ability.

EVENT REPRESENTATION IN SYMBOLIC PLAY

Pretending simulates and transforms routine events from family life, story-books, and television. However, the ability to represent these scripts (and their distortions and transformations) does not emerge fully fledged. With development, there is a marked increase in the number of roles and the order and co-herence of actions reproduced in make-believe, accompanied by a decreasing reliance on veridical props.

Role, action, and object representation are here treated as separate dimensions of pretend play even though, at the simplest level, they are not completely dis-sociable. An action always requires an agent and frequently an object. Yet it is possible to enact a relatively complex role structure (two teddy bears engage in interaction) with a simple action structure (e.g., the two bears kiss each other). Similarly, a complex action structure such as the performance of a lengthy breakfast sequence can be enacted with a simple role structure (the sole actor is the child him- or herself).

Role and action representation are initially affected by the availability of re-alistic props. Later, objects can be mentally transformed into other objects and imaginary props can be created through miming or language.

ROLES

Piaget (1962) outlined a systematic progression from self-representation to the representation of more complex role structures. As previously noted, what Pi-aget saw in these findings was an increasing ability to distance symbolizer and symbolized. Viewed from a different perspective, the same data document the child's developing ability to represent roles, beginning with single roles and moving on to the representation of several interacting roles. Although Piaget's observations were based on the behavior of only three children, his findings have since been corroborated by many others (e.g., Fenson & Ramsay, 1980; Kagan, 1981; Nicolich, 1977; Watson & Fischer, 1977, 1980; Wolf, 1982). Not all of these investigators have agreed on which fine distinctions can and should be drawn, nor have they necessarily interpreted their findings in the way I have presented them here. My aim has been to integrate the different viewpoints, note reasons for disagreements where these exist, and suggest possible resolutions.

Self-representation

There is general agreement with Piaget (1962) that pretend activity begins with self-representation, wherein a child produces a behavior such as sleeping, but outside the going-to-bed context and without being tired. To count as a symbolic scheme rather than practice of a known behavior the child must indicate awareness of pretense in some way (see Nicolich, 1977; Piaget, 1962). A very clear example is Jacqueline's behavior at the age of 15 months.

> She saw a cloth whose fringed edges vaguely recalled those of her pillow; she seized it, held a fold of it in her right hand, sucked the thumb of the same hand, and lay down on her side, laughing hard. She kept her eyes open, but blinked them from time to time as if she were alluding to closed eyes. Finally, laughing more and more, she cried "nene" [Piaget, 1962, Observation 64a, p. 96].

In the preceding example laughing and blinking communicate awareness of make-believe. In other cases the presence of sound effects (lip-smacking in the course of "eating") and exaggeration of symbolic gestures may distinquish this behavior from earlier recognitory gestures (Nicolich, 1977).

It is not always easy to decide whether chidren are playing at being themselves or whether symbolic schemes are derived from observation of other people. For this reason a number of investigators (Fenson & Ramsay, 1980; Jeffree & McConkey, 1976; Kagan, 1981; Largo & Howard, 1979; Lowe, 1975; Watson & Fischer, 1977) have not attempted to distinguish between pretending at one's own or another person's behavior. This definitional problem is addressed in the next subsection.

Representing Another's Behavior

Piaget (1962) described an unambiguous example of other-representation. At 19 months, Lucienne (Observation 76a) "read" the newspaper, pointing to certain parts of the sheet of paper she was holding while muttering to herself. Unfortunately the distinction between self-pretending and other-pretending is not always so clear. Take, for example, pretend-telephoning. An infant might have acquired the scheme not through observation but from direct instruction with a toy telephone (parent holding the receiver to the child's ear). In this case it would probably be wrong to infer that the child is representing another person's actions. By contrast, when an infant pretends to drink from an empty cup it is natural to jump to the conclusion that the child is engaging in self-representation. That this may not be the case is illustrated by Fein and Apfel's (1979) study. A majority of 12-month-olds, most of whom were not permitted to use a spoon at home and who were for the most part bottle-fed, chose to "eat" from an empty spoon and disdained pretend-use of the bottle in favor of a cup. They were representing others' behavior, not reenacting their own.

The distinction between self-representation and other-representation, although problematic, is important. Pretending at a behavior that is unambiguously that of another person can be regarded as the beginning of role-play (or trying out the world from another vantage point).

Others as Passive Recipients of the Child's Action

Piaget (1962) and Nicolich (1977) agreed that projection of the child's own behavior onto another person or a doll (feeding mother or doll) is conceptually similar to projection of another person's behavior onto the self (both involve decentration). However, neither Piaget nor Nicolich distinguished between live and inanimate recipients of action.

Fein and Apfel (1979) undertook a direct comparison of play with a person (mother or experimenter) and an inanimate other (a doll). At 12 months, 80% of the infants engaged in self-directed pretend feeding, 32% fed mother or experimenter, and only 19% fed a doll (the various forms of pretending were not mutually exclusive so they add up to more than 100%). These findings, corroborated by Shimada, Sano, and Peng (1979), suggest that it may be easier to project a scheme onto a live partner than onto a doll, with important implications. If infants use a person as recipient of a symbolic scheme before they use a doll in the same fashion, we have stronger grounds for assuming that the infant is treating the doll as a human figure when doll-directed behavior does emerge.

I also suspect (in accord with Fein, 1978) that behaviors directed to a doll or person take slightly different forms, although this has not been formally investigated. For example, it is my impression that infants expect an adult to cooperate when holding a cup toward his or her mouth, but that they do not have this expectation of a doll. Regardless of what the child expects, an adult who is offered a "drink" from an empty cup is likely to cooperate by producing language and sound effects ("Mmm. That's yummy . . . all gone"). These interchanges therefore constitute the first examples of infant-initiated collabo-rative make-believe.

A related question is whether the child is merely projecting his or her own behavior onto a doll or whether the child is pretending at care giving. Piaget (1962) clearly assumed the former:

> In projecting his own behavior onto others (making dolls cry, eat, drink or sleep) the child himself is imitating the actions they do when they reproduce his own actions! [p. 123].

Notwithstanding Piaget's notion of egocentrism, this statement sounds remark-ably like a description of role taking or seeing oneself from the viewpoint of the other (Mead, 1934). Such issues aside, when infants "feed" a doll or person in the same way in which they feed themselves one cannot decide with certainty whether the behavior constitutes role taking or care taking. However, when infants put a doll to bed and tuck in its blankets there is a much stronger pre-sumption that this represents care-giver behavior directed to a doll as passive recipient. The distinction is important. If the child regards the doll as a partner, rather than a symbolic representation of the self, we are dealing with the rep-resentation of *two* roles (self in relation to other) and thus a higher level of role-representation.

Parallel Roles

Nicolich (1977) noted that once children have mastered the projection of schemes onto others, they tend to include themselves and the partners in the same action (feeding themselves, then mother, then a doll). This could be re-garded as a further step toward representation of reciprocal interaction with the other person or the doll. Wolf (1982), in a case study, also drew attention to this type of behavior.

> O. presents a bag of toy implements to J. at 1:4. Each one that he tries out he tries first on himself and then on a big doll. He takes out a comb and combs the back and then the front of his hair, then the doll's. He takes toy scissors, clipping at the hair around his and then the doll's ears [p. 314].

The Use of the Replica as Active Recipient

This level of role representation is sometimes not distinguished from the pre-vious level (passive recipient) and sometimes included with the next level (active agent). I see strong grounds for treating it as a separate category, however. Mere holding of a bottle to a doll's mouth differs conceptually from doll feeding accompanied by talking to the doll and/or by ascription of feelings and perceptions to the doll (see also Wolf, 1982). Piaget (1962) provides a striking example of the kind of behavior I have in mind:

> At 2; 1(13) she [Jacqueline] fed it [her doll] for a long time in the way we used to encourage her to eat her own meals: "a little drop more, to please Jacqueline. Just eat this little bit" [Observation 81, p. 127].

Although the doll is treated as a human figure, the child is not yet vicariously acting *for* a doll. This constitutes the next level.

Use of a Replica as Agent

When the child acts for the doll or pretends that a doll can act on its own (feed itself) the child becomes a vicarious actor. Such behavior has been described by Fenson, (Chapter 9, this volume), Fenson & Ramsay (1980), Inhelder, Lézine, Sinclair, and Stambak (1972), Lowe (1975), and Watson and Fischer (1980), although it is not always distinguished from use of a figure as active recipient. Several instances of animation were described by Wolf (1982). Curiously, the act of talking for the doll is seldom discussed in this connection, perhaps because of a desire to consider enactive and verbal representation in terms of separate symbol systems. Again, Piaget provides an example:

> At 1; 6(30) J. said "cry, cry" to her dog and herself imitated the sound of crying. On the following day, she made her bear, duck, etc. cry [1962, Observation 75a, p. 121].

Assuming Another Person's Role

I here conceptually equate the child's acting for the doll with the ability to pretend at being another person, although empirical data to support this hunch are not yet available. Both activities constitute role play: In the case of animating a doll, role play is vicarious; in assuming another person's role, it is direct. Piaget described early forms of this identification, which he called "assimilation of the ego to others":

> At 1; 9(20) J. rubbed the floor with a shell, then with a cardboard lid, saying: "Brush Abebert" [like the charwoman]. The same day she pulled her hair back as she looked at herself in the mirror, and said, laughing "Daddy" [Piaget, 1962, Observation 76a p. 122].

As Piaget (1962) noted, such behavior transcends imitation because the child does not merely copy the behavior of others while continuing to be him- or herself, but identifies completely with others. Huttenlocher and Higgins (1978), who drew the same distinction, required that the child make a *verbal* statement indicating identification with the other, terming this behavior role-play to set it off from its developmental precursor, role-enactment. Huttenlocher and Higgin's definition was used by Miller and Garvey (Chapter 4, this volume) as well as by Dunn and Dale (Chapter 5, this volume). It may, however, be possible to create nonverbal criteria for role-play.

Use of a Doll as Active Partner

A more complex form of role-representation than either activation of a doll or assumption of another role is to engage in reciprocal interaction with the "active" doll or to assume a complementary role to another person (discussed in the next subsection).

In playing the active partner to an active doll the child has, in effect, to enact two roles that complement one another. I have not been able to find appropriate examples in Piaget's work. However, Miller and Garvey (Chapter 4, this volume) provide several illustrations of this ability around 30 months (a child mothers a baby doll, but also speaks and cries for it).

A striking example of this type of behavior at an earlier age appeared in Wolf's (1982) case study.

> J. at 1:9 develops a new pattern of interaction with his jack-in-the-box. If, when he presses down the lid on top of the jack, its hand is poking out of the corner of the lid, J. calls out, "Ouch, ouch. Boo-boo" [his word for a hurt]. He then quickly cranks the lid so that it pops open, rubs the clown's hand and kisses it, before carefully stuffing it back down into the hole, hand and all [Wolf, 1982, p. 319].

Simple Collaborative Role Play

When assuming a role vis-à-vis another person the child need only enact one role, not two, as in replica play with two figures. On the other hand, joint role-play requires the child to coordinate his or her event schemata or scripts with those of another person. This constitutes implicit representation of at least two roles, a task that can at first be mastered only with more experienced partners such as older siblings or parents who tend to engage in frequent coaching; see chapters by Dunn and Dale (5), Miller and Garvey (4), and O'Connell and Bretherton (12), this volume.

To illustrate this level, I again resort to Wolf's case study (although in this example the child coaches the parent, not vice versa).

> J., at 2:0, is sitting at his little table in his room with his father in a nearby rocker. J. walks up to his father, draws him toward the little table and tells him: "Eat ice cream." J. reaches into an empty canister and takes out a handful of air. "Daddy eat ice cream . . . Me, too." When his father does not immediately understand or follow, J. insists again, "Daddy eat ice cream." Then his father catches on and "digs in" [Wolf, 1982, p. 324].

A somewhat more advanced example (Jacqueline is assuming her mother's role) is furnished by Piaget:

> At 2; 4(8) she was her mother, "it's mommy", and said to me "come kiss mommy," and kissed me [1962, Observation 79 p. 125].

Replica Play with Several Interacting Roles

The development of spontaneous and prompted play with small figures or replica play has been extensively studied by Wolf and her colleagues (Rubin & Wolf, 1979; Wolf, 1982; Wolf, Rygh, & Altschuler, Chapter 7, this volume). Watson and Fischer (1980) covered some of the same ground, but their findings were exclusively based on play elicited through modeling and are discussed in a later chapter (Bretherton, O'Connell, Shore, & Bates, Chapter 10, this volume). Rubin and Wolf emphasized that not until the third year do children come to animate small figures without themselves participating in the plot as actor. First attempts at activating two figures often consist of casting them in parallel roles. The subsequent mastery of doll play with several interacting figures about whom the child talks as narrator and for whom the child talks as vicarious actor marks a great step forward whose implications are discussed later. An example of this simple form of story telling can be found in Wolf's (1982) case study:

> J. at 2:0 has a parent figure and a child figure. 0. has also given him some doll furniture. He lays the child in bed, making the parent walk over and kiss the child. Then he makes the child hop out of bed and run off to under the table. He makes the parent figure chase after the child calling out "Get you" [p. 320].

With further development the roles assigned to the replicas tend to become more differentiated (a nasty lion may chase a frightened boy, but is also capable of feeling lonely; see Rubin & Wolf, 1979). Alternatively, each replica can assume more than one social role (a boy can be the doctor's son as well as patient; see Watson & Fischer, 1980). Miller and Garvey (Chapter 4, this volume) describe an analogous development in collaborative play: A 30-month-old girl plays "mother" to "baby" and "wife" to "husband" while coaching "husband" in how to perform the role of "father."

Collaborative Play with Several Interacting Roles

In analyzing collaborative role-play in preschool children between the ages of 3 and 5 years, Garvey (1977) found it useful to distinguish functional roles from character roles. Garvey's *functional roles* define only the behavior of the person in the present situation, for example, driver and passenger of a pretend car, not a permanent identity. Functional roles that resemble what Watson and Fischer (1980) called *behavioral roles*, Rubin and Wolf (1979) called *pragmatic roles*, and Huttenlocher and Higgins (1978) called *role enactment*, precede character roles in development. However, even though older children are capable of impersonating a character role, they do not always choose to do so. Hence functional roles persist after the mastery of character roles.

Diverging slightly from Garvey's scheme (she made a distinction between character and family roles) I suggest that the definition of *character roles* include family roles (mother, father, baby), occupational roles (doctor, nurse), or fictional roles (Superman, witch). In Garvey and Berndt's study, fictional and occupational roles tended to be played with much less attention to detail than family roles. Sometimes nonfamilial character roles were merely indicated by putting on the appropriate costume (a girl playing "bride" put on a veil without enacting a wedding script). The younger preschool children in Garvey's study tended to limit themselves to roles that they had personally experienced as agents or recipients (e.g., parent–child roles). Older preschoolers, by contrast, also enacted family roles based purely on observation (husband and wife), in addition to trying more occupational and fictive roles.

In summary, simple forms of role taking and playing are present as soon as the infant goes beyond self-representation. These activities include, in the second half of the second year, clear evidence that people are understood as experiencers as well as agents (Wolf, 1982). At the end of the third year children are capable of much more. In performing a drama including several interacting dolls, the child has to play an event from several points of view (play and take roles). In collaborative make-believe the situation is comparable. The child must coordinate her or his viewpoint of the make-believe event with that of other children.

ACTIONS

Actions have temporal and spatial characteristics; that is, they are directed by agents to recipients or objects in a more or less obligatory temporal order. In addition, actions take place in spatial settings. The first symbolic actions consist of single schemes or miniscripts, which become elaborated into complex sequences. However, as in role-representation, the decision as to when there is one scheme or several schemes in combination is not always as easy to make as one might wish.

Single Schemes

The question that usually arises with regard to single schemes like "drinking" is whether the child is merely performing the appropriate action with an object or pretending at the function (drinking a pretend liquid) as well. Infants' first functional schemes with objects are often cursory, as if to indicate "I know what you do with this." However, even when there are indications that the infant is pretending, the meaning of the make-believe action probably depends on the object with which the infant is playing. The question is relatively easily resolved in the case of "drinking" because the child presumably notices that the cup holds no liquid. Many 1-year-olds given an empty cup will actually feel its inside before proceeding to "drink" (personal observation). I am convinced, however, that in pretend-telephoning, infants do not understand the function (communication) until much later, even though they know, at 1 year of age, that the receiver is held somewhere near the neck–face area and that one says something like "hi." Thus, whether the child pretends at the function (as understood by an adult) as well as the outward action depends on how well he or she understands the real-world function of particular objects.

Scheme Combinations

Most investigators (Fenson & Ramsay, 1980; Nicolich, 1977)) have reported the first scheme combinations late in the second year. However, in one study (Bretherton, Bates, McNew, Shore, Williamson, & Beeghly-Smith, 1981) very simple scheme combinations during play with single objects were noticed in 13-month-olds (45% of the infants both hugged and/or kissed, rocked, and cooed to a teddy bear or doll; 50% lifted a telephone receiver to their neck–face area and said "hi.") These are admittedly simpler scheme combinations than examples previously described in the literature. Yet they undeniably constituted two separate behaviors (each could also be shown singly), suggesting that we may have to distinguish finer qualitative levels in the development of scheme combinations. Moreover, as the examples given earlier indicate, the combination of manual and vocal schemes in the representation of actions cannot be disregarded even at this early stage.

Two types of scheme combination have been extensively described in the literature. First to emerge are single-scheme combinations in which the same scheme is applied to several objects (the infant stirs in the cup, then in the pitcher). According to Nicolich (1977), these have been mastered by most children at around 19 months, and are followed, between 19 and 24 months, by multischeme combinations. Multischeme combinations consist of several related actions carried out in sequence—that is, pouring from a pitcher to a cup and then drinking from the cup. In most cases infants acquire the component schemes long before they combine them into a sequence (Fenson & Ramsay, 1981). It is therefore not paucity of schemes that delays the onset of multischemes.

Ordered Multischemes

Fenson and Ramsay (1980) hypothesized that the execution of scheme combinations should progress from random to real-world order. When they examined their data for supportive evidence they were surprised to find very few nonordered sequences even at 15 months. Examples of ordered multischemes were pouring "tea" into a cup and then "drinking" from it, or placing a pillow on the doll-bed and then laying the head on the pillow as if to go to sleep. To count as ordered, the sequence had to reflect a logical or ecological order. Most but not all combinations defined as ordered were unidirectional, that is, they were not meaningful when the position of the two component acts was reversed. Unordered multischemes were actions such as placing the doll in bed and then combing its hair (Fenson & Ramsay, 1980). Fenson and Ramsay's findings regarding ordered sequences are in accord with Nelson and Gruendel's (1981) study, in which 3-year-olds tended to report the component acts of scripts in the correct order.

There are few systematic studies of the further development of multischemes, yet it is surely necessary to distinguish a mere two-scheme sequence such as feeding and burping of a baby doll from the following example provided by Inhelder *et al.*

> Thus Pierre, at 22 months, imitates in detail how his mother feeds her baby as he puts the nipple of the bottle to the baby-doll's mouth with a well-coordinated movement, lifts up the baby's head which is resting in the crook of his arm, then holds up the bottle and pulls on the nipple as if it had collapsed, looks at the bottle, shakes it like an adult feeding a baby and "checks" the level of formula in the bottle, then returns the bottle to the baby's mouth, pushing the nipple forcefully against its mouth [1972, p. 217].

Fenson (personal communication, March 1983), who studied spontaneous multischemes in 20- to 31-month-olds, found that 50% of his sample performed two-scheme sequences at 20 months. At 26 and 31 months this percentage had risen to 71%. In addition, 33% of the 31-month-olds enacted three-scheme and 17% four-scheme sequences. Rheingold and Emery (1983) observed multischemes somewhat earlier. In their study, all 18-month-olds achieved two-scheme sequences. At 30 months all of the children performed meaningful five-scheme sequences. The cause for this discrepancy may lie in the prolonged observation perioid (30 minutes) used by Rheingold and Emery.

Episode Combinations

Some of the longer sequences in the two studies just discussed may have consisted of several subepisodes, but so far, hierarchical sequence structures have not been systematically investigated. Inhelder *et al.* (1972) briefly alluded to the emergence during the third year of longer sequences created by producing several multischeme episodes in a meaningful order (e.g., bathing the baby doll after having fed it). Unfortunately, no detailed examples are given. However, Wolf's case study described what I consider to be episode combinations. In the first example the episodes are accident/treatment; in the second they are arriving/going to bed/having an accident.

> J., at 1;8, had a minor accident in which he cut his forehead. For several weeks thereafter he re-enacts the specific details of falling, crying, being stitched up, wearing a bike helmet to protect the cut using a large doll [Wolf, 1982, p. 314].

> J., at 1:10, picks out a little figure and walks it up to the door of a small playhouse, knocking on it. J. opens the door and lets the figure in. He walks the figure up the stairs and lays it down in bed, saying "Shhh, go Ni-ni." The figure rolls out of bed. J. says, "oh-oh, need a bandaid" [Wolf, 1982, p. 320].

The content of early pretending is drawn from and reproduces the infant's everyday experience (sleeping, eating, telephoning, going for a ride). The 3- to 5-year-olds studied by Garvey had a considerably larger repertoire, but a few general themes accounted for the greater proportion of make-believe acts; treating–healing, averting a threat, packing, taking a trip, going to the store, cooking, having a meal, and repairing were especially popular themes. A theme, it should be noted, is a more abstract framework than a basic-level script. Hence, several different scripts may be instantiated to enact the theme of averting threat (the threat can be a monster, fire, getting lost).

Throughout this period, actions based on everyday family scripts were much more highly elaborated than those associated with occupational and fictive roles. The instantiation of a particular script was often inspired by the presence of a specific object or set of objects, although during the third and later years scripts became less and less dependent on realistic props.

OBJECTS

Infants' first efforts at pretending appear to require prototypical objects such as spoons, telephones, or baby dolls (Nicolich, 1977; Piaget, 1962; Vygotsky, 1966). Later, such realism is less and less necessary to sustain the make-believe reality, although many children seem to need tangible placeholders to stand for imagined objects. Empty-handed miming tends to be infrequent in spontaneous play until at least the middle of the third year (Fenson, Chapter 9, this volume).

The presence of realistic objects seems to provide perceptual–tactile–spatial support for the performance of the first miniscripts like sleeping or eating. Without such support, 12-month-olds are unlikely to engage in pretending at all. Later in the second year, children begin to substitute one object for another. Several studies have attempted to identify those features of the substitute object (appearance, function) that interfere most with substitution. A number of these studies have used modeling as an eliciting technique and are discussed in a later chapter (Bretherton *et al.*, Chapter 10, this volume). Here I focus on studies of spontaneous substitution.

Object Substitution

Several explanations for the emergence of object substitution have been offered. Piaget considered assimilation of one object to another (use of a shell as a cup) to be conceptually equivalent to assimilation of another person to the ego (e.g., assuming the maternal role). His interpretation resembles Vygotsky's (1966) notion that substitute objects serve as "pivots" whose function, in symbolic terms, is to sever the meaning of an object from the real object. Not all objects, Vygotsky claimed, can function as pivots. Whereas a stick that permits the enactment of riding can become the pivot for a horse, a postcard could never serve in this fashion. Nevertheless, object substitution, from a Vygotskyan perspective, implies that meaning has come to dominate over appearances. Nicolich (1977) took a somewhat different approach by classifying object substitution under the rubric "planful" behavior. In her study, infants' first object substitutions, late in the second year, coincided with other foresightful acts such as announcing the "script" to be enacted or searching for toys relevant to a planned script.

Neither Piaget nor Nicolich spoke of object substitution when infants use a toy that recognizably resembles a realistic object, even though it is not a "good" prototypical exemplar. This weaker form of substitution is possible even for 13-month-olds (Bretherton *et al.*, 1981). Most infants of that age performed some symbolic schemes with pared-down but recognizable versions of cups, spoons, telephones, dolls, and cars. But note that, for 1-year-olds, even this simple form of object substitution is more difficult than play with realistic objects.

Jeffree and McConkey (1976) conducted a longitudinal study of 10 children who were observed in a playhouse situation at 6-month intervals, beginning at 18 and ending at 42 months. Two sets of toys, one prototypical and the other consisting of junk material (cans, boxes, rags, pieces of paper, sticks, and a rag doll) were presented to the children for 5 minutes of spontaneous play. Junk material, less suggestive than the abstract toys used by Bretherton *et al.* (1981), led to a significant decrease in the frequency of play schemes, but did not affect the highest level of symbolic behavior. Unfortunately, the findings were not broken down by age. It is therefore not possible to tell whether the divergence between behavior with realistic and junk materials decreased with age, as observed by Kagan (1981). When Kagan compared spontaneous play with realistic and unrealistic toys in 13- to 25-month-olds, symbolic acts with realistic toys exceeded those with unrealistic toys at all monthly sessions from 13 to 25 months. However, by 25 months there was no longer a difference in the proportion of time devoted to symbolic acts with both toy sets.

In both of these studies, children played with a whole set of realistic or a whole set of abstract toys. There is only one investigation which compared the effect of single and multiple substitutions. Fein (1975) invited 26-month-old children to play with prototypical and abstract versions of a horse and eggcup. Almost all children spontaneously fed the prototypical horse with the prototypical cup. Seventy-nine percent of the toddlers "fed" the prototypical horse with the abstract cup (a clamshell), and 61% fed the abstract horse (a metal horse shape) with the realistic eggcup. By contrast, double substitutions (feeding the abstract horse with the shell) were much more difficult; only 33% of the toddlers performed them.

Miming

Investigators (e.g., Elder & Pederson, 1978; Overton & Jackson, 1973) generally agree that empty-handed miming, unsupported by perceptual–tactile cues from an object, emerges later than use of tangible substitutes, be they pared-down versions of the real thing, placeholders such as blocks or sticks, or even counter-conventional objects that differ from the symbolized object in form and function (a comb used as a spoon). Fenson found miming to be virtually nonexistent in the spontaneous play of 21–31-month-olds (see Fenson, Chapter 9, this volume).

It is therefore surprising that Piaget (1962) reported an instance of miming at 12 months:

> At 1; (20) J. scratched at the wall paper in the bedroom where there was the design of a bird, then shut her hand as if it held the bird and went to her mother: 'Look (she opened her hand and pretended to be giving something). —What have you brought me?— a birdie." [Observation 74, p. 119].

Other examples of miming described by Piaget (1962) occurred after the age of 2. At 2:0;2 Jacqueline moved her finger along the edge of a table, saying "finger walking, horse trotting." Note that she verbally described the transformation (finger to horse) and that she used a body part (the finger) to stand for agent-action (horse trotting). At 2:3;8 Jacqueline made a circular movement with her fingers, saying "bicycle spoilt," followed by another circular gesture accompanied by "bicycle mended." Here the gesture appeared to depict the object (the wheel or perhaps the rolling of the wheel as well) whereas the script (breakage–repair) was verbal. At 2:5;25, Jacqueline, in preparation for giving her sister a make-believe bath, mimed an undressing sequence without ever touching Lucienne's clothes. At 2:6; 22 she pretended to have a baby in her arms and put it down on an imaginary bed. What is noteworthy about the latter two examples is that they are pure pantomime, in the sense that the child did not depict the object but merely the action on the object. Work by Overton and Jackson (1973) suggested that pure pantomime constitutes a higher developmental level than use of a body part to depict both object and action, although their results are based on a verbal prompting paradigm, not observation of spontaneous behavior.

In the course of my own studies I have observed a 13-month-old boy build a tower consisting of several blocks, and then alongside it construct an imaginary tower of equal height. The same child was also reported to play pebble-tossing games that began with real pebbles but continued with imaginary ones. These examples, taken together with Piaget's observations, suggest that it might be useful to look for instances of spontaneous miming at earlier ages. Indeed, Fenson (Chapter 9, this volume) points out that miming *with* object support is quite common, but has not generally been interpreted as such. Thus a child who "pours" from pitcher to cup (perhaps shaking the pitcher to remove the last drop) is miming or inventing the presence of an imaginary liquid. Invention with object support is also involved when a child picks up imaginary food from a plate and holds it to a doll's mouth. Sometimes invented substances are further specified by naming (Bretherton *et al.*, Chapter 10, this volume; Fenson, Chapter 9, this volume; see also Matthews, 1977). Such verbal invention in the presence of perceptual support becomes very frequent during the third year and deserves further study.

Individual Differences

Wolf and Grollman (1982) suggest that a child's preference for tangible substitutes over imaginary (mimed or named) objects and realistic or semirealistic substitutes over placeholders and counterconventional objects may, beyond the second year or so, be partly a matter of cognitive style rather than developmental level. For some children, these authors have claimed, the objects' tangible presence and physical features are necessary to support fantasy. For others, language and gestures suffice to create a fictive world almost independent of the immediate physical environment.

Object-dependent children, as described by Wolf and Grollman, will put a few small blocks in a bowl rather than pantomime the presence of batter in an empty bowl. Red beads are transformed into cherries, a jagged piece of felt into the ocean bordering the edge of the rug. Such children tend to search for "good" substitutes, denying the presence of cake on a plate until a small rectangular block is placed on it. Object-dependent children also tend to maintain the transformed identity of objects, once it has been agreed upon. Object-independent children, by contraast, are much less concerned with the appropriateness of the substitution. A tiny cube can serve as bath towel because it still affords the necessary rubbing action. Rather than searching for good substitutes and conserving their identity, object-independent children make the same object fill diverse functions as the action requires. A clothespin can serve as spoon, pothandle, and knife in rapid succession. Object-independent children are also far more likely to pantomime objects or create them verbally.

Although play with nonveridical objects and miming become more common with age, realistic objects continue to play an important role. In a study of collaborative pretending, Garvey and Berndt (1977) found that the presence of a realistic prop often led to the instantiation of a related script (their term is *action-scheme*). However, once make-believe was underway it was most often the ongoing script that came to determine subsequent object transformations. In their study of 3–5-year-olds, a three-legged stool with a magnifiying glass in its center was transformed into a telescope (to spot a fire), a toilet (to take care of baby), a workchair (while performing a household task), a trailer (packing for a trip) and a milk carton (while shopping for provisions). The last two substitutions did not appear to be inspired by the perceptual properties of the transformed object. However, there was no age trend indicating progress from object dependence to object independence, a finding supporting Wolf and Grollman's notion that object dependence–independence may, during the preschool years, be a function of individual style rather than of developmental level.

THE INTEGRATION OF ROLES,
ACTIONS, AND OBJECTS

Nicolich's (1977) study of spontaneous pretense between the ages of 14 and 19 months suggests that progress in role representation (making others the recipients of one's action, enacting others' behavior) generally takes place before the emergence of multischeme sequences. It seems sensible to hypothesize, however, that there may be a trade-off between the two dimensions (roles and actions). For example, a child might be able to represent two interacting roles, provided sequencing was not also required. Likewise, sequences might first appear in conjunction with self-representation (the lowest level of role perfor-

mance). Analogous findings have been reported in studies of language acquisition. Children in the two-word stage can verbally express action–object,
agent–object, agent–recipient, or agent–action relations (Greenfield & Smith,
1976). At the same period the encoding of three-part relations using the same
components (e.g., agent–action–object or agent–action–recipient relations) is not
yet possible within the confines of a single utterance. If similar trade-offs occur
in early symbolic play, a child might, for example, be able to make a big bear
kiss a small bear good night (represent an interaction between two replicas)
without being able to embed this event in a longer teddy bear interaction sequence. To study such trade-offs requires resolution of some of the definition
problems discussed in the secions on role and action representation.

The level of event representation (in terms of roles and actions) is also influenced, at least in the early stages, by the realism of the available props. Infants
may be able to act out a sequence or represent another role, provided they have
access to veridical toys, but revert to single-scheme play or self-representation
with a substitute object (see also Watson, in press). This may hold only during
infancy and toddlerhood, however. During the later preschool years nonsugges-
tive toys may help rather than hinder (Phillips, 1945; Pulaski, 1973; also reviewed in Fein, 1981). Studies in which role-, action-, and object-representation
in children's spontaneous play are examined as separate but interacting dimensions still remain to be done.

One aspect of event representation in pretense which I have so far neglected,
but which becomes very prominent during the third and fourth years, pertains
to procedural rules. In collaborative play children not only enact make-believe
sequences, but plan, negotiate, and coordinate their enactment. The term
metacommunication was coined by Bateson (1955/1972, 1956/1971) to refer to
messages that communicate to co-players that "this is play" as opposed to "not
play." The content and use of metacommunication in the pretense of preschoolers is reviewed in the next section. I would like to draw attention to the
fact, however, that the precursors of this ability can be traced to a much-earlier
age, although systematic studies of metacommunicative signals during the second and third years are still lacking. I suggest that the very same criteria that
allow an onlooker to judge whether a child is engaging in a literal or nonliteral
act (Nicolich, 1977) can also be interpreted as metacommunication about play.
Several relevant instances are described in Piaget (1962). For example, Jacqueline at 15 months "alluded" to closed eyes by blinking as she put her head on
a blanket in pretend sleep (Observation 64a). At 28 months she announced her
transformed identity to her father ("It's Mommy"), assuming a third-person
bystander role, before requesting that Piaget give "Mommy" a kiss (Observation
79). Yet when transforming herself into a cat at 32 months (Observation 79),
she merely crawled into the room on all fours saying "Miouw." Perhaps overt
metacommunication is less necessary when the enactment itself is clarification

enough. Several further illustrations of metacommunication during the third year can be found in Miller and Garvey (Chapter 4, this volume) and Dunn and Dale (Chapter 5, this volume). Very early comprehension, as opposed to production, of metacommunicative signals is suggested by Fein and Moorin's (in press) case study of a 15-month-old girl who responded appropriately to verbal pretend invitations to "feed" a doll or adults. Notwithstanding early precursors, the metacommunicative ability truly comes into its own during the preschool years. Event representation now seems to proceed on two levels, planning and enactment, a topic more fully discussed in the next section.

MAP AND TERRITORY: TWO LEVELS OF EVENT REPRESENTATION IN SYMBOLIC PLAY

Because acts of pretending often resemble their real-world counterparts closely it is necessary to mark the make-believe reality as simulation or fiction. Bateson (1955/1972) first drew attention to the fact that pretense, to set it off from not-play, must somehow be identified or framed by the message "this is play." Metacommunicative signals enable coplayers or onlookers to distinguish real actions or mood signs from those that resemble them but are not meant in the usual sense of the word. The acts of make-believe are, Bateson (1955/1972) pointed out, characterized by a logical paradox, which he paraphrased as follows: "These actions in which we now engage do not denote what the actions for which they stand would denote" (p. 180) or put more concretely, "This nip is not a bite." Although such metacommunicative statements represent logical nightmares for philosophers, they are apparently quite transparent to children.

In discussing metacommunicative signals, Bateson (1955/1972, 1956/1971) uses two metaphors: the frame and the map. The message "this is play" frames play, indicating that material contained within the frame is to be interpreted as different from the surround. However, as Bateson pointed out, although the two levels (out-of-frame metacommunication and within-frame acting) are logically distinct, in actual play these levels are often intertwined. Play-acts and utterances therefore tend to carry multiple levels of meaning, which can only be disentangled conceptually.

Bateson's second metaphor refers to the same logical distinction. Make-believe, he claims, is to everyday reality as a map is to a territory. The analogy holds in the sense that the played or simulated reality is a representation (map), but the limitations of the map–territory metaphor are revealed upon closer analysis of the map's content. Pretending, I suggest, hardly ever constitutes straight re-production of event schemata. Whereas scripts and specific memories provide the raw material for make-believe scenes, play is not usually an attempt at faith-

ful reconstruction. Rather, make-believe consists of making new maps by transforming old ones (a point that is elaborated in the last section of this chapter).
The map–territory distinction is still useful, however, in discussing differences
between the actual and the fictional as a problem of levels.

Although map and territory, to continue the metaphor, are logically distinct,
the levels have a way of becoming tangled in play. Frightening make-believe
themes may become so "real" that a player feels compelled to step outside the
playframe or refuses to enter it, as the following conversation between two preschoolers, taken from Garvey and Berndt's (1977) protocols, illustrates;

Pretend there is a monster coming, OK?
No, let's don't pretend that.
OK, why?
'Cause it's too scary, that's why.

On the other hand, real-world concerns may intrude into the make-believe
world in a number of ways (through the themes that are enacted, how the roles
are distributed, bits of external reality incorporated into the play). As Hofstadter
(1979) pointed out, the paradoxical tangling of levels possible in human representation has preoccupied many artists and writers. A most striking depiction
of the paradox is Escher's lithograph *Print Gallery* (see Figure 1). The picture
shows an art gallery. Looking into the gallery from outside we see a young man
who is looking at a picture of a town. The picture-within-the-picture bursts out
of its frame, however, to merge with the "real" town, the town that contains
the art gallery in which there is a boy. . . . Hofstadter graphically clarifies the
paradox depicted by Escher's print (Figure 1) in the abstract diagram of Figure
2. The young man is *in* the gallery which is *in* the town, but the town is also
in the picture (graphic representation) which is *in* the young man (mental representation).

The management and tangling of map and territory in pretend play has been
addressed in three major studies concerned with the conduct of collaborative
make-believe (Garvey & Berndt, 1977; Giffin, Chapter 3, this volume; Schwartzman, 1978). All three studies emphasize metacommunication or frame negotiation, but in somewhat different ways. In addition, Scarlett and Wolf (1979)
have reflected on the same question as it applies to play with small doll figures
(replica play).

Garvey and Berndt (1977) went beyond Bateson (1955/1972). They emphasized that the joint creation of a make-believe reality requires more than the
message "this is play." In order to pretend with companions, children need
techniques for negotiating about content: what theme or script is to be played,
and where as well as how the theme is to be realized. Garvey and Berndt studied
48 acquainted dyads in which partners were of similar age, but ages ranged from
34 to 67 months. The children were observed during 8 minutes of spontaneous,
joint make-believe play in a laboratory playroom. From this material Garvey

Figure 1. M. C. Escher's *Print Gallery* (as illustrated in Hofstadter, 1979, p. 715). Printed with permission. Copyright © BEELDRECHT, Amsterdam/V.A.G.A., New York, Collection Haags Gemeentemusem—The Hague, 1981.

and Berndt developed a system for categorizing the behaviors (mostly verbal statements) through which children regulate the content and conduct of play. Aside from preparatory or procedural statements such as "do you want to play with me" or "It's my turn now," players explicitly inform each other (metacommunicate about) roles, plans, and props. Garvey (1977) and Garvey and Berndt (1977) distinguished the following metacommunicative messages:

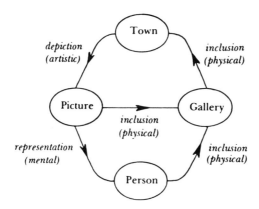

Figure 2. Abstract diagram of M. C. Escher's *Print Gallery* (from Hofstadter, 1979, p. 715).

(1) Mention role	other's	"Are you going to be a bride?"
	own	"I'm a lady at work."
	joint	"We can both be wives."
(2) Mention plan	other's	"Pretend you hated baby fish."
	own	"I gotta drive to the shopping center."
	joint	"We have to eat. Our dinner's ready."
(3) Mention object	transform	"This is the train,"putting suitcase on sofa.
	invent	"Now this is cheese," pointing to empty plate.
(4) Mention setting	transform	"This is a cave,"pointing to wooden structure.
	invent	"We're there," about imaginary picnic site.

Garvey and Berndt pointed out that roles, actions, and objects are sometimes only mentioned, not acted. For example, the role of grandmother can be brought into the game by calling her on the telephone.

Entry into the pretense world is not only explicitly instituted, but can also be explicitly terminated by statements that negate make-believe roles ("I'm not the dad"), actions ("I'm not dead"), props ("that's not a car") and settings ("we're not at the beach"). Especially interesting are back-transformations ("It's not a cake anymore"; "Please don't push me 'cause I'm not the dragon anymore"). Such exits from the make-believe world were also analyzed by Matthews (1978).

Giffin's study (Chapter 3, this volume) focused not so much on the content of metacommunication but on *how* children use a variety of metacommunicative options to coordinate shared meanings. Careful analysis of 31 play episodes produced by 38 previously acquainted preschool children in groups of two to five players suggested that collaborative make-believe may be guided by an unspoken rule not to expose the pretend illusion unnecessarily. Giffin identified categories of metacommunication that lay on a continuum from deeply within-frame to completely out-of-frame.

Whereas enactment itself can, through exaggerated gestures and postures, convey the message "this is play" (see also Garvey and Berndt, 1977), it may be less obvious how the content of play can be redirected without stepping out-of-frame. Giffin discovered that children were able to do just that. What she terms *ulterior conversation* looks like enactment but is really a surreptitious way of suggesting a change of script. For example, the question "Is it lunchtime?" is ulterior conversation if the children are not already playing at having lunch. A somewhat more overt form of metacommunication, which has the appearance of being within-frame, is *underscoring*. Statements such as "I'll pour the milk" spoken as a pitcher is tipped over an empty cup informs the playmate that the pitcher "contains" milk as opposed to juice. Such statements do not jar, especially if spoken in character-voice. Remarks such as "I'm crying" said in a wailing tone of voice disturb the illusion somewhat more obviously, although they do not explicitly step out of the playframe. Giffin noticed that some types of underscoring statements were rhythmically chanted (e.g., "wash—wash—wash" accompanied by rubbing clothes or "cooky—cooky—cooky" accompanied by a few stirring motions above a pot.) Such *magicking* is interpreted by Giffin as a theatrical device, wherein chanting both metacommunicates about and partially stands for an abbreviated make-believe action.

A special singsong cadence also characterizes *storytelling*, which, interestingly, tends to be couched in the past tense. This sophisticated form of verbal pretending permits the development of more elaborate plots, such as "and you went to bed right after supper. . . . I went to bed later than you. . . . I went to bed three hours later than you. . . . and the kitty went to bed even before you" (Giffin, 1981, p. 99). Giffin speculates that the cadence keeps the players psychologically within the play-reality, but at the same time detached enough to create it. Volterra (Chapter 8, this volume) describes the fantasies of a 2-year-old, which were almost entirely of this verbal variety.

There are occasions when it becomes necessary for a player to step completely out-of-frame to clarify or "improve" the joint performance. *Prompting*, often done with lowered voice, is a technique whereby one player instructs a partner how to act and what to say while temporarily abandoning the play identity— (for example "You didn't talk like that. You say (sweetly) 'What's the matter,

Mother?'" (from Giffin, Chapter 3, this volume). One of Garvey and Berndt's (1977) protocols illustrates a girl of 3:3 prompting a boy of 2:9!

Finally, Giffin identified *implicit* and *formal pretend proposals*. These are closest to the categories described by Garvey and Berndt (1977). In *implicit proposals* the frame is not stated, but the designation of roles ("I'm the mommy"), of settings ("this is the kitchen") or of objects ("this is my key") clearly constitutes communication about the play to ensue, not an already established theme. *Formal pretend statements* are even more explicit (e.g., "Let's pretend (say, play) we were monsters"). According to Giffin formal pretend proposals occur much less frequently than one might expect and are most likely to be employed at the start of play.

Once a play-episode has begun players tend to resort to more indirect forms of managing the pretend reality. Skilled players, as defined by Giffin, know when they can afford to metacommunicate within-frame and when it is necessary to step out of frame even though this breaks the illusion conservation rule. An example is the direction "Pretend that I was dead, but you thought I was alive" (made by a child of 3:9). It is difficult to see how an idea of this complexity could have been conveyed by mere acting (lying still). Further studies are now necessary to find out in what order the various metacommunicative options are acquired and to pinpoint developmental changes in the skill with which they are used.

Independently of the work on collaborative symbolic play, Scarlett and Wolf (1979) examined how children manage the boundary between make-believe and reality in play with small human and animal figures. Instead of playing the dual role of producer and actor, the child who animates small figures assumes the dual-level roles of narrator (to a real or imagined audience) and vicarious actor. Yet we find that many devices, such as narration, occur not only in collaborative play (in the form of underscoring and storytelling), but also in play with small figures.

Perhaps because they observed younger children than those who particpated in the three studies of collaborative pretending just reviewed, Scarlett and Wolf (1979) noted that the two planes—reality and pretense—are, at first, difficult to keep apart and tend all too easily to blend into one another. In their study of spontaneous and prompted play with small human and animal figures, 2-year-olds frequently backed away with genuine fear when the observer animated a small toy alligator. Children at this age were not able to cope with the pretend threat on its own terms (for example by making a lion chase the observer's alligator). At other times young children entered the story scene as deus ex machina to rescue a figure "endangered" by the observer's play. This behavior is conceptually similar to Garvey and Berndt's example of a child who refused to play monsters because "it's too scary." Confusion of levels (reality and simulation) is especially likely if the thematic content of play is highly emotional. But is this really as surprising as it may seem? After all, even adults weep during dramatic presentations and adults, not merely children, sometimes treat symbolic objects (a flag, a cross) as if they were that for which they stand (Bateson, 1956/1971). Fictive reality does arouse genuine emotion and particpation. It is never completely detached except in the logical sense. Indeed, it would carry little meaning if it were.

The ability to keep out-of-frame and within-frame roles (narrator and vicarious actor) distinct develops concurrently with a greater facility to weave back and forth between levels. Wolf (1981), in a meticulous longitudinal study of five children, found that 24 month olds begin to narrate what the vicariously activated human and animal figures are doing. Toward the end of the same year children narrate what the figures did in the past and what they are about to do. At the same time the literary device "she said" is introduced when speaking for the figures (e.g., "I can't," said the girl). In the fourth year Wolf observed the emergence of metanarrative, where the child briefly steps out of the narrator role to instruct the audience how the props are to be taken (a piece of wood is cheese). The formula "let's pretend" also occurs in this connection. In short, by the end of the preschool period the bulk of fictive meaning is not primarily carried by activation of the figures but by what the children say about or for the characters, including their plans, and motives (see Wolf et al., Chapter 7, this volume, for an extensive discussion of this topic).

Note that Wolf's (1981) categories are remarkably similar to those developed quite independently and in a somewhat different context by Giffin. There is of course a reason for this: Play with small human and animal figures and collaborative play with other children are not as distinct as I have pretended so far. Make-believe with small figures can be (and often is) collaborative—that is, there may be two cooperating narrators. Conversely, collective make-believe frequently includes dolls and stuffed animals whom the children vicariously animate in addition to playing their own assumed in-frame roles and managing out-of-frame roles as writers, directors, and prompters.

Just as Escher collapsed his paradoxical representation of an intertwined three-dimensional and two-dimensional reality onto one two-dimensional surface in the lithograph *Print Gallery* (Figure 1; Hofstadter, 1979), so children collapse several levels of event representation (out-of-frame planning and within-frame acting) in their conduct of make-believe play. They do this so effortlessly that the presence of several conceptual levels has, until recently, quite escaped our notice. Sutton-Smith (1979) has suggested that all play be considered a quadralogue in which an individual player must keep track of four prototypical parties: actor, co-actor, director, and audience. Although his position is similar to the one proposed here, his model omits the emphasis on levels of event representation. Conceptually the relationship of actor and co-actor is situated within the playframe, whereas the relationship of director and codirector is conducted outside the playframe—even if, as in prompting, stepping outside the playframe is brief and intermittent or, as in ulterior conversation or underscoring, only implicit.

Yet another perspective on the problem of levels in make-believe play is provided by Schwartzman (1978). In studying a group of low socioeconomic status children in a day-care center over a period of 18 months, she found that the relationship of the players to each other outside the play context (friendships, dominance) affected the content and process of collaborative pretend play. These findings led Schwartzman to claim that play can be regarded as text and context. Play as text is the creation of a make-believe reality within the real-world context of the day-care center. Play as context is play as a commentary on the everyday relationships of the players as children in a day-care center.

> In order to be a successful player, one must be able to communicate information that simultaneously (and paradoxically) defines one as a player *subject* (e.g., adopting the play role of witch, mother, etc.) and as a person in the defining social context (e.g., the day-care center) and therefore a play *object*. For example, a child (Linda) must be able to communicate to other players and that she is both Linda (i.e., a person who leads, dominates, and directs activities, as she is known for this in the general classroom setting) and not-Linda (i.e., a witch or mother) in a play situation [Schwartzman, 1978, p. 236].

This emphasis on the social relations of the players led Schwartzman to pay attention to the manner in which different children used metacommunicative statements to enter and exit from a joint make-believe reality. Whereas Garvey and Berndt's (1977) primary interest was in what had to be communicated and Giffin's in the degree to which metacommunicative messages were in or out of frame, Schwartzman focused on when and how specific children used the following set of statements.

1. Formation statements: "Let's play house."
2. Connection statements: "Can I be the daddy?"
3. Rejection statements: "You can't play here."
4. Disconnection statements: "I'm not the sister anymore."
5. Maintenance statements: "The daddy burnt himself, quick bring a band-aid."
6. Definition statements: "I'm cooking dinner."
7. Acceptance statements: "OK, I'm eating it."
8. Counterdefinition statements: "No, this is meat, not rice."

Schwartzman noticed that these statements were used differentially by high- and low-status group members. High-status children could join ongoing play by peremptorily adopting a role or defining an activity, whereas low-status children had to ask for permission to join and play particular roles ("Can I be the witch?"). Moreover, the roles children played tended to reflect the actual authority struc-

ture of the group. Those who frequently played mothers and fathers were the
most popular children in the classroom. By contrast, the role of pet ("kitty" or
"doggy") was often assumed by one of the less-popular children, although there
were exceptions to this rule. The leading child in the day-care center sometimes
paradoxically defined herself in a submissive role even as she continued to direct
activities of her co-players. In short, Schwartzman found that the process and
content of pretending was strongly influenced by the children's out-of-frame
social relationships.

Schwartzman's notion that pretend play can be interpreted as a commentary
on co-players' nonplay relations is derived from anthropology, which has noted
such phenomena in larger social contexts. For example, Geertz (1972/1973) has
suggested that certain rituals may be interpretive of the culture that created
them. In Geertz's view the Balinese cockfight mirrors, and at the same time
defines, aspects of the structure and functioning of Balinese society while permitting the expression of strong emotions that must be controlled in everyday
interactions.

If Schwartzman is correct that co-players remain cognizant of their everyday
relationships as they engage in make-believe (and the findings of Dunn and
Dale, Chapter 5, this volume, corroborate Schwartzman), we have to add yet
another layer of meaning to an already complicated situation. I have previously
stated that the construction of joint pretense requires that children take and play
roles on two levels: as out-of-frame writer–directors of make-believe events and
as within-frame actors. In play with small figures children engage in similar
multileveled role playing and role taking as narrators and vicarious actors. If
play activities also reflect real-world relationships of the participating children,
the multiple meanings embedded in the representation of make-believe events
begin to assume mind-boggling proportions. This is not all, however. The events
represented in pretense are fictive: The roles children play are often not their
own, the objects serving as props are frequently not what they purport to be,
and the scripts may represent physically impossible worlds. The simulated territory of symbolic play is not necessarily a straight reproduction of real-world
maps.

THE REPRESENTATION OF SUBJUNCTIVE
EVENTS IN SYMBOLIC PLAY

The term *make-believe* is used in several different ways. First, it serves to
distinguish the level of everyday reality where one actually eats, drinks, and
sleeps from the fictive here one merely simulates these behaviors. It is in this
"as-if" sense that I used make-believe in the previous section. In a somewhat

different sense the label make-believe refers to transformations of reality into fictive worlds where a spoon can be a telephone, toddlers can be mother or father, animals speak, and people can fly or become invisible. In this section I talk about make-believe in this second "what-if" sense.

Hofstadter (1979) has pointed out that human beings constantly manufacture mental variants on the situations they face. Unconsciously manufactured subjunctives, Hofstadter proposed, represent some of the richest potential sources of insights into how humans organize and categorize their perceptions of the world. I agree with him. Yet this "subjunctive" capacity has not, to my knowledge, been formally studied. To quote Hofstadter,

> The manufacture of "subjunctive worlds" happens so casually, so naturally, that we hardly notice what we are doing. We select from our fantasy a world which is close, in some internal mental sense, to the real world. We compare what is real with what we perceive as *almost* real. In so doing we gain some intangible kind of perspective on reality. . . . Think how immeasurably poorer our lives would be if we didn't have this capacity for slipping out of the midst of reality into soft "what ifs"! And from the point of view of studying human thought this slippage is very interesting, for most of the time is happens completely without conscious direction, which means that observation of what kind of things slip, versus what kinds don't, affords a good window on the unconscious mind [emphasis in orginal; 1979, p. 643].

Hofstadter proposed a hierarchy of conditions in which the lowest levels (e.g., a specific behavior) can slip quite easily, higher levels (e.g., the context for the behavior) are more resistant to slippage, and the highest levels (e.g., the laws of gravity, causality, three dimensional space) hardly slip at all.

Oddly, Piaget, who was a master at noticing interesting problems others had overlooked, took the ability to engage in counterfactual representation completely for granted. The cognitive implications of the phrase *assimilation to the ego* (distorting reality according to one's wishes) are nowhere elaborated. It appears that assimilation of reality to the ego is something children are simply able to do for the pleasure of mastering reality, to liquidate conflicts, to compensate for unpleasant experiences, to take revenge on reality:

> But why is there assimilation of reality to the ego instead of immediate assimilation of the universe to experimental and logical thought? It is simply because in early childhood this thought has not yet been constructed, and during its development it is inadequate to supply the needs of daily life [Piaget, 1962, p. 166].

Yet even wishful thinking, it seems to me, requires a cognitive capacity to create alternative worlds, at least in a small way. There is subjunctive thought when pretense serves to correct reality, as illustrated by the following two examples of "compensatory" symbolic combinations.

> At 2; 4(8)., J., not being allowed to play with the water being used for washing, took an empty cup, went and stood by the forbidden tub and went through the actions saying: "I'm pouring out water." At 2;6 (28) she wanted to carry Nonette (i.e., L. who had been

born shortly before). Her mother told her she could try later on. J. folded her arms and said: "Nonette's in there. There are two Nonettes." She then talked to the imaginary Nonette, rocked her etc. [Piaget, 1962, Observation 84, p. 131].

The same is true when symbolic play is employed to liquidate a disagreeable event by "reproducing scenes in which the ego ran the risk of failure, thereby enabling it to assimilate them and emerge victorious" (Piaget, 1962, p. 134). In the following example Jacqueline alters reality by projecting an unpleasant experience onto another recipient:

J., at 2; 1(7), was afraid when sitting on a new chair at table. In the afternoon she put her dolls in uncomfortable positions and said to them: "It doesn't matter. It will be allright," repeating what had been said to her [Piaget, 1962, Observation 86, p. 133].

Counterfactual play did not, in Piaget's view, require a cognitive explanation. Yet distortion of reality whether for the sake of mastering emotional conflict (Erikson, 1963; Peller, 1952/1971) or for the sake of power reversal, admiration, and the mere fun of generating paradox (Sutton-Smith, 1979) must be based on already-existing event schemata, albeit transformed by substitution of alternative and sometimes paradoxical actors, recipients, objects, or actions into routine scripts. In many cases such substitution is deliberate, although some fantastic events produced in play may merely reflect the child's level of misunderstanding.

Nelson and Gruendel (1981) as well as Nelson and Seidman (Chapter 2, this volume) downplayed the fantasy aspect of make-believe by claiming that much pretending consists of the playing through of scripts. Certainly the research on *early* pretense supports them. The first transformations (self-representation) are merely "as-if" transformations in which routine events are simulated. The substitution of unlikely agents (a toddler plays an adult, an inanimate object is treated as a living person) and unlikely objects (a stick is a spoon, a box is a plate) are low-level "what-if" transformations, which do not create impossible or distorted scripts. Indeed, in the second year pretense seems to become more realistic and organized, not more fantastic in the sense of deliberate play with the laws of time, space, and causality.

However, we know from Garvey's (1977) work that fictive roles and actions become increasingly common during the preschool years. Material from Scarlett and Wolf's (1979) case study also supports the notion that "impossible" subjunctive worlds become more internally consistent with age, that fantasy undergoes cognitive development. It may be that in order to create coherent fantasy one has first to gain a coherent understanding of everyday reality.

Yet, even when the make-believe ability is well developed, there are limits on the extent to which reality is allowed to slip (in Hofstadter's sense). In preschoolers "slippability" seems to have more to do with the socioemotional significance of particular transformations for particular children than with the hierarchy of conditions proposed by Hofstadter (1979). In general, preschoolers appear far more willing to transform their generational status than their gender (Garvey & Berndt, 1977). In mixed sex dyads boys steadfastly refused the role of mother but accepted the role of father. In single-sex dyads boys did sometimes play functional roles normally assumed by females (server of food) but without overtly identifying with a female character role. When mixed sex dyads played "averting threat" the boy, true to stereotype, was usually cast in the role of defender and the girl in the role of victim. Along similar lines, Schwartzman (1978) found that high status children tended to resist being cast in roles which contravened their everyday social status. Some of Giffin's findings are also relevant here. Giffin (Chapter 3, this volume) noted that in the creation of pretend transformations co-players seemed to operate on the basis of an unspoken principle which she termed the *incorporation rule*. When a player did not want to assume the unpleasant role of victim vis-à-vis the other player's monster, both could become monsters chasing imaginary victims.

Children's resistance to emotionally distasteful or threatening transformations derives from the tangling of levels (reality and simulation) to which I referred in the previous section. The out-of-frame world also intrudes into the play world in other, less emotionally charged ways. Some of the plot changes (retransformations) described by Giffin (Chapter 3, this volume) were precipitated by the wish to admit new players. When a "car" to be taken on an imaginary journey became too small to hold all the players who were eager to join, a "camper" was added to accommodate them. In one case, two children created the synthetic role of doctor–mommy, which enabled them to play the family and doctor scripts simultaneously and thus satisfy both children's plans. In addition, out-of-frame events (a child falls over) are often taken into the frame by adjusting the plot (the child is taken to a "hospital"). This phenomenon was also noticed by Schwartzman (1978) and by Wolf and Pusch (1982). Such transformations of transformations in response to real-world events or real-world constraints again bring home the paradoxical intertwining of out-of-frame and within-frame content, of map and territory.

Whereas much remains to be discovered about the *reasons* for particular transformations, we can be somewhat more specific about the *structure* of transformations. Persons and objects can be transformed without necessarily creating an outlandish script. A toddler can play "mother" to a baby doll by feeding it with a block. The script here, although acted by unlikely agents and with the aid of unlikely props, may be fairly ordinary and routine. Action transformation, by contrast, does not work in quite the same way. It is true that make-believe actions may be unrealistic in the sense of being stylized, ritualized, or abbreviated. Flapping the arms once or twice *can* stand for flying. However, one action cannot stand for a different one in the same way that a prop can stand for something that does not resemble it at all. When make-believe actions suspend the laws of time, space, and causality they transform the script itself.

There is, of course, a reason why this is the case. Think, for example, of how scripts are generally described. Schank and Abelson (1977) defined the socalled restaurant script by the actions (being seated, ordering, eating, paying, leaving). Nelson and Seidman (Chapter 2, this volume) follow the same procedure. This makes sense only because the mention of actions imposes fairly severe constraints on possible agents, recipients, and objects. The act of flying implies an actor who can fly (a bird or Batman). The act of driving implies a driver and a vehicle. Because actions often serve actually to *create* role and object transformations they cannot themselves be transformed without transforming the script. In talking about fantasy it may thus be useful to make a distinction between the enactment of fairly realistic scripts in which the agents and objects are not what they purport to be (low-level "what-if" play) and fantasy scripts (high-level "what-if" play). The latter can be produced by inserting unlikely actions into real-world scripts, by linking the component actions of a script in causally or temporally inappropriate or paradoxical ways or by creating scripts that, akin to parables, disguise a realistic event while retaining aspects of its relational structure. These are, of course, but a few of the many possibilities.

CONCLUSIONS

In considering symbolic play in terms of the intertwining of map and territory and the creation of subjunctive realities, we have moved a long way from the discussion of make-believe in terms of mere role- and action-representation. In what way are these more complex phenomena related to social understanding?

I suggest that the ability to engage in "serious" mental trial and error ("what if I did it this way, rather than that way") and the ability to engage in make-believe are two different facets of the same representational function. In other words, organisms who can create mental alternatives prior to action are ipso facto able to play with this ability, just as organisms with delicate voluntary control over motor actions can and do play with their motor skills (Fagen, 1981). Indeed, Piaget (1962) makes much the same claim, noting that because representation enables children to go beyond the perceptual field they can distort reality according to their wishes and subordinate it to the ends they want to achieve. I differ from him only in claiming that the complexity of subjunctive thought is rooted in and thus reflects real-world understanding.

Not all children seem willing to play with their representational ability to the same degree (Wolf & Grollman, 1982)). Past infancy the imaginative disposition appears to be more a matter of cognitive style than of cognitive level. Some individuals refuse to contemplate fanciful ideas or repress them before they even come to mind, whereas others enjoy toying with subjunctive thoughts, however outlandish these might be. Nevertheless, the quality of fantasy an individual can produce ought to be related to the coherence and sophistication of his or her real-world knowledge. The ability to create imaginary worlds (even of the low-level "what-if" variety) should not, I believe, simply be taken for granted as it was by Piaget (1962).

A second major component of make-believe is the ability to engage in subjunctive event representation for and with others, creating both the possibility for sharing one's inner world (Bretherton & Beeghly, 1982) and the possibility for deceit or pretense. Bateson (1955/1972) pointed out that pretense (and communication as we know it) becomes possible only when an organism realizes that mood signs (and I would include all actions) are signals that can be trusted or distrusted, falsified or denied, amplified or corrected. Thus make-believe is linked to the capacity to lie, to "put on a show," to deceive, and, at the other end of the value scale, to engage in sacred ritual. In the case of lying the communicator hopes that the addressee will not perceive the deception. In the case of make-believe and ritual the participants jointly agree to create an alternative reality.

It is presumably because of its close association with deceit that children's make-believe play creates both enchantment and unease in adult onlookers. A further reason for unease in the face of pretense is the incompleteness of the map–territory distinction. By claiming that "a behavior is only pretend," real-world antagonisms can be surreptitiously acted out. The real is tranformed into apparent "make-believe," a process that can also work in the reverse direction. What started as deliciously thrilling make-believe can become frighteningly or distressingly real. Adults, as noted before, are not immune from this effect. Indeed, it may be that the tendency for map and territory to blend is an inevitable part of the capacity to simulate reality in order to entertain alternative courses of action.

Mature artists, in their fictive event representations, play much more consciously with potential map–territory confusions and distinctions and with the paradoxes of metacommunication than do young children. Some try to pack as many layers of meaning into a literary work or painting as possible. Others try to eliminate meaning altogether and play only with the texture of paint or language. Some try to imagine alternative worlds or utopias, others tease an audience with inappropriate or omitted metacommunication, and yet others explore the paradox of levels of creating plays within plays and pictures within pictures. Preschoolers do not yet exploit these devices with the conscious artfulness of a writer, poet, or painter, but there are occasional glimpses of play with the paradoxes involved in pretense. Giffin's (1981) protocols describe a small boy holding up a match-box car while warning his companion "this is a real fire, this car is burning up." A "real" pretend fire! Likewise, one of the preschoolers in Garvey and Berndt's (1977) study teased another by claiming she had "stealed" her partner's nonexistent cake. The partner nonchalantly retorted that it was not cake anymore.

I suggest that the ability to create symbolic alternatives to reality and to play with that ability is as deeply a part of human experience as the ability to construct an adapted model of everyday reality. Indeed, the successful building of accurate models may often involve prior play with a number of alternative possibilities. Conversely, the complexity and quality of subjunctive thought (whether in symbolic play or other contexts) is likely to depend on already existing cognitive structures. It is presumably for this reason that creativity, cognitive flexibility, and divergent thinking have frequently been linked to a fantasy predisposition (Dansky & Silverman, 1975; Lieberman, 1977; Singer, 1973; Sutton-Smith, 1968).

If symbolic play is not straight event reproduction but play with social reality, its interpretation as an index of social understanding poses problems. But these are more apparent than real. Much play seems to consist of a large admixture of reality with a much smaller admixture of fantasy. Where there is distortion of real-world scripts, we may need to look at script understanding and play separately to discover the extent to which a child is toying with reality and the extent to which what seems to be fantasy and imagination is really a representation of social misunderstanding. More importantly, however, the ability to create "what ifs," to function in the subjunctive and simulative mode, is itself a vital aspect of human experience and hence of social understanding, one that deserves much more extensive study.

As Steiner, the linguist, phrased it,

> We hypothesize and project thought into the "if-ness," into the free conditionalities of the unknown. Such projection is no logical muddle, no abuse of induction. It is far more than a probabilistic convention. It is the master nerve of human action . . . . Ours is the ability, the need to gainsay or "un-say" the world, to image and speak it otherwise. . . to define the "other than the case," the counterfactual propositions, images, shapes of will and evasion with which we charge our mental being and by which we build the largely fictive milieu of our somatic and social existence [1975, pp. 217, 218, 222].

Children do not just say it otherwise, they play it otherwise.

ACKNOWLEDGMENTS

I would like to express my gratitude to Elizabeth Bates, Judy Dunn, Larry Fenson, Lorraine McCune-Nicolich, Barbara O'Connell, and Cecilia Shore for helpful comments on previous versions of this manuscript. Special thanks are due to Greta Fein for a detailed and influential critique.

During the writing of this paper I received support from the Spencer Foundation, a Biomedical Research Support Grant and the MacArthur Foundation Network on the Transition from Infancy to Early Childhood.

REFERENCES

Aebli, H. *Denken: Das Ordnen des Tuns* (Vol. 1). Stuttgart, Federal Republic of Germany: Klett-Cotta, 1980.

Bates, E., Benigni, L., Bretherton, I., Camaioni, L., & Volterra, V. *The emergence of symbols: Cognition and communication in infancy.* New York: Academic Press, 1979.

Bateson, G. The message "This is play." In R. E. Herron & B. Sutton-Smith (Eds.), *Child's play.* New York: Wiley, 1971. (Reprinted from B. Schaffner (Ed.), *Group processes: Transactions of the second conference.* New York: Josiah Macy, Jr. Foundation, 1956.)

Bateson, G. A theory of play and fantasy. In G. Bateson, *Steps to an ecology of mind.* New York: Chandler, 1972. (Reprinted from *American Psychiatric Association Research Reports*, 1955, *II*, 39–51.

Bloom, L. *One word at a time: The use of single word utterances before syntax.* The Hague, The Netherlands: Mouton, 1973.

Bretherton, I., & Beeghly, M. Talking about internal states: The acquisition of an explicit theory of mind. *Developmental Psychology*, 1982, *18*, 906–921.

Bretherton, I., Bates, E., McNew, S., Shore, C., Williamson, C., & Beeghly-Smith, M. Comprehension and production of symbols in infancy. *Developmental Psychology*, 1981, *17*, 728–736.

Brown, R. *A first language: The early stages.* Cambridge, MA Harvard University Press, 1973.

Dansky, J. L., & Silverman, W. I. Play: A general facilitation of associative fluency. *Developmental Psychology*, 1975, *11*, 104.

Elder, J. L., & Pederson, D. R. Preschool children's use of objects in symbolic play. *Child Devel**opement*, 1978, *49*, 500–504.

Erikson, E. H. *Childhood and society.* New York: Norton, 1963.

Fagen, R. *Animal play behavior.* New York: Oxford University Press, 1981.

Fein, G. G. Pretend play in childhood: An integrative view. *Child Development*, 1981, *52*, 1095–1118.

Fein, G. G. Play revisited. In M. Lamb (Ed.), *Social and personality development.* New York: Holt, Rinehart & Winston, 1978.

Fein, G. G. A transformational analysis of pretending. *Developmental Psychology*, 1975, *11*, 291–296.

Fein, G. G. & Apfel, N. Some preliminary observations on knowing and pretending. In M. Smith and M. B. Franklin (Eds.), *Symbolic functioning in childhood.* Hillsdale, NJ: Erlbaum, 1979.

Fein, G. G. & Moorin, E. R. Confusion, substitution, and mastery. In K. Nelson (Ed.), *Children's language* (Vol. 5). Hillsdale, NJ: Erlbaum, in press.

Fenson, L., & Ramsey, D. Decentration and integration of the child's play in the second year. *Child Development*, 1980, *51*, 171–178.

Fenson, L., & Ramsay, D. S. Effects of modeling action sequences on the play of twelve-, fifteen-, and nineteen-month-old children. *Child Development*, 1981, *52*, 1028–1036.

Garvey, C. *Play.* Cambridge, MA: Harvard University Press, 1977.

Garvey, C., & Berndt, R. Organization of pretend play. JSAS *Catalog of Selected Documents in Psychology*, 1977, *7*, (Ms. No. 1589).

Geertz, C. Deep play: Notes on the Balinese cockfight. In C. Geertz, *The interpretation of cultures.* New York: Basic Books, 1973. (Reprinted from *Daedalus*, 1972, *101*, 1–37.)

Giffin, H. *The metacommunicative process in collective make-believe play.* Unpublished doctoral dissertation, University of Colorado, Boulder, 1981.

Greenfield, P. M., & Smith, J. *The structure of communication in early language development.* New York: Academic Press, 1976.

Hofstadter, D. R. *Gödel, Escher, Bach: An eternal golden braid.* New York: Basic Books, 1979.

Huttenlocher, J., & Higgins, E. T. Issues in the study of symbolic development. In W. A. Collins (Ed.), *Minnesota Symposia on Child Psychology* (Vol. 11). Hillsdale, NJ: Erlbaum, 1978.

Inhelder, B., & Lézine, I., Sinclair, H., & Stambak, G. Les débuts de la fonction symbolique. *Archives de Psychologie*, 1972, *163*, 187–243.

Jeffree, D., & McConkey, R. An observation scheme for recording children's imaginative doll play. *Journal of Child Psychology and Psychiatry*, 1976, *17*, 189–197.

Kagan, J. *The second year: The emergence of self-awareness.* Cambridge, MA: Harvard University Press, 1981.

Kintsch, W. *The representation of meaning in memory.* Hillsdale, NJ: Erlbaum, 1974.

Largo, R., & Howard, J. Developmental progression in play behavior in children between 9 and 30 months. *Developmental Medicine and Child Neurology*, 1979, *21*, 299–310.

Lieberman, J. N. *Playfulness: Its relationship to imagination and creativity.* New York: Academic Press, 1977.

Lowe, H. Trends in the development of representational play in infants from one to three years: An observational study. *Psychology and Psychiatry*, 1975, *16*, 33–47.

Mandler, J. H. Categorical and schematic organization in memory. In C. K. Puff (Ed.), *Memory organization and structure.* New York: Academic Press, 1979.

Mandler, J. M., & DeForest, M. Is there more than one way to recall a story. *Child Development*, 1979, *50*, 886–889.

Matthews, W. S. Modes of transformation in the initiation of fantasy play. *Developmental Psychology*, 1977, *13*, 211–216.

Matthews, W. S. *Breaking the fantasy frame: An analysis of the interruptions and terminations of young children's fantasy play episodes.* Paper presented at the meeting of the Eastern Psychological Association, Washington, DC, March 1978.

Mead, G. H. *Mind, self, and society.* Chicago: University of Chicago Press, 1934.

Nelson, K. Social cognition in a script framework. In J. H. Flavell & L. Ross (Eds.), *Social cognitive development.* Cambridge: Cambridge University Press, 1981.

Nelson, K., and Gruendel, J. Generalized event representations: Basic building blocks of cognitive development. In A. Brown & M. Lamb (Eds.), *Advances in developmental psychology* (Vol. 1). Hillsdale, NJ: Erlbaum, 1981.

Nicolich, L. M. Beyond sensorimotor intelligence: Assessment of symbolic maturity through analysis of pretend play. *Merrill-Palmer Quarterly*, 1977, *23*, 88–99.

Overton, W. F., & Jackson, J. P. The representation of imaged objects in action sequences: A developmental study. *Child Development*, 1973, *44*, 309–314.

Peller, L. E. Models of children's play. In R. E. Herron & B. Sutton-Smith (Eds.), *Child's play.* New York: Wiley, 1971. (Reprinted from *Mental Hygiene*, 1952, *36*, 66–83.)

Phillips, R. Doll play as a function of the realism of the materials and the length of the experimental session. *Child Development*, 1945, *16*, 145–166.

Piaget, J. *Play, dreams and imitation in childhood.* New York: Norton, 1962.

Pulaski, M. A. Toys and imaginative play. In J. L. Singer (Ed.), *The child's world of make-believe.* New York: Academic Press, 1973.

Rheingold, H. L., & Emery, G. N. The nurturant acts of very young children. In J. Black, D. Olweus, & M. Radke-Yarrow (Eds.), *Aggression and socially valued behavior: Biological and cutural perspectives.* New York: Academic Press, 1983.

Rubin, S., & Wolf, D. The development of maybe: The evolution of social roles into narrative roles. In D. Wolf (Ed.), *New Directions for Child Development* (Vol. 6). San Francisco: Jossey-Bass, 1979.

Scarlett, W. G., & Wolf, D. When it's only make-believe: The construction of a boundary between fantasy and reality. In D. Wolf (Ed.), *New Directions for Child Development* (Vol. 3). San Francisco: Jossey-Bass, 1979.

Schank, R. C. & Abelson, R. P. *Scripts, plans, goals and understanding.* Hillsdale, NJ: Erlbaum, 1977.

Schwartzman, H. B. *Transformations: The anthropology of children's play.* New York: Plenum Press, 1978.

Shimada, S., Sano, R., & Peng, F. A longitudinal study of symbolic play in the second year of life. *Bulletin of the Research Institute for the Education of Exceptional Children,* Tokyo Gakugei University, December 1979.

Singer, J. L. (Ed.). *The child's world of make-believe: Experimental studies of imaginative play.* New York: Academic Press, 1973.

Stein, N. L. The comprehension and appreciation of stories: A developmental analysis. In S. Madeja (Ed.), *The arts and cognition* (Vol. 2). St. Louis, MO: Cemrel, 1978.

Stein, N. L., & Nezworski, M. T. The effect of organization and instruction on story memory. *Discourse Processes,* 1978, *1,* 177–191.

Steiner, G. *After Babel: Aspects of language and translation.* New York: Oxford University Press, 1975.

Sutton-Smith, B. Piaget on play: A critique. *Psychological Review,* 1966, *73,* 104–110.

Sutton-Smith, B. Novel responses to toys. *Merrill-Palmer Quarterly,* 1968, *14,* 151–158.

Sutton-Smith, B. *Play and learning.* New York: Gardner, 1979.

Volterra, V., Bates, E., Benigni, L., Bretherton, I., & Camaioni, L. First words in language and action: A qualitative look. In E. Bates, L. Benigni, I. Bretherton, L. Camaioni, & V. Volterra, *The emergence of symbols: Cognition and communication in infancy.* New York: Academic Press, 1979.

Vygotsky, L. S. Play and its role in the mental development of the child. *Voprosy Psikhologii,* 1966, *12,* 62–76.

Watson, M. W. Agent and recipient objects in the development of early symbolic play. *Child Development,* in press.

Watson, M. W., & Fischer, K. W. A developmental sequence of agent use in late infancy. *Child Development,* 1977, *48,* 828–836.

Watson, M. W. & Fischer, K. W. Development of social roles in elicited and spontaneous behavior during the preschool years. *Child Development,* 1980, *18,* 483–494.

Wolf, D. *How to speak a story: The emergence of narrative language.* Paper presented at the Eleventh Annual Conference of the Jean Piaget Society, Philadelphia, May 1981.

Wolf, D. Understanding others: A longitudinal case study of the concept of independent agency. In G. Forman (Ed.), *Action and thought: From sensorimotor schemes to symbol use.* New York: Academic Press, 1982.

Wolf, D. & Grollman, S. Ways of playing: Individual differences in imaginative play. In K. Rubin and D. Pepler (Eds.), *The play of children: Current theory and research.* New York: Karger, 1982.

Wolf, D., & Pusch, J. Pretend that didn't happen: Children's responses to interruptions in play. In A. Pellegrini & L. Galda (Eds.), *Play and Narrative.* Hillsdale, NJ: Ablex Publishers, 1982.

PART II

Cooperative Symbolic Play

CHAPTER 2

Playing with Scripts*

KATHERINE NELSON
SUSAN SEIDMAN

INTRODUCTION

The language of play comes in many varieties (Garvey, 1977). One form of particular interest for both its cognitive and its language implications is fantasy play. Much that is subsumed under the terms *fantasy* and *pretense* appears to be a recapitulation or simple variation of reality observed or experienced. Playing Cowboys and Indians or Cinderella (no less than their modern counterparts Star Wars or E.T.) requires the establishment between the players of a shared fantasy world that has little or no basis in the child's experience. In contrast, playing house or school or other themes from everyday life requires only that the players instantiate the same or a similar model of what such real-life situations involve. This point is hardly novel. Nor is the related point that the establishment of pretense on the level of variations on the child's experience may be a necessary prelude to the establishment of pretense on the level of a fantasy world.

However, the requirements for establishing a shared world within which play

*Preparation of this paper was supported by NSF Grants no. 78–25810 and 79–14006 to the first author and by an NICHD Training Grant Fellowship (Grant No. 5732HD07196) to the second author.

can proceed need to be examined more closely. Briefly, these requirements are that both participants have available a representation of some event drawn from experience, each similar enough to the other's that they can communicate about that world and maintain a coherent scenario within it. These requirements are more demanding than those for solitary play, and play with peers demands more than does a similar form of play with parents. In solitary play the child has freedom to establish any sort of pretense, to declare any act or object to stand for something else, and to carry out any series of actions and discourse that occur to him or her. (That there may be constraints placed on these choices in terms of the child's own implicit rule system does not negate the general point.) When playing with parents, the child retains great freedom, both because the parent usually grants the child's right to establish the context, and because the parent, having provided the experiential base, shares to a very large extent the child's world. Although parent and child obviously have different world views or perspectives on the same "objective" reality, the parent usually has enough insight into the child's perspective to understand the requirements of the reality temporarily being established in play. In contrast, peers, even when they are familiar playmates, each have different experiential backgrounds, and thus the establishment of a shared reality may be more problematical. (We would expect siblings to lie somewhere between parents and peers on this continuum.) Our interest in these matters concerns how preschool peers establish and maintain a context within which a shared reality-based pretense takes place.

This analysis implies that the most basic requirement for carrying out pretense with peers successfully is to establish a context of shared knowledge within which play and its talk takes place. There are many levels of possible shared knowledge. For example, there is the here-and-now context that children share when playing with blocks, using clay, painting, or engaging in other side-by-side activities that may be carried out together or in parallel. The topic of discussion in these contexts is usually focused on the objects themselves, and as Piaget (1955) and others following noted, such talk often appears egocentric, taking the shape of a collective monologue. Object-centered talk need not, of course, be egocentric in Piaget's sense; participants may engage in action-centered dialogues as well.

If objects do not provide the context of shared knowledge, this context must be established through talk itself. It is also possible to use talk to establish a context that overrides the singular perspective of each participant in object play and turn the collective monologue into a dialogue organized around the shared context of pretense. As noted previously, in order to be successful in establishing a context of shared knowledge, both children must bring to the situation some representation of the reality that is to be established in pretense, and these representations must match sufficiently well so that the talk and actions of the partners can be coordinated, and differences in understanding or interpretation can be negotiated, if necessary.

Where do the necessary representations come from? Obviously some are gleaned from stories, TV characters, or movies. But most basically, and perhaps most successfully, children appear to use their own experience as the basic element of their early pretense play. We have used the concept of a script for familiar events to describe the way in which experiential representations are organized. Scripts (Nelson, 1978, 1981; Nelson & Gruendel, 1981; Schank & Abelson, 1977) are composed of a sequence of acts organized around goals and specifying actor roles, props, and scenes. In a series of studies we have found that preschool children readily talk about their experiential knowledge in script-like form, and that the hypothesized scripts affect the way in which they interpret and remember stories and everyday events.

It has been suggested (Nelson & Gruendel, 1979) that conversations between preschoolers would be *successful* (that is, would be characterized as true dialogues, maintaining topic coherence across turns) when the participants used shared script knowledge as a framework for their discourse. To illustrate this, we analyzed several examples of conversations in play contexts by 4- and 5-year-olds in a preschool. Our focus was on the way in which the shared script knowledge provided the background for play and talk. Talk in these contexts tended to concern issues that needed to be negotiated, with the script assumed implicitly as the framework for play. Two examples will illustrate this point. In the first example (Nelson & Gruendel, 1979, p. 76) two 4-year-olds are talking on toy telephones:

G. Hi.
D. Hi.
G. How are you?
D. Fine.
G. Who am I speaking to?
D. Daniel. This is your daddy. I need to speak to you.
G. All right.
D. When I come home tonight, we're gonna have . . . peanut butter and jelly sandwich, uh, at dinnertime.
G. Uhnmm. Where're we going at dinnertime?
D. Nowhere. But we're just gonna have dinner at 11 o'clock.
G. Well, I made a plan of going out tonight.
D. Well, that's what we're gonna do.
G. We're going out.
D. The plan, it's gonna be, that's gonna be, we're going to McDonald's.
G. Yeah, we're going to McDonald's. And, ah, ah, ah, what they have for dinner tonight is hamburger.
D. Hamburger is coming. OK, well, goodbye.
G. Bye.

We commented,

> This example illustrates the important point that to sustain a dialogue the participants must each assume a shared topic context within which that dialogue is structured. This shared context determines such things as what is expressed and what is left to inference, the particular answers that follow from a given question, and the particular semantic and syntactic links that will be established between utterances. Shared context may derive from two primary sources—the immediate situation, including objects and people present, and background knowledge about the topic of the discourse. Either or both of these may serve to cement the individual contributions to the conversation. Both are evident in the telephone exchange. Indeed, this particular conversation reveals a multiply-embedded structure which relies upon shared context at several levels.
>
> First, a pretend-play context is established within which a conversational exchange then takes place. The contextual focus of the conversational exchange, the telephone context, itself invokes a particular type of dialogue which in the real world is independent of visual cues. In fact Daniel and Gay obeyed this constraint in their pretend realization, but we do not know whether this was intentional or not. Finally, the primary dialogic context of mother and father making dinner plans is then invoked. Thus the levels involved may be represented in the following embedded structure:
>
> (Pretend (Conversation (Telephone (Dinner plans))))
>
> Each of the embedded levels may be seen to involve its own structural characteristics and to rely on substantive event knowledge, all of which are shared by the young participants. Shared context in this exchange thus goes far beyond the immediate here and now which initially helps to ensure that conversational exchanges are held "on track" [Nelson & Gruendel, 1979, pp. 76–77].

A second example from this study illustrates other ways in which scripts enable children to keep play on track. In this example, two 3-year-old girls are playing with a toy model of a school and appropriate toy people (Nelson & Gruendel, 1979, pp. 83–84).

Part I

(1) G 1. (Rings the bell). Stop!! The school is open! (rings bell) School is open. Walk, walk, walk, walk, walk in. Whoops!

(2) G-2. You shut up this end. (Closes the front flap of the schoolhouse.)

(3) G-1. Yeah, shut up this end and let's get all these things ready.

(4) G-2. Yeah, it's nighttime. We have to go home now.

(5) G-1. Yep. Now where's the other person? Put it, put it on, now, yeah. (Brings people out of school) Now close this up.

(6) G-2. They have to go home! Why do you think they have to stay in school! They have to go home!

(7) G-1. (Laughs)

(8) G-2. And the teacher has to go home, too. What do you think she's in there. She likes to sleep in a school. Nobody sleeps in a school.

(9) G-1. Nooo.

Part II

(10) G–2. OK. Here's her house and she's sleeping right here. She's in here. OK. Here comes . . . She's right next to the school (walks Teacher to school) Right here. She doesn't have to walk too far.

(11) G–1. (Rings bell) School's open!

(12) G–2. Ding. Ding! Go in.

(13) G–1. Having snack.

(14) G–2. (Rings bell loudly)

(15) G–1. Having snack, no. I want to ring the bell for snack. (rings it)

(16) G–2. Here, here.

(17) G–1. What's that?

(18) G–2. In case she sits right there (?) (Puts people in chairs at tables)

(19) G–1. Whoops. School is closed.

(20) G–2. All the people out. (Moves them out) Out.

(21) G–1. School is closed. (Rings the bell)

(22) G–2. Walking home! Walking home! (Both sing-song this way as they move F–P[1] people around the room.)

(23) G–1. Back at school, back at school! (Rings the bell)

(24) G–2. Walking home, walking home.

Part III

(25) G–1. School is ready.

(26) G–2. School is ready! Uh-oh, ba-sketti-oh!

(27) G–1. The door's closed, because it's not locked up. But you can walk in this door. (Walks person in) And, but no one there has a (?). Not snack time, yet. First, you take your coat off.

(28) G–2. Here I come to school, walk. The TEACHER! (Walks teacher into school)

(29) G–1. THEN, then you play, then you play.

(30) G–2. This is the teacher. This is the teacher. She's looking out the window.

(31) G–1. These guys are playing outside now. Now people are playing outside.

(32) G–2. No, they're taking a nap now. Put 'em in! They're going to take a nap now. Teacher, the teacher's rubbing her back. The teacher's . . . rubbing . . .

(33) G–1. She . . . this is the teacher, and she's walking ouside to get something from her car. Ba-doop, ba-doop (walks teacher to pretend car.) Get something out from her car. Laughs. Walk back inside. OK.

(34) G–2. Her mother's car is broken, so let's ride in the teacher's car.

(35) G–1. Yeah. Rubbing your back, rubbing your back. (Moves teacher rub children's backs) Ooops, school's closed!

(36) G–2. School's closed! Wake up everybody. Time to go ouside, time to go ouside. WHEEE!!! (Everyone is moved outside the school)

Several points about this example should be noted. First, there is high preference for agreement (indicated by "yeahs") even where the participants do not apparently agree on action. The school day is represented in very general, almost

---

[1]F–P people refers to Fisher-Price figures, a brand name of small dolls.

skeletal terms: you come, you play, you snack, the teacher rubs backs at nap, you wake, go outside, and then go home. These script scenes are instantiated in action as well as talk. The absence of detail in both modes and the repeated cycles of coming and going may serve many functions and have many determinants, but among other functions they tend to ensure agreement among participants on the representation they are engaged in coconstructing. Cycling is one of the characteristics that is the focus of analysis in the study we report later. In this dialogue, the three cycles of arrival to departure are expanded by the children from the beginning of the sequence to its end, through the inclusion of first one, then several intermediate event components in different parts of the script structure. This is illustrated in Figure 1.

It should be noted also in this sequence that the two girls sometimes run off their own scripts independently of each other (see Turns 23–32).

> The shared script which previously directed and supported the joint conversation and active play also allows the two to proceed within the script independently of one another without noting the independence until there is an actual conflict over the placement of the props . . . after the two children have been running through their own individual scripts and come to disagree. G–2 incorporates information about the teacher's car, while G–1 goes back to pick up the "rubbing back" component introduced by G–2 on turn 32. Thus the dialogue converges again and ends in agreement [Nelson & Gruendel, p. 86].

Although the original focus of the analysis of these examples from Nelson and Gruendel (1979) was in terms of the development of dialogue, the dialogues emerged as the talk of pretend play by peer dyads. Our present studies were designed to extend these analyses to a standard pretend-play context within which we could determine what aspects of the context were supportive of sustained play sequences. We use context here, as described earlier, to include the chil-

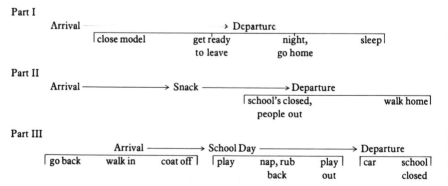

Figure 1. Cycles of script events. Conversation 4, from Nelson and Gruendel, 1979.

dren's representations of the reality to be instantiated as well as the physical and social context of the play itself.

On the basis of the initial analysis of script-based dialogues, we made predictions about when talk between preschool peers would result in coherent sustained dialogue and when it would lapse into monologic fragments. We proposed that three components of conversational context would contribute to maintenance of dialogue: presence of objects, shared topic, and shared script knowledge. By extension, we propose that sustained play sequences will rely on these components as well.

Where objects themselves are the focus of play, as in using clay, paint, or blocks, they are likely to be the focus for each child independent of the other and conversations are likely to be limited to requests for objects, claims of possession, or comments on the child's own construction. However, if objects serve as the setting or as props for pretense, as with telephones, household toys, vehicles, or the sandbox play used in the present study, they may aid in sustaining a coherent sequence of play and its accompanying dialogue. Thus the role of objects in supporting dialogic sequences cannot be understood apart from their role in the play itself.

By definition, conversation takes place around a shared topic. Conversational episodes are defined in terms of topic shifts, which begin and end each episode. Thus shared topics are necessary to sustained dialogue. However, conversations around shared topics vary in both coherence and length. Topic itself cannot explain these variations, because the occurrence of variations in topic length suggests that certain informational contents are more supportive of discourse than others. It is likely that some forms of knowledge provide a more fertile basis for topic sharing than do others.

In order to account for the variable potential of topics to sustain play-related discourse, we need to invoke the notion of the shared script. When a script becomes the topic of play it provides the structure within which a coherent sequence of activity and talk may proceed. Note that a script alone is not sufficient to maintain a dialogue. That is, it is not enough for one member of the dyad to propose a script, for example, to suggest "Let's play going to Disneyland," if the other member does not share the Disneyland script. In that case, either one partner will engage in continuous direction or both will run off independent and sometimes conflicting contributions. Conversational episodes are likely to be brief.

The shared script, in contrast, contributes a background context within which roles are defined, props are specified, and a sequence of actions is understood. One partner may say to the other, as in playing grocery store (Gearhart, 1983), "You be the clerk" and the other partner, accepting or not, is able to pick up the role and carry it through. Available props can be given designated parts in the script (as in "pretend this is the cake"—see succeeding text) and be accepted without conflict because they are understood to be relevant to the script that has been instantiated.

Because young children are still in the process of building up scripts for everyday events, they seem disposed to use them as conversational topics and as the basis for pretense play. We expect that older children would be more disposed to "background" their script, to assume shared knowledge, and to "foreground" the novel, the fantastical, and the mysterious. Script-based play may then be largely confined to the early childhood period, although establishing scripts *for* play may continue on into later childhood and even into adulthood. For example, all of the childhood fantasy games of dolls, armies, and so on, as well as organized dramatic games like dungeons and dragons, rely on shared scripts, some of them highly elaborate.

Our analysis here is confined to the simple scripts instantiated by preschool children in their everyday play in a day-care setting. We report two studies carried out to explore further the propositions set forth in Nelson and Gruendel (1979). In the first study, 4-year-olds were observed at play in three different play contexts. The analysis focused on the comparison between the longest and the shortest segments of continuous discourse in each dyad in each context. In the second study young (3-year-olds) and older (4-year-olds) children were observed in a specially arranged sandbox play context. Discourse based on object-and-activity-centered and on event-centered (script-based) sequences were analyzed. These analyses were based on the talk accompanying play on the grounds that they reflect the thematic episodes of play itself.

STUDY 1: THE LONG AND THE SHORT OF PLAY

METHOD

Subjects

Six white, low-SES children participated in the first study. They were all recruited from the same classroom of a public day-care center. Three unsystematically selected children were matched by their teacher with a friend. Two dyads consisted of girls (Dyad A, ages 50 and 48 months; Dyad B, ages 55 and 54 months) and the third dyad was mixed-sex (Dyad C, ages 57and 58 months).

Procedure

Each dyad was audiotaped in its center during 15-minute play periods on three successive days. In the first session, dyads were invited to the housekeeping area and provided with a small cookie sheet, toy rolling pin, little bowls, and two cans of play dough. On the second day, the pairs were recorded during sandbox play with two shovels, a plastic bucket, a measuring cup, and a large spoon. In the final session, two toy telephones were provided for play in the housekeeping center. Before each session the class was told that only two children were allowed in the observed play center. This ensured that only the talk of the subjects was recorded. For all sessions, the experimenter, who was familiar to the children, sat in an unobtrusive corner of the play area, observing and recording the context of the pair's verbalizations.

Audio recordings were transcribed. The speech was divided into exchanges, defined as sequences of two conversational turns in which a turn was taken by each partner. Each turn was classified as belonging to either continuous or discontinuous discourse. Continuous discourse was defined as more than one turn linked by topic collaboration. Discontinuous discourse occurred when a speaker did not engage him- or herself in the topic expressed in the preceding turn, and addressed a set of unrelated topics (Keenan & Schieffelin, 1976). Two or more turns of continuous discourse constituted a conversational epidsode and the longest and shortest segments of continuous discourse were extracted from each transcript for further analysis.

Data Analysis

The analysis focused on a comparison of the topics of the longest and shortest conversational episodes. The purpose of this analysis was to explicate the relationship between the knowledge used in discourse and the resulting play. All conversations were classified as either scripted or nonscripted. Scripted discourse was defined as conversational episodes that contained specific proposals for instantiating events in play. Play events were defined as jointly instituted play episodes by the dyad. They were identified by examination of the dyad's play talk and action. For example, in the exchange "A: Want to cook? B: Yes, let's make pancakes," the play events would be "cook food" and "make pancakes." After play events were identified, play scripts were determined. These were organized, multievent play sequences, comprising all the interrelated play events. Nonscripted discourse was discourse containing no play events.

RESULTS

The results are presented in terms of the descriptions of the play episodes in each context. Table 1 lists the event of the longest discourse sequence for each dyad in each play session. As the table shows, with one exception (Dyad B, telephone context) pairs invoked a common script for all of their extended verbal interactions.

Play Dough Context (Long)

In the play conversations within this context, all dyads responded contingently to each other's statements, and their scripts for play guided their actions and moved them toward a common goal.

The conversation of Dina and Michael illustrates how children used an event structure ("make food") to collaborate in the creation of a shared fantasy. (Numbers identify exchanges of turns.)

(1) M. Make food!
     D. Yeah. And everybody get to see a Big Mac. I'm making a Big Mac.
(2) M. And we'll sell the food.
     D. Yeah, but what if the truck don't take the food. The truck has to

Table 1

Scripts and Topics of Longest and Shortest Conversations in Three Play Contexts

	Play dough		Sand box		Telephone	
Dyad	Longest script	Number of exchanges	Longest script	Number of exchanges	Longest script	Number of exchanges
A	Baking	5	Birthday	5	Planning visit	8
B	Making cookies	7	Birthday	2	None	—
C	Making food	8	Birthday	10	Planning visit	12
Dyad	Shortest topic	Number of exchanges	Shortest topic	Number of exchanges	Shortest topic	Number of exchanges
A	Requests for materials	2	Requests for materials	4	Calling doctor	2
B	Requests for materials	1	Playing catch	1	Expressions of feelings	2
C	Information on materials	2	Requests for materials	2	Planning visit	6

deliver the food. And the grocery store. And the truck will deliver to the house.

(3) D. Mister from the truck, will you take it please, please, please.
     M. He said yes, he said yes.
(4) D. I'm making a lot of hamburgers. Here you go. It's almost ready.
     M. This has to go to a different house. You doing yours for a different house. I gotta put this back.
(5) D. Where?
     M. The can of meat balls.
(6) D. I do too. The can of meat balls.
     M. All finish.
(7) D. Got to shake it a little, then we take it out. Then we put some blue in here. Then shake it.
     M. Almost flatter.
(8) D. It ready.
     M. I know it's ready.

In this conversation, Michael initially sets the pretense context ("Make food!"). This topic immediately becomes elaborated by Dina, and over the next seven exchanges collaboration between the two is smoothly carried out, invoking various roles (e.g., truck driver), locations (grocery store, house), objects, and actions that plausibly belong to a shared script. Note that the pretense here, including the identification of props and roles, is implicit. The children use definite articles, pronouns, and names to refer to elements of the script that have not been explicitly introduced—"the truck" (2), "the grocery store" (2), "the house" (2), "Mister" (3), "the can of meat balls" (5)—and these are smoothly picked up by the other partner and incorporated into the script. This segment of play might be based on previous experience by these two in acting out a similar scenario; nonetheless, it nicely illustrates the way in which a shared script can flawlessly direct pretense play and its accompanying dialogue.

Table 2 shows the way in which the play events within the longest segments for each dyad in each context were scripted. Dyad C (the example just given), produced a long and detailed food sequence; the sequences produced by Dyads A and B were less detailed, but these dyads also focused on making food in this context and used this script to structure their play.

Sandbox Context (Long)

Play in this context was also goal directed. Participants attended to each other's actions and talk and worked together toward a common goal. The "make cake" dialogue of Peggie and Evelyn illustrates these features.

Table 2

Play Events and Scripts of Longest Discourse Segments in Three Play Contexts

Context	Dyad A	Dyad B	Dyad C

Play dough	Add ingredients
	|
	Roll cookies
	|
	Request cookie
	|
	Taste cookie
		Make gingerbread man
		|
		Take if off table
		|
		Pick out your cookie
		|
		Make a big cookie
			Make food
			| \
			Sell it Hamburger
			| |
			Truck Shake
			delivers |
			it Flatten
			     |
			    Finish

Sandbox	Request butter | Get butter | Say "Happy Birthday" | Taste cake	Make cake | Add ingredients	Make cake | Add ingredients | Mix | Put in pan | Put candle in cake | Say "Happy Birthday"
Telephone	Greeting | Invite for visit | Ask permission | Confirm parental permission | Say goodbye		Greeting | Say not home tomorrow | Say going on a date with boyfriend | Date with superhero | Say goodbye

(1) P. Give me some butter. Some butter, OK?

    E. OK.

(2) P. Evelyn the butter.

    E. OK.

(3) P. Get the butter!

    E. OK. Where is the butter? (She hands P. a tub of sand.)

(4) P. We have to get a little bit, not a lot. (P. is standing with a bucket of sand in front of her.)

    E. OK, happy birthday.

(5) P. It taste good.
     E. The candles are gone. I'm not playing anymore.

In this segment, even though Peggie did not verbalize the event of her play explicitly Evelyn understood that she was making a cake (Exchange 4). When a scripted event structures play, partners can understand the play goals even when they were not overtly announced. Again note the definite reference—"the candles" (5)—for an implicitly introduced element.

As Table 1 shows, birthday scenarios directed all of the children's play in this context.

Telephone Context

Two of the three dyads planned visits in these conversations. The scripts for their dialogues are shown in Table 2.

A noteworthy exception was the conversation of Dyad B (Ines and Emmanuella), who did not utilize the telephones in this play session.

(1) I. That's not a real phone.
     E. I have a game at home.
(2) I. I have a whole bunch.
     E. I have a game at home.
(3) I. Me too.
     E. I have a whole bunch.

As this dialogue indicates, the longest continuous dialogue segments were not always very long and were not always scripted. Contrast the impoverished structure of this exchange to the previous examples, in which an assertion was followed by repetition, which was followed by a reassertion, producing a circular structure. Conversational movement toward a common goal never occurred, and there were no jointly instituted play achievements.

SHORTEST CONVERSATIONS

The longest discourse segments yielded a mean length of exchange of 6.3 turns, and the mean for the shortest segments was only 2.4 turns. Short conversations were generally requests for play materials, as shown in Table 1. The requests were present in the conversations of all children, as shown in these examples.

Dyad A (Play dough)

(1) E. Give me! (Refers to rolling pin.)
     P. No.
(2) E. I'm not your friend.
     P. You could get some.

Dyad B (Play Dough)

     I. Let me do it.
     E. I didn't finish.

Dyad C (Sand box)

     M. I need a bean.
     D. This is a bean

Requests for materials occurred outside a scripted topic. The focus on materials accompanying these statements usually engendered conflict, and it appeared that this inhibited, at least temporarily, the establishment of a joint play goal.

Expressions of emotion were also a topic of the short discourse segments, as illustrated by the exchange between Ines and Emmanuella in the telephone context.

(1) I. I got the big one.
     E. I'm not your friend then.
(2) I. Here. (Sulking, she hands E. the phone.)
     E. You're not my friend anymore?

The expression of negative affect resulted in the termination of the interaction, as Ines left the play context shortly after this incident.

It is important to note that the shortest continuous dialogue segments were not always very short. A high percentage of the discourse of Dyad C reflected scripted topics, and their talk was most often directed to a common goal. They had few short dialogue segments, as they developed their events of play across their entire corpus of talk.

DISCUSSION

The first hypothesis, that the majority of the longest segments of continuous discourse would be scripted, was supported. Conversations accompanying manipulation of play dough contained scripts for food preparation. In sandbox play the event that structured play was a birthday party, and for telephone talk planning a visit was the theme. The scripts functioned to structure the interactions, allowing all the participants, confident in their knowledge of the sequence of events of the scripted topic, to play and talk interactively for an extended period of time. Further, within the scripted exchanges the mean length of the conversations was 12.6 turns. Thus scripted conversations were much longer than 4 turns, which has previously been reported as the mean episode length of 4-year-olds in their nursery school conversations (Shields, 1978). Coherence was maintained within dialogues by both implicit and explicit references to own and others' prior turns and to elements of the script implicitly understood.

It is noteworthy that there was commonality across children in the play event utilized within a given context. This suggests that children have specific scripts for play in different contexts.

The second hypothesis, that the majority of the shortest segments of continuous discourse are concerned with nonscripted topics, was also confirmed. These brief peer interactions consisted of requests for materials and expressions of negative affect, and had an average length of only 4.8 turns.

In summary, scripts in discourse service play in a way that nonscripted discourse can not. When using their play scripts, children accept each other's proposals, and play develops. In contrast, nonscripted talk and play functioned either to establish a desired state (requests for material) or to state a fact (expressions of emotion). Thus nonscripted talk did not generate elaborate, sequential, sustained pretense. In the second study, a direct examination of the structure of play sequences that were fantasy based or related to objects was carried out.

STUDY 2: STAGING PLAY THROUGH ACTION AND DIALOGUE SEQUENCES

METHOD

Subjects

The participants in the second study were 20 white English-speaking children of both genders, from low-SES families. All children were recruited from the same public day-care center. Teachers from three classrooms nominated pairs of children they had previously observed talking and playing together who were within 2 months of each other in age. From the nominated pairs, 5 younger dyads (range = 36–45.5 months, M = 42.1) and 5 older dyads (range = 49–63 months, M = 58.1) served as subjects.

Materials

Children were audiotape recorded during play in a small room of their day-care center. A large sand-filled tub was placed in the corner of the room. Two shovels, a plastic bucket, a measuring cup, and a large spoon provided the props for play with the sand. The only other subjects in the room were an adult-sized desk and chair.

Procedure

The observer, who was familiar to all the children, brought the dyads to the observation room. They were told they could talk and play together using the sandbox and the props, but were asked not to talk to the observer because she would be working. Following these instructions the audiotape session began. The observer sat at the desk near the children and recorded the action context of the pair's verbalizations. All dyads spontaneously played for at least 12 minutes.

The first 12 minutes of each dyad's talk was transcribed by the observer. The speech was divided into utterance units (Garvey & Hogan, 1973), the utterances were numbered on the transcript. All relevant utterances and conversational episodes identified with pretend play and physical object play themes were examined. The discourse units were defined as follows.

1. *Relevant Utterance.* Child utterances, coded within and across each child's turn, that were sensibly connected to the speaker or listener's prior utterance, and that sustained conversational continuity and flow.
2. *Episode.* An unbroken succession of relevant utterances that was maintained over at least one child–child turn. An episode was terminated by an irrelevant utterance, and consisted of the number of relevant utterances within the episode boundaries.
3. *Pretend Play.* Utterances that evoked a fantasy or imaginative context, or episodes that contained a majority of pretend play theme utterances.
4. *Physical Object Play.* Utterances that were reality based, dealing with the manipulation of sound and/or play materials as objects in themselves, and episodes that contained a majority of physical object play theme utterances.

Interrater Reliability

Interrater reliability in coding the utterances for thematic content was established by independent coding of 20% of each transcript for each subject. The reliability for pretend play units was 95% and for physical object units was 97%.

Data-Analysis Procedures

Pretend and physical object play talk accounted for over 60% of the discourse in the sandbox setting (Seidman, in preparation, 1983). The purpose of the analyses was to determine the structure of these two types of play.

Within the pretend play discourse, all play events and scripts were derived from the transcripts (see Study 1). Following this, all pretend play utterances were categorized as either scripted or nonscripted. Scripted utterances were those that had been used to create a play scene of sequential elaborated activity, based on knowledge of a familiar event. Similarly, all the play actions were derived from the transcripts for the physical object play discourse. For example, in the exchange "A: I'm using the shovel. B: OK, put the sand in here," the play actions would be "use shovel" and "pour sand." As with pretend play, physical object play utterances were classified as either action sequences or not. Action sequence utterances were those that had been used to describe interrelated sequences of play actions accompanying physical object play, based on the manipulation of familiar objects.

RESULTS

A one-way analysis of variance was performed to compare the number of utterances within scripted and nonscripted pretend play. This analysis revealed a significant difference between the number of utterances in these categories, $F(1, 18) = 9.04, p < .01$; 79% of the pretense utterances were elements of a play script. Similarly, within physical object play there was a significant difference between sequenced and nonsequenced play, $F(1, 18) = 7.82, p < .05$; 69% of these utterances were embedded in a play sequence.

Content of Scripted and Action-Based Play

Table 3 lists the content of the scripts of pretend play and action sequences of physical object play instantiated by the 10 preschool dyads during sandbox play. Of the 10 dyads, 8 had conversational episodes in which scripts for making play dough, egg salad, Jell-O, and cake were used to create complex fantasies. Additionally, 60% of the dyads' talk contained physical-object play episodes wherein their reality-based play described or maintained the players' joint or separate actions on their play materials. Samples of discourse with script-based and action-based structures illustrate the qualitative differences between pretend and physical-object play.

Table 3

Content of Play Sequences

Action	Pretend play		Physical object play
Made	Cakes, cookies, bakery shop, birth-day parties, egg salad, corn meal, pancakes, meat balls, Jell-O, play dough, castle	Actions described	Pour: sand into and out of bucket Open: bucket Give: bucket, more sand, seven cups of sand Take: sand from bucket Mix: sand, using shovel Lift: bucket
Establish	Water, egg, chicken, rice, refrigerator, ice cream, coffee		Look: at sand in bucket Move: sand Fill: cup up to eight
Role played	Mother, father	Activities described	Drawing in sand: circle, shark Pouring: one cup of sand Working: with sand, with hands Helping: with sand play Throwing: sand in air

Pretend Play Themes in an Event Sequence

Making cake was the most common script for pretense, occurring in 4 of 10 dyads. Three of these dialogues are presented to illustrate the form of the scripted dialogue and elaboration at different ages.

"Making Cake" Conversations. Two girls, 36 months of age, started off their play episode with the following conversation.

(1) A. More (requesting more sand).
    B. What you doing?
(2) A. Get the cake.
    B. What? Get the cake?
(3) A. Yeah.

This was the only episode of pretend play of this dyad. The same theme is repeated by another dyad, 36 months old. Their pretend play episodes had an event-based structure and the friends recycled back to the same scripted topic in two conversational episodes.

(1) C. Yeah, I know. You making cake.
    D. Yeah! (chanting) Who wants cake?
(2) C. No it's not finished. You have to get more.
    D. No, look it!

(3) C. OK. (singing) "Happy Birthday." That cake.
   D. OK. Oh, Oh.

Recycle 1

(1) C. You have to pick up all this. NO!
   D. The cake. It all ready. (singing) Happy Birthday to FaFa.
      Look it!
      OK.
      I make bigger and bigger and bigger.
      Oh Ah!
(2) C. OK (singing) "Happy Birthday, Happy Birthday to you."
   D. It's too much.
(3) C. I have to make. I'm making. I making coffee.
   D. Yeah. We're pretending. Pretend.

Recycle 2

(1) C. Want to put it in (referring to pretend cake).
   D. OK. Hold on.
(2) C. (singing) "Happy Birthday to you."
      Sing, sing Diana!
   C. and
   D. "Happy Birthday to you."
(3) C. I made happy birthday right?

The third dyad, two girls who were 58.5 months old, created the following event-based play activity.

(1) J. Want to play bakery? Want to play bakery shop? Wanna play bakery shop?
   L. Then we need something else.
(2) J. A what?
   L. Make a cake?
(3) J. Yeah.
   L. We can make a cake with the measuring cup.
(4) J. Oh yeah. You have doing and I'll have doing.
   L. Yeah but. We have to play bakery shop.
(5) J. I know. Make the cake.
   L. Put in one or more? (referring to cup of sand).
(6) J. No, put the cake in.
   L. OK. I put the cake in there.
(7) J. Put some sugar too.
   L. OK.

(8) J. Put some sugar.
    L. Have to mix it up.
(9) J. OK.
    L. How 'bout peanuts.
(10) J. No, no peanuts. Just a little peanuts.
    L. OK. A little more.

Recycle 1

(1) J. Want to give it to the truck now?
    L. OK.
(2) J. Now we have to make another one now.
    L. I'll make another.
(3) J. Make believe we have a truck.
    L. OK, come on. (both make truck noises) Brrrooommm.
(4) J. Now pour it in.
    L. This is chocolate. Chocolate my flavor.
(5) J. No don't put chocolate.
    L. A little chocolate.
(6) J. That's chocolate?
    L. OK, this, this is grape.

Recycle 2

(1) J. Put it in the truck. Put it in the truck.
    L. OK, I get. Truck, I got it in. OK, its in the truck.
(2) J. OK.
    L. Get up on the truck.
(3) J. Come on, I'm gonna leave you.
    J.. and
    L. Brrrooommm (Both drive away.)

All age groups used a script structure. However, when the "make cake" dialogues were analyzed in terms of number of different play events they contained—where each play event contributes an additional bit of information—an increase with age was found. As Table 4 shows, only 3 play events can be derived from the youngest dyad's conversation, whereas the oldest children's dialogue contains 15 play events.

Additional analysis revealed that the scripted themes of each dyad's talk persisted across multiple episodes. Of the five dyads who produced two or more pretend play episodes, four repeated and developed the same event-based content in *all* their pretense episodes.

Table 4

Play Events Derived from the "Make Cake" Conversation of Three Dyads at Pretend Play

Dyad's age	Number of play events	Cycle 1	Recycle 1	Recycle 2
36 Months	3	Add more sand		
		Name it cake		
		Bring the cake		
46.5 Months	6	Make cake	Identify cake	Make cake
		Invite people to eat cake	Sing "Happy Birthday"	Sing "Happy Birthday"
		Sing "Happy Birthday"	Make bigger cake	Announce party
			Sing "Happy Birthday"	
			Make coffee	
58.5 Months	15	Announce play	Cake to truck	Cake in truck
		Bakery shop	Make cake	Drive away
		Make cake	Locate pretend truck	
		Get measuring cup	Make cake	
		Add cups to bucket	Make chocolate cake	
		Put cake in bucket	Make grape cake	
		Add sugar		
		Mix		
		Suggest peanuts		
		Add peanuts		

*Physical Object Play Themes
in an Action-Referenced Sequence*

There was greater commonality across the content of the 10 dyads' scripts for play than across their play exercises. However, there was one play action that was referenced in the conversations of 3 dyads.

"Fill Shovel–Pour Sand into Bucket" Conversations. Our youngest players in the "make cake" dialogue also produced the following physical object play conversation.

(1) A. More (sand).
    B. A little bit. More sand.
(2) A. Me too, sand.
    B. Yeah.
(3) A. Me too.
    B. Me too!
(4) A. More.
    B. I add sand too.
(5) A. Sand.
    B. I want a. -- a.
(6) A. Sand.
    B. Yeah.
(7) A. Put some sand here.

Despite the length of this conversation, it contains only two ideas, as shown in Table 5.

By 46 months, however, players were able to label objects used to fill their buckets.

(1) F. There no more (sand) then.
    S. OK then.
(2) F. That cup, that same cup.
    S. OK. OK. Give me more (sand).
(3) F. This is my shovel. Look here.

Table 5

Play Action Derived from the "Fill Shovel-Pour Sand into Bucket" Conversations of Three Dyads at Physical Object Play

Dyad's age	Number of play actions	Cycle 1
36 Months	2	Add sand
		Request more sand
46 Months	4	Observe empty bucket
		Obtain cup
		Fill bucket
		Identify shovel
56 Months	5	Empty bucket
		Fill bucket
		Use shovel to fill, not hands
		Obtain sand
		Request turn to add sand

Once these children completed this action sequence, it never re-emerged in subsequent play. The youngest dyad that explicitly stated their procedure for filling the sand bucket was 56 months of age.

(1) J. Wait Louise.
      L. Take some (sand) out, Take some out. (J. removes sand.) O.K. Now fill it. Don't do it with your hands. Jamie watch. (L. adds sand with shovel.) Do it with the shovel.
(2) J. Louise, *I'll* get the sand.
      L. I got it.
(3) J. Why didn't you give me a chance? (to fill the bucket).

Although all age groups used an action-referenced structure, there was an increase in the number of play actions that accompanied the "fill shovel–bucket" conversations. However, of the four dyads who had two or more physical object play episodes, *none* had repeated physical object play content in any subsequent object play episodes.

DISCUSSION

These data provide further evidence that children from 3 to 5 years of age utilize scripts to structure their extended dialogic exchanges of fantasy play. Although children were able to engage in coherent discourse when they requested play materials or expressed feeling, these conversational exchanges were short lived. Furthermore, eight of nine pretense play conversations were based on context-specific events (i.e., making food or having a birthday).

Comparison of the structures of pretend and physical object play revealed that although event sequences structured pretend play, action-referenced sequences structured physical object play. Moreover, the conversational episodes on these themes were qualitatively distinct. Scripted, eventful play was expansive. Scripted themes were used to unify children's play interactions—they repeated and developed the event-structure theme throughout the entire course of their play interaction. In contrast, the action-referenced conversations of physical object play had a discontinuous, local influence on the interactions of the dyads. The descriptions of current actions that constituted these dialogues directed and sustained play action. However, because these actions accompanying physical object play were free to vary and similar action sequences generated conversations with varying content, these conversations had no history beyond their initial emergence.

GENERAL DISCUSSION

Beyond describing the qualities of pretend and physical object play discourse, these studies suggest a model of how children are able to use their knowledge to engage in conversation. A number of investigators in the area of mother–child discourse have documented that adults "bootstrap" children's discourse to promote the sharing of meaning (Bloom, Rocissano, & Hood, 1976; Brown, 1980; Bruner, 1975; Cross, 1977). Presumably, when young children are engaged in discourse with peers they have to rely on each other to share meaning and convey ideas. It has been shown that even toddlers share meaning through action and that as the length of peer interactions increases, shared meaning becomes more frequent (Brenner & Mueller, 1982). Previous reports have indicated that verbal episodes with peers were rarely sustained over more than four exchanges (Shields, 1978). However, our subjects, when engaged in scripted pretense, consistently were able to maintain play-centered dialogue at or beyond four exchanges, and they shared many new propositions in their talk. During physical object play, their action-referenced conversations were less detailed and elaborated.

The analysis of these discourse segments suggests that peers use multiple strategies to share topics. First, they can use "holding" discourse. There are two forms of this strategy: (1) bilateral holding, in which each partner repeats the content of the other's talk, resulting in the sharing of the *same* topic again and again; and (2) unilateral holding, in which one partner develops meaning by proposing new ideas, and the other child simply repeats or affirms the ideas; in this way they share the same topic, but only one member of the pair develops it. Holding was infrequent in pretend or physical object play. Second, peers can use "activated" discourse; this was the most common type of discourse accompanying physical object play. This strategy consisted of talking about joint or separate actions on play materials, with the child directing her partner's attention to what she was doing in play. Although this is common in physical object play, it was uncommon in pretense play. Finally, peers can use "scripted" discourse, which was the most common conversational form accompanying pretend play. This strategy required participants to find an event whose structure was known to both participants. Once events for play were introduced, children were able to develop these themes throughout the course of their interaction. The course of the play episodes examined here suggests that the presence of objects may serve to bring forth a particular script as a play theme. Once suggested, the script serves as a continuous background framework within which both participants can play their roles. Because this frame is a constant for both children it enables the dyad to construct episodes jointly that develop and elaborate the pretense play based on it.

If these strategies are taken as a general model of how children engage in child–child discourse, it becomes possible to generate specific hypotheses about the way in which different contexts and situations affect peer interactions. Employment of the holding, activated, and scripted discourse strategies implies that in a play situation the children's available forms of knowledge include their conceptual representations of events, their actions, and the ideas verbalized by their discourse partner. Situational or contextual factors alter the probabilities that specific conceptual representations and actions will be utilized to share meaning. For example, different play props may access different events for play (as shown in Study 1), and thus afford different sorts of actions as well as different script possibilities. The differences in the content of the pretend conversations across the three play contexts were a manifestation of contextual modification at work.

Clearly, the young children in these studies used both descriptions of actions and event knowledge to sustain peer interactions. However, in contrasting the scripted to the activated discourse it was apparent that eventful play had a greater capacity for developing extended, recycled themes of talk containing numerous ideas that were shared in play.

Our conclusion that scripts support extended play sequences is similar to the conclusion reached by Gearhart (1983) in a study of preschool children's negotiations of play in a grocery store context. She also found that children used scripts in jointly constructing a play sequence. However, she argued that even within the elaborated scene provided by the grocery store props the constructions were not true collaborations. Although our present analysis has not focused on the dimension of collaboration, both studies suggest that shared script knowledge may provide a bridge between solitary play and collaborative play by providing the context within which each partner can make contributions that are understandable to the other. A major difference between Gearhart's study and the present one is that the children in her study were told to play store, whereas in the present studies children were free to initiate any fantasy they could. Interestingly, almost all did so, and they instantiated scripts that were context-specific (e.g., "birthday party" in the sandbox context). In our situation children were not constrained to a given play theme; thus they may have been better able to instantiate a script familiar to both participants that could serve the shared knowledge function essential to successful collaboration.

The analysis of play in terms of shared script knowledge is similar also to Garvey and Berndt's (1977) analysis of play in terms of schemas, which they specifically define as "an abstract plan or representation of an event sequence" (p. 8). They note that "Once a schema is formed, it is productive, i.e., it generates specific action formats that control the performances" (p. 8). Our concept is clearly related to this notion. In extension of this idea, it is important to note (1) that the script must be shared to sustain coherent play and (2) that it not only generates action formats but also serves as the basis for transformations of familiar events. Sharing the basic script knowledge is what enables the two children to coconstruct transformations of it.

The data we have presented are still largely illustrative of this thesis. A more rigorous test of the script model would require a more detailed account of its operations based on specific structural characteristics (see Nelson & Gruendel, 1981), as well as a comparison of play constructions around unscripted events in contrast to scripted ones. However, we believe that even in its present state the model has heuristic value and deserves further exploration.

ACKNOWLEDGMENTS

We are grateful to the children and staff of the cooperating preschools. We would like to acknowledge the help of Sahli Cavallero in the analysis of the data and in providing comments on a previous draft of this manuscript. The data reported here were presented in a different form by the second author at the biennial meeting of the Society for Research in Child Development, Detroit, Michigan, April, 1983.

REFERENCES

Bloom, L., Rocissano, L., & Hood, L. Adult-child discourse: Developmental interaction between information processing and linguistic knowledge. *Cognitive Psychology*, 1976, *8*, 521–552.

Brenner, J., & Mueller, E. Shared meaning in toy toddlers' peer relations. *Child Development*, 1982, *53*, 380–391.

Brown, R. The maintenance of conversations. In D. Olson (Ed.), *The social foundation of language and thought: Essays in honor of J. Bruner*. New York: Norton, 1980.

Bruner, J. The ontogenesis of speech acts. *Journal of Child Language*, 1975, *2*, 1–19.

Cross, T. C. Mother's speech adjustments: The contribution of selected child listener variables. In C. E. Snow & C. Ferguson (Eds.), *Talking to children*. Cambridge: Cambridge University Press, 1977.

Garvey, C. Play with language and speech. In S. Ervin-Tripp & C. Mitchell-Kernan, *Child discourse*. New York: Academic Press, 1977.

Garvey, C., & Berndt, P., Organization of pretend play. CSDP *Catalog of Selected Documents in Psychology*, 1977, *7*, (Ms. No. 1589)

Garvey, C., & Hogan, R. Social Speech and social interaction: Egocentrism revisited. *Child Development*, 1973, *44*, 562–568.

Gearhart, M. *Social plans and social episodes: The development of collaboration in role playing*. Unpublished doctoral dissertation, City University of New York, 1983.

Keenan, E. O., & Schieffelin, B. Topic as a discourse notion: A study of topic in the conversations of children and adults. In C. Li (Ed.), *Subject and topic*. New York: Academic Press, 1976.

Nelson, K. How young children represent knowledge of their world in and out of language. In R. S. Siegler (Ed.), *Children's thinking: What develops?* Hillsdale, NJ: Erlbaum, 1978.

Nelson, K. Social cognition in a script framework. In J. Flavell & L. Ross (Eds.), *Social cognitive development.* New York: Cambridge University Press, 1981.

Nelson, K., & Gruendel, J. At morning it's lunchtime: A scriptal view of children's dialogues. *Discourse Processes,* 1979, *2,* 73–94.

Nelson, K., & Gruendel, J. Generalized event representations: Basic building blocks of cognitive development. In M. Lamb & A. Brown (Eds.), *Advances in developmental psychology* (Vol. 1). Hillsdale, NJ: Erlbaum, 1981.

Piaget, J. *The language and thought of the child.* New York: World, 1955.

Schank, R. C., & Abelson, R. P. *Scripts, plans, goals, and understanding.* Hillsdale, NJ: Erlbaum, 1977.

Seidman, S. *Child to child: Discourse content in a single context.* Manuscript In preparation, 1983.

Shields, M. D. Some communication skills of young children: A study of dialogue in the nursery school. In R. N. Campbell & P. T. Smith (Eds.), *Recent advances in the psychology of languages: Language development and mother child interaction.* New York: Plenum Press, 1978.

CHAPTER 3

The Coordination
of Meaning in the
Creation of a Shared
Make-believe Reality

HOLLY GIFFIN

INTRODUCTION

Heather, almost 5 years, and Kathy, $3\frac{1}{2}$, crouch in the corner of the dress-up room in their preschool. Andy and Laura, 4-year-olds, stand nearby. They are playing make-believe. In the course of the subsequent 20 minutes they transform themselves into "daughter," "father," "gramma," "mother," and "police." They transform the room into a "dance hall," "a house," a "jail," and "heaven." Perhaps most importantly, they transform the meaning of their behavior to evoke and resolve compelling but complex conflicts: between parents, between parent and child, between parent and police, between police and child.

Throughout the playing, these transformations are accomplished collectively. The children at preschool age are able to construct a shared metaphoric system of meanings and interact within that system, conjointly sustaining and developing it. The impetus for this study is the two-part question, "How do they know what the transformed meanings are?" and "How do they manage to coordinate with each other to sustain those meanings?"

SYMBOLIC PLAY

The apparent answer is that they *tell* each other. They negotiate concerning how to interpret the materials of make-believe, that is, the people, objects, environment, actions, in their transformed sense. In other words they metacommunicate. Bateson defines *metacommunication* as "communicating about communication" (Bateson, 1951, p. 209). It is communication that indicates to others how to interpret and how to respond to events. Metacommunication refers to and explicates the "psychological frame" of an interaction (Bateson, 1955/1972, p. 88). The *frame* is the set of shared organizational principles that places behavior and events in a context. The frame makes behavior comprehensible and prescribes appropriate response (Goffman, 1974).

One of the most significant aspects of the framing of make-believe play is the metacommunicated message "this is play." Understanding that behavior is symbolic enables others to respond appropriately "as if." Merely establishing the fact of play is not sufficient for collective make-believe, however. Specific transformations of specific objects, persons, time, space, action, and rules must be understood for an imagined event to be conjointly represented. These constitute a complex frame within which children must operate. This study focuses on the metacommunicative process through which meanings are transformed conjointly. It describes some of the metacommunicative options available to players and some rules that influence which option is selected.

LITERATURE REVIEW

The literature suggests developmental significance in the ability of children to metacommunicate during make-believe play. Piaget noted that ability to announce a pretend role marks a significant structural change in the development of symbolic play because it indicates the intention to symbolize and thus a greater cognitive awareness of the symbolic nature of the activity (Piaget, as cited in Nicolich, 1978). In addition, literature in developmental psychology suggests two related areas of maturation in play: (1) children begin to play collectively (Gowen, 1978; Parten, 1971; Sanders & Harper, 1976) and (2) children increasingly base their play on internal and more complex action plans (Garvey & Berndt, 1975; Hulme & Lunzer, 1966). It seems that the skills of metacommunication develop to meet the need for interpersonally communicating and negotiating complex internal images of what should happen. Thus development of skill in metacommunication seems integral to the development of make-believe play.

Few investigations have attempted to describe the process in detail. The concern of many studies has been cognitive ability rather than skill in make-believe play for its own sake. This emphasis elicits a different set of questions and a different set of categories. If the activity of children is viewed as an aspect of a distinct child culture rather than as a precursor to adult abilities, questions can focus on describing the activity from the point of view of its actors.

The concept of a child culture has been articulated by Fein. She observed that "children create an informal culture which changes in structure with increasing maturity" (Fein, 1976, p. 60). Make-believe play is a phenomenon within this culture. Fein commented, "In the privacy and safety of play with its principles of entry and organization children coordinate their movement toward mastery of basic social conventions and principles" (Fein, 1976, p. 60). The social conventions are the scripts borrowed from adults but the principles of entry and organization, which constitute the frame of play and are expressed metacommunicatively, are indigenous to the child culture. When they "coordinate their movement" they may be practicing cultural skills.

Assuming a child-cultural perspective allows us to examine closely *how* children conduct make-believe play prior to explaining *why* or *when* they do so. This perspective brings to light the cultural–social nature of the play group and presents collective make-believe play as a social activity requiring its own set of social skills. If we assume the values of the players, behavior that is skilled is behavior that contributes to the players' goals. Tracing the development of skill in doing make-believe and relating that skill to skills of mature adulthood are important steps, but they should not precede adequate description of the phenomenon itself.

Two studies that have, independently of each other, focused specifically on the process of conducting make-believe play among young children are those of Garvey and Berndt (1975) and of Schwartzman (1978). Garvey's study explained that "the point to be made about the communication of pretending is that a great deal of speech is devoted to creating, clarifying, maintaining or negotiating the social pretend experience" (Garvey & Berndt, 1975, p. 10). Her research has identified the *content* of this metacommunication, the elements subject to transformation (i.e., role, object, action plan). Social pretend play is organized around these transformations. She did not systematically describe the metacommunicative process itself, the communicative behavior. That task is undertaken in the present report.

Schwartzman's research took what she called the "sideways perspective" (1978, p. 237). This perspective, which refers to how players behave in regard to each other, enabled her to describe the social group and how players establish their relationships through the playing. She identified several kinds of metacommunicative statements that can be made in the construction of make-believe play (e.g., "definition statements," "counter definition statements"; Schwartzman, 1978, p. 237). The statements suggest how each player is relating to the other players.

Schwartzman's focus was not so much on how children metacommunicate to construct the play world as on how they do so to construct the play *group*. Schwartzman emphasized how children indicate, or metacommunicate, their social position in the play group (e.g., leader, contender for leadership) through participation in the collective making believe. However, one of the distinguishing characteristics of make-believe play is that it is itself essentially a metacommunicative activity. Participants communicate to each other how to interpret and how to respond to the transformed elements of their shared make-believe world. The focus of the present research is to investigate the metacommunication process at this task-oriented level: how children metacommunicatively define the play world rather than how they define themselves in the play group.

Like the work of Garvey and Berndt and of Schwartzman, this study attempts to describe some aspects of make-believe play from a child-cultural perspective. It probes further, however, into the actual metacommunicative process. The questions indentified as the basis for this research are process questions: *"How do children communicate transformed meanings?" How* do they coordinate to develop and sustain the make-believe reality?" Finding a methodology that enables the researcher to describe and interpret the process is the appropriate first step for research to take. Communication scholar Hawes has argued that "social science need not equate method with a way of coming to know" (Hawes, 1977, p. 34). The method of research can provide perspectives on phenomena through description and interpretation. "It can bring to light unexamined presuppositions, ultimately disclosing previously concealed features of the phenomenon and its world" (Hawes, 1977, p. 34). The following section presents in detail the descriptive methodology used in this study.

METHOD

SAMPLE

Approximately 20 hours of observation produced 31 episodes of make-believe play involving 38 children. All were between the ages of 3 and 5 except for one 7-year-old girl; 22 children were students at a local preschool and 7 were friends of the researcher who had volunteered to participate in the study. Each episode observed involved children who had previously played together. Groups ranged in size from two to five members; the usual size playgroup was two or three. All children were of United States middle-SES (socioeconomic status) background. Ages and sex of children are listed in Table 1.

Table 1

Characteristics of Children in Study

Ages (years:months)	Girls	Boys
2:10–3:5	6	2
3:6–3:11	4	5
4:0–4:5	3	10
4:6–4:11	2	1
5:0–5:6	2	2
7:0–7:1	1	0

DATA COLLECTION

Two methods of collecting data were used in this study: videotaping in a laboratory playroom and audiotaping augmented by taking notes at a local preschool. The initial method of collecting data was videotaping children's transactions in the laboratory playroom of the local university. Six interactions of pairs of children were collected in this way. The method had the advantage of allowing the researcher to check observations. It attuned the researcher's observation skills for noticing salient material when it arose during field observation.

The bulk of the data was then collected through direct observation of naturalistic behavior at a local preschool. Tape recordings were made of children's make-believe play interactions during free-play periods in the dress-up room or on the playground. The researcher would sit quietly nearby, interacting with the children in a friendly but minimal way. The children were accustomed to having adult teachers constantly nearby, so they were able to accept the researcher's presence. They appeared to play unselfconsciously. The tape recorder was turned on when it seemed that the play both was collective and involved transformation. As the theory began to evolve, the research used participant observation techniques to clarify observations and test hypotheses.

DATA ANALYSIS METHOD

As a framework for generating descriptive categories this research relied on the grounded theory method developed by sociologists Glaser and Strauss (1967). This approach provides a method adaptable both to the requirements of describing and interpreting the communication process and to the requirements for controlled research.

The focus of the grounded theory method is to generate formal or substantive theory. Whereas formal theory is general, substantive theory offers a description of the functioning of a particular phenomenon that later may provide the grounding for more generalized theory. Theory building is seen as an organic process of developing increasingly comprehensive categories and hypotheses based on direct experience with the data. The process is controlled by the requirement for constant comparison. Data is collected until categories are saturated (i.e., until the same phenomenon is observed repeatedly). Categories may be initiated from observation of one incident, but they cannot become saturated without comparison to other incidents. "The adequate theoretical sample is judged on the basis of how widely and diversely the analyst chooses his groups for saturating categories" (Glaser & Strauss, 1967, pp. 63–64).

Understanding theory-building as an ongoing research process forces the researcher to be conscious of constructing categories and drawing relationships and thus to allow them to be continually subject to transformation and refinement. Openness to new data is preserved because researchers are not struck prematurely in a given set of categories. The object of research is not to document precisely how many times a certain category of behavior occurs, but to incorporate as many categories as possible, thus providing a more comprehensive theory that may later be tested statistically.

The grounded theory method combines collection, testing, and analysis of data in the process of generating theory. Throughout the analytical process in this study, examples were compared to each other in order first to generate and then to confirm, refine, and relate emergent categories. Transcripts were made from the videotaped data and then analyzed utterance by utterance in terms of the question "How do they manage to coordinate meanings?" The theoretical answers were the categories and structures that emerged from analysis of the videotapes. These were tested against data collected in the natural setting. Analysis of field data led to saturation of several of the existing categories of metacommunicative behavior and metacommunication rules and to the developement of others. Constant comparison continually refined the categories.

Examples of categories as they spontaneously occurred in the field were sought, and participant observation techniques were used in the second-stage data collection in order to generate behavior that would reflect existing categories. This was particularly important for checking the accuracy of hypothesized rules. According to communication scholar Shimanoff (1980), the best way to demonstrate the existence of an implicit rule is to provide data in which a deviation from the rule is negatively sanctioned. In order to elicit negative sanctions, the researcher sometimes entered the play with the children's permission and purposefully violated suspect rules. Because the researcher was a novice player, the apparent lack of knowledge concerning the rules was understandable. In general this technique produced the predicted negative response.

The appropriate results of such a method of research is the substantive theory itself, that is, the identification of descriptive categories and an explanation of the relationship among them. The remainder of this chapter is devoted to describing some categories of metacommunicative behavior and explicating a system of metacommunicative rules that interrelates those behaviors. This represents a substantive theory of how players coordinate meanings in the creation of shared make-believe realities.

FINDINGS

Results of the analysis are: (1) a description of a range of metacommunicative verbal and nonverbal behaviors and (2) the identification of a system of rules that influence the choice of metacommunicative options. The analytical process that produced these results follows.

The major expectation of this research was that metacommunication would play a significant role in the achievement of the coordination of meaning. Analysis of the transcripts made it evident that much verbal behavior in pretend play had metacommunicative functions, which did indeed contribute to coordination but did not fulfill the requirements of overt metacommunication (i.e., verbal commentary on the playing as playing). In order to describe and distinguish this behavior a continuum ranging from within-frame to out-of-frame metacommunication was developed. The attempt to explain why one metacommunicative option should be chosen over others led to the construction of a tentative organization of rules guiding the establishment of transformations. Because the system of rules cannot be adequately discussed without reference to the categories of behavior, a description of metacommunicative options precedes an explanation of implicit rules that influence which option is chosen.

METACOMMUNICATIVE OPTIONS

The analysis of the 31 episodes of make-believe play considered in this study generated the following categories of transformation-proposing metacommunication. These categories can be located along a continuum from within-frame communication to out-of-frame communication. In other words, some metacommunication overtly reveals the pretense and other options tend to conceal it. A diagram of such a continuum might look like Figure 1.

Where on the continuum a particular category of behavior is placed depends on both the verbal and the nonverbal components of the message. All com-

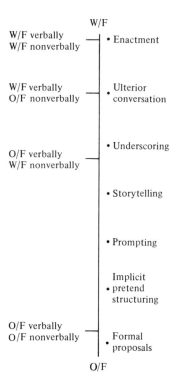

Figure 1. Continuum of within-frame (W/F) to out-of-frame communication.

munication behaviors can be described in terms of verbal and nonverbal components. A transformation proposal tends to be out-of-frame verbally if the verbal content of the message is inappropriate to the play script. It may be illogical or redundant in terms of the play text. It may refer directly to the frame by stating the fact that this is play or by stating the rules governing the playing. In addition, the duration of time in which players speak directly about their procedure influences how out-of-frame their behavior may be considered. A transformation proposal also tends to be out-of-frame if nonverbal behavior is incongruent with the imagined role or event, that is, if it would not be acceptable or necessary in real life. However, nonverbal behavior might be indicating the play state and thus would be appropriate only to a play situation and still not within the play frame.

Returning to the play episode with Laura, Heather, Kathy, and Andy described at the beginning of this chapter (see transcript in Appendix, p. 96), it is possible to identify the various options used to create and develop the text of their play. As discussed earlier, in the actual application of the categories to a transcript it becomes apparent that the metacommunicative options as defined are not mutually exclusive. They can overlap; they can be combined. When clear examples of categories are not available in this particular transcript other episodes will be used for clarification. The use of one episode provides a model for demonstrating how the categories can be used to explicate the conjoint coordinated transformation process.

Enactment

In the case of enactment both verbal and nonverbal behavior are within-frame. Players are enacting a shared script and thus each action automatically and implicitly metacommunicates the appropriate response. No transformations are being proposed. All necessary transformed meanings have been previously established either by preceding discussion or by tradition.

For example, after she has established the action plan at a more out-of-frame level ("and I make you some cake"), Heather announces to Kathy, "Mommy, I did something nice for you. I made you a wedding ring cake." The expectation is that Kathy will accept the cake and thus enable Heather to enact doing "nice things" for mother. Another example of enactment is observed among children relying on a traditional action format: "chase." (The existence of traditional action formats is discussed by Garvey & Berndt, (1975). The girls shout "help!" and the chaser, a boy, responds appropriately "I'm gonna getcha this time!"

Ulterior Conversation

Once players have established a basic script that they are playing, such as "playing family," they then must fill in the details by transforming specific objects and events in supportive ways. The play text, script, or action plan is thus developed, explored, and experienced. Ulterior conversation enables players to adhere verbally and often nonverbally to the play definition while simultaneously constructing that definition. As part of the playing, players profess to be mere respondents to events. The ulterior purpose of their behavior however is to create and orchestrate events.

Ulterior conversation differs from enactment because it is used intentionally to propose transformations and develop the action plan in ways that have not been previously conjointly established. Like enactment, ulterior conversation is behavior that is consistent with and appropriate to the pretend definition of the situation. Thus, while developing the episode the players can behave "as if" they were merely responding to developments. Ulterior conversation in play may be similiar to communicative behavior of adults in some social circumstances when they are covertly attempting to define apropriate response (e.g., "wouldn't you like to come to the table now?").

For example, one way players influence the development of the play episode is by asking questions that contain implicit answers. After they have set the scene "crying in the wedding place," Heather asks Kathy "What's the matter? You want to get married is why?" Ulteriorly she is laying the basis for an action plan involving Kathy and Andy "getting married." Without even waiting for Kathy to reply verbally, Heather instructs Andy in the appropriate response, "She wants to get married so she's crying. You should get married." Later Heather helps Andy develop his idea of "calling someone else." She asks, and ulteriorly suggests, "the police?" Andy incorporates her suggestion with "yes." In this way they introduce "police" into the developing action plan.

Another way the text may be developed is through reporting warning, threatening, or foretelling as if in response to real uncontrolled events. Actually, these behaviors function to add the events to the ongoing action plan. After suggesting that Andy call the police, Heather warns "Better not I don't want my mother to get hurt." Andy again picks up the disguised suggestion. He prophesizes, and thus establishes, that "she's going to get hurt, and she's going to die." This conversation precipitates an exciting episode of "hiding mother from the police."

Andy elicits support for a new role and a new action plan by reporting to Heather that he called the mother's "gramma" and she going to "keep care of her every day." Heather confirms this as part of the action plan by reporting it to Kathy. Each part of Andy's report is echoed by Heather, thus further establishing the plan.

Not only action plans but also definitions of role and object can be established implicitly within-frame. Players refer to the person or the object using the transformed name. When Heather cries "Gramma, come save me" to Laura, she automatically gives the role of "gramma." In this way roles can be assigned without interrupting the flow of action. Likewise, objects may be assigned meaning through naming. Heather points to an object on the table and exclaims "Quick, get her alive with that stuff." She has just defined the object as "get-alive stuff."

Underscoring

The option of underscoring allows players to define their action or state of being verbally while enacting it nonverbally. This behavior tends to expose the playframe more than ulterior conversation does because it is often not quite appropriate within the play definition. Often underscoring draws too much attention to obvious or irrelevant details, detracting from the accepted focus of the event. Further, whereas in ulterior conversation communication is directed toward other players, underscoring has more the character of a monologue. The player often seems to be talking to him- or herself although communicating transformations to anyone who happens to overhear them. Underscoring seems similar to the convention of the soliloquy in traditional theater, and thus slightly less supportive of the pretend social situation. More than ulterior conversation or enactment, underscoring tends to reveal the artificiality of the activity.

Some examples from the "bad mother" transcript include when Heather underscores her enactment of crying by wailing "I'm crying!" and Andy underscores his acting of making a telephone call by announcing aloud to himself "I'm calling her gramma." These comments, which define the players' actions, would be unnecessary for real life. Heather's delineation of her crying is redundant but useful in terms of the play. It clarifies the grief she is trying to represent. The underscoring points to the representation, however, and thus tends toward the out-of-frame position. Andy's talking to himself is useful for clarifying to himself, and to any others who might overhear, the symbolic meaning of his actions. Realistically, however, it should not be necessary for him to talk at all.

Later Andy announces to the others in a gruff voice, "All right, the police are going to come." He is simultaneously the police who are not there yet and the one who warns about their coming. This is a situation in which underscoring and ulterior conversation are combined. The paradox of being there and yet not being there strains the believability of the situation and thus makes the statement more out-of-frame, closer to underscoring.

Underscoring does not have to rely on whole sentences or even on words at all. Frequently sound effects serve to underscore the action. For example, Andy makes a shooting noise to enhance his pantomime of shooting a gun. In other episodes in the study, children were heard accompanying their action with chanting. Three-year-old Penny sang to herself, "glass of milk! Get a glass of milk!" as she played with toy dishes. In this case the symbolic meaning of the action was reinforced through child-made sound. Thus, underscoring exposes the pretense even while it attempts to enhance the experience.

In a separate episode a 7-year-old girl played "tea party" with her 5-year-old sister. She underscored her action of tipping an empty pitcher over a toy cup by saying "I'll pour the milk." Such a statement could be considered within-frame because it would not be inappropriate to the conversation in many real-life tea parties. It thus does not disturb the illusion. The statement is underscoring, however, because the player is defining some essential elements of the pretend situation—who she is: "one who pours the milk," the object in the pitcher: "milk," and what she is doing while she is performing the act. The statement is not essential in real life because it would be obvious that milk was in the pitcher. However, the statement could serve to focus attention on the performer and the action. There may be status and relationship implied in being the one to pour the milk. It may be that underscoring is used similarly in real life to define role and relationship. However, if such statements were used too frequently in adult interactions they would probably draw an uncomfortable degree of attention to role and relationship and to the one who is overly concerned with defining them.

In other episodes players were observed using symbolic words to give meaning to cryptic gestures. A boy who announced he must fix his tricycle touched the handlebar and said "fix." The magic word has allowed the player to represent what might otherwise be an impossible or too time consuming a task. It has also allowed him to experience success at a task that in reality is beyond his capability. "Magicking" is a type of underscoring that is more obviously out-of-frame. In fact, magicking relies on players' ability to access the playframe. Players must be aware that they have the power to substitute a symbol for the reality. They must distinguish between the restrictions of reality and the much more adaptable requirements of the play script. Magicking enables players to experience the pretend situation without being bogged down in uninteresting or disconfirming details.

Although it may expose the pretend nature of the activity, the function of underscoring is actually to enhance the experience of the play situation. Underscoring allows players to stay emotionally within the play world while clarifying definitions. Although in real life this redundant verbalization would disrupt the experience of the event, in make-believe play the verbalization deepens it. Reality abounds with concrete details that often must be supplied symbolically in play through verbally defining actions and states of being. Further experience of the details is often more important in play than the professed point of activity. Being the one who makes a telephone call may indeed be a more central purpose to playing telephone than the ostensible reason for making a call. Being the one who is crying is at least as interesting as the reason for crying.

Storytelling

As in underscoring, the metacommunication option of storytelling allows players to propose transformations verbally without entirely abandoning the experience of the play. Storytelling is distinguished by a peculiar singsong cadence. Phrases are usually preceded by the word *and* and several phrases will be strung together. The end word of each phrase is accented almost as in a question. This cadence functions to keep players involved in the play world while simultaneously detached enough to create it. It cues other players to hear the message as a narrative, about the play world but not of it.

Heather uses the storytelling cadence as she describes rather than enacts the events following the fight with "mother," "and I closed the door . . . and you start to cry . . . and I make you some wedding cake." She then enacts giving "mother" some "wedding ring cake." Kathy uses the cadence when she attempts to establish the following situation: "pretend I was crying at the wedding place because you . . . you guys yelled at me." Heather uses it again to clarify her ascent to heaven and resurrection: "and I was crying up in heaven . . . and I got back alive . . . . And I was crying."

Unlike underscoring, storytelling does not usually refer to a specific action or state of being. Rather, it allows players to abstract from the immediacy of the here and now. Transformations are frequently proposed in the past tense as in a narrative style. The narrative style may enable players to become more detached from the play text, and thus allowing them greater range and flexibility in developing it further. Players are able to develop more elaborate and complex plots than would be possible to communicate within-frame. These more complex action plans may become the basis for future activity or may substitute for such action. Although it is addressed more to other players than is underscoring, storytelling is a means of communicating transformations rather than a tool for negotiating about them. If a player has something to add to the narrative, he or she can do so using the same cadence: conjoint storytelling. However, rarely do players overtly disagree while maintaining the storytelling mode.

Prompting

In the course of developing and enacting an episode, it is sometimes necessary for a player to break out of the playframe briefly in order to clarify meanings and give directions. Often players refer directly to the frame. Nonverbally, players abandoned character voices and posture. They momentarily assume their own voices, though often at lowered volume. A lowered but normal voice indicates that they are no longer speaking according to the play script, but rather speaking about the script. The lowered voice also suggests a desire to reduce awareness of overt metacommunication.

Symbolic-play prompting functions much as asides to the audience and prompting work in the theater. The comments are generally very short and action is resumed immediately within the play text as if the comments had not been made. Prompting provides necessary information overtly. However, participants understand that consciousness of the break from the play world is to be dismissed as soon as the message is heard. The message usually refers to the specific enactment currently under way. Events may thus be most efficiently defined and directed in midprocess.

Heather prompts Kathy to "make the crying sound" and then immediately assumes role to ask "what's the matter?" Later, Heather interrupts Andy's enactments of a telephone call to "gramma" in order to correct him: "No, her name is Annie." Andy resumes his call using the corrected name, as if there had been no interruption. Kathy prompts Heather with "You said 'What's the matter, Mother?'" She then interrupts Heather's performance to correct it. "You didn't talk like that." Heather repeats her lines with the appropriate intonation and carries on with the playing.

Prompting is characterized primarily by its very brief duration. However, behavior that begins as prompting may develop into more overtly out-of-frame metacommunication if conflict arises forcing negotiations to continue. It also is distinguished from other options by the fact that players are specifically directing their communication to each other and nonverbally are behaving as themselves in reality rather than as roles in the play.

Implicit Pretend Structuring

Implicit pretend structuring refers to negotiations that overtly establish the major elements of the action plan but still do not verbally acknowledge the pretense. Nonverbally, players behave as themselves, not yet enacting the role or situation under discussion. The negotiations go on at length. Frequently they precede enactment of the script. If they occur in midepisode the pretense is suspended indefinitely until the necessary transformations of persons and objects and the action plan are conjointly established. Only the avoidance of verbally stating the pretense keeps the interaction from being completely out-of-frame.

In their initial conversation, Andy, Heather, and Kathy attempt to set up the conjoint definition of the play world. Much of their negotiation is accomplished without the use of such phrases as "let's pretend" or "let's say." The "as-if" preface is assumed. For example, in response to the pretend rule stated as "you have to come and dance," Andy announces, "No, I Dad." Heather then adjusts the situation by redefining the role of "dad" to include "and he can't dance." This conversation is by nature out-of-frame because it defines the frame within which situation and roles may be enacted. Yet the knowledge that this is pretend remains tacit, allowing players to be slightly closer to the experience than they could be if "pretend" prefaced each statement.

In another example, conflicting definitions force Kathy and Heather to abandon enactment of the play, but they still do not find it necessary to admit the pretense. Heather attempts to prompt Kathy to act alive after the medicine has been administered. She announces "You're alive now." However, Kathy replies "I'm still dead." Prompting is replaced by more serious implicit pretend structuring as the situation must be redefined. Heather restructures the action plan, "If you're going to be dead would you please get out of my room." The pretense is still admitted only implicitly.

Other options also rely on assumption of the pretend definition; however, they have other characteristics that also contribute to keeping metacommunication partially within-frame. Prompting, although in many respects identical to implicit pretend structuring, is of shorter duration and is distinguished by the lowered voice. In underscoring players are nonverbally still enacting the pretend situation. Like prompting, it elucidates a particular action at a particular moment during the playing. Implicit pretend structuring has no other element to keep it from exposing the playframe. It does not necessarily focus on the immediate action and thus is useful for negotiating the larger overall structure of the episode, such as the roles, the major events, future circumstances, or the setting.

Overt Proposals to Pretend

At the far end of the metacommunication continuum is the option of making an overt proposal to pretend. This behavior acknowledges the pretendedness of the activity with such phrases as "let's say," "pretend that," "let's play that." They frequently end with a request for confirmation, such as "OK?" Nonverbally, players behave as themselves in real life. Communication thus is completely out-of-frame.

The overt proposal is the most direct way to communicate transformations and ascertain cooperation from other players. Players talk openly about the playing. No attempt is made to conceal the fact that they are conjointly choosing the play definitions. Heather makes overt proposals when she wants to establish events that would have already occurred. "Let's say you guys were already married, OK?" "Let's say you gave me a spanking, Kathy O'Neil." Kathy uses an overt proposal to establish a specific and rather subtle action plan. "Pretend you thought I was alive but I was dead."

The options of overt proposals and implicit pretend structuring are extremely important in make-believe play. These metacommunicative options release players from the constraints of the play definition. Because they are outside the frame of play they can collectively and radically restructure that frame if they wish. They can move ahead in time; they can replay past events in different ways. They can adapt the script to be more compatible with their needs or to resolve differences among collaborators. They can abandon one script and try another. The ability to move collectively outside of the playframe through the use of overtly out-of-frame metacommunication enables players to control the make-believe world.

In summary this section has identified metacommunicative options that enable children to coordinate meanings during make-believe play. They were described in terms of placement on a continuum from within-frame to out-of-frame metacommunication. Some of the options allow players to indicate transformations and suggest developments in the script without abandoning or only partially abandoning the pretense. Other options allow players to negotiate directly about the play from outside the play world.

Given this range of metacommunicative behavior the question remains, Why should one metacommunication option be chosen over any other one? One hypothesis is that a system of implicit appropriateness rules guides the selection of metacommunicative behavior. The shared metacommunicative vocabulary provides a partial answer to the question of how children coordinate meanings in the creation of collective make-believe. The second part of the answer is provided by rules that facilitate and influence how coordination is achieved.

RULES FOR CONSTRUCTION
OF MAKE-BELIEVE PLAY

It is assumed in this study that the purpose of playing make-believe with others is to sustain and experience collaboratively a transformed definition of reality. Rules function to enable players to achieve this goal most effectively.

Illusion Conservation Rule

The range of metacommunicative options identified in make-believe play can be explained by the paradox inherent in collaboratively creating and experiencing a pretend situation. Communicating transformation and ascertaining agreement from other players is achieved most clearly through out-of-frame metacommunication. However, sustaining the experience of those definitions requires within-frame behavior. The rule dealing with how to resolve the paradox has been termed the *illusion conservation rule.* This rule can be stated

> When constructing make-believe play, players should negotiate transformations with the least possible acknowledgment of the playframe.

The illusion conservation rule is preferential. It allows for the fact that problems in communicating complex transformations or in reaching agreement require the clarity of out-of-frame metacommunication. The preference for within-frame behavior also accounts for development of the array of metacommunicative options that are partially within and partially outside of the playframe.

The existence of hypothesized rules was determined throughout the study by observing whether rule-violating behavior was systematically negatively sanctioned. In one episode the researcher offered to carry a child's stick. She (the researcher) was told to refer to the stick as a "gun." Only when she rephrased her proposal using the proper term was it (gratefully!) accepted. The researcher had unnecessarily disconfirmed the pretend definition and this was not to be tolerated no matter how appealing her idea.

The illusion conservation rule is violated only a few times in the "bad mother" episode described in this report. In general the rule is upheld, however. At one point Kathy rebukes Heather for calling her by her real name rather than her pretend name "Annie." Heather complies by adjusting her behavior, thereby suggesting that she acknowledges the existence of an illusion conservation rule. In general the rule is upheld during this episode and most episodes of make-believe. Existence of the rule can only be indicated by the fact that attempts are indeed made to preserve the illusion through the use of partially within-frame metacommunicative options. One of the reasons that sanctions against rule violations may be lacking is that sanctioning itself inevitably relies on out-of-frame metacommunication. Discussing rules of interaction is discussing the frame of the interaction. It thus disturbs the illusion possibly as much as a rule violation.

Implicit Pretend Rule

Whereas the illusion conservation rule offers an explanation of why partially within-frame metacommunicative options exist, a complementary set of rules, termed *coordination rules,* facilitates and encourages their use. The coordination rules prescribe how to interpret and respond to metacommunicative behavior in make-believe play. Three ways in which the illusion of the pretend world can be jeopardized are (1) through continual reminders that "it's only pretend," (2) inappropriate behavior that belies the pretend definition of the situation, and (3) frequent out-of-frame negotiations of the pretend definitions.

One of the reasons players are able to metacommunicate partially within-frame is that they can expect others to understand the pretend framing without an explicit explanation that "this is play." They rely on an *implicit pretend rule* that guides all players to interpret statements during make-believe play as if they were prefaced with the words "pretend that." It can be stated

> When engaged in make-believe play, players should interpret statements that transform real meanings as implicit requests to pretend and should respond within the playframe.

Thus, Heather can offer an empty cake pan, saying "Here's some wedding ring cake," and expect that Kathy will understand the implicit request to pretend that the empty pan holds cake. To demonstrate sanctioning against violation of the implicit pretend rule a similar episode can be described. Another child, Maggie, and the researcher were playing "house." Maggie offered the researcher an empty pan, saying "It's time for lunch. Here, eat it." Purposely violating the rule, the researcher responded "But Maggie, there's nothing in it!" In an exasperated tone Maggie replied "Just pretend!" When players do not have to say they are pretending they can proceed with increased engrossment in the framed activity, the object of make-believe play in the first place.

Script Adherence Rule

When play is based, as it most often is, on some shared transactional script, the necessity for clarifying meanings and defining appropriate response is reduced. The rule prescribes that players should only propose transformations or action plans that are consistent with the general script. The strength of the rule depends on how detailed and specific is the script the participating players have in mind. If the script is not defined in detail, many more behaviors are acceptable than if players have specific expectations for how the pretend situation should be played. The rule also prescribes that players respond to appropriate proposals according to the established script without overt direction.

For example, when Andy announces that "the police are going to come," Heather knows she is to respond by crying out a warning and hiding the "mother." Likewise, when Heather reports to Andy "Daddy, I'm crying cause my mother gave me a spanking and she yelled at me," he knows he is to come to her aid. (His response, "I'll kill her!" may seem extreme to realists, but is apparently acceptable to the players.) Script prescriptions are usually general rather than specific. In each case proposals of action were appropriate to the established pretend definitions, the family relationship, and the threat of the police. Thus other players could have a general idea of how to respond without being told.

A favorite minor script in the "bad mother" episode is the pattern of one person crying and another person responding by asking sympathetically "what's the matter?" and then doing something to resolve the problem. Heather sets up such a script in the beginning of the episode when she has Kathy "make the crying sound" and procedes to ask "what's the matter?" Later in the episode she violates the script adherence rule concerning this very pattern. As described earlier she responds to Kathy's "crying" with inappropriate anger in her tone of voice. As indicated earlier, this behavior strains the illusion. It does so because it is an inappropriate response to the scripted action and thus disconfirms the pretend definition of the situation. The behavior is thus more specifically a violation of the script adherence rule. Again, when sanctioned, Heather repeats her performance in the proper way, that is, according to the script.

Incorporation Rule

The third threat to conserving the illusion mentioned was frequent out-of-frame negotiations during the process of collective make-believe play. Any time awareness is directed toward the frame of the playing itself, engrossment in the activity defined by the frame is diminished. An implicit rule therefore encourages players, to the extent that their ingenuity and the script will allow, to adapt their personal definitions of the play in order to incorporate each other's proposed transformations. Further, it encourages players to incorporate any event or element of the real world environment that might otherwise disconfirm the play. This is called the *incorporation rule* and can be stated

> When a player introduces an appropriate transformation, other players should adapt their own definition of the pretend situation in order to incorporate it and respond in ways that confirm the conjoint plan.

The incorporation rule allows the details that fill out the general script to evolve through the process of playing. It facilitates the use of partially within-frame metacommunication because players can expect that their transformations will be supported and thus do not have to step out-of-frame to elicit cooperation overtly from others. When Andy reports that the grandmother will take care of the mother, Heather and Kathy immediately accept this as a fact rather than a suggestion. Because they accept his statement, in accordance with the incorporation rule Andy can propose a development of the situation without overtly asking for support for this pretend definition.

An example of masterful adherence to the incorporation rule occurs when Heather orders Laura to "get her alive with that stuff" and Laura objects that "this is poisonous." Nonplussed, Heather immediately accepts the change of definition and adapts her image by creating some "other stuff" that will do the job: "Well get her alive with that other stuff." Because Heather was able to incorporate Laura's transformation, conflicting definitions did not interrupt the flow of the playing. It was not necessary to abandon the pretense in order to negotiate agreement.

The major sanction against violation of the incorporation rule is that the collective playing disintegrates. If a player's ideas are consistently rejected, she or he is likely to refuse to play further. Play between two 3-year-old girls ended abruptly after about 15 minutes of setting up the event, during which one child rejected every idea the other suggested. Eventually the rejected playmate ran away.

Prior to abandoning the play, negative sanctioning may take the form of intentional disruption of the illusion. For example, Kathy refuses to incorporate Heather's action plan by coming alive after the "stuff" is administered. Rather than stopping the playing entirely, Heather ostensibly accepts Kathy's counterproposal while rendering it unbelievable. She insists "if you're going to be dead would you please get out of my room." Subsequently Heather proposes out-of-frame an action plan that includes Kathy's idea. Kathy is very cooperative.

This section has described the system of rules governing coordination efforts during collective make-believe play. An illusion conservation rule has been formulated that prescribes choosing within-frame or partially within-frame options to the extent possible in the process of collectively transforming meanings. In addition an implicit pretend rule, a script adherence rule, and an incorporation rule have been identified that facilitate and encourage use of within-frame metacommunicative options by preestablishing meanings and encouraging adaptability.

However, the preferential nature of the illusion conservation rule was also stressed. It allows players to choose overtly metacommunicative language to the extent necessary for the purposes of playing. As discussed earlier, the purpose of collective make-believe play is to realize a conjointly held definition of a pretend world. Players in collective make-believe play are interdependent in achieving that experience. The sustaining of a conjoint make-believe reality depends not only on understanding but also on cooperation among players. Although coordination rules may facilitate communication they are not sufficient if the action plan is too complex or if players are not willing to accept the suggested transformations. The more out-of-frame the metacommunicative choice, the more clearly players can define the situation and the more directly they can attempt to elicit confirmation from each other.

This study suggests that construction of make-believe reality depends on the availability of the full range of metacommunicative options. Skilled players move out of the play world as coordination needs arise and move back in as they are resolved. The appropriate metacommunicative choice enables players to reach understanding and agreement as well as to support the ongoing pretense. Skilled players are continually conscious of two levels of meaning: that of themselves as participants experiencing the play world and that of collaborators creating it. The final section of this chapter reexamines the sample episode, the "bad mother" (see Appendix), in an effort to describe the metacommunicative choices of skilled players in the process of making believe.

METACOMMUNICATION IN PROCESS

This section demonstrates how the interplay between the necessity to preserve the illusion and difficulties in collectively transforming meaning causes players to vacillate between within-frame and out-of-frame behavior. The frame shifts during the "bad mother" episode are traced to provide an explanation of how conjoint make-believe is metacommunicatively constructed.

Coordination problems often arise during the initial setting up of the play situation. The play group is found trying the establish roles, relationships, and a dramatic conflict. Players agree on the questions of who the others are, what they are doing, and what the action plan is. However, the impulse in play seems to be to act rather than organize if at all possible. Heather and Kathy use prompting to establish the setting "wedding place" and the immediate action "making the crying sound." Then they play the scene out as far as possible. However, Andy's role has not been clarified. To do this Heather steps back from the play definition and attempts to prompt Andy into taking the role and action that would be confirming to the girls' scenario.

The problems of coordination, however, involve more than mere clarification. Willing cooperation must be elicited. When Andy refuses to "get married," Heather steps completely out of the play frame in order to redefine circumstances more acceptable to Andy. She relies on overt proposals of pretend to transfer the entire scene ahead in time to a point at which Andy and Kathy are "already married." This strategy would allow the relationship "married couple" to continue but would appease Andy by skipping the wedding part. Without the ability to metacommunicate overtly, to step outside of the play frame, Heather would not have been able to communicate clearly something as structurally significant as a leap into the future.

Unfortunately, this redefinition is not acceptable to Andy either. The conversation continues at an implicit pretend structuring level. Kathy suggests a rule for the conducting of the episode, "You have to come and dance with me Andy," which Andy has no intention of recognizing.

Heather, however, picks up on whatever transformations Andy does suggest and makes them into part of the role requirements. Thus he "*has* to put on the song" and he "*can't* dance" because he's "Dad." Heather manages to adapt the play script so that Andy's announcements are incorporated and no longer disconfirm the emerging pretend situation. The access to the playframe provided by the option of out-of-frame metacommunication allows Heather the flexibility to adjust relational definitions and the means to communicate such changes directly. This strategy is successful at involving Andy in the play.

Once Andy has agreed to an acceptable role, Heather immediately coaches him in the appropriate response and immerses herself in the play situation again. She "cries" and attempts to establish through ulterior conversation that "my mother yelled at me." Then apparently she senses that she should elicit Kathy's cooperation in establishing a history that precedes her scene with "Dad." Heather steps back out-of-frame briefly, prompting to establish "Let's say you gave me a spanking." After a short successful negotiation of what Kathy should be called during the playing, Heather and Andy resume the scene enactment.

During the remainder of the episode, the playframe is transcended sporadically but briefly for the purposes of clarification and of eliciting confirmation.

The option of making overt proposals is useful when recoordinating after a conflict. After the conflict over Heather's misperformance of "what's the matter?" and again after the disagreement over whether or not the mother is dead, Heather prefaces her suggestions with a direct "let's say." It seems that after conflict the recoordinating requires greater clarity and specific requests for cooperation. Kathy prefaces many of her suggestions about the action plan with "pretend," directly making the request for confirmation. She may fear that her suggestion will not be incorporated by the others and sense that a direct attempt to elicit cooperation is in order. She even combines the overt proposal with the storytelling cadence at one point: "pretend I was crying at the wedding place because you . . . you guys yelled at me." This suggests conflicting need for direct elicitation of cooperation and desire to stay emotionally in touch with the developing scenario.

At other times the players move toward out-of-frame metacommunication not because cooperation is in doubt but in order to construct more elaborate or subtle action formats. When Kathy wants Heather to pretend that "you thought I was alive but I was dead," she must interrupt the flow of action because this situation might not be possible to arrange within-frame. Heather uses storytelling to speed up, develop, and clarify an elaborate action plan that involves her mother's death and her own ascent and descent to and from heaven. The storytelling allows Heather to fill in the background, which then frames her performance of pleading "Gramma, save me!"

Much of the episode, however, is developed through use of the more within-frame communication options, that is, through ulterior conversation and underscoring. Establishing that the daughter "is nice" to the mother, that the "Gramma" will "keep care of her," that the police are coming to shoot the mother, and that the daughter hides her are all accomplished essentially without exposing the pretense.

The question of whether the mother lives or dies requires negotiation. Each player seems to resolve the problem separately. Heather mourns the death of the mother and calls for the grandmother to save her. Andy offers to call the police to tell them not to shoot Heather. As she doesn't respond he decides to shoot her himself. When both of his attempts to develop the action within-frame fail he returns to reporting to the telephone, a situation in which he perhaps feels more influential. Kathy attempts to prompt Heather to say something but is interrupted by Heather's refusal and implicit pretend structuring of her situation "I'm dead and I want my grandmother." Rather than overtly terminating the playing, the children let the pretending become less collective, each playing out her or his own fantasy line without adapting to others. The play dissolves.

This episode is an example of fairly highly skilled playing. The script as it is developed through the process of playing is extremely complex. Although Heather is obviously the most influential player, other players' ideas were for the most part incorporated, demonstrating Heather's skill as a leader and a player. The children managed to develop much of the action of the play without transgressing the playframe. However, they also exhibited a facility with the full range of metacommunicative vocabulary. They were able to step outside the playframe but did not do so when a more within-frame option would suffice. The ultimate indication of skill is that they managed to sustain a shared make-believe reality collectively through several developments and for an extended duration of time.

CONCLUSIONS

This study presented a substantive theory in the manner of Glaser and Strauss (1967), based on naturalistic observation, of metacommunicative behavior during the collective make-believe play of children. It proposed a theoretical metacommunicative continuum ranging from within-frame to out-of-frame, as a means to understanding, describing, and relating the variety of metacommunicative behaviors identified. Further, it suggested that a system of implicit rules guides choice of metacommunicative behavior and encourages and facilitates movement along the continuum.

The purpose of substantive theory is to provide a framework of categories as a perspective from which phenomena may be described. Because the categories proposed were generated from direct observation of many interactions performed by many different children, the requirements of saturation and of constant comparison were met. The resulting theoretical structure provides categories and relationships among categories that would probably not have been identified without the open-ended methodology. However, because of the strict closeness to the data, the theory provides some potentially useful insights into the nature of collective make-believe play that may be tested in future research. Future work should be done to enlarge and refine further the repertoire of behaviors already identified. This research has performed the important primary step of articulating a theoretical framework on which subsequent investigation may be based.

The cultural perspective was deliberately chosen for this research in order to identify the skills of constructing make-believe play from the point of view of the player. Again, once the substantive theory has been articulated, developmental implications can be drawn. Viewing the child as a competent cultural member brings into focus social abilities.

Mead has suggested that the function of play is to learn to take the role of the other and thus learn how to respond in socially appropriate ways (Mead,

1934/1967). Role taking is a prerequisite ability to social maturity. Play itself involves another level of social ability, however. Bateson has suggested that play is a step forward in the development of human communication because a primary and metaphoric level of meaning can be both equated and discriminated. Communicators are more detached from their symbols and thus have greater control over them (Bateson, 1955).

The ability of children to communicate symbolic meanings, know that those meanings are symbolic, yet interact as if they were not may be considered, then, an evolved form of communication. Bretherton has suggested that the facility with multiple levels of meaning in collective symbolic play demonstrates a capacity for multiple levels of role taking among players (Bretherton, Chapter 1, this volume). A player must take the role of the other as a character in the pretend situation in order to understand how to enact the ongoing shared script successfully. Simultaneously, a player must take the role of the other as co-creator and anticipate what transformations need to be clarified and how to elicit this collaborator's cooperation. Skills of make-believe play may then be more than precursors to script competency in adulthood. They may be instrumental to the development of more highly evolved skills in human communication, those involved in multiple levels of role taking. This study has contributed a description of those skills in operation.

APPENDIX

"BAD MOTHER"

(Heather, Kathy, Andy, and Laura are playing in the dress-up room.)

(1) H. (to K.) You're crying in the wedding place.
        [. . .][1]
        Make the crying sound.
        (K. "cries.")
(2) H. What's the matter? You want to get married is why?
        (to A.) She wants to get married so she's crying. You should get married.
        Let's say you guys were already married, OK?

[1]Ellipses in brackets refer to unintelligible speech.

(3) A. No! I'm going to put on the song.
         (The play stove has become a disco booth.)
(4) H. Andy has to put on the song and then he'll dance with you.
         (to A.) Give me the song.
(5) K. You have to come and dance with me Andy.
(6) A. No I [. . .] Dad.
(7) H. And he can't dance.
         And you say what's the matter with me, Andy.
         (H. "Cries.")
(8) H. My mother yelled at me.
         Let's say you gave me a spanking, Kathy O'Neil.
(9) K. No, my name is Annie.
(10) H. Annie, let's say you gave me a spanking. And I call you Mom.
         (to A.) Daddy, I'm crying 'cause my mother gave me a spanking and
         she yelled at me.
(11) A. I'll kill her!
(12) K. . . .² Pretend I was crying at the wedding place because you . . . you
         guys yelled at me. . .
(13) H. No I just told Daddy. I didn't yell.
         You aren't [. . .] since I told Daddy what happened.
         Mother, I did that because!
         (A. settles in a corner with a toy telephone)
(14) A. I'm calling her gramma to keep care of her, every day.
         Hi, Kathy. . .
(15) H. No, her name is Annie.
(16) A. Annie. . . [. . .]
(17) K. You said "What's the matter."
(18) H. I know I did!
         What's the matter, Mother?
(19) K. You didn't talk like that.
         You say (sweetly) "What's the matter, Mother?"
(20) H. (imitating) What's the matter, Mother?
         'Cause I told Dad and all 'your crimes'
         [. . .] Well I had to tell Dad.
(21) K. Let's say I was really bad to you.
(22) H. Mother I'm sorry about that!
         I'm very angry!
         Bye!
(23) H. And I closed the door . . .

²Ellipses preceding and following speech indicate storytelling cadence.

And you start to cry . . .

And I make you some wedding cake . . .

(24) H. Mommy, I did something nice for you.

I made you a wedding ring cake that you can eat for your own self.

(She offers empty angel food cake pan.)

(25) A. (to "phone") So she can bring all of her toys.

(26) H. You can eat it with a spoon if you want.

I made something cute for you.

(27) K. No, I'm not crying yet.

(28) H. I made something cute for you.

Here's one piece of candy.

(A. continues to talk on the "phone.")

(29) H. She's my mother.

I do nice stuff for her.

(30) A. Heather, I called her gramma.

And she's gonna keep . . . she gonna keep care of her.

(31) H. Gramma's gonna keep care of you.

(32) A. And she can bring all her toys.

(33) H. Yay!

(34) K. She is?

(35) H. . . . And she can bring all her toys.

(36) A. And bring all her clothes.

(37) H. And bring all her clothes.

She's gonna take care of you, mother.

(38) A. And I told she spanked you.

Now I'm going to call somebody else.

And tell she yelled at you.

(39) A. Now I'm going to call somebody else.

(40) H. The police?

(41) A. Yeah.

(42) H. Better not.

I don't want my mother to get hurt. Or get in jail.

She's a very good mother.

(43) A. And she's going to get hurt and she going to die.

They're going to shoot her.

(44) H. (gasp) Oh they're going to shoot you mother! Quick!

Get in here and we'll lock the door.

(H. indicates the "room" she has constructed with chairs.)

(45) A. They can smash down the window.

They can get it.

(46) H. We don't care.
We're going to hide.
[A segment was missed.]

(47) H. She's in jail!
(to K.) Lie down there and I'll cover your head so they don't know OK?
Now lie down
And you can drink that tea cup.
Now don't wiggle or the blankets will come off.
Get into this over your head, OK?

(48) A. (gruff voice) All right! The police are going to come.

(49) H. Oh no! Put that over your head.

(50) K. Pretend you thought I was alive but I was dead.

(51) H. Ah! She's dead she's dead she's dead.
(to L.) Get her alive with that stuff.

(52) L. This is poisonous.

(53) H. Well get her alive with that other stuff.

(54) H. You're alive now.

(55) K. I'm still dead.

(56) H. If you're going to be dead would you please get out of my room 'cause I want to sleep with the baby all the time.
Take your purse!

(57) H. Let's say you fell dead outside.

(58) K. Yeah.

(59) H. . . . and you were outside . . .
. . . and you saw the police . . .

(60) K. Yeah.

(61(H. . . . and she was dead . . .
. . . and she'll stay dead forever, . . . I thought.
. . . and she did . . .
Oh, she's dead and I think she'll stay dead forever! I'm crying!

(62) A. I'll call the police and tell them not to shoot her.

(63) H. (to L.) Gramma, come save me and help me so the police don't shoot me.

(64) H. . . . And I was crying up in heaven . . .
. . . And I got back alive . . .
. . . Grandmother, Gramma, save me!
. . . And I was crying . . .
(A. makes shooting sound.)

(65) A. I shot you!

(66) K. Heather, I told you say . . .
(67) H. No. I'm dead and I want my grandmother!
(68) A. (on "phone") Leave it alone and I will call you.

ACKNOWLEDGMENTS

This chapter is based on doctoral research conducted at the University of Colorado, Boulder, Colorado. I would like to thank my dissertation advisor, Dr. Janice Rushing, and my dissertation committee, Dr. Thomas Frentz, Dr. Elise Boulding, Dr. Inge Bretherton, and Dr. Elaine Yarbrough, for their advice and support. I would also like to thank the children who contributed to this study.

REFERENCES

Bateson, G. Information and codification: A philosophical approach. In G. Bateson & Reusch, J. (Eds.), *Communication: The social matrix of psychiatry.* New York: Norton, 1951.

Bateson, G. Toward a theory of play and fantasy. In G. Bateson (Ed.), *Steps to an ecology of mind.* New York: Ballantine, 1972. (Reprinted from A.P.A. *Psychiatric Research Reports*, 1955, II.)

Fein, G. *The social competence of play.* Paper presented at the annual meeting of the American Education Research Association, San Francisco, April 1976.

Garvey, C., & Berndt, R. *The organization of pretend play.* Paper presented at the annual meeting of the American Psychological Association, Chicago, August 1975.

Glaser, B., & Strauss, A. L. *The discovery of grounded theory.* Chicago: Aldine, 1967.

Goffman, E. *Frame analysis.* Cambridge, MA: Harvard University Press, 1974.

Gowen, J. *Structural elements of symbolic play of preschool children.* Paper presented at the annual meeting of the American Psychological Association, Toronto, August 1978.

Hawes, L. C. Toward a hermeneutic study of communication. *Communication Quarterly, 25,* 1977, 34.

Hulme, I., & Lunzer, E. A. Play, language, and reasoning in subnormal children. *Journal of Child Psychology and Psychiatry,* 1966, *7,* 107–123.

Mead, G. H. *Mind, self, and society.* Chicago: University of Chicago Press, 1967. (Originally published, 1934).

Nicholich, L. M. *Methodological issues in studying symbolic play.* Paper presented at the biennial meeting of the Southeastern Conference on Human Development, Atlanta, April 1978.

Parten, M. Social play among preschool children. In R. Herron & B. Sutton-Smith (Eds.), *Child's play.* New York: Wiley, 1971.

Piaget, J. *Play, dreams and imitation in childhood.* New York: Norton, 1962.

Sanders, K. & Harper, L. Free play, fantasy behavior in preschool children: Relations among gender, age, season, and location. *Child Development. 47,* 1976, 1182–1185.

Schwartzman, H. B. *Transformations: The anthropology of children's play.* New York: Plenum, 1978.

Shimanoff, S. B. *Communication rules: Theory and research.* Beverly Hills, CA: Sage, 1980.

CHAPTER 4

Mother–Baby Role Play: Its Origins in Social Support*

PEGGY MILLER
CATHERINE GARVEY

INTRODUCTION

Much research has been devoted to understanding the cognitive bases of young children's play (e.g., Fein, 1975, 1981; Fenson, Kagan, Kearsley, & Zelazo, 1976; Lowe, 1975; Nicolich, 1977, 1981; Sinclair, 1970). Comparatively less attention has been given to the portrayal of roles. This is rather surprising, as social role-play has been widely documented in children aged 3–5 years (Corsaro, 1979; Greif, 1976). In its ontogeny, role portrayal is social in two ways: (1) it embodies social (conventional) knowledge and (2) learning to play occurs within the context of interactions between young children and their care givers, siblings, and peers. The present study investigated spontaneous performances of the reciprocal roles of mother and baby, focusing specifically on developments

*This research was supported, in part, by a National Institutes of Mental Health Grant No. 1ROMH34413–01 to the first author and a Spencer Foundation Grant to the second author. We wish to thank Judy DeJong and Anca Nemoianu for help in processing the data.

101

during the third year of life. There were two objectives: (1) to generate hypotheses about the changes in content and technique of role portrayal and the possible contributions of caregivers and peers to this acquisition and (2) to describe the communication that accompanies mothering play, with particular focus on pretend motherese as the primary technique of role portrayal.

Several studies (El'Konin, 1969; Garvey & Berndt, 1975; Nelson & Gruendel, 1979) have indicated the importance of shared social knowledge for the conduct of peer relations and especially for the development of playful and nonplayful conversations. One type of shared resource is knowledge of social roles, including relational or family roles. The first social role to be portrayed is the role of Mother. Garvey (1979, p. 70) examined this role as adopted by a 3-year-old girl in relation to a second child who assumed the pretend role of Baby. This episode began with explicit assignment of the Baby role ("Won't you be my baby, OK?") and implicit adoption of the reciprocal role of Mother. The child in the make-believe role of Mother not only engaged in conventional domestic and nurturing activities but was also highly attentive to Baby, asked her numerous questions, and even anticipated her needs and interests. Perhaps the most significant finding was that most of Mother's behaviors were made in *response* to Baby's changing behaviors. For example, when Baby asked, "Is this baby's food?" Mother replied, "Do you want your baby food?" And when Baby picked up a hat, Mother immediately said, "That's a hat. Put it on." This flexibility in situated interaction is evidence that the child was operating on the basis of a complex and productive mental representation of the Mother–Baby relationship. The actual portrayal, however, was interactive and reciprocal. In addition, the pretend Mother's speech, which reflected several of the features of motherese, indicated that speech register is an important means of role portrayal.

An important question that remains to be answered concerns the early developmental history that precedes role-play of this kind. What are the developments that lead up to the explicit adoption, at about 3 years of age, of reciprocal roles in spontaneous interaction? In this connection, Huttenlocher and Higgins (1978) have made a useful distinction between *role enactment* and *role-play*. They caution that behavior deriving from conventional action patterns, such as rocking or hugging a doll, is not sufficient evidence from which to infer that symbolic processes are involved. Such behavior, which they call *role enactment,* does involve mental representation but merely exemplifies a category of action. By contrast, role-play is genuinely symbolic; the child's behavior designates the behavior of another person. The most persuasive evidence of role-play, as distinguished from role enactment, occurs when the child makes an advance verbal announcement, such as "I'll be the mother." Following Huttenlocher and Higgins, we reserve the term *role-play* for those more mature performances that are marked by a prior verbal naming of roles, as in the Mother–Baby episode described earlier, and use *role enactment* for performances that do not meet this criterion.[1] We use the terms *performance* and *portrayal* as general terms, referring to both role enactment and role-play.

LEARNING TO PORTRAY MOTHER–BABY ROLES

Much of the work on early pretense has focused on the individual player. This has obscured the importance of interpersonal experience in the development of role-play. In a review of the literature on pretend play, Fein (1981) concludes that there is little evidence that parents teach or model pretense for their young children. However, several studies indicate that care givers do, indeed, provide support for pretend activity (Dunn & Wooding, 1977; Kavanaugh, Whittington, & Cerbone, 1981; Rocissano, 1982; Sachs, 1980).

It is our contention that care givers in many communities assist young children, particulary girls, in learning to portray mother–baby roles. They arrange situations in which the play takes place, provide dolls and other props, readily accept pretend overtures, and help the child to extend her efforts by guiding, structuring, modeling, and teaching. Before the child is able to adopt the Mother role consciously, she has already experienced extensive enactment practice and considerable training and encouragement from care givers. This experience provides her with a repertoire of conventional mothering behaviors for role enactments as well as some of the communicative techniques necessary for the social conduct of such play.

In this chapter we attempt to describe more precisely how care givers contribute to the process of learning to portray mother-baby roles and to specify how care giver assistance prepares the child for the transition to role-play with age-mates. Initially, the peer partner provides some of the types of support that the care giver had provided at the earlier stage, namely the encouragement and even the prompting of an interested audience. Toward the end of the third year of life, the peer is actually incorporated into the reciprocal role, and mature role-play is attained. Communication is critically important to this achievement.

COMMUNICATION IN MOTHER–BABY
ROLE PORTRAYAL

The conduct of social pretend play depends heavily on communication. First, roles, themes, and objects are negotiated verbally by the players (Garvey, 1977;

[1]In order to emphasize this distinction we capitalize only in reference to role-play (e.g., "The 3-year-old girls adopted both Mother and Baby roles"), not in reference to role enactment (e.g., "The child enacted mothering behaviors in relation to doll as baby").

Pellegrini, 1982). Second, there is overt representation of the characters and their actions in both verbal and nonverbal behavior, with speech-in-role (i.e., the production of certain features from the role-appropriate speech register) a major means of representation in social role portrayal.

Findings concerning the acquisition of motherese or baby talk are relevant here.[2] Students of speech to young children have shown that children as young as 3 and 4 years old talk differently to babies than to peers or adults (e.g., Dunn & Kendrick, 1982; Gleason, 1973; Shatz & Gelman, 1973). Children's use of features of motherese has been discussed mainly in terms of what it reveals about the developing ability to adjust speech to different categories of listeners. However, motherese is not only the first alternative speech style to be acquired, it also figures importantly in pretend portrayals of the mother role, the first social role to be represented. Sachs and Devin (1976) reported that four children, aged 3–5 years, used some features of motherese in speaking to a pretend baby (doll) as well as to a real baby. In the present chapter, we attempt to demonstrate that during the third year of life pretend motherese emerges as the primary technique of portrayal in mothering play and, as such, provides a sensitive measure for assessing early changes in social role portrayal.

Related to the issue of the development of pretend motherese is the question of the functions motherese serves in pretend and nonpretend contexts. Brown (1977) identified two major components of motherese: communication-clarification and expressive–affective. Use of simple constructions, slowness of delivery, and high rate of repetitions, for example, serve a communicative function, whereas such features as euphemisms and "nursery tone" serve an expressive function. In a description of speech to infant siblings, Dunn and Kendrick (1982) reported consistent use of clarification features by children aged 34–36 months, but individual variation in the use of expressive features of baby talk. Only those subjects with particularly warm relations with the sibling used diminutives, endearments, and playful repetitions. For the present analysis, we use a modified version of the Dunn and Kendrick measures in order to explore the expressive and communicative dimensions of pretend motherese.

In addition to speech-in-role, social role portrayal also includes a great deal of communication about the play. Players issue invitations to play, assign pretend identities, adjust or improve the production, and terminate the performance. Through these production and regulation techniques, the player assists herself or himself in conducting the play and provides co-present others with opportunities to interpret messages and to extend the play (Garvey, 1982). In mothering play, children also talk about baby to self and to partner. They draw

---

[2]The terms *motherese* and *baby talk* have been used interchangeably. In order to avoid confusion, we use *motherese* to refer to the speech register used by mothers when talking to young children. That is, *motherese* refers to speech appropriate to the mother role. The reciprocal register—speech appropriate to the baby role—we call *speech as baby*.

attention to baby, offer a running commentary on baby's behavior, describe the pretend mother's activities in respect to baby, inquire about baby's state, and direct the partner in how to behave with baby.

In sum, the emergence of mature role play at about 3 years of age is undoubtedly a cognitive achievement. What has not been adequately acknowledged is the degree to which role-play has its roots in interpersonal experience. The use of role-appropriate speech registers, the importance of communication for the social conduct of role portrayal, and the contributions of caregivers and peers in learning to play all point to the social origins of role play. In this chapter we examine these origins by reference to systematic observations of spontaneous mothering play by young girls and their families and friends.

PROCEDURES

In order to ensure that the description was broadly valid, the investigation was based on video-tape-recorded observations from three sources.

Study 1 (2-year-olds). A longitudinal study of three girls from low-SES families provided data on the earliest period under investigation. Age at the beginning of the study was 18 months for Amy, 24 for Wendy, and 25 for Beth. Interactions with mother and other care givers were recorded at home every 3 weeks for a period of about 8 months. Each recording session lasted for 1 hour. Procedures are described more fully in Miller (1982). The present analysis was baed on Samples I, III, V, VII, IX, and XI, for each of the children, for a total of 6 hours of observations per child.

Study 2 ($2\frac{1}{2}$-year-olds). A longitudinal study of three middle-SES girls provided data that overlap the upper age range covered in Study 1. Age at the beginning of the study was 25 months for Sarah, 28 for Judy, and 31 for Anne. Interactions with mother at home and with a same-age friend at home and in the laboratory playroom were recorded at monthly intervals for about 5 months. Procedures are described more fully in Garvey (1982). The present analysis was based on four 1-hour-long observations for each of the following: Judy with a male friend in the laboratory playroom and Anne with a male friend in the laboratory playroom. Sarah's friend was a girl who was considerably older and more skilled at pretense than Sarah, the youngest child in the $2\frac{1}{2}$-year sample. Because Sarah's interactions with her friend were not comparable to those of Anne and Judy with their friends, only Sarah's interactions with her mother are described in this chapter. These totaled 4 hours of observation over the 5-month period.

Study 3 (3-year-olds). A cross-sectional study provided data on 12 previously acquainted peer dyads, all from middle-SES backgrounds. From this sample, five dyads involving the three oldest girls were selected for the current analyis: Meg (37 months) with a same-age boy, Meg with Carrie (37 months), Carrie with a boy, Mary (38 months) with a boy, and Mary with a second boy. The interaction of each dyad was recorded on a single occasion in a laboratory playroom with no adult present. The recording session for each dyad lasted 15 minutes, providing a total observation of 30 minutes for each of the three girls. Procedures are described more fully in Garvey and Berndt (1975).

Together the data cover ages 18–38 months and include observation of caregiver–child interaction for the youngest group, peer–peer interaction for the oldest group, and both caregiver–child and peer–peer interaction for the middle group.

The videotapes were transcribed in detail, including speech, paralinguistic, and nonverbal behaviors. (See Miller, 1982, for transcription procedures.)

The tapes and transcripts were examined for performances in which the child engaged in conventional mothering behaviors in relation to a doll or a human partner. *Mothering* was defined as the performance of any behavior appropriately directed to infants or young children, if performed in a manner that conformed to the status differential of the mother–child relationship. Preliminary inspection of the videotapes resulted in a number of behavioral codes. These codes were grouped into four categories: affectional (e.g., hug, kiss); nurturant (e.g., feed, burp, dress); control (e.g., spank, scold, prohibit); and teach (e.g., show, elicit speech, tell name of object). Procedures for analyzing speech are described subsequently.

Performances of mothering were easily identified for the older children whose talk clearly established the nature of the play. For the younger, less verbally sophisticated children it was easy enough to distinguish performances in which mothering behaviors were directed to the doll from those in which the doll was treated as any other object might be treated, (e.g. inspected or moved from one location to another). Somewhat ambiguous, in the absence of relevant talk, were instances in which the doll was treated like a human but not necessarily like a baby (e.g. given a ride in a truck, made to sit down), and these were omitted from the analysis.

GENERAL DESCRIPTION OF MOTHERING PLAY

Mothering play accounted for a significant amount of the children's activity in both home and laboratory settings but varied in frequency from one sample to the next. For the youngest group, mothering play occurred in 17 of the 18 samples. The only exception was Beth XI, during which Beth's newborn sister was present. Speech accompanying mothering play accounted for as many as 0.20 of Amy's intelligible utterances in any given sample, 0.41 of Wendy's, and 0.30 of Beth's. On the average (across the six samples per child), 0.11 of Amy's intelligible utterances accompanied mothering play, 0.16 of Wendy's, and 0.20 of Beth's. The middle group engaged in mothering play in all eight samples. Accompanying speech accounted for an average of 0.32 of Judy's intelligible utterances and 0.18 of Anne's. In the oldest group, speech accompanying mothering play accounted for 0.45 of Mary's utterances with one boy partner and 0.28 with the other boy. When paired with the boy partner, Meg produced only 0.11 of her utterances in accompaniment to mothering play, but when paired with Carrie the proportion increased to 0.69. Similarly, Carrie's proportion with the boy was 0.26 but rose to 0.62 when paired with Meg. For the 3-year-olds, it appears that characteristics of the partner (e.g., gender, skill at and predisposition to role-play) influence the amount of role portrayal a child displays.

The 2-year-olds engaged in both solitary and joint performances, with the typical portrayal of the mother–baby relationship involving child, doll, and mother. In addition to mothers, other caregivers also served as partners in mothering play. These included Amy's aunts, grandmother, and 5-year-old cousin; Wendy's mother's friends; and Beth's 5-year-old cousin. A few episodes involved several interactants such as child, mother, and cousin or child, aunt, and grandmother. (The investigators also participated in some episodes of mothering, usually at the child's instigation.)

The children acted as mother to doll, using verbal, nonverbal, and paralinguistic means of enactment. Amy, at 18 months, said, "drink," and put a cup to the doll's mouth. Wendy, at 28 months, said, "Pattycake, pattycake, bakerman," marking it with the conventional rhythm and guiding the doll's hands through the pattycake motions. These behaviors are usually taken to indicate attribution of agency to an inanimate object (Watson & Fischer, 1977). The doll was consistently called "baby" and was also referred to by personal pronouns. ("Baby" was also applied to stuffed animals, which were occasionally treated in nurturant ways.) The child directly addressed the baby and talked to self and to caregiver about baby. However, there was no evidence at this age of genuinely symbolic representations of mothering or that the child regarded herself as the pretend Mother.

The same was true in the middle group. The $2\frac{1}{2}$-year-old girls continued to enact mothering with dolls, but their performances were more complex. The elaboration of mothering play was best seen in the verbal performance accompanying relatively simple action lines. That is, although the child picked up, held, and changed baby's diaper, the *talk* was most revealing of maternal activity—comforting, crooning, inquiring about wants, requesting feedback, telling baby about future activities, or verbalizing the meaning of care giving actions.

The boys were interested and asked relevant questions but did not become actively involved with baby. Often, in fact, the girls would warn the boy not to touch or disturb the baby. Both boys and girls in this group appeared to recognize the girls' "responsibilities" and rights to care for baby.

In the 3-year-old group we find the first clear evidence of role-play, in which the child transformed her identity in imagination. The child explicitly adopted the Mother role in relation to another child who was cast in the role of Baby, prefacing the performance with a statement or proposal in which the pretend role was named, such as "Won't you be my baby, OK?" That is, at this point the child was able to propose and negotiate a mutual portrayal in which the partner was incorporated into the reciprocal role. Each girl in this group adopted at least one family role and assigned a reciprocal role to the partner. In addition, they continued to engage in mothering play with dolls and were observed to converse with a baby doll, speaking in alternating turns as Baby and as Mother, for example, alternately crying and comforting.

At the same time that Mother–Baby role play was observed, the child showed the ability to adopt both roles. Further, the Mother role was now multiply defined so that Mother stood in simultaneous reciprocal relationships to Baby and to Father or could serve as Mother both to Baby (doll) and to partner as older Sister. Although no 3-year-old girl identified herself as Wife, as was the case among 4- and 5-year olds (Garvey & Berndt, 1975), the 3-year-olds did portray their (motherly) relationship with Baby and simultaneously treated a male partner as Father of the Baby (see Example 3, under *Pretend Motherese*) often addressing him as "daddy." Versatility of role-play was further evidenced by the same child's playing Baby to Father (a male partner) as well as Mother to Baby (a female partner) in different observation sessions.

CONTENT OF ROLE PORTRAYAL

The content of mothering, as portrayed in relation to dolls, was mainly nurturant and affectional. This was true for all three age groups. Baby dolls were fed, burped, dressed and undressed, given baths, put to bed, diapered, and taken to the toilet. They were rocked, patted, hugged, kissed, smiled at, swung, bounced on lap or knee, sung and crooned to. In addition, the children sometimes tried to control, direct, or punish baby by, for example, spanking or angrily shaking it. Least frequent, and increasing developmentally, were behaviors that involved teaching or informing—for example, showing baby an interesting picture, explaining an object's use or function, or planning the day's events ("We're going to the park and then we're going to have a picnic.")

When peers were incorporated into the Baby role (by the 3-year-olds), the content of mothering differed somewhat. Peers were treated not as young "lap" babies but as slightly older children. Peers, unlike dolls, were not "handled" (i.e., diapered, swung, bounced). They were nutured (e.g., offered food, dressed, taken to potty), controlled (e.g., spanked), and taught (e.g., informed of plans) but received relatively little affection.

With respect to the organization of content, there was a clear developmental progression. In our earliest data (18 months), the child enacted a single mothering behavior, such as feeding the doll or brushing its hair. Next, we observed enactments of multiple behaviors, such as putting the doll to sleep, comforting it, and playfully bouncing it. By the age of 2 the children were able to represent mentally complexes of mother-like behaviors. There were best exhibited in solitary performances in which the children, in play with dolls, enacted sequences of mothering behaviors. For example, at the age of 24 months Wendy enacted the following sequence on her own: puts doll to sleep, holds on lap, expresses affection to, speaks harshly to, comforts, makes doll dance, sings to doll, makes it dance. At about 30–36 months, linear sequences or goal-directed activities began to appear as the child, for example, enacted the steps in toileting the doll. Later developments included (1) the incorporation of larger numbers of role-relevant behaviors and (2) further elaborations within the steps of linearly arranged sequences. Moreover, at this age sequences were usually verbally planned in advance, and the actions subordinate to the governing plan were subsequently portrayed. For example, in one of the 3-year-old dyads Mother announced that she was taking Baby to Sunday School and then took out Baby's clothes and pretended to dress her.

VERBAL TECHNIQUES OF ROLE PORTRAYAL

Although nonverbal means of portrayal continued to be used during the third year, speech became increasingly important in mothering play. Three types of speech were identified.

PRETEND MOTHERESE (SPEECH AS MOTHER)

The child directly addressed the baby doll or the partner, producing aspects of the register appropriate to the mother role. Identifying features included vocatives, second person pronouns, high pitch, exaggerated intonation, gaze at baby's face, leaning toward baby, and holding the baby doll in face-to-face position while speaking.

Example 1³ (Wendy I, 24 months)

ACTION	WENDY	MOTHER'S FRIEND
		Give the baby some.
W. turns, direct gaze at doll	want some?/	
W. extends toy dish	hm?/ good/	

Example 2 (Wendy IX, 30 months)

ACTION	WENDY
W. holds doll appropriately	here/
W. looks into doll's face	baby cryin, OK?/ - - - cryin/ gonna take you a walk/
W. picks up another doll	do you want me to?/ come on/ I take you/

Example 3 (Mary, 38 months)

ACTION	MARY
M. carries doll over to the car in which the boy partner is riding	hey baby/
M. moves doll's arm up and down as if waving goodbye to partner	say goodbye to your daddy/ say bye bye/
M. hugs doll while making it wave, chanting bye-bye in singsong	bye bye/ bye daddy daddy/ bye bye daddy/

---

³The following format is used for all examples: The sample is identified by Roman numeral indicating the number of the sample (for the longitudinal data only) and by child's age. Column 1 contains a description of nonverbal and paralinguistic behaviors, with the actor identified by first initial. Column 2 contains the target child's utterances. Each utterance boundary is indicated by a slash. Column 3 contains other speakers' utterances. An unintelligible utterance or portion of an utterance is indicated by three hyphens: - - - cryin/.

PRETEND SPEECH AS BABY

The child spoke for the baby doll or as baby as she herself portrayed the baby role. That is, she produced aspects of the register appropriate to the baby role. Identifying features included first person pronouns, high pitch (usually higher than that used with speech to baby), and a good deal of crying and whining, Frequent also in the baby role were demands for services and for help, such as "I need. . ." or "I want. . . "

Example 1 (Judy III, 31 months)

ACTION	JUDY
J. holds doll, addresses boy partner	this baby's crying/
J. high pitch	(cries)
J. puts doll in cradle, addresses partner	she has to go home/

Example 2 (Mary, 38 months)

ACTION	MARY
M. speaks to boy partner, whom she has called "daddy," whining, demanding tone	I want my teddy bear/

Example 3 (Carrie, 37 months)

ACTION	CARRIE
C. having accepted role of Baby, addresses female partner in role of Mother, gazing directly at Mother	mommy, I need to go to the bathroom/

Example 4 (Carrie, 37 months)

ACTION	CARRIE
C. acting as Baby, addresses female partner in role of Mother while trying to open purses	how do we open these, mommy?/

SPEECH ABOUT BABY

Child talked to self or partner about baby or about the parent–baby relationship. Included were descriptions of baby's behavior, feelings, or appearance; queries about partner's behavior toward baby; and directions about what to do with baby.

Example 1 (Beth I, 25 months)

ACTION	BETH	MOTHER
		Go on. Talk to the baby. See if it peed. See if it peed. Did it?
B. touches doll's crotch	wet/	
		Well, you better clean her.

Example 2 (Beth IX, 30 months)

ACTION	BETH	INVESTIGATOR (PEGGY)
B. gives small container to P.	here this, Peggy/	
	wash the baby's hair/ wash the baby's hair/	
		What?
	wash the baby's hair/ wash the baby's hair/ yeah/	
P. pretends to wash doll's hair		Oh. Like this?
	yeah/	
		Oh, alright.
	that pretty hair/	

Example 3 (Mary, 38 months)

ACTION	MARY	BOY PARTNER
M. sits on sofa with doll, singing to it		
B. reaches for baby bottle	no, that's the bottle for the baby/	
M. with B watching, takes off doll's bonnet	does she look pretty when she takes it off?/	
		no/

M. readjusts bonnet	she looks prettier/
	now does she look
	pretty?/

Sometimes the child made use of more than one of these techniques in a given episode, for example, talking about baby and then directly to baby.

Each child utterance was coded as pretend motherese, pretend speech as baby, speech about baby, speech not relevant to mothering play, or ambiguous. Intercoder reliability estimates were computed based on (1) 300 consecutive child utterances from each of three samples for Amy, Wendy, and Beth; (2) 50 consecutive child utterances from each of two samples for Judy and Anne; and (3) 50 consecutive child utterances from one sample for Mary, Meg, and Carrie. Proportions of agreement were as follows: Amy I, 0.88; Amy V, 0.86; Amy XI, 0.96; Wendy I, 0.82; Wendy V, 0.97; Wendy XI, 1.00; Beth I, 0.90; Beth V, 0.88; Beth XI, 1.00; Judy I, 0.96; Judy IV, 0.94; Anne I, 0.94; Anne IV, 0.92; Mary, 0.96; Meg, 0.98; Carrie, 0.96.

Even the youngest group made frequent use of speech to baby and speech about baby. However, none of the two year olds talked as baby. This technique was used by one of the $2\frac{1}{2}$-year-old girls and by two of the 3-year-old girls, whose role flexibility was displayed in rapid alternation of mother–baby talk as the child portrayed both Mother (speech as mother) and Baby (speech as baby) vis-à-vis Father as partner. Of all speech accompanying mothering play by the girls, the proportion of role-appropriate speech (as mother and as baby) increased across the three age groups from an average of 0.31 among the 2-year-olds to 0.54 among the $2\frac{1}{2}$-year-olds and to 0.75 among the 3-year-olds. (There was no evidence of consistent increase within age groups.) In other words, pretend motherese was the first role-appropriate register to emerge in mothering play, and it remained the most important throughout. Toward the end of the third year, the children added the reciprocal register (pretend speech as baby) to their repertoires. Note, however, that the use of role-appropriate speech does not in itself constitute evidence of role-play, as we define it. To count as role-play, rather than role enactment, the performance must be prefaced by an explicit reference to the adopted role (e.g. "I'll be the mommy.").

PRETEND MOTHERESE

In this section we take a closer look at pretend motherese in an attempt to discover whether the two major functions that have been found to characterize speech to real babies also apply to pretend motherese. In order to facilitate comparisons with the Dunn and Kendrick (1982) study of 3-year-olds talking to infant sibling, we constructed the following measures, based partly on their measures:

Expressive features—proportion of utterances directed to baby that included one or more of the following: (1) explicit expression of affection (e.g., "love you," "don't cry," "give kiss,"); (2) paralinguistic expression of affection (e.g., affectionate or gentle tone of voice); (3) endearments, diminutives, and playful names (e.g., "you fat thing," "dear," "thizzy"); (4) rhymes, songs, and playful repetitions (e.g., pattycake pattycake baker man," "baby baby baby baby baby," "big, big girl").

Clarification features—proportion of utterances directed to baby that included one or more of the following: (1) questions: utterances in interrogative form, including utterances having terminal rising intonation (e.g., "want some?" "OK?" "Awright?" "understand me, baby?"); (2) attention-getting and attention-holding devices: utterances that include such words as *hey, see, hi, look, hear, watch,* and listener's name as attention getters and *now, OK, c'mon* as attention holders (e.g., "you hear me?" "baby!!"); (3) imperatives: utterances that direct or command (e.g., "You stay right here, baby"; "Baby you're going to Sunday school, baby. Let me get you some clothes on"; "Go ahead and pee-pee right there.")

This analysis revealed that the children used expressive features when talking to baby dolls or to child partners in the Baby role. This was true even of the youngest group. The frequency of expressive features seemed to vary considerably across children. Among the 2-year-olds, for example, the proportion of utterances to a baby doll that contained one or more expressive feature ranged from 0.11 for Beth to 0.38 for Amy. A similar range was obtained among the 3-year-olds (0.08 to 0.39). In addition, the frequency of expressive features also varied across situation. For example, Judy's ($2\frac{1}{2}$-year-old) talk to baby doll contained as few as 0.16 (Sample II) expressive features and as many as 0.64 (Sample III).

The boy partners of the $2\frac{1}{2}$- and 3-year-old girls talked very little if at all to the pretend baby. The one (3-year-old) boy who adopted the family role of Father used none of the affectionate features when addressing his female partner in the Baby role but did use stern or angry features.

The proportion of utterances that contained one or more clarification feature was computed only for the $2\frac{1}{2}$- and 3-year olds. Because the 2-year-olds routinely produced incomplete sentences (e.g., omitting sentence subjects), it was not possible to reliably identify the imperatives in their speech, particularly in the early samples. However, such utterances as "don't cry," "don't wake up," "sit up," and "hold still" were recorded. In addition, the 2-year-olds addressed questions to baby dolls (e.g., "cry?" "wanna drink?" "cold?" "allright?" "do you want me to?" "you want some?") and used attention-getting and attention-holding devices (e.g., "look," "see, baby, bottle," "look, baby, tiger," "baby!").

Among the $2\frac{1}{2}$- and 3-year old groups, clarification features were common, appearing on the average in about half of their utterances to baby. Moreover, in many cases a single utterance contained multiple clarification features, such as question and attention-getting device. For example:

(Meg, 37 months)

MEG	FEMALE PARTNER (CARRIE)
I'm ironing/	
do you got a shirt	
that needs ironing,	
baby?/	
	yeah/
okay, where is it?/	
where is it, baby?/	

ROLE PORTRAYAL IN INTERACTION

In the remainder of the chapter we focus on the interactional features of joint performances, that is, performances involving one or more partner. How do child and partner together construct performances of mother–baby behaviors? And how do different kinds of partners, namely care givers and peers, contribute to these portrayals?

2-YEAR-OLDS WITH CAREGIVERS AT HOME

Caregivers created the context in which mothering play occurred at home. They arranged the situation in which such play took place and provided dolls and other props, including toy replicas of clothing, dishes, bottles, and so on. In addition, they readily accepted the child's appropriation of nonplay objects for pretend purposes. It was the children, however, who initiated the majority of episodes of mothering play, and these overtures were consistently positively received by caregivers. In some cases, the child solicited the care giver's participation by, for example, taking doll to mother, or by directing talk to mother about baby (e.g., "cryin"). In other cases, what started as doll play involving the child alone was transformed into a joint performance as the caregiver spontaneously entered into the play.

Caregivers provided support for the children's portrayals, helping them to achieve fuller realizations of mothering. This support took various forms, including a great deal of explicit instruction and direction. Caregivers identified or explained props (e.g., "Here. Here. Use this as a baby bottle"), told the child how to behave with baby (e.g., "Pat the baby"), what to say to baby (e.g., "Say 'chew it up. Tell the baby, say 'chew it up' "), and how to say it (e.g., "Go 'aw' "). In addition, caregivers explicitly demonstrated mothering behavior. In the following episode, Beth's mother demonstrates how to burp the baby.

(Beth I, 25 months)

ACTION	MOTHER
At B.'s request, M. gives B. a small object to use as bottle	
B. feeds doll	There. Feed the baby.
M. demonstrats burping	Burp it. Burp the baby. Burp the baby. Like this. Burp her. Put her on your shoulders and burp her. Go on. How you do Kathryn (B.'s infant cousin). Burp her. She had enough. Burp her. You're gonna cut her mouth open.
B. feeds doll again	Burp her. OK. She's, she's ate enough. Here.
M. puts doll against B.'s shoulder and moves B.'s hand through patting motion	Put her on your shoulder and burp her like this.
B. pats doll's back	Burp her. Until she burps. Don't stab her!

Occasionally, the caregiver herself enacted mothering behaviors in relation to dolls, thereby modeling mothering play for the child. In the following episode involving four participants, Aunt Norma carefully holds the doll on her lap as though it were a real baby. She explicitly expresses affection for baby ("Aw, I like that baby") and directly addresses baby ("Aw. Hi, George"), gazing into baby's face and speaking in an affectionate tone.

(Amy VII, 23 months)

ACTION	AMY	OTHER SPEAKERS
	baby/	
		AUNT N. Give me that baby.

Aunt N. takes doll
  from A.
Aunt N. holds doll on
  lap like real baby
Aunt N. uses   AUNT N. Aw, I like that baby.
  affectionate tone
                        cry/
                                          AUNT N. What's her name?
                        (laughs)
                                          AUNT N. What's her name?
                                          MOTHER It looks like a boy,
                                              don't it? Look at the
                                              face.
                                          AUNT N. What's her name?
                                              What's his name?
                                          MOTHER. Say "George."
                        George/
                                          AUNT N. George?
Aunt N. gazes into   AUNT N. Aw. Hi, George.
  doll's face, uses
  affectionate tone
Aunt N. leans   AUNT N. Look at him sleep.
  forward, gazing
  closer at doll's face
Cousin K. gazes at
  doll's face
                                          AUNT N. He's waking up.
                        ---/
                                          AUNT N. He's waking up, oh he
                                              went back to sleep.
A. and Cousin K.
  giggle
                                          AUNT N. I guess he's tired.
                        yes he is/
Aunt N. uses   AUNT N. Yes he is? Aw.
  affectionate tone
                                          AUNT N. Did you give him a
                                              bath?
                        yeah/
                                          AUNT N. You got some jammies
                                              on him?

	yeah/	
		COUSIN K. No.
Aunt N. looks at doll		AUNT N. What you feed him?
and then at A.		
		AUNT N. What did you feed him?
	yes he is/	
		AUNT N. Yes he is. What do you
		feed him?
	egg/	
		AUNT N. Eggs.
		MOTHER. Say "baby cereal."
	baby cereal/	
		AUNT N. Baby cereal? You eat
		baby cereal?
	yeah/	
		AUNT N. Are you a baby?
	yeah/	

In addition to supporting enactments of mothering, caregivers also facilitated the social conduct of joint performances. At this age, the children were already capable of communicating in rudimentary ways to caregiver about baby. They solicited her attention, requested props, and made brief informational comments. Caregivers made requests for more information about baby and about child's activity. After the child had laid the doll on a blanket, mother asked, "What's the baby doing?" If the child was able to answer, mother might suggest further relevant actions. If the child was not able to answer, mother answered for the child, offering an interpretation of baby's behavior. In the example just given, Aunt Norma inquires about baby (What's his name?) and about Amy's treatment of baby ("Did you give him a bath?" "You got jammies on him?" "What did you feed him?"), and Mother elicits from Amy appropriate responses to these queries. When modeling mothering behavior for the child, the caregiver provided a running commentary on what she was doing or what baby was doing or feeling. In the same example, Aunt Norma says, "Look at him sleep. He's wakin up. He's wakin up. Oh he went back to sleep. I guess he's tired." Caregivers thus linked motive or internal state with appropriate behavior. They led the child toward intelligible accounts of the doll play actions, emphasizing conventional procedures, miniscripts, and conventional techniques for interpreting actions. In these ways they conveyed to the child that it is necessary to keep one's partner informed. This is one of the fundamental notions that the child must grasp in order to create social performances with a partner.

$2\frac{1}{2}$-YEAR-OLDS WITH CAREGIVERS AT HOME

As the children approached the age of $2\frac{1}{2}$ years, there was evidence of less reliance on caregivers' assistance. We find this in the later data for the 2-year-olds and the early data from the $2\frac{1}{2}$-year-olds. The children were able to enact elaborate mothering behaviors, such as toilet training baby, and to communicate more fully to caregiver about baby. Caregivers were often approving spectators to these performances. However, they continued to direct, coach, and encourage the children to enact more detailed and realistic mothering procedures, such as heating milk before feeding baby, putting the right number of blankets on baby in its cradle, or singing a lullaby as baby goes to sleep. Judy's mother gave a lesson in burping, much as Beth's mother had done (in the example given earlier), but her explanations were more complex (she explained why a baby must be burped periodically during feeding). Caregivers also seemed to take these occasions to teach other scriptlike information about practical social action. They explained how to set the table for a pretend meal, what kinds of food are eaten at different mealtimes, and that if someone is hurt the doctor must be called or the injured child taken to the hospital.

In addition, caregivers tended to make more attributions about baby (e.g., "She's gotta burp") and about child's treatment of baby (e.g., "Oh, you made the baby cry"). This is the first time that caregivers made explicit references to child as mother, saying, for example, "You're the mommy." In one such instance, Beth's mother instigated a role reversal, taking the role of Baby in relation to Beth, whom she addressed as "mommy."

(Beth VII, 29 months)

ACTION	BETH	MOTHER
B. has been pretending to cook		Well, feed me.
M. uses insistent tone, modified pronunciation		I'm hungry, mommy. I'm hungry, mommy.
B. prepares meal in nesting bowls	OK!	
M. uses insistent tone		Here's spoon. Feed me.
B. gives bowl to M.	this it/	

		Oh, this is it? Mmm.
B. feeds M.	eat that/	
M. uses insistent tone, modified pronunciation		I'm hungry.
	OK!/	
M. whines		Well, feed me.
	I feed you/	
B. prepares meal in bowl		Alright then. Come on. I'll starve by the time you finish. I'm mad 'cause I'm hungry and you won't feed me.
B. continues to cook	uh oh/	
M. uses insistent tone		Mom!
	OK!/ I gotta cook/	
		(laughs)
M. uses insistent tone, modified pronunciation		You gotta cook. Well, hurry up! I'm hungry.
B. continues to cook	wait cook/ I cook/ you wait?/	
		(to Investigator). Now you see she's learnin that. She knows when I'm cookin somethin for her she's gotta wait. (laughs)
M. uses insistent tone, modified pronunciation		I'm hungry.

	OK!/	
M. uses insistent tone		Well, feed me!
M. bawls		Yah!- - -/ Yah! (laughs)
	- - - food?/	
B. brings "food" to M.		Oh boy what do you got for me?
	a chicken/	
M. makes eating sounds		
		What? A chicken?
B. feeds M.	no/	
M. protesting tone		One bite? I ain't full.
M. protesting tone		I'm still hungry. Alright, thank you. I'm full.

This episode continues as Beth resumes "cooking," Baby protests that the food isn't done, Beth pretends to serve her coffee, and Baby insists on feeding herself, saying "I'm a big girl. I want to feed my own self." Thus, Beth was able to achieve a sustained enactment of mothering, in relation to mother as Baby, through a lengthy cooking and feeding scenario.

Sarah, the youngest child in the $2\frac{1}{2}$-year-old group, was observed to enact a virtually identical episode at the same age (29 months). Sarah had not shown readiness to adopt the role explicitly (i.e., had not said, "I'm the mother"), and, in fact, had rejected her mother's attempts to assign that role to her explicitly. She was able, however, to enact feeding, as her own mother portrayed the role of Baby (not infant) and, much like Beth, gave her mother milk, cooked an egg for her, and acceded to her mother's whining and petulant demands for "more. I want more." When her mother pretended to spill the milk, Sarah wiped up the (pretend) mess.

$2\frac{1}{2}$-YEAR-OLDS WITH PEER IN LAB

Beth's performance at age 29 months and Sarah's performance at age 29 months were the first in which the child enacted mothering in relation to a human partner (i.e., mother) rather than a doll. However, there was no evidence at this age of comparable performances of mothering in relation to a human partner of the same age. Rather, in our earliest peer interactions, which involved girl–boy dyads at just under $2\frac{1}{2}$ years, the girls still portrayed mothering in relation to dolls. Although they did not attempt to incorporate the boy partner into the play in any pretend capacity, they did treat him as audience, keeping him informed of their own and of baby's behavior.

(Judy I, 29 months)

ACTION	JUDY	BOY PARTNER
J. lays doll down and speaks to doll, sternly	baby, you have to go to bed/	
		is that a baby?/
B. approaches		
J. speaks to B., holding doll	no, don't touch cuz the baby's tired/	
		is the baby tired?/
J. sets doll down	no, the baby's not tired/	
J. moves to sofa with doll	I'm gonna put her into bed and then- - -/	
		what's Judy gonna do with the baby?/
	I'm gonna take the baby for a walk/	

The boys were interested in the girls' mothering activities and made appropriate responses that revealed considerable knowledge of the mother–baby relationship. Unlike the caregivers, whose speech contained a large proportion of directions, the boys' interest was expressed mainly in the form of queries and comments about partner's activity. Moreover, these verbal contributions appeared to structure and further the girls' mothering play. For example, when the girl made comfort noises to the doll, the boy asked, "What's the matter with the baby?" She replied that the baby is tired and must go to bed. On another occasion the girl commented that the baby is crying and the boy asked why and she gave a reason. Eventually, the partner's interest—"where's her mommy?"—led the girl to state for the first time, "I'm the mommy." The boy then inquired about the father, "Where's the dada? Is the dada at work?"

Thus, in these peer interactions the girls first included the boy partner as audience. They kept him informed, and his feedback helped them to structure the activity with baby. His interest as witness gradually drew him in as helper (e.g., he got the baby's bottle at mother's request) and eventually as a possible role partner (that is, as father). But throughout the girls maintained the lead and sustained the only active involvement with baby. (Although the girl–boy dyads did not engage in reciprocal role enactment at this point, they did cooperatively engage in other make-believe performances, e.g., taking a trip together, jointly eating dinner.)

3-YEAR-OLDS WITH PEER IN LAB

Role portrayal in 3-year-olds varies somewhat in quality, depending on the capabilities and inclinations of the peer partner to adopt and portray a complementary role (Garvey, 1979). With boy partners, the girls in the 3-year-old group continued to take the lead, instigating and directing the role-play episodes. In the following example Meg tried to involve the boy in doll play, referring initially to the doll as "a baby Indian" and later as "our baby Indian."

(Meg, 37 months)

ACTION	MEG	BOY PARTNER
M. sees doll in cradle and approaches it		
	there's an Indian/	
B. comes to look		
		what Indian?/
M. shows doll to boy, holding it like a baby	here/ this is a baby Indian/ see?/ it's a baby Indian/	
B. leaves cradle		it don't have a ---/
M. interrups B., carries doll to ironing board		
		will you - - - can I get some water? it wants some milk
B. climbs on car		
M. places doll on ironing board and turns to B.	our baby Indian/ an let me lie it down/ where shall I lie it?/	
B. climbs off car and looks for milk, in crib		where the milk?/

M.	now has bottle in hand	I got - uh - uh I'll get
	and shows it to B.	the milk/

B.	points toward sofa		here, there's the milk/

M. feeds doll with bottle

The three males in the 3-year-old group steadfastly refused to adopt the Baby role, although they did assume the Father role at the girl's suggestion.

In a well-matched and compatible female dyad, Mother portrayed the role relationship with Baby in considerable depth and scope. As she reacted to Baby's initiations, she displayed flexibility in meeting the demands of the role. Although the 3-year-old's use of the motherese register was still inconsistent and incomplete, she did address more imperatives and more questions concerning wants and needs to Baby than to child partner when the pair was not in role. Mother also produced more self-repetitions than in her nonrole speech. For example, Mother (Meg) asked Baby (Carrie) where her shirt is: "Where is it? Where is it, baby? Where is your clothes? Inside here? (looking in drawers) Is it inside here ones? Is it inside here ones?" Note that she addressed Baby as "baby," rather than using a proper name as real mothers would do. When Baby did speak, Mother reponded promptly and appropriately (e.g., Baby: "Mommy, I need to go to the bathroom." Mother: "Okay, I'll take you, baby. Here. I'll take you"). The topics of talk were primarily those of nurturance, instruction, and control (as contrasted with issues of sharing or the discussion of toys that occupy non-role-playing partners.)

In portraying Mother in relation to a doll as Baby, the 3-year-old girls supplied the speech for Baby as well as for Mother, often in rapid alternation. For example, Mary (38 months) spoke first in a whiny, lisping voice as Baby, "I want my Kathy doll," and then clearly and sternly as Mother to Baby doll, "If you will just go to sleep." She then turned to her boy partner, and in a normal speaking voice directed him to speak to the Baby, "Say 'Go to sleep, now.'" Through the remainder of the episode, Mary acted as Baby vis-à-vis her male partner as Father and alternated her speech as Baby with out-of-role stage directions to the boy as to how he should portray his role of stern Father.

The 3-year-old girls, then, vocally marked their performances in ways appropriate to the role persona, and they did so with both dolls and child partners in the reciprocal roles. The most sustained and elaborate portrayals of Mother–Baby roles were achieved in relation to female partners. Male partners refused to play the Baby role. When Mary addressed one of her male partners as "baby," he quickly replied, "I not baby." She then found a doll to fill that essential role and later assigned him the role of Father. The boys did, however, accept the role assignment of "daddy," thereby enabling the girls to play Mother (or Baby) to Father.

DISCUSSION

These observations suggest several developmental steps in the child's understanding of roles, as expressed in mother-baby role portrayal. At the earliest stage (2 years), the children enacted the behavior of mothers, treating dolls as babies. At $2\frac{1}{2}$ years, two children showed the ability to act as mother to a caregiver who assumed the role of Baby, although in these interactions it was the caregiver who directed and prompted the performance. In sessions with peers, the $2\frac{1}{2}$-year-old children enacted mothering behavior to doll as baby, but also demonstrated the ability to alternate the use of speech as mother (motherese) and speech as baby, thus portraying by explicit verbal means a reciprocal role relationship with the doll. At $2\frac{1}{2}$ years, however, the peer partner was not incorporated into a role relationship, although the peer partner and the pretending child did exchange frequent and often extended communications *about* the mother–baby play. Not until the age of 3 years (37 and 38 months) was role-play with a peer partner observed. At this time it could be said that the child was able to assume a social role in relation to a partner who assumed a reciprocal pretend role. And at this time not only did the criterial behavior of explicit role assignment occur, but the girls also displayed flexibility in playing either role, Baby to Father (male peer) or Mother to Baby (female peer). Further, the girls at this time also acted as Mother to Baby doll and incorporated a male partner as Father, thus indicating some understanding of the dual relationship the pretend Mother held to Father and to Baby. On occasion the 3-year-old girl dyads, portraying a Mother–Baby episode, spoke about the (absent) Father, who might be "at work" or expected home for dinner.

A similar progression was obtained by Watson and Fischer (1980), using an experimental paradigm of modeled elicitation of role performance with dolls as characters. The ability to represent the perspective of an "agent carrying out a behavioral role" (p. 492) which corresponds to role enactment in our terms, appeared prior to the ability to take the perspective of an "agent filling a social role" which corresponds to role-play in our terms. A final development in the Watson and Fischer scheme is the ability to take the perspective of a "more individualized agent filling several social roles at once." Although Watson and Fischer did not use the term *role relation* and did not describe the use of real persons in pretend roles, their results do parallel our findings in the sequencing of developments. However, in our data the achievements were accomplished at earlier chronological ages.

During the period under study the content of mother–baby role portrayal with dolls changed relatively little. All three age groups portrayed a mother–baby relationship that was primarily nurturant and affectional, with occasional efforts to control, discipline, or punish baby. Teaching, informing, or planning for baby was the least frequent content domain and the only one that tended to increase developmentally. However, when the peer rather than the doll was cast as Baby (by the 3-year-olds), Baby was portrayed not as an infant but as a somewhat older child. The peer as Baby was nurtured, controlled, and taught but received relatively little affection.

Developments in the organization of content are consistent with those described by Nicolich (1981). Portrayals of a single mothering behavior occurred first, followed by representations of multiple behaviors at about 2 years of age. Linear sequences began to appear at about $2\frac{1}{2}$ years; for example, the child prepared food and then fed baby or reproduced the ordered steps in toileting baby. By about 3 years, the children not only produced longer and more elaborate linear sequences but prefaced the sequence by an explicit plan that organized the subsequent actions.

Although prior verbal naming of roles and planning of joint action sequences were not observed until about 3 years of age, verbal means of portrayal figured importantly in mothering play from the beginning. This was especially evident in the use of role-appropriate speech registers. The first register to appear was motherese. Even the 2-year-olds displayed some understanding of this register. When acting as mother to doll, they directly addressed baby, using both expressive and clarification features of motherese. An important development, occurring around $2\frac{1}{2}$ years of age, was the increasing reliance on pretend motherese as the primary technique of portrayal. Although action lines remained rather simple, the elaboration of enactment was apparent in the accompanying talk to baby doll. The girls comforted the doll, crooned to it, inquired about wants, requested feedback, and announced future plans. At the same time, we find the first instance of a child speaking for the baby doll (i.e., speech as baby). Later, when the 3-year-olds adopted the Mother role in relation to a peer partner as Baby, speech as mother was elaborated into a more realistic rendering of motherese. Moreover, at this point, command of both registers was evident in rapid alternation of mother–baby talk as the same child portrayed both Mother and Baby to partner as Father. To a large degree, then, the overt representation of the mother–baby relationship was accomplished through the use of role-appropriate speech registers, with pretend motherese emerging earlier and more fully than the reciprocal register of pretend speech as baby.

Do these findings about the development of pretend motherese reveal anything about the acquisition of motherese in general? One might expect speech to pretend baby and speech to real baby to be similar insofar as both involve knowledge of the mother–baby relationship, and, indeed, our observations indicate that many of the expressive and clarification features previously identified in speech to real babies occurred in the pretend situation as well. As Sachs and Devin (1976) pointed out, use of motherese when no real baby is present to provide feedback indicates that the child has acquired some abstract understanding of a speech style that is appropriate for babies.

Beyond this, however, there are some possible differences in the use of motherese in pretend and nonpretend contexts. First, speech to pretend baby may be governed not only by rules for speaking to babies but by rules specific to mothering play, that is, conventions of pretense. For example, the children tended to address the pretend baby as "baby" in situations in which a real baby would be addressed by its proper name. Second, the child does not necessarily stand in the same relation to a pretend baby as she does to a real baby. In our make-believe episodes the child acted as mother, treating the doll or the role-playing partner as her *own* baby. All of the children used expressive features when talking to their pretend babies although there was individual variation in the frequency of such features. An infant sibling or friend, on the other hand, may be treated primarily as rival or playmate rather than baby. This is supported by Dunn and Kendrick's (1982) finding that expressive features were used only when the relationship with the infant sibling was particularly warm. What is needed in order to resolve these issues are comparative data on the same child's use of motherese in pretend and nonpretend contexts.

Most of the observed episodes of mothering play were not conducted by the child alone. Rather, they were social performances, involving the cooperation of at least one other person and requiring communication between the participants. These performances were achieved with the support, first, of caregivers and, later, of peers.

With 2-year-olds, care givers actively fostered mothering play. They created an inviting context for play, arranging situations, providing props, permitting the use of nonplay objects, and readily accepting the child's pretend overtures. They coached, guided, modeled, and explicitly taught mothering speech and behavior. Although the 2-year-olds were already able to initiate talk about baby, care givers helped them to provide more intelligible accounts of their own actions and of the baby doll's behaviors.

Caregivers continued to offer many of the same kinds of assistance to the $2\frac{1}{2}$-year-olds. The difference at this age was that the children knew more about mothering and could conduct some performances more independently. Care givers provided the support of interested, approving spectators who could, nonetheless, intervene with ideas for elaborating the play or making the portrayal more realistic. Similarly, in peer interactions at this age the boy served as audience, providing the impetus for the girl to communicate about her pretend activities with the baby doll.

By the time that genuine role-play occurred at age 3 years, the girls had had a year or more of practice in representing the mother–baby relationship and had experienced considerable instruction and encouragement from care givers. In addition, they had learned to keep the play partner informed, first from the care giver's explicit direction and modeling and subsequently from the experience of communicating to an audience of care giver or peer. Not only had they experienced the necessity of providing an ongoing, interpretative account of the meaning of pretend actions, but they had also learned to mark changes in role identity and continued portrayals with appropriate features from the linguistic registers. Further, the 3-year-olds were remarkably similar in their use and comprehension of the verbal conventions of social play. Even the male partners, who adopted roles less frequently, knew the conventional formulas for transforming role identity (e.g., "You be X and I'll be Y" and "Pretend you were the Father") and spaces and props (e.g., "This is our kitchen"; "This can be the table").

In respect to learning the content of social roles (i.e., the appropriate properties of persons, their reciprocal obligations and rights, their characteristic and proper activities and abilities), here too we detect continuity from the earlier mothering play of child and care giver and the subsequent social role-play of peers. In the lengthy example of Amy VII at age 23 months, Amy's mother and aunt are defining the universe of discourse of the mother–baby relationship. They model and elicit from the child not only what it is that babies need, want, and do, but also what mothers are responsible for providing, what they must be concerned with, and how they should act. The instruction goes beyond the little scripts for practical action such as burping, diapering, or feeding to include the attribution of internal states and the demonstration of appropriately fond or affectionate attitudes. The $2\frac{1}{2}$-year-olds similarly described the baby doll to their partners as "tired," "hungry," and "wanting her mommy," and showed concern for reassuring the baby and calming it.

The 3-year-olds' role-play exhibited a far more complex role relationship. Baby was sometimes portrayed as petulant, naughty, or interested in the names or functions of objects or the whereabouts of other persons. They began to communicate plans to Baby for "going to the park" or "to the mountains." Mother had many more responsibilities. Not only did she instruct and inform (e.g., "That's not baby's food. That's big people's food"), but she also communicated to her pretend Baby her own concerns about going shopping, getting ready for a meeting, or preparing for company. Pretend Mothers at 3 years of age also appeared to recognize the Baby's interest in where Daddy was and what he was doing, and they expected Daddy to say "goodbye" or "goodnight" to the Baby. They expected the Baby to be unhappy when Daddy went away. Thus, by 3 years, the appropriate attributions for the role relationship of Baby and Father were also represented by the pretend Mother.

In sum, in this chapter we have indentified some of the steps leading up to the achievement of Mother–Baby role-play. In order to attain this milestone, the child has to be able to represent the content of the mother–baby roles, including role-appropriate speech registers, and to communicate to her partner about the pretend actions and identities. These skills, we have tried to show, originate in the child's prior experience of enacting mother-baby roles in co-operation with others. With the support first of caregivers and later of peers, the child learns to transform her identity in imagination, explicitly adopting a social role for the first time.

REFERENCES

Brown, R. Introduction. In C. Snow & C. Ferguson (Eds.), *Talking to children: Language input and acquisition.* Cambridge: Cambridge University Press, 1977.

Corsaro, W. A. Young children's conceptions of status and role. *Sociology of Education,* 1979, *52,* 46–59.

Dunn, J., & Kendrick, C. The speech of two and three year olds to infant siblings: 'Baby talk' and the context of communication. *Journal of Child Language,* 1982, *9,* 579–595.

Dunn, J., & Wooding, C. Play in the home and its implications for learning. In B. Tizard & D. Harvey (Eds.), *Biology of Play.* Philadelphia: Lippincott, 1977.

El'Konin, D. B. Some results of the study of the psychological development of preschool-age children. In M. Cole & I. Maltzman (Eds.), *A handbook of contemporary Soviet psychology.* New York: Basic Books, 1979.

Fein, G. G. A transformational analysis of pretending. *Developmental Psychology,* 1975, *11,* 291–296.

Fein, G. G. Pretend play in childhood: An integrative review. *Child Development,* 1981, *52,* 1095–1118.

Fenson, L., Kagan, J., Kearsley, R. B., & Zelazo, P. R. The developmental progression of manipulative play in the first two years. *Child Development,* 1976, *47,* 232–236.

Garvey, C. *Play.* Cambridge, MA: Harvard University Press, 1977.

Garvey, C. An approach to the study of children's role play. *The Quarterly Newsletter of the Laboratory of Comparative Human Cognition,* 1979, *1,* 69–73.

Garvey, C. Communication and the development of social role play. In D. Forbes & M. Greenberg (Eds.), *New directions in child development: The development of planful behavior in children.* San Francisco: Jossey-Bass, 1982.

Garvey, C., & Berndt, R. The organization of pretend play. Paper presented at the symposium on Structure in Play and Fantasy, American Psychological Association, Chicago, September 1975.

Gleason, J. B. Code switching in children's language. In T. E. Moore (Ed.), *Cognitive development and the acquisition of language.* New York: Academic Press, 1973.

Greif, E. Sex role playing in preschool children. In J. S. Bruner, A. Jolly, & J. Sylva (Eds.), *Play: Its role in development and evolution.* New York: Basic Books, 1976.

Huttenlocher, J., & Higgins, E. T. Issues in the study of symbolic development. In W. A. Collins (Ed.), *Minnesota Symposia on Child Psychology* (Vol. II). Hillsdale, NJ: Erlbaum, 1978.

Kavanaugh, R., Whittington, S., & Cerbone, M. Mother's use of fantasy in speech to young children. Paper presented at the Biennial Convention of the Society for Research in Child Development, Boston, April 1981.

Lowe, M. Trends in the development of representational play in infants from one to three years—an observational study. *Journal of Child Psychology and Psychiatry,* 1975, *16,* 33–47.

Miller, P. J. *Amy, Wendy, and Beth: Learning language in South Baltimore.* Austin: University of Texas Press, 1982.

Nelson, K. & Gruendel, J. M. At morning it's lunchtime: A scriptal view of children's dialogues. *Discourse Processes*, 1979, *2*, 73–94.

Nicolich, L. M. Beyond sensorimotor intelligence: Assessment of symbolic maturity through analysis of pretend play. *Merrill-Palmer Quarterly*, 1977, *23*, 89–101.

Nicolich, L. M. Toward symbolic functioning: Structure of early pretend games and potential parallels with language. *Child Development*, 1981, *52*, 785–797.

Pellegrini, A. D. The construction of cohesive text by preschoolers in two play contexts. *Discourse Processes*, 1982, *5*, 101–108.

Rocissano, L. The emergence of social conventional behavior: Evidence from early object play. *Social Cognition*, 1982, *1*, 50–69.

Sachs, J. The role of adult-child play in language development. In K. H. Rubin (Ed.), *Children's play*. San Francisco: Jossey-Bass, 1980.

Sachs, J., & Devin, J. Young children's use of age-appropriate speech styles in social interaction and role-playing. *Journal of Child Language*, 1976, *3*, 81–98.

Shatz, M., & Gelman, R. The development of communication skills: Modifications in the speech of young children as a function of listener. *Monographs of the Society for Research in Child Development*, 1973, *38* (5, Serial No. 152).

Sinclair, H. The transition from sensory-motor to symbolic activity. *Interchange*, 1970, *1*, 119–126.

Watson, M. W., & Fischer, K. W. A developmental sequence of agent use in late infancy. *Child Development*, 1977, *48*, 828–836.

Watson, M. W., & Fischer, K. W. Development of social roles in elicited and spontaneous behavior during the preschool years. *Developmental Psychology*, 1980, *16*, 483–494.

CHAPTER 5

I a Daddy: 2-Year-Olds' Collaboration in Joint Pretend with Sibling and with Mother*

JUDY DUNN
NAOMI DALE

According to Piaget, pretend play is initially a solitary symbolic activity [Stage 1]. Sociodramatic play [i.e., collective symbolism, Stage 2] does not begin until the latter part of the third year of life. . . . Indirect evidence suggests that a shift from solitary to social pretense may occur at about 3 years of age.

Fein, 1981

INTRODUCTION

The ability to take part in joint pretend play—requiring the construction and maintenance of a shared fantasy framework—has been widely regarded as a relatively sophisticated form of pretend play, beginning as children reach their third birthday. But in fact very little is known about the early development of

*Dale's study was conducted while the author was supported by a Medical Council Research Studentship and a grant from the Wellcome Foundation. The study by Dunn and Munn is supported by the Medical Research Council. We are very grateful for the help of the families in the sample.

such play or its precursors because it has been chiefly studied in children over 3 years, playing with peers in a preschool or laboratory setting. Miller and Garvey's (Chapter 4, this volume) important study of the development of the "mother" role in young children, which included a longitudinal study of children playing at home with their mothers, is one of the very few that have focused on the beginnings of role play in a family setting. They traced the development first of *role enactment* (play in which the child's role identity can be inferred from a combination of speech and behavior) and then of *role-play* (play in which the adoption of an identity other than the self is announced by the child; see Huttenlocher & Higgins, 1978) in the context of play between mother and child. Playing at "mothers and babies" first took the form of the child acting as "mother" to a doll, performing nurturing, affectionate activities and calling the doll "baby," with her own mother providing support and tutoring and herself enacting "mothering" toward the doll.

By the age of 30 months, the children had come to rely less on the mother's assistance and the mothering sequence became more realistic and detailed. Nevertheless, the mothers continued to act as approving spectators to the performances and to offer teaching directions and encouragement. At this age the authors noted, for the first time, that the mothers made explicit references to the child as mother, such as "You're being the mommy." And at 28 months the first enactment of "mother" to a human partner—the real mother—was observed. Explicit reference by the children to their own transformed identity was not observed until the children were at least 30 months old. With peers, role enactment was not observed until at least 34 months. At about 3 years the first clear evidence of reciprocal role play was observed: The girl explicitly transformed her identity to the "mother" role, in relation to another child to whom she assigned the role of "baby."

Miller & Garvey (1981) argued that two changes led to the performance of reciprocal role play: (1) the transformation of self into the role persona and (2) the incorporation of another person, the peer, into a reciprocal role. The first change could be observed independently of the second change, and in the authors' observations, the first change preceded the second by a number of months. Realization of the second change depended on the understanding and willingness of the play partner and on the communicative skills of each partner. Before the self was explicitly transformed into a different identity the child had experienced extensive practice in acting the role, and considerable training, modelling, and supportive encouragement by the mother. Miller and Garvey (1981) emphasize that the configuration of Mother-with-Child behavior, attitudes and activity "scripts" was learned before the critical transformation of self into the role persona. Both mothers and peers provided the encouragement and prompting of an interested audience before the children transformed themselves into different identities and later were observed to set up reciprocal role games. The children were able to carry out role enactment to the mother as partner long before they were able to perform similar reciprocal games with the peer as partner.

This demonstration by Miller and Garvey is of central importance: The earliest rudiments of role enactment of the "mother" role appear to emerge within social interaction with the mother, with the mother providing a tutoring and modeling framework to the child's own performance. Many months before the children were able explicitly to adopt a pretend role identity, they were involved in social exchanges and play activities that appeared to be closely related to this ability.

How general are the implications of this study—a study that concerns the development of one specific role game in the context of one specific family relationship? Many children grow up not only with a mother, but also with a sibling as play partner, a child with whom they have a close familiar relationship. Do developmental changes in pretend play with a sibling follow the same pattern as that described by Miller and Garvey for child and mother? What part does the sibling relationship play in the development of the ability to share a fantasy framework with transformation of identity and negotiation of roles and rules in a nonliteral world?

It has been argued that the process and context of pretending is influenced by the nonplay relationship between children and their partners (Schwartzman, 1978; also cited by Bretherton, Chapter 1, this volume). Schwartzman showed that differences in the relationships between the children outside the play context were systematically related to differences in the quality of their joint pretend play, and in an elegant analysis of the play of one 5-year-old boy, Martlew and her colleagues demonstrated clear differences in the nature of his play with mother, with a friend, or alone (Martlew, Connolly, & McCleod, 1978). If differences in social pretend are closely linked to the nature of children's relationships with their play partners, then one would expect marked differences in the nature of a child's pretend play with mother and with sibling. The very features of the sibling relationship that make it so distinctive—the familiarity of the children, their shared world of daily routines, the salience of the older sibling as a model for the younger, the reciprocal aspects of the relationship (Dunn, 1983)—all suggest that it may be a relationship in which joint pretend play flourishes. Differences in the joint pretend play of different sibling pairs might also be expected, because there are very marked differences in the quality of the relationships among young siblings (Dunn & Kendrick, 1982).

In this chapter, then, we consider differences in the nature of 2-year-olds' pretend play with mother and with sibling, drawing on two studies conducted in Cambridge, England. Both are based on home observations; one is a study of 20 2-year-olds (Dale, 1983), the other an ongoing study of 40 sibling pairs observed when the secondborns were 18, 24, and 36 months old (Dunn & Munn, in preparation). Dale's study examined in detail a range of issues raised by the observations of the children playing with mother, with sibling, and alone: the

sources of individual differences in the nature of pretend play and the significance of the children's gender, linguistic ability, and of differences in their affectional relationships within the family. Two of these issues are discussed here:
(1) the differences in initiation, thematic content, pretend transformation, and
partner participation in pretend play with mother and with sibling and (2) the
evidence for joint enactment and role play in the families. We argue, on the
basis of Dale's systematic findings and the illustrative material from the study
by Dunn and Munn, that (1) the observations of joint play of mother and child
clearly parallel and support those of Miller and Garvey (Chapter 4, this volume);
(2) there are, however, distinctive differences in the child's play with mother
and with sibling; (3) the study of 2-year-olds playing in the context of the familiar and supportive relationship with a sibling indicates that children may
begin to understand, cooperate in, and contribute to joint pretend play considerably earlier than supposed; and (4) a concentration on solitary play in children
under 3 may have led to a misleading picture of the development of symbolic
play.

METHOD

SAMPLES

Dale's sample was composed of 20 families living within the city of Cambridge, England. All families were white and of Caucasian origin. The families
covered all classes of the Registrar General classification of socioeconomic class
(SES) position, and there was a roughly equal distribution of low- and middle-
SES families. Each family had a 2-year-old child with an older sibling aged 4
or 5 years old. The mean age of the 2-year-old children was 26 months (range
22–30 months) and the mean age of the older children was 53 months (range
38–61 months). In the majority of families the older sibling was the firstborn
child and the younger child was the secondborn one, but in six of the families
there was another, older sibling above 6 years of age (these latter siblings were
not included in the study). In one family there was an infant younger than the
2-year-old child. The target 2-year-old is here referred to as "the child' and the
older 4- to 5-year-old as "the sibling." There was no significant difference in
the chronological age of the male and female 2-year-olds, and there was no significant difference in the chronological age of their older siblings. The mean
language level of the 2-year-old children was 25 months (range 13–36 months),
assessed by the Reynell Language Scale. The female children of the study scored
significantly higher on the language measure ($M = 28.4$ months) compared with

the male children (M = 23.8 months) (Mann–Whitney test, U = 19, N = 8 and 12 respectively, p < .05 level).

The children in the second study, from which illustrative but not systematic findings are reported here, were from very similar families: The target second-born children were seen first at age 18 months, then at 2 years.

PROCEDURE

In both studies the observations were conducted in the home, and were un-structured. The observer carried a portable stereo tape recorder to pick up the children's speech and family conversations. Immediately after the observation the observer transcribed the tape recording. During Dale's observations a nar-rative record of the children's pretend play was made in a lined notebook, in which each line represented 15 seconds. An electronic beeper provided time signals (a method based on that of Clarke-Stewart, 1973). The analyses reported here are based on three 1-hour observations in each family.

Before considering the differences in mother–child and sibling–child pretend play and the evidence for role enactment, it should be noted that pretend play was relatively frequent in the observations in Dale's study, filling 21% of ob-servation time, and that 59% of play episodes involved some participation of mother or sibling; 33% involved mothers, 16% involved siblings, and 10% in-volved both. Individual differences in the participation of mothers and siblings with the children in pretend play were very marked in both studies. The origins of and influences upon these individual differences are not discussed in this chapter, but it must be emphasized that joint pretend play with the siblings was closely related to the affectional quality of the relationship. It was much more frequent in those families in which the relationship between the siblings was, according to maternal interview, very friendly (Table 1). For details of the cat-egorization of sibling relationships, coding, and reliabilities, see Appendix 1.

FINDINGS

Differences in the children's play with mother and with sibling were striking (for details, see Dale, 1983). Three aspects of these differences are summarized here: First, the differences in the manner in which the joint play was set up with the mother or with the sibling and in the role of object props in pretend play with the two partners; second, differences in the themes of joint pretend play with mother and with sibling; third, differences in the nature of the par-

Table 1

**Comparison of the Frequency of Intervals
of Joint Pretend Play by Quality
of Sibling-Child Relationship**[a]

Quality of relationship	N	M
Very friendly	5	10.0
Somewhat friendly	9	1.8
Unfriendly	6	.7
df	2	
H	8.2*	

[a] Kruskal-Wallis test.
*$p < .01$.

ticipation of mother and sibling. Finally, evidence for collaboration in social role play by 18-month-olds and 24-month-olds is presented.

INITIATIONS OF JOINT PRETEND PLAY
WITH MOTHER AND WITH SIBLING

Although 48% of the mothers' initiations of joint play involved encouraging the child to label a replica object, or to carry out an appropriate action on a replica object, siblings were significantly less likely to start play in this way. Only 30% of sibling initiations were of this type. Unlike the mothers, they showed much interest in setting up pretend games involving transformations of role identity, location, or psychological state. The difference between mothers and siblings was marked: 41% of sibling initiations involved such transformation, as compared with only 12% of mother initiations.

Parallel differences were apparent in the children's behavior to the two partners. For instance, 89% of the children's initiations to their mothers involved the child drawing the mother's attention to an object, but only 23% of their initiations to the sibling were of this kind. Of the children's initiations to the sibling, 38% were imitations of the sibling's pretend actions or comments; the children were never observed to initiate joint play with their mothers in this way. The highest proportion of sibling-child games began with the sibling setting up a pretend game and inviting the child to join.

The importance of objects in the pretend play with the mother was evident not only in the initiation of the play, but throughout the episodes. Of the bouts of joint pretend play with the mother, 97% were either focused on replica objects or had an object prop as a vital part of the game, and the objects provided a focal topic for instruction by the mother. The evidence that the children set up so many of these play bouts with the mother by drawing her attention to an object suggests that the 2-year-olds had already gained some kind of expectation that this form of referential communication provided a successful and appropriate method of attaining the mother's interest during pretend play.

In contrast, 27% of the play bouts with the sibling did not involve objects at all, but were sustained through linguistic or nonverbal actions without reference to object props. Most play with the mother involved the use or discussion of replica objects, but with the sibling all types of pretend transformation were equally common. And one category of pretend transformation occurred only with the sibling—the transformation of role identity, location, or psychological state.

THEMES OF THE JOINT PRETEND
WITH MOTHER AND WITH SIBLING

There were also differences in the *themes* of the pretend games that children played with their mothers and those they played with their siblings. In 58% of the total episodes of pretend play observed, the 2-year-olds carried out a sequence of pretend actions with a coherent theme. A plan, or logical temporal order of events, was identifiable either by the child's explicit comments on the plan or by an obvious relation between actions (e.g., filling a bath with "water," immersing the doll, drying her with a towel). Most of these bouts consisted of only 2 or 3 actions related by a unifying theme, but the length and complexity of acts carried out within a single theme varied very much with individual children; the range was 1–20 actions. The part played by mothers in supporting long bouts of pretend play has been noted in previous studies (Dunn & Wooding, 1977; Martlew et al., 1978; Trevarthen & Grant, 1979; Valentine, 1937). The observations in Dale's study paralleled these findings, and showed moreover that in some families child and sibling also engaged in very long bouts of play together. One child sustained a sequence of 17 different actions when playing a tea-party game with his elder brother.

A classification of themes was developed by Dale, which is included in Appendix 2. Certain of these themes were extremely popular with the children, and within the games in each thematic category there was a striking similarity in the children's choice of actions, comments, props, and sequential ordering of events. Even when animating miniature people while playing alone, the children used very similar phrases when pretending that the people were talking. Sequences of making and preparing tea, telephoning, cooking, and feeding and putting the doll to bed were also very similar when played by different children; the similarity in theme and content across the children suggests that they had taken part in similar social practices and shared similar representations—or "scripts"—of these experiences.

It is possible of course that the similarity of the pretend games in the different families reflected not only a similarity in the children's experiences of real social practices, but also a similarity in the direction of their partners in play—the mothers and siblings. Very similar suggestions were indeed made by their mothers. For example, a number of mothers suggested that the child talk to an absent family member during the telephoning sequence, and outlined a common sequence during the tea-preparation game (first pouring the pretend tea and milk into the cup, then handing the cup to the play partner). When the child was putting the doll to bed, most mothers suggested that the child give the doll a kiss after putting it under the blanket. Siblings were also observed making very similar explicit directions about the order and content of the pretend game, particularly in those sequences that involved performing everyday routines and household activities and role-play games. Both the mothers and the siblings were then marking culturally salient constituents and sequences of social practices within the pretend game.

The most common theme for the play bouts with the mother was that of nurturing a doll or toy.[1] This was the theme for significantly more bouts of mother–child than sibling–child play—33% of mother–child play bouts compared to 10% of sibling–child play bouts. With the sibling, the most common theme was that of everyday routines and household activities. This was the theme of 46% of the sibling play bouts, compared to 13% of bouts with the mother. The question of whether these differences primarily reflected differences in the partners' interest or whether they also reflected differences in the expectations that the 2-year-olds held for play with mother or with sibling is difficult to answer. The siblings were in fact particularly interested in initiating everyday routines and household activity games, and over a quarter of their initiations involved setting up these games. In contrast mothers showed less interest in initiating such games than siblings, and they were more likely to initiate nurturing doll or stuffed animal games than the sibling. It was clear however that gender differences were important here: Mothers of daughters initiated games of nurturing and everyday routines and household activity relatively frequently (34% of initiations to daughters) compared to mothers of sons (8% of initiations to sons). Actions on vehicles were encouraged in mothers' initiations to sons, but not in those to daughters (15% of mothers' initiations to sons; 0% of initiations to daughters).

Similarly, siblings showed a higher proportion of initiations encouraging actions on vehicles to younger brothers than to sisters (26% to brothers and 0%

---

[1] The theme of nurturing doll, toy, or person includes all four subcategories of mothering distinguished by Miller and Garvey (Chapter 4, this volume).

to sisters). Notably, neither mothers nor siblings encouraged games with vehicle replicas when initiating a game with a female child. So, although mothers and siblings did differ in the themes of the games they initiated with the child, the gender of the child also influenced each partners' interests and intentions.

How far did the 2-year-olds adapt their own playful initiations to the interests of their partners? As the children were in fact responsible for initiating relatively few of the bouts of joint pretend play with the siblings, it is difficult to assess the extent to which they were sensitive to the interests of their partners. However, it was clear that gender was again important. Although almost a third of the initiations of daughters to their mothers were of the nurturing theme, none of the sons' initiations to their mothers were of this theme. Thus, the daughters appeared to show some anticipation of their mothers' interest in playing nurturing games with the dolls—their enthusiasm for mother–baby games, which was such a feature of the mother–daughter relationship. Sons, in contrast, were either uninterested in nurturing games or anticipated their mothers' lack of interest in performing such games with them.

DIFFERENCES IN THE PARTICIPATION OF MOTHER AND SIBLING

Differences in the nature of the participation of mother and sibling in joint play with the child were also evident. Two categories of participation were distinguished. In the "spectator" role, the play partner offers relevant pretend suggestions and comments on the child's play actions but does not enter the joint game as a full participant. The partner does not perform pretend actions and/ or adopt a pretend identity, even if she or he makes comments on the child's pretend identity. The only action participation within this role is to mend or construct an object or equipment to be used in the pretend game, to assist the child in a particular action (e.g., dislodging a vehicle replica blocked behind the sofa), or to take and give the child a replica object without adding any further pretend actions with the object. In the "complementary actor" role the partner enters the joint game as a full participant by performing pretend actions and/ or adopting pretend identities complementary to the child's pretend performance (e.g., drinking pretend tea at a tea party, actively joining the child in washing and drying a doll, pretending to be a customer in a shop, pretending to be in the "mother" or "teacher" role).

Siblings often entered the pretend play as complementary actors and their games involved the close meshing of each partner's verbal and nonverbal actions. In contrast mothers usually remained in the role of interested spectator, offering relevant comments and suggestions but avoiding the adoption of pre-

Table 2
Partner as Spectator or as Complementary Actor: Mean Percentages
of Mother and Sibling Play Bouts in the Two Roles [a]

Type of role	Joint bouts with mothers (N bouts = 90)	Joint bouts with siblings (N bouts = 48)
Partner as spectator	85	40
Partner as complementary actor	15	60*

[a] Wilcoxon test.
*p < .001.

tend actions or identities (Table 2). Pretend play with the mother involved alternation of the speaker–listener roles, but the actions were generally performed by the child and required little coordination with the mother partner's contribution.

COLLABORATION IN ROLE PLAYING

When 2-year-olds played pretend games with their siblings the themes, initiation, and participation of the two partners were, as we have seen, different from those of the games played with the mother. One particular category of social pretend play was strikingly evident in a few sibling–child pairs: the joint pretend play that involved role enactment or adoption of a role identity, a change in psychological state, or a change in location. The participation of children as young as 2 years old in such play is remarkable, and we look next at four questions raised by these observations.

First, were these social role-taking games a distinctive feature of the children's play with the siblings, or were they also observed in the play between mother and child? Second, how common were these games among the 2-year-olds? Third, what part did the partner play in initiating and maintaining the social role-play with the 2-year-olds? Fourth, how do the observations of social role-play with the 2-year-olds relate to the developmental sequence proposed by Miller and Garvey (1981) from their studies of children's play with mother and peers?

The answer to the first question is clear. This category of play was observed only in play with the sibling, and not with the mother. Second, such play was observed in only 4 of the 20 2-year-olds in Dale's sample and 13 of 40 2-year-olds in Dunn and Munn's sample, although maternal interview material suggests that other children in the samples did in fact engage in such play with their siblings. The problems of sampling such play between very young children and their siblings are obvious and present serious difficulties to the researcher. But although role enactment and role-play were observed in only a minority of the 2-year-olds with their siblings, the occurrence of this play in such young children is sufficiently unexpected and interesting to justify a closer look at the sequences of play.

Consider the following examples from the Dunn and Munn sample, recalling that role designation was not observed in play with mothers until 30 months, and with peers until several months later in Miller and Garvey's study. The child in each example is 24 months old and is playing with an older sibling.

Example 1

RICHARD'S SISTER. The gates have shut (pulls cushion down). Train's coming.
RICHARD. Where?
RICHARD'S SISTER. (pulls cushion up). That gate's not shut but a train's coming.
    Choo choo! Choo choo! . . . I open the gates in a minute Richard.
RICHARD. Train coming now.
RICHARD'S SISTER. Choo choo. I wonder when they're going to come.
    Do you know?
RICHARD. Yes.
RICHARD'S SISTER. There's one going this way and one going that way.
RICHARD. Go London.
RICHARD'S SISTER. Look Richard. Got a little tunnel (of cushions).
RICHARD. (drives tractor into tunnel) Rrrrrrrrrrrrr.
    Dege degedegedege. . . . Broom broom. Engine broke down.
RICHARD'S SISTER. Richard, can you get some more petrol? The train's got
    stuck. Doesn't start. No you try.
    Go and get some more petrol.
RICHARD (puts "petrol" in). Sssssssssssssss.
RICHARD'S SISTER. Not here it keeps leaking. Try it here near my finger.

'Cos you're the petrol man. You've got to sit next to me.
RICHARD. No I run out.
    . . .I'm a driver.

Example 2

LAURA'S SISTER (lying on her back). Change my bottom Laura.
    Change my bottom.
LAURA. Yes (pulls her pants off) That's stinky!
    . . . Wee-wee! Wee-wee!
LAURA'S SISTER. Yes. Put some cream on here.
LAURA. Come on Baby. I put the cream on. Get in (pretend bed).
    . . . (gives "food").
MOTHER. What you doing? What you giving her?

LAURA'S SISTER. She's giving me an egg.
(to Laura): Give me more egg.
LAURA. She ate my egg! I got no more left.
LAURA'S SISTER. (high voice). Mum. I want that bib. Bib. Bib.
LAURA. Which one?
LAURA. (pretends to read book to Baby). I read. I read.

In both of these examples, drawn from the study of Dunn and Munn (1984, in preparation), the 2-year-old cooperates effectively with the older sibling and makes innovatory contributions to the pretend play. In the train game, Richard not only accepts the directions of his older sister, refueling the train and making appropriate noises, but also drives the train through the tunnel of cushions, suggests where the train is going, and introduces the first breakdown. He announces his own role as driver. In the second example Laura followed her sister's commands to change her, but she herself "fed" her sister as the "baby" and "read" to her from an imaginary book without these actions being suggested to her.

It is entirely possible that these sequences were familiar and repeated routines for the children, and that the apparently innovatory contributions of the younger children were in fact actions that had been suggested to them by the older child in previous games. But whether or not the 2-year-olds' contributions were in fact originally acts remembered from previous games, the ability of the 2-year-olds to cooperate within a shared framework and to dispute and negotiate the rules is without question. It is particularly striking that such young children do, in the context of joint play with the sibling, make explicit reference to the role identity they have taken on. Richard announced his role as driver; John, the 2-year-old in the next example from the Dunn and Munn sample is addressed as Henry (his father's name) by his older sister, and not only responds to this name but explains to the observer that he is the "daddy."

Example 3

JOHN'S SISTER. I know, you can be the daddy and I can be the mummy. Yes?
JOHN. Yes.
JOHN'S SISTER. Right, we've got a baby haven't we?
JOHN: Yeah.
JOHN'S SISTER. (addresses him by real father's name). Henry.
JOHN. Yeah?
JOHN'S SISTER. Have you got any babies?
JOHN. (inaudible reply)
JOHN TO OBSERVER. I a Daddy.

And in another family from the Cambridge study the 2-year-old Martin, playing at being trains with his older sister, repeated his announcement "I'm Gordon" no less than eight times—Gordon being a particular railway engine in a story that he had recently been read.

The third question concerned the part played by the partner in setting up and maintaining the joint role games. The majority of the role designations and negotiations were performed by the siblings, particularly at the start of the game, with an explicit role designation announcement made by the older sibling.

Example 4

SARA'S SISTER. (after she had followed Sara into the space
   behind the garden hut). Sara, I'm going to be the school teacher.

Some interactions were started by the child venturing into the sibling's play area, for example, sitting in the stroller being used by the sibling or sitting on the row of chairs set out by the sibling. These entries were usually resisted initially by the sibling.

Example 5

LENNY'S BROTHER. Lenny, there can't be two drivers in an aeroplane.

But after resigned acceptance of the child's entry into the area the sibling would announce the role identities of the game.

Example 6

LAURA'S SISTER. (after Laura had set herself in the stroller).
   Baby, the baby is Laura.

It was also quite common for some siblings to attempt to set up a joint role game with the child by designating the child with a pretend role identity, and for the attempt to fail because the child ignored the role designation and continued with her or his own activity.

Example 7

LENNY'S BROTHER. Lenny, you're the airport driver.
   (Lenny does not respond and continues to ride his tricycle).

Example 8

JAMIE'S SISTER. Dog's got to lay down (shows Jamie toy dog lying down). Look,
   lay down and sleep, Jamie.
   Tell him to got to bed. Bed—you're going straight to bed (to dog).
JAMIE. What?

JAMIE'S SISTER. We're playing doc docs (doctors). (Jamie goes on with his own play activity.)

Some of the siblings continued to refer to their own identity or that of the child during the role-enactment itself. The reminders appeared to occur particularly when the child or partner started to perform an inappropriate action.

Example 9

(Lenny raises a spade as "wheel" during pretend driving.)
LENNY'S BROTHER. You must put— (resignedly) alright put that in there, then. There's the passenger.
Lee drive! You're the pass—I'm the passenger.

The role designation was also used by the sibling to communicate recognition of the child's role enactment. Karen's brother responded to her initiation of a role enactment (by saying "woof, woof") with a role designation.

Example 10

KAREN. Woof, woof.
KAREN'S BROTHER. Oh! not that dog again. Woof, woof.
KAREN. Woof, woof.
KAREN'S BROTHER. I'm the big dog. Woof woof (said in deep voice).

Negotiation or argument over the role designation by the 2-year-olds was uncommon, but was observed in both Cambridge studies. A particularly interesting instance of the ability to play with role identities is given in the next example from the study by Dunn and Munn (in preparation). The older sister has three imaginary friends, a striking trio named Lily, Allelujah, and Peepee. In the course of an observation her 24-month-old sister Rose announces that *she* is Allelujah. Her sister disputes this, protesting that *she* is Allelujah, and that Rose is Lily.

Example 11

ROSE. Allelujah! Allelujah! Me Allelujah!
ROSE'S SISTER. Who's Allelujah?
MOTHER. Rose thinks she's Allelujah.
ROSE'S SISTER. Who's Lily? Who's Lily?
MOTHER. I don't know. You tell me.
ROSE'S SISTER. Who's Lily, Mummy?
ROSE. I'm Allelujah.
ROSE'S SISTER. (to Rose). Who's Lily? I'm Allelujah.
ROSE. No, I'm Allelujah.

Later in the observation Rose teased her sister by repeatedly announcing that she was Allelujah.

In the next sample Sara appeared to allocate a role identity to the sibling that was refused by the sibling, who offered an alternative identity.

Example 12

SARA'S SISTER. Sara, I'll be the school teacher.
SARA. School. School. Baby, me baby.
SARA'S SISTER. You're a little schoolgirl, aren't you?
SARA. Sissy (sister) boy.
SARA'S SISTER, No, I'm not—I'm a, you're a school teacher.

Although it is not clear whether the child actually intended to offer role designation labels to herself and her older sister, her sister did in fact respond as if the child had these intentions within the pretend game.

In most of the episodes of joint role play, the sibling was the announcer of the plan of the game. The sibling assigned relevant actions to the child and herself.

Example 13

LENNY'S BROTHER. Lenny, drive. We are not going home yet. Lenny, you must
    drive.

Example 14

SARA'S SISTER (as teacher). I'll go and get a story book. I'll go and get a story
    book. (in exaggerated play voice) I've just got to go home. You stay there.
    . . . (later) . . . (ordinary voice) Here comes your teacher. (in authoritarian
    teacher voice) I'm going to read a story now.

Some episodes were initiated with role designation, and the actions relevant to the adopted roles were carried out during the game without prior announcement of a main plan. In a mother–baby game, Laura's sister announced that Laura was the baby, and then proceeded to perform nurturing activities, feeding Laura and a boyfriend with real sweets, giving the children a blanket, advising the children to go to sleep, pushing the children in a double-seated stroller (pushchair), and kissing the children. Laura's sister marked the entry into a new action sequence within the overall mother–baby game by statements or questions.

Example 15

LAURA'S SISTER (before a sequence of feeding the "babies"). Now are you hun-
    gry?
    (to boyfriend, when giving the "babies" clothing material) Be a sister. Can
    you do shoes up?
    (pushing the "babies" in the stroller) We *are* going.

It was relatively rare for the 2-year-olds themselves to announce the overall plan or components of the plan during the joint role game. Nevertheless, their presence was not passive during the game; they generally accepted the plan proposed by the sibling and performed actions that were appropriate to the overall plan and complementary to the sibling's own intentions within the game. Although many of the actions were preceded by explicit directives from the siblings, some of the children added independent material to the game, as Examples 1, 2 and 9 illustrate. In Example 9 Lenny was instructed to drive an airplane. He then added an innovatory action by raising a spade and pretending it was a driving wheel. This object transformation was initially resisted by his brother, who later conceded that the spade was indeed the wheel.

Apart from compliance with the sibling's directions and the addition of some independent comments and actions, the children's active involvement depended on *acceptance* of the sibling's intentions within the plan. One child refused to comply with unpleasant demands.

Example 16

LAURA'S SISTER (gives Laura, as "baby," a blanket). A blanket to put over your head.
LAURA (fusses). Why?
LAURA'S SISTER (to boyfriend). Say Laura is a naughty baby.
BOYFRIEND. Laura is a naughty baby.
LAURA'S SISTER. Cry Laura.
LAURA. No (climbs out of stroller).

In some of the games, such as mother–baby games, communication of the pretend location was not important for the execution of the role enactment. In others, such as the games of teacher–pupil and airplane pilot–passenger, the roles were linked to a location, and in these games either the child or the sibling announced the pretend locations.

Example 17

SARA'S SISTER. Sara, I'll be the school teacher.
SARA (announces location). School, school.

Siblings took a strong-handed managerial role in the game through the use of frequent role instructions (conveyed in an ordinary voice) and commands within the role (stated in a pretend voice). They often switched from the play voice to an ordinary voice a number of times during the game, thus communicating when they were "in role" or had temporarily relinquished the role. The following examples show the siblings issuing commands and instructions to the child, both in a role-appropriate and in an ordinary manner.

Example 18

SARA'S SISTER (as teacher). Here comes your teacher. (in exaggerated play-voice) I'm going to read a story now, teacher. (switches to ordinary voice)—No, you can't sit there, you'll have to sit here. You'll have to sit just facing me. Alright, sit here and I'll read you a story.

Example 19

LENNY'S BROTHER (in ordinary voice). Off now. No, you must still drive. (Switches to exaggerated play voice)—Thank you very much, see you later . . . (in ordinary voice) Get in now, you get in—get in the driving seat. Right. No, Lenny (shouts) that's not the driving seat! That's it! . . . Not yet. Come on. Get off. Go on! (shouting).

Example 20

LAURA'S SISTER (in ordinary voice). Laura, talk just like Peter (friend)—say (adopts high-pitched "baby" voice), Can I have some more sweeties? . . . (in authoritarian "mother's" voice) Look boys and girls, good girl, good girl, go to sleep . . . Now pick up your sandals. Good girls, babies.

The siblings who adopted the roles of "teacher" and "mother" were able to give role commands to the child within role, because their adopted roles were of a more powerful status than the complementary role of baby and school pupil. In the airplane game, the sibling's role as a passenger did not permit this form of command within role, and most of the instructions were issued in an ordinary voice outside the role enactment.

The siblings also responded to the child's role enactment performance with complementary actions or comments.

Example 21

LAURA (in high-pitched "baby" voice). Can I have some more sweeties?
LAURA'S SISTER. Chocolate (gives sweets to "babies").

None of the 2-year-old children in Dale's study issued any commands or instructions during the joint games with the sibling.

A number of the siblings made normative comments—statements about how things usually are—to justify their actions and intentions within the game.

Example 22

LENNY'S BROTHER. Lenny, there can't be two drivers in an aeroplane.

Example 23

LAURA'S SISTER. Babies who are hungry, they should cry.
BOYFRIEND. Babies do have milk.

In contrast, no 2-year-old children made normative statements during the role games.

In summary, the 24-month-old children's performances within the role game was usually that of appropriate role enactment, rather than discussion of the plan and role designation of the game, although explicit role designations were occasionally made. The games were maintained by the active, directive contribution and management of the sibling, but the children did offer some independent original actions appropriate to the role-game. Although about half the children's actions were imitations of the sibling's act, or actions in compliance with the sibling's directions, the other actions were spontaneous within the game. The children showed that they could perform actions that were different and complementary to those of the siblings, such as playing "baby" with the sibling as "mother," or "mother" with the sibling as "baby," or "schoolchild" with the sibling as "teacher." When the children were no longer interested in the joint game, they removed themselves abruptly and the game collapsed. Their presence in the game was voluntary and the maintenance of the game seemed to depend on the active contributions and presence of each partner.

It is difficult to ascertain exactly what the children understood of the joint role game, and it is not clear how much they appreciated the identity transformations of themselves or the other partner. In the mother–baby and teacher–schoolgirl games, the children seemed to have some understanding of the non-literal nature (Garvey, 1974) of the "mother's" and "teacher's" commands. It is unlikely that the children would have complied with the sibling's stern authorative commands and prohibitions unless they had recognized their playful element. What we can conclude is that some 2-year-old children were able and willing to offer some independent role-appropriate actions to a joint game in which the sibling partners had explicitly transformed their own role-identities.

The fourth question raised by these observations concerned the course of the development of role-play proposed by Miller and Garvey (1981). Miller and Garvey emphasized that the children needed to have extensive practise of role-enactment, with supportive onlookers, before they began to transform their own identity into the role-persona, and later to incorporate a partner into a reciprocal role-game. In a number of respects the observations from both of the Cambridge samples parallel those of Miller and Garvey. For instance, in some families the siblings were attempting to engage the secondborn children in role-play well before the children were 2 years old, instructing and supporting their first essays into role-enactment. The next example comes from an observation of an 18-month-old girl, Mary, with her older sister. The older sister has set up a "birthday party" with a cake made of sand in the garden. Both children are singing "Happy Birthday."

Example 24

MARY'S SISTER. Dear Mary! You're three now.
MARY (nods). Mmm.
MARY'S SISTER. You can got to school now.
MARY (nods). Mmm.
MARY'S SISTER. Do you want to got to school now?
MARY. Mmm.
MARY'S SISTER. All right then. (play voice) Hello Mary
    I'm Mrs. Hunt. Do you want to help me do some of this birthday cake do
    you? (ordinary voice) We'd better help do our birthday cake hadn't we?
MARY (sings appropriately). "Happy Birthday . . . ."
    (both children walk hand in hand around the garden singing.)
MARY'S SISTER. We're at church now. We have to walk along. I'm like Mummy
    and you're like Baby. I'm Mummy.
    (play voice) What, little one? We'd better go back to our birthday then.
MARY (sings again). "Happy Birthday. . . ."
    (Mary holds her hands up to her sister to be carried.)[2]
MARY'S SISTER (play voice). That's alright little girl. Are you going to sleep?

Instruction of this kind was observed in 6 of the 40 families with 18-month-olds.
A second parallel with the Miller and Garvey study concerns the mother–child interaction in nurturing games with dolls. The sequence described by Garvey started with an initial period of role-performance with a doll, with the mother acting as an attentive spectator to the game. Very similar nurturing episodes between children and dolls, with the mothers attending to the activity, were noted in both Cambridge samples. These sequences rarely involved the sibling. None of the children designated themselves as "mother" during these games (see, too, Miller & Garvey, Chapter 4, this volume). However, at the same age that they were engaging in these games with the mother as spectator, some of the children were participating in *joint* role games with the siblings. These games were very different in content and style from the nurturing episodes with the doll. First, the sibling partners changed their own role-identity, whereas mothers remained as spectators. Second, the sibling partners expected the children to *coordinate* their role actions with the partner's. Third, the chil-

[2]Mary was not observed to hold up her arms to be carried by her sister *out* of the context of pretend play in the role of "baby" in the course of six 1-hour observations. According to a maternal interview, this behavior was directed to her sibling only in the context of mother–baby games with her sibling as "mother."

dren were expected to conform with the partner's instructions and to show some evidence of transformed role-identity.

We are not suggesting that the 2-year-old children were demonstrating the sophisticated role flexibility shown by some 3-year-old children, who could perform a role simultaneously reciprocal to two other roles or who adopt two complementary roles at different times (Miller & Garvey, Chapter 4, this volume). It would be unjustified to infer that the 2-year-olds could construct a "cognitive representation of the role, together with its consonant acts, attitudes, rights and obligations" (Garvey, 1979, p. 69). But the evidence that such young children engage in joint role-games with the sibling does lead us to question whether the children needed to be able to transform their own role-identity with *explicit self-designation* before being able to enter a joint role-game with another person. It appears that with a sibling, role-enactment in a joint game can take place before explicit self-designation is achieved.

The observations also raise the question of whether it is appropriate to place such emphasis on *explicit* self-designation in role-play with a sibling. The children, who play together every day, are so familiar with one another and their customary games that they may well not need such explicit comments. Announcement of roles may, in these familiar games, be unnecessary.

One other difference between the findings of the studies by Miller and Garvey and the two Cambridge studies concerns the themes of the early role-play. Garvey suggested (1979) that the "mother" role was the first role to be enacted fluently and perhaps the first to be conceptually elaborated. Yet in our observations the 2-year-olds were designated and enacted the roles of "baby," "schoolgirl," "father," "airplane pilot," "car driver," "train driver," "dog," "zoo keeper," "farmer," "doctor," "garage man," "policeman," "shopper," and assorted named imaginary friends.

What the observations suggest is that the experience of playing with a sibling during the second year may provide one route—not of course the only route— by which children discover and explore in play the power and delight of role transformation and shared role-play. Whether this comparatively early initiation into the world of shared pretend, with its possibilities for exploring and exploiting the social rules and roles of the real social world, has implications for later-born children's socio-cognitive development is of course a matter for empirical study.

Finally, a speculative point on the distinction which Bretherton (Chapter 1, this volume) makes between make-believe in the "as-if" sense and in the "what-if" sense. It is our strong impression that the pretend suggestions made by mothers are largely of the "as-if" type. Mothers seem eager to guide their 2-year-olds' pretend play along lines of simulating reality or of following conventional play themes. The focus of their suggestions and contributions is to stress the question "Is that how it is in real life?" In contrast, the make-believe of children playing on their own or with a sibling is far more anarchic and is much more likely to explore the "what-if" of make-believe. The significance of this distinction is discussed elsewhere (Dunn, 1981). Here we would simply stress the importance of examining children's make-believe within different social contexts, with close attention to the relations between the different kinds of pretend transformation in which the child engages and the nature of the particular social relationship between him and his partner in play.

CONCLUSIONS

The importance of these observations lies, we suggest, in the following points.

1. The observations demonstrate that children as young as 24 months old can, in the context of the sibling relationship, take part in joint role enactment and joint role-play. They can make explicit a transformation of their own identity and can share a framework of pretend play with another person.

2. The findings suggest that there may be different developmental routes to the achievements of social understanding upon which joint role-play depends, and that it presumably fosters. The quality of particular family relationships, whether with mother or with sibling, may be of considerable significance in influencing the pattern of development of this aspect of social understanding.

3. The distinctive features of young children's relationships with their siblings are presumably of major importance in accounting for *why* such young children can take part in joint role-play with another person. It is likely that the familiarity of the social world of sibling and child, the saliency of the sibling as a model for the child, the affection and support of the sibling, and the older sibling's powerful status and proficiency in the world of pretend are all of significance. We should take seriously the importance of these features of the sibling relationship for a broader consideration of young children's cognitive development (Dunn, 1983).

4. Individual differences in the quality of the sibling relationship are related to the nature and complexity of the joint pretend play in which they engage. The direction of causal effects here is unclear; it is possible that the quality of the relationship is influenced by the experience of shared role play together, as well as vice versa.

5. The gender of the child and partner influence the theme and roles enacted in joint play by not only mother and sibling but by the 2-year-old; these findings here precisely parallel those of Miller and Garvey (Chapter 4, this volume).

6. Finally, the observations clearly support the argument of Miller and Garvey (Chapter 4, this volume) that the degree to which role-play has its roots in interpersonal experience has not been adequately studied or acknowledged. The view of the relative significance of solitary and social play expressed in the quotation with which this chapter began must surely be reconsidered. If we are to understand the early development of symbolic play we must certainly focus on *both* solitary and social play. For the development of role-play and the social understanding on which this play depends, both the studies of Miller and Garvey and those reported here support Vygotsky's contention that "what the child can do today in cooperation tomorrow he will be able to do on his own" (1962, p. 104).

APPENDIX 1

CATEGORIZATION OF
THE SIBLING–CHILD RELATIONSHIP
FROM THE MATERNAL INTERVIEW

The maternal interview included questions on (1) whether child and sibling liked doing many things together, or preferred doing things separately; (2) what kinds of play they engaged in together; (3) how boisterous and excited they became when playing together; (4) how helpful each child was towards the other; (5) whether each child missed the other in his/or her absence; (6) whether the child or sibling minded the other playing with his or her toys; (7) whether each child went to the other for comfort; (8) the frequency and course of arguments and fights between the children; (9) the interest the child showed in the sibling's play; and (10) whether the mothers thought the child and sibling were good friends and how well they got along together. The agreement between mothers' replies to such questions on the relationship between young siblings and other sources of information such as direction observation and child interviews are demonstrated and discussed in Stillwell and Dunn, 1983.

Very Friendly Relationship

The sibling–child pair was categorized having a very friendly relationship if their mother reported that they were very close, intimate, good friends, engaged in frequent joint play, and had many shared games. The children in this category were reported to miss the sibling if he or she was absent from the home, the sibling was able to keep the younger child occupied and happy, the child seemd interested in joining in the sibling's play, and the sibling shared items with the child and helped to comfort the child.

Somewhat Friendly Relationship

The sibling–child pair was categorized as having a somewhat friendly relationship if their mother reported that they engaged in some joint activities but did not do many things together, if she described them as quite close but not good friends and as usually independent or separate from one another.

Unfriendly Relationship

The sibling–child pair was included in this category if the mother reported that they were not close or intimate, did not engage in much joint play, and engaged in frequent disputes when together. In this category the sibling did not usually help the child to play, the child did not miss the sibling when absent, and there was little sharing or comforting by the older sibling.

CRITERIA IN CLASSIFYING JOINT PRETEND PLAY
(DALE, 1983)

The following criteria were used in classifying a joint pretend bout.

1. Each participant contributes actions that develop a joint game, through coordinated actions, turn taking, exchanging vocalizations and play materials, and other forms of complementary activity.
For example, a child gives her mother a toy cup and says "tea," and the mother pretends to drink from the cup. Or, a child and sibling push vehicle replicas across the floor. The sibling pushes a car into the child's car and says "Beep, beep," and the child pushes her car towards the sibling and says "Beep. Brmm." Or, a sibling lies on the floor and says "I'm going to sleep. Good night." The child imitates the sibling and lies down next to the sibling. The child says "Night night" and pretends to snore.
2. One participant is involved in the joint game with physical actions and verbal comments, but the other participant contributes to the course of the game through making verbalizations relevant to the game.
For example, a child holds her doll, and the mother looks at the child and

says "Is your dolly sad? Give her a cuddle." The child cuddles her doll and says "Dolly happy." Or, a child pours the teapot towards the cup and then says "Mummy—cup." The mother looks at the child and replies "Cup—yes. Could I have a cup of tea please?" Or, a sibling raises a receiver of a toy telephone to her ear and says "Hello, it's the policeman here." The child repeats "Hello" and then says "Bye." The sibling says "Bye bye" and then lowers the receiver.

3. A participant (other than the child) helps the child set up or mend some replica material being used during the game and both the child and her partner make verbalizations or actions relevant to the course of the pretend game.

For example, a child gives her mother a car replica to mend, saying "Car broke." The mother replaces the wheel on the car and then pushes it on the table, saying "Brmm, here it comes." The child takes the car and pushes it on the table, saying "Brmm."

Note: At least one action or verbalization relevant to the course of the joint pretend game and directed at the other partner must be contributed by each participant if the interaction is to be counted as joint pretend play. This formula applies to all joint pretend play, whatever the original criteria used to substantiate its existence. Other contextual evidence, such as the proximity between the child and the partner, the nature of the activity of the partner, and the directed gaze towards each other, are also used to infer whether the interaction is a joint game, fleeting joint attention, or uncoordinated and independent activity by each individual.

INTEROBSERVER AGREEMENT

Fourteen videotapes of 2-year-olds playing with their parent or sibling in the home setting (these videotapes did not form part of the data collection of the study) were coded separately by the observer (Dale) and another research worker trained in using the precoded categories. The codings by the two independent observers were then compared. The reliability measure was the ratio of the number of agreements in coding to the number of agreements plus the number of disagreements. A disagreement was scored if there was disagreement regarding the nature of the particular behavior that had occurred or if one observer recorded an instance of a behavior that the second observer did not record. Table 3 illustrates the interobserver reliabilities for a number of the principal observational categories. For further details of coding see Dale, 1983.

Table 3
Interobserver Agreement

Observational category	Interobserver agreement ratio
Interactional measures	
Parent–child	
% of intervals in joint pretend play	.87
% of intervals in joint attention during pretend play	.74
Sibling–child	
% of intervals in joint pretend play	.85
% of intervals in parallel pretend play	.83
Child behavior during pretend play	
% of intervals in pretend play	.93
Imitates action by other	.78
Shows object to other	.81
Performs appropriate action with replica object	.85
Pretends toy is performing action	.82
Pretends absent object is present	.86
Pretends present object is another object	.93
Carries out a role enactment	.76

APPENDIX 2

CLASSIFICATION OF THEMES

1. *Performing everyday routines and household activities.* The child engages in an action or sequence of actions linked by the notion of an everyday activity usually performed in the domestic setting. The activities may include personal routines usually performed by the child (but ouside his or her usual context) or those usually performed by another member of the family (such as household activities carried out by the mother or father). The thematic category includes actions applied to the child or another play partner, but not applied to a toy partner.

Examples: Having a pretend tea party; pretending to go to sleep and then to get up for breakfast; holding a pretend telephone call with an imaginary or real person; pretending to have a bath; pretending to be sweeping the floor; pretending to be cooking a cake or ironing clothes.

2. *Nurturing doll or stuffed animal.* The child engages in an action or se-

quence of actions linked by the notion of caring and looking after the well-being of a toy partner, such as a doll or stuffed animal. The child may discuss the doll's inner psychological states within the same category, and these comments are included as part of the related actions. The category does not include performing actions on miniature people or animal replicas.

Examples: Cuddling, feeding, dressing, and brushing the hair of a doll; placing a teddy bear in the pram and wrapping a blanket around it.

3. *Riding large replica with appropriate pretend noises.* The child engages in an action or sequence of actions linked by the notion of being a rider or driver of a large replica and making appropriate noises indicating the mechanized or animate motion of the replica. The child's actions assume the adoption of the action role of driver or rider of the replica, but without necessarily making explicit verbal reference to this identity.

Examples: Riding a tricycle or sit-in car and going "Brmm brmm"; sitting on a rocking horse and going "Gee up, gee up."

4. *Going to a pretend location.* The child engages in an action or sequence of actions linked by the notion of being in a location other than the current one. The child indicates the theme by verbally announcing the identity of the pretend location. The enacted actions are relevant to the adopted location.

Examples: Being in a shop and buying food; being in a bus and taking a ticket from the driver; being at school and reading a schoolbook.

5. *Military games.* The child engages in an action or sequence of actions linked by the notion of shooting or killing using military methods, fighting, and adopting the action role of victim or aggressor.

Examples: Pretending to shoot another person with a toy gun; pretending to be the victim of an attack from a gun and pretending to die.

6. *Animating doll or stuffed animal.* The child engages in an action or sequence of actions devoted to treating the doll or stuffed animal as an active, animate partner. The child's comments and actions are directed to animating the toy partner and do not include indirect references to the toy's psychological or animacy, such as saying that the doll is sleeping.

Examples: Talking or singing directly to the doll; pretending that the doll or teddy bear is talking, watching, eating, crying, or sleeping (and taking the toy partner through the relevant actions symbolizing these actions and intentions).

7. *Animating miniature people or animals.* The child engages in an action or sequence of actions in which a miniature person or animal is treated as animate and made to engage in actions symbolizing animation. This category does not include indirect references to the animacy or psychological state of the replica.

Examples: Pretending that the miniature person is talking to another miniature person; pretending that the person is walking; pretending that a miniature horse is eating grass.

8. *Actions on miniature people or animals.* The child engages in an action or sequence of actions in which the child performs actions on miniature people and animals but does not subject them to acts of animation.

Examples: Miniature horse and cow are pushed into a stable and then into a field; miniature people are placed inside a selection of vehicle replicas; miniature people are placed on chairs around a table.

9. *Actions on vehicles.* The child engages in an action or sequence of actions in which the child performs actions on vehicle replicas. The replica may be treated as animate, in the sense of assuming being driven by a driver with intentions.

Examples: Pushing car replica to garage and giving the car fuel from a pump; pushing a car up the ramp of a garage and then down again; crashing one car replica into another car; placing car replicas onto a transporter vehicle and then pushing the transporter across the floor; pushing a car and announcing that the "car is going to the shop."

REFERENCES

Clarke-Stewart, A. Interaction between mothers and their young children: Characteristics and consequences. *Monographs of the Society for Research in Child Development*, 1973, (Serial No. 153).

Dale, N. Early pretend play within the family. Unpublished doctoral dissertation, University of Cambridge, 1983.

Dunn, J. Playing with speech. In C. Ricks & L. Michaels (Eds.), *The state of the language.* Berkeley: University of California Press, 1981.

Dunn, J. Sibling relationships in early childhood. *Child Development*, 1983, *54*, 787–811.

Dunn, J. & Kendrick, C. *Siblings: Love, envy and understanding.* Cambridge, MA: Harvard University Press, 1982.

Dunn, J., & Munn, P. *Longitudinal study of pretend play in siblings.* Manuscript in preparation, 1984.

Dunn, J., & Wooding, C. Play in the home and its implications for learning. In B. Tizard and D. Harvey (Eds.), *The biology of play.* London: Spastics International Medical Publications/Heinemann Medical Books, 1977.

Fein, G. G. Pretend play in childhood: An integrative review. *Child Development*, 1981, *52*, 1095–1118.

Garvey, C. Some properties of social play. *Merrill-Palmer Quarterly*, 1974, *20*, 163–180.

Garvey, C. An approach to the study of children's role play. *Quarterly Newsletter of the Laboratory of Comparative Human Cognition*, 1979, *1*,(4), 69–73.

Huttenlocher, J., & Higgins, E. T. Issues in the study of symbolic development. In W. A. Collins (Ed.), *Minnesota Symposia on Child Psychology* (Vol. 11). Hillsdale, NJ: Erlbaum, 1978.

Martlew, M., Connolly, K., & McCleod, C. Language use, role and context in a five-year-old. *Journal of Child Language*, 1978, *5*, 81–99.

Miller, P. & Garvey, C. *Learning to mother at two.* Paper presented at the biennial meeting of the Society for Research in Child Development, Boston, April 1981.

Schwartzman, H. B. *Transformations: The anthropology of children's play.* New York: Plenum Press, 1978.

Stilwell, R & Dunn, J. Continuities in sibling relationships: patterns of aggression and friendliness. Submitted for publication.

Trevarthen, C., & Grant, F. Infant play and the creation of culture. *New Scientist,* 22 February 1979, pp. 566-569.

Valentine, C. N. A study of the beginnings and significance of play in infancy. *British Journal of Educational Psychology,* 1937, 7, 285-306.

Vygotsky, L. S. *Thought and language,* Cambridge, MA: MIT Press, 1962.

CHAPTER 6

Shared Pretend:
Sociodramatic Play at
3 Years of Age*

SUSAN K. STOCKINGER FORYS
LORRAINE McCUNE-NICOLICH

DEFINITION AND DEVELOPMENTAL ISSUES

We can learn much about young children's social abilities and their social knowledge by watching and listening to their spontaneous play together. This is particularly true in the case of interactive play in which pretend enactments are attempted and successfully maintained. Sociodramatic play requires both social-interactive and social–representational abilities. Successful engagement in this form of play requires that each player have the social and communicative skills needed to sustain ongoing interaction with the other players. It further requires that each player possess sufficient representational knowledge of social roles and of specific social events to allow for their expression in language and action. Each of these categories of abilities can be exercised separately in other types

*The research reported here was partially supported by Grant Number HD1731 from the National Institutes of Child Health and Human Development and by a Busch Grant from Rutgers University.

159

of play (i.e., in nonpretend peer play and in solitary pretend play, respectively). However, in social pretend play the social interactive and the representational must be integrated by each player, and must be coordinated with the other players—as exemplified in the following play sample, adapted from Smilansky (1968, p. 155).

> *SETTING:* A doctor's office. A mother and her friend have brought a sick baby to see the doctor.
> *MOTHER.* Doctor, maybe you give her an injection?
> *DOCTOR.* No need for injections, I will examine her.
> *MOTHER.* (to child) There darling, the doctor is only examining you. Don't cry!
> *DOCTOR.* (gives injection with some long object) I did it already, I finished the injection!
> *MOTHER'S FRIEND.* You already did it?
> *MOTHER.* Yes, she did it well, (to child) don't cry sweety, sweety it is alright!
> *DOCTOR.* Give me some cotton, she is bleeding!
> *MOTHER.* (as she hands cotton to doctor) There. Oh poor baby, she is bleeding. (to child) Sit nicely, I will change your cloth. [p. 155]

From Smilansky's report we know that this scene took place in the "doctor's corner" of a preschool classroom, where three little girls, probably about 4 years old, took the roles of "mother" to a doll, "doctor," and "mother's friend" in enacting a scene that may be based on their own real experience as well as on previous shared play in their classroom. This is not an exceptional sample of shared pretend, but it embodies many of the major hallmarks of sociodramatic play that have been identified in research on play (Fein, 1981; Garvey & Berndt, 1977; Rubin, Fein, & Vandenberg, 1983; Schwartzman, 1978; Smilansky, 1968).

The players were conducting themselves with obvious ease, as if they were in a doctor's office while they actually played in a corner of the school room. Such out-of-context activity, in this case supported by several props, is recognized as a major defining criterion for pretend activity at all ages (Fein, 1979; Matthews & Matthews, 1982). The theme or *script* (Schank & Abelson, 1977) enacted by the children is fairly typical, portraying familiar events from the children's everyday lives. This is revealed by the shared knowledge of medical practice expressed in their actions and conversation as well as by the appropriate temporal order and logical congruence with reality.

Integral to the enactment of the script was the assumption of pretend roles and the appropriate pretend social interaction among the role-players. The identities of the roles assumed by the children were most clear for the "mother" and the "doctor," who displayed the language and functions appropriate to their respective roles. The identity of the third child's role, dubbed as "mother's friend," is less clear to the observer. However, it is notable that it was played out within the pretend theme and did not usurp the functions of the other players' roles. The fourth role in the drama was "played" by an inanimate object, the doll, to whom role-appropriate biological conditions (illness, blood) and a (human) affective state (crying) were attributed.

Most children show the ability to treat doll-like figures as *active recipients* by endowing them with animate qualities, or as *active agents* by portraying their motoric actions, by 24 months of age. This skill has been extensively researched in studies in which an experimenter modeled brief scenes and observed the children's subsequent play with the same materials (e.g., Bretherton, O'Connell, Shore, & Bates, Chapter 10, this volume; Fenson, Chapter 9, this volume). Similar instances of doll use have been reported in descriptions of sociodramatic play, but aspects of doll animation have not been a specific focus of research in this area.

The types of roles enacted in the episode excerpted earlier were typical of the roles played by preschool children, who most frequently select familial roles and roles involved in relationships in which they have been participants (Garvey & Berndt, 1977). The intercoordination of three different social roles (i.e., "mother," "child," "doctor"), which was demonstrated in the episode, suggests considerable symbolic maturity in these players. Multiple role coordination has not been examined in detail as it develops in sociodramatic play. However, in experimental research in which single subjects portrayed multiple roles using cardboard replicas, representation of more than two roles in complementary relationships was first observed at about 5 years of age (Watson & Fischer, 1980).

An instance of the transformational activity of object substitution, in which inanimate objects were imbued with new identities, occurred in the episode with respect to the "long object" used as an injection syringe, with which it shared certain perceptual characteristics. Although experimental symbolic maturity research has shown that children of about 4 years of age are capable of transforming objects that lack perceptual similarity to the object signified (Elder & Pederson, 1978; Jackowitz & Watson, 1980), it is also known that objects with some similarity to the referent are preferred by most children (McCune-Nicolich & Fenson, 1983), and that in social pretense object transformations are usually motivated by the theme and action sequence requirements (Garvey & Berndt, 1977).

A necessary aspect of sociodramatic play that was not readily observed in the excerpted episode pertains to the manner in which the players communicate the message that they are pretending. Metacommunications serve to establish and maintain a psychological frame within which pretend behavior can be enacted and separated from real-life behavior (Bateson, 1956). They are also used by the players to decide on pretend themes, to execute role and object transformations, and to negotiate the development of the script throughout pretend episodes (Fein, 1979; Garvey & Berndt, 1977; Giffin, Chapter 3, this volume; Rubin *et al.*, 1983; Schwartzman, 1978).

A look at the interaction of the children just prior to the doctor–patient episode recounted earlier reveals the metacommunications used in the initial planning of that episode. As described subsequently, all three children were present when the verbal negotiations for the episode began. Because they had not yet assumed pretend roles, in this segment they are labeled Child A, Child B, and Child C. These labels correspond to the pretend identities of "mother," "mother's friend," and "doctor," respectively.

> *SETTING:* The "doctors' corner" in a preschool classroom. A girl (Child C) is busy with the medicine case. Enter two girls (Child A and Child B), holding two dolls.
>
> (1) A. (to B.). Ruth, that is your baby (hands her a doll).
> (2) B. Let's pretend both had measles.
> (3) A. (to C.). Why do you take this?
> (4) B. You cannot take it, it is the doctor's case.
> (5) B. (to C.). Tamar, all right, you know, she is sick, she has the measles. No, no, she has the flu!
> (6) C. If she has the measles, then she shouldn't eat any oil.
> (7) B. But she has the flu. My mommy has the flu too, really!
> (8) A. It is my turn now, I am number 65. You are 66!
> (9) A. (in mother role, as earlier). Doctor, maybe you give her an injection? [adapted from Smilansky, 1968, p. 155]

Because these children were familiar with the "doctor's corner" as a classroom setting for pretend play concerning this theme, merely going to that area implicitly conveyed the intention to engage in such play. In this contextually supportive setting the three children negotiated the roles and plans for their play verbally using both explicit and implicit messages, some of which were within the pretend mode and others out-of-pretend. The clearest instances of metacommunication were those that were explicit and outside the play frame (e.g., Line 2, "Let's pretend . . ."). Taking the doctor's case was apparently a nonverbal role adoption signal by Child C, which was questioned with out-of-pretend remarks in Lines 3 and 4 and finally confirmed by Child C's pretend statement in Line 6.

In this relatively brief exchange, the three children successfully set the stage for the pretend enactment that followed through the use of the setting, inanimate objects, and verbal and nonverbal messages. The success of their metacommunicative activity was evidenced by the certainty in their orderly role assumptions and playing of the doctor–patient theme.

We have presented this play sample and our interpretive commentary on its characteristics as a working definition of well-formed social pretend play and as a standard of comparison for use throughout the remainder of this chapter, which is specifically focused on immature social pretend play. Examination of the research literature revealed that few studies of sociodramatic play included subjects below the age of 4 years. Where younger children were included, data were often not reported by age. Hence a normative age for onset of sociodramatic play cannot be specified, although the existing literature, as well as anecdotal accounts in this literature (e.g., Piaget, 1946/1962; Rubin et al., 1983; Smilansky, 1968) suggested that this ability emerges late in the third or early in the fourth year of life. At all ages numerous contextual variables influence the occurrence of such play.

FAMILIARITY

In play between same-age peers, both the extent of familiarity of the pair and the familiarity of the play setting are likely to affect the incidence and maturity of their sociodramatic interaction. In the extreme, children who are best friends and play together frequently from toddlerhood are likely to develop some joint play themes that can be launched and maintained with little effort, whereas children who are introduced for the first time in an unfamiliar playroom may need to establish a degree of social understanding before exhibiting sociodramatic skill, regardless of their individual symbolic ability. Research concerning this contrast remains to be conducted. However, when familiar and unfamiliar peers have been compared, social interaction between familiar peers has been shown to be both more frequent and more intense at several points between 1 and 4 years of age (Doyle, Connolly, & Rivest, 1980; Lewis, Young, Brooks, & Michalson, 1975; Schwartz, 1972.) Similarly, research focused on the effects of settings on social behavior suggests that familiar play settings enhance the positive social interaction of young children (Jeffers & Lore, 1979). Doyle et al. (1980) further reported more behavior in Parten's (1932) interactive categories, and a greater frequency of sociodramatic play between familiar partners than unfamiliar partners. Matthews (1977) found short-term familiarity effects such that over play sessions on 3 consecutive days, initially unacquainted children increasingly initiated pretend play by ideational or verbal modes, rather than relying on material objects.

Given the sensitivity of young children to social context it was not a simple matter to design a study that would begin to specify the structural properties of early sociodramatic play. Indeed, it was not entirely clear how these properties should be conceptualized developmentally in order to describe early manifestations of this skill. In our view what was needed was a study that would elicit the richest sample of play possible while controlling for the familiarity of subjects included in the study. Because children differ in the extent to which they have a frequent play partner and such partners differ by age and gender, it was necessary to pair initially unacquainted children to control this variable. This design provided the additional advantage of allowing study of the manner in which the children would overcome their initial unfamiliarity and engage in interaction.

Thus our study evolved to include both this social interaction question concerning children's *entry* into play and the study of *structural properties*. To summarize, the structural properties of interest were: (1) pretend role assumption, (2) enactment of themes, (3) object substitution and invention, (4) social interaction within pretend, and (5) metacommunication, or the manner in which children conveyed to one another the message "This is play" (Bateson, 1956). We wondered in particular whether children would need to establish social contact on a realistic level prior to entering the play sphere or whether mutual pretending would provide a vehicle for such entry.

CONDUCTING THE PLAY SESSIONS

On 2 consecutive days, same-sex pairs of children, who were unacquainted prior to the study, played together in a laboratory playroom. The children were from middle-SES two-parent families, and all were within 1 month of their third birthdays. The two girl pairs, who will be designated throughout this discussion by single initials, were L.&A. (who were one day apart in age) and J.&K. (whose third birthdays were 9 weeks apart). One boy pair, designated by double initials, AA.&JJ. were 4 weeks apart in age. Originally a second boy pair was included in the study, but one of these children was unable to stay in the playroom for any reasonable length of time on either of 2 days, which necessitated dropping the pair from the study.

The children played in a 3.6- by 5-meter carpeted room, located in a small house on the Rutgers University Campus, that doubled as a preschool classroom for language-impaired children. A one-way mirror extended along one wall of the room, and a microphone hung from the center of the ceiling.

The room was well stocked with toys and equipment selected for their known ability to elicit social pretend play and/or social interaction in children of this age. A play kitchen area contained a small table, a high chair, and child-size wooden appliances stocked with toy food, dishes, pots, and utensils. Adjacent to the kitchen were a child-size wooden doll bed, and a smaller cradle, both with mattresses, pillows, and blankets. A variety of male and female hats and clothing, jewelry, mirrors, combs, and brushes were available in a dress-up area, and there was a block corner with blocks, trucks, cars, tools, and a toolbench. Several dolls, stuffed animals, and puppets inhabited the room. The most popular of these were a doll that cried when jostled and three panda bears of different sizes. A large wooden apparatus, which could be either a rocking boat or a stable platform with stairs on two sides when flipped over, was located in the middle of the room. This apparatus was always in the stairs position at the start of a play session, and was flipped over to the boat side only as a last resort to keep the children in the room. Other toys the children used frequently were two flashlights, two adult-size paintbrushes, a set of real keys on a key ring, a fur stole, and a wooden toaster with two wooden slices of toast, which could be activated with an attached lever.

Before entering the playroom, the members of a dyad were introduced to one another and spent 5–10 minutes in a nearby waiting room. They were told that the playroom was for children and that their mothers would remain out of the room. There were differences in individual children's reactions to this prohibition, ranging from a lack of concern to strong protest. In the latter cases, mothers were allowed to sit on chairs just outside the playroom, near the opened door.

One of the authors escorted the children into the playroom, gave them a brief tour of the toy areas, and invited them to play with anything they wished. The experimenter exited the playroom as soon as the children appeared to be comfortable. The play sessions were planned to continue for at least 30 minutes, but in many cases the sessions continued for a longer time (range: 35–75 minutes) because the children were happily absorbed in their play activities.

All sessions were videotaped with a two-camera system that used a special effects generator to create a split-screen recording of the play. One camera was located in the room, providing a stationary wide-angle view, and the other was located behind the one-way mirror. Videotape recording of each session began when the experimenter entered the room with the children.

RESULTS: ENTRY INTO PLAY

Our first examination of the videotaped play sessions focused on the manner in which each dyad negotiated this "strange" social and nonsocial situation. How would the children establish social interaction and enter into shared pretend? We had anticipated both individual differences by dyad and Session I versus Session II differences, but were unprepared for the extensive variability displayed as each dyad revealed its unique "personality."

We initially considered the children's behavior during an orientation period in which the adult introduced them to the room. This analysis, to be described anecdotally, focused on their interest (both social and nonsocial), exploratory behaviors, and affective responses in this new situation. Within the play session proper we examined the temporal sequencing of a set of behavioral events expected to be related to social pretending. These social and pretend behaviors were defined as follows.

Social Utterance (SU). Verbalization of one child directed to the other.

Verbal Social Interaction (VSI). An exchange between two children consisting of a minimum of one verbal turn each (additional verbal and nonverbal turns optional), and in which each successive turn was contingent on the previous turn of the partner.

Verbal Social Pretend (VSP). An exchange between two children in the pretend mode, consisting of a minimum of one verbal turn each (additional verbal and nonverbal turns optional) and in which each successive turn was contingent upon the previous turn of the partner.

Social Bid (BID). Explicit verbal request or command to the partner to join in pretend or nonpretend play. (This designation represents a special form of SU as described earlier.)

Nonverbal Social Pretend (NVSP). An exchange between two children in the pretend mode consisting of a minimum of one turn each, that might include some verbalization but fails to meet the criterion of two verbal turns required for VSP.

Nonverbal Social Interaction (NVSI). An exchange between two children consisting of a minimum of one turn each, in which each successive turn is contingent on the previous turn of the partner and that might include some verbalization but fails to meet the criterion of two verbal turns required in VSI.

Solo Pretend (SOLO). An enactment of a pretend sequence as defined by McCune-Nicolich (Nicolich, 1977, Level 4 or 5.2) by one child that was not imbedded in a social interaction or social pretend episode.

The emphasis on verbal behavior in these categories reflects the importance traditionally ascribed to language in the sociodramatic play literature (e.g., Garvey & Berndt, 1977; Schwartzman, 1978; Smilansky, 1968), where language has been considered the primary vehicle for sociodramatic play.

For two of our three dyads the verbal categories nicely captured their varied strategies for engaging one another. However, for the third dyad, J.&K., a substantial portion of social negotiation was nonverbal. The NVSP and NVSI categories were devised as an essential means for characterizing the interaction of this dyad, but did not prove useful when applied to the other dyads. No doubt, with a larger sample this category would reflect the behavior of some noticeable proportion of dyads.

Our analyses of the play session proper identified the timing of the *first* occurrence of each of these behaviors and all occurrences of BIDS prior to the dyad's first VSP. These events were organized in the form of time lines for each dyad, both individually and as partners, as shown in Table 1, to reveal the relationship between pretending and social engagement.

Table 1

Temporal Patterns[a] for Social and Pretend Behavior in Sessions I and II[b]

Dyads	Minute 1: Seconds			Minutes						
	0–20	21–40	41–60	2	3	4	5	6–10	11–20	21+
L.&A.										
Session I L.	SU									
L.&A.										
A.	SU	BID		VSI SOLO	SOLO	VSP(27)				SOLO
Session II L.	SU									
L.&A.	VSI–VSP(36)									
A.	SU							SOLO		
AA.&JJ.										
Session I AA.	SOLO									
AA.&JJ.						SU/BID BID	BID BID	VSI–VSP(9)		
JJ.								SU SOLO / SOLO		
Session II AA.				SU						
AA.&JJ.			VSI–VSP(15)					SOLO		
JJ.			SU							
J.&K.										
Session I J.	SOLO				SU/BID BID	BID BID BID	BID BID			
J.&K.				NVSI				VSI–VSP(11)		SOLO
K.								SU / SOLO		
Session II J.				SOLO	SU/BID					
J.&K.	NVSP					VSI–VSP(21)				
K.			SOLO			SU				

[a] These time lines show the approximate time of occurrence of each behavioral event. No attempt was made to represent absolute points in time. Abbreviations are explained in text in the section "Results: Entry into Play." Numbers in parentheses indicate number of social turns.

[b] Abbreviations are explained in text in the section "Results: Entry into Play." Numbers in parentheses indicate number of social turns.

To our surprise, the first social interaction in five of the six sessions was a pretend interaction. That is, the first social exchange (VSI) *co-occurred* with social pretend (VSP), rather than being a prerequisite to pretend interaction. These occurrences appear in Table 1 as clusters of behaviors because SUs from one or both partners as well as social and verbal interaction by the dyad occurred in the same event.

A Session I versus Session II comparison by dyad showed earlier occurrence of social interactive events (VSI and VSP) in the second session for each pair, despite differences in the absolute time of occurrence of these behaviors. This supported short-term familiarity effects previously reported in the literature.

Within Session I the three dyads demonstrated a pattern of social engagement that was strikingly similar, despite strong differences in extent of verbalization, activity level, and other aspects of style. We identified an aspect of temporary social leadership, which was demonstrated by one member of the pair as soon as the session began and continued until the children entered social interaction. We have termed this partner *initially socially dominant;* we will develop the definition of this term by example in subsequent discussion.

Within each dyad, one child was initially more socially dominant than the other child who, in all cases, was not merely "less dominant" but also appeared to be reticent in the new situation. The initially socially dominant children (A. in dyad L&A., AA. in dyad AA.&JJ., and J. in dyad J.&K.) exhibited the individual behavioral events (e.g., SU and SOLO) earlier in the session than did their initially reticent partners. Additionally, all three delivered a series of BIDs to their partners that culminated in the pair's first interactive episodes. It seemed that the initially socially dominant child, through a series of persistent but nonintrusive social maneuvers, gradually pulled the reticent child into a social interaction. This initial asymmetry did not consistently typify the social balance in each dyad for the remainder of Session I, nor was there a consistent pattern of dyadic social balance in Session II.

The most consistent interdyad similarity in the second session, in addition to earlier social interactive events, was later occurrence of SOLO episodes. In the case of dyads L.&A. and AA.&JJ., first SOLOs in Session II were enacted after all other behavioral events and showed a close similarity in timing. For both dyads, the initially more socially dominant child performed the first SOLO in each dyad, and the SOLO of the initially more reticent child occurred much later in the session. Thus, in dyad L.&A., A.'s SOLO occurred 9 $\frac{1}{2}$ minutes into the session, and L.'s SOLO was enacted at the 38th minute of the session. Similarily, in dyad AA.&JJ., AA. enacted his first SOLO 7 minutes into the session, but JJ.'s did not occur until 23 $\frac{1}{2}$ minutes had transpired. This pattern was not shown in dyad J.&K.'s Session II play, where both girls enacted their first SOLOs prior to engagement in social interaction. The difference in the timing of second session SOLO episodes appeared to be due to the degree to which the children were mutually engaged during that session. Both L.&A. and AA.&JJ. exhibited substantially more interactive behavior than J.&K. in the second session, and the later timing of their SOLOs seemed to indicate their preference for sustained interactive play over SOLO enactments. J.&K., on the other hand, had engaged in the least amount of social interaction across the first session and did not establish a strong sense of mutual engagement until later in Session II.

Each dyad demonstrated unique qualities in their adaptation to the social and nonsocial features of the play situation, both during the orientation period and during the play session proper. Information concerning their orientation behavior sets the stage for interpretation of events within the play session proper. Descriptions of first instances of the social and pretend occurrences in each session will provide a more realistic picture of how these behaviors unfolded sequentially. A somewhat detailed description of L.&A.'s Session I play serves as a model and a point of comparison for brief descriptions of the remaining sessions.

L.&A.

The girl pair, L.&A., was the most gregarious dyad in the study and engaged in more-frequent, longer, and less-stereotypic episodes of social pretending than the other dyads. Yet their social interest and skills were not directly expressed in their orientation behavior in either session. On the first day, they readily entered the playroom with the adult and in a self-assured manner began exploring the room, both visually and by moving at a moderate pace, each to different play areas. Each focused on the physical environment, and showed no visual or verbal notice of the other. Likewise, they paid little attention to the adult, although their compliance with her requests to look at areas of the room indicated that they were listening to her instructions. Similarly, they took little notice of the announced exits of the adult and L.'s mother, who had been standing in the doorway.

In contrast, when the play session proper began L.&A.'s behavior was characterized by alert interest in each other, which occurred sooner than for the other dyads. As the adult left the room, A., who was near the fish tank, directed an SU to L., who was bent over the jewelry case in a different area of the room: "I see some fish." (Points) "I looking into the fish bowl." (Turns and starts to walk toward L., who has now looked up and faced A.) "I saw some fish." Immediately, L., began to walk toward A., and said: "Hi, A.," with a slight smile as she looked away and fumbled with her shirt.

Although these SUs were temporally contingent, they were not judged to constitute a VSI, but rather to be discrete acts of social recognition independently executed by each child. The events that followed are of note because they exemplify a pattern seen in all three dyads. A. continued to be socially active and directed BIDs to L., whose behavior following her first SU became somewhat constricted. L. ignored A. and began slowly handling the jewelry with none of the alert interest that characterized her orientation behavior. A. moved to a position next to L., put on a bracelet, looked at L. and said:

A. C'mon girl, let's get goin.
L. (furtively looks at A., then returns gaze to jewelry).
A. (takes mirror, looks at self). C'mon girl, let's get goin.
L. (ignores A., handles jewelry).
A. (puts mirror down). C'mon, *lets get going!*
L. (ignores A.).

A. then walked to a bucket containing two flashlights, took one, and turned it on. L. walked to the bucket and stood, watching A., who again directed a BID to her.

A. (takes second flashlight, holds out to L.). C'mon, take 'erself a light and put it on.
L. (stands motionless staring at A.).
A. (withdraws second flashlight). Take 'erself an own—on—light—off. (Turns first flashlight off, returns it to the bucket.)

A. then walked to the nearby kitchen and enacted a SOLO in which she baked cookies and cupcakes in the toy oven, and provided an animated narration of the entire sequence. L. stood nearby watching passively. However, immediately following A.'s SOLO, L.&A. engaged in a brief VSI, initiated by L., in which they commented on the "pretty goldfish" in the fish tank.

At this point L. came to life. She opened cupboard doors decisively, found a pan, slammed the doors and proceeded to enact a complex cooking SOLO, also narrating her actions as she made pancakes. A. moved close to L. and watched but did not attempt to enter her play. L. ended her SOLO holding a pan of "soup," which she carried away from the kitchen, saying as an aside to A., "Anybody have a baby?" A. then set off for the doll beds where L.&A. began a lengthy VSP (27 turns), in which they engaged in a series of care-taking acts with the dolls characterized by extensive negotiations and the use of several themes and several areas of the room.

Following this VSP episode, L.&A. interacted almost continuously and mostly in a pretend mode for the entire first session, which lasted over an hour. The initial social balance, wherein L. was more reticent and A. more dominant, did not typify the session: The balance was relatively equal in most episodes; however, L. slightly exceeded A. in dominance, both in her influence on the direction of the play and in her frequency of verbalization.

On the second day, L.&A. confidently entered the playroom at a faster pace than on the previous day. In the orientation period, both showed an interest in the social and nonsocial environment. A. first spoke happily to the adult and then moved to the doll corner, and L. went immediately to the jewelry as on the previous day. L.'s social interest was revealed when she immediately became so upset when the adult left the room that a visit to her mother and the promise of a snack were needed for her to return to the playroom. After L. conversed with the adult, telling her of the previous day's activities, the adult was able to leave the room with little attention from either child. As Table 1 indicates, at this point L.&A. engaged in interactive play that subsumed all the social categories (i.e., SUs, VSI, VPI) and continued for 36 alternating turns. However, this episode as well as several others throughout the session were terminated when L. became upset for no discernible reason and required her mother's presence. For about 40% of the session her mother sat just inside the door reading a book, and skillfully deflecting L.'s (and sometimes A.'s) requests for attention. L. was then able to resume her play, which as on the first day was almost entirely of a social pretend nature.

A. did little playing when L. was upset and most frequently wandered around in proximity to L., watching her. On several occasions A. tried to comfort L. with gentle comments (e.g., "Now don't be so crying. Don't be sad"), and pats on the back. Late in the session, A. tried a stronger tactic and told L. that "If you cry too much, you'll get sick," which resulted in a debate on the veracity of this thesis that never reached resolution.

The maintenance of lengthy social pretend sequences by L.&A. in the presence of strong negative emotional arousal was quite remarkable, and seemed to be due to the ability of both girls to use the pretend state to deal with their conflicts. A. was preoccupied throughout the session with her inability to stop her "baby's" crying (the doll that cried as she jostled it). L. was uncompromising in many of the pretend episodes (e.g., "You *have to go* to the meeting") and sometimes introduced discord into the pretend play (e.g., "Your baby likes me, but she doesn't like you"). Comments such as these usually did not result in the termination of pretend interaction because both children employed strategies such as ignoring, moving to another topic, or restoring a more cooperative mood, showing considerable social interactive skill. Thus L. reworded her previous statement about A.'s baby (somewhat ambiguously): "Your baby likes you, but she likes you."

AA.&JJ.

JJ.'s difficulty in separating from his mother to enter the playroom resulted in a lengthy orientation period (more than 5 minutes) in the boys' first play session. He did not accompany AA. and the adult as they entered the room, but stayed near the doorway during most of the period. He fully entered the room only after the adult had left, and thus his entry signaled the beginning of the play session proper. Once inside the room, JJ. stood in the grooming area with his back to AA. and handled the grooming materials. AA., who had entered the room with the adult, appeared happy and interested in the physical environment as well as in JJ. and the adult. He explored the room freely, and spoke occasionally to the adult and to himself. Early in the period, he shared one of two paint brushes with JJ. who was in the doorway, but paid no further attention after JJ. took the brush and exited to his mother.

At the start of the play session proper, AA. executed an elaborate cooking SOLO while JJ. remained across the room in the grooming area. Soon after the SOLO, AA. directed an SU to JJ. which was also a BID: "Oh, it's time for tookies (cookies), JJ. Oh it's time for tookies." As Table 1 indicates, the SU was followed by a series of BIDS that induced a smaller series of familiarization responses in JJ. as were shown by L. in response to A.'s BIDs. JJ. first looked at and then slowly walked to AA., and finally directed an SU to AA. that developed into a pretend interaction (i.e., VSI–VSP) centering on food preparation.

The remainder of Session I was characterized by the occasional enactment of brief interactive episodes with little thematic development, which increased in frequency over the session, and by solo pretending by both boys. The social balance in the dyad shifted slowly over the first session. AA. was more dominant in the first half, and JJ. literally followed him around the room. JJ. gradually asserted himself over the last half of the session; toward the end the majority of BIDs were being delivered by JJ. and were usually attempts to induce AA. to cook dinner for him. AA.'s ignoring of many of the invitations to pretend were the major instigation of conflict between the boys, and caused JJ. to make brief visits to his mother from time to time.

Session II began with a brief orientation period, during which the adult remained in the doorway, giving instructions as AA.&JJ. entered the room. Both boys were happy, calm, and confident as they entered, and immediately went to different parts of the room to play. JJ. showed only slight separation upset, which was resolved by keeping the door open. AA. calmly watched JJ. during this time, then returned to his play when the problem was solved. Neither child appeared to notice the adult's exit from the room, and within the first minute were engaged in a pretend interaction (VSI–VSP), initiated by AA.'s SU, which continued for 15 turns. Shortly after the first VSP, JJ. requested that AA. feed him. AA. cooperated after only one request from JJ. and the two engaged in a second VSP.

In general, these events typified the quality of the play in the first half of the session, wherein the boys engaged in longer and more integrated episodes of social pretend than at any other time. The second half of the session was characterized by conflict. Several fights occurred, which disrupted the play and required adult intervention for the continuation of the session. The most disruptive of the conflicts were two occurring at the end of the session at a point when JJ., for the first time, was engaged in cooking dinner for himself. He became absorbed in arranging pots on the stove; he made multiple trips to the refrigerator to get play food, which he put in the pots, saying to AA. "I'm cooking dinner" and, later, "Ah, dinner's cookin." AA. began to take the pots from the stove and dump the food onto the floor. The first time this happened, JJ. became very angry, but then proceeded to pick up the food and pots and again arrange them on the stove. When AA. again began to dump the dinner on the floor, JJ. screamed angrily; when AA. did not stop, he joined him in dumping everything on the floor, and then went crying from the playroom while AA. began marching around the room banging pots together. The play session, which was terminated at this point, was the shortest of the six sessions, lasting approximately 35 minutes.

J.&K.

As mentioned earlier, the girl dyad, J.&K. exhibited the least amount of verbal behavior of the dyads in our study; as Table 1 indicates, their first VSI and VSP episodes occurred at later points in both sessions. Neither child uttered a sound during either orientation period. In Session I, they stood together near the door as the adult gave the instructions. J. soon walked out into the room, first stopping at the wooden "stairs" where she picked up a doll, smiled to herself, and then went to the kitchen and began playing. K. remained near the adult for a longer time and then walked very slowly to the jewelry area where she stood, finger in mouth, watching J. who was absorbed in play and seemed oblivious to the presence of K. and the adult. Neither girl looked when the adult announced her exit, but K. then walked slowly to stand next to J.

With K. watching, J. immediately executed a multi-action sequenced SOLO at the sink. The girls maintained complete silence for the next two minutes, when J. uttered her first SU, which was also a BID. As can be seen in Table 1, prior to J.'s first SU the girls engaged in a nonverbal interactive sequence of five turns (NVSI) in which K. gave instrumental assistance to J., who was setting the table. Following this interaction, K. retreated to a chair in the corner where she sat and stared impassively at J. who initiated a series of 10 verbal BIDs aimed at engaging K. in a feeding interaction. J. spoke in a soft voice, looking at K. and smiling as she asked "What's you wanna eat?" several times and then showed K. a variety of "foods," each time asking if K. wanted one to eat. K. never responded, but seconds after J. issued her last BID, K. left her chair and joined J. at the high chair. J.&K. then engaged in their first interaction (VSI–VSP) as they jointly put a doll into the high chair. K. uttered her first words during this sequence (i.e., "I'll put her in here"), but most of her participation was nonverbal.

J.&K.'s entire first session was characterized by a low level of verbalization of any kind, with J. engaging in substantially more verbal behavior than K. whose utterances were usually only a few words. J. thus remained the socially dominant child in this dyad; however, as the session continued, K. began to assert herself more and several nondisruptive, silent object struggles, accompanied by glaring and grimacing, occurred.

On the second day, J.&K. entered the playroom in a state of eager anticipation. As on the previous day, they stood together as the adult spoke to them; but when the adult announced her exit, they simultaneously went into action, moving to opposite sides of the stairs, where they knelt facing each other. K.'s behavior appeared to be an imitation of J.'s Session I behavior, as she picked up a doll, smiled at J., and walked rapidly to the sink. J. followed K. to the sink where they engaged in a nonverbal pretend interaction (NVSP) that closely resembled J.'s SOLO of the previous day. Again there was total silence for the first few minutes, which was broken by J.'s first SU as she showed K. some jewelry. K.'s SU, which followed shortly, occurred in a struggle over a bracelet in which her nonverbal gestures had been unsuccessful in conveying her wishes. The utterance proved successful and initiated a lengthy exchange (VSI–VSP) of 27 turns.

The first portion of J.&K.'s second session was similar to the first session on many dimensions, including the dyadic social balance and the degree and type of social and pretend behavior. Midway through the session, a social turning point occurred in which K. began to assert herself in a vigorous manner in nonpretend social interaction. She sat in the rocking boat, which had been turned in an attempt to elicit social interaction, and began calling to J. to join her: "C'mon here, OK?" was repeated many times in an increasingly loud voice until J. responded. J.&K. then engaged in a lengthy period of social interaction characterized by periods of silliness and the exchange of factual information. As the session was coming to an end, they began to engage in more balanced, complex, and lengthier social pretend sequences than had occurred in their prior play.

SUMMARY

The children in this study were strongly motivated to engage in interaction, and in the majority of cases, both social bids and initial social engagement occurred in the pretend mode. The finding that pretending facilitated the social interaction of unfamiliar young peers has not been reported previously. Because most studies of social interaction have not examined the role of pretending, and because of the small number of subjects in the present study, this finding is considered a tentative one, pending replication with a larger sample.

Despite substantial differences in the social skills exhibited by these 3-year-olds, several common patterns of social interaction were identified. In order to overcome initial first-session inhibitions, each pair showed surprising skill in managing a leadership–followership relation that was not characteristic of the social interaction observed throughout the sessions. In every case the initially socially dominant child showed great sensitivity to the more reticent child's need to warm up by bidding nonintrusively, but persistently, until initial social engagement occurred. Although all pairs did eventually play in a reasonably balanced and sustained fashion, only L.&A. engaged quickly in both sessions. In contrast J.&K. only achieved this level of play halfway through the second session, and AA.&JJ. displayed it in occasional episodes that increased in length and frequency across two sessions.

We found Session I by Session II differences based on increased familiarity. In Session II all dyads became socially engaged in less time and explored the playroom with a quickened pace, as compared to their Session I behaviors. Both J.&K. and AA.&JJ. showed an increase in social interaction and social pretend play in Session II, whereas L.&A., whose Session I play was predominantly interactive, exhibited similar behavior in Session II.

In addition, second session happenings showed an interesting content relationship with the initial sessions. Many of the pretend sequences played by a dyad in Session I were reinstated in easily recognizable form in Session II, sometimes by different partners. Even in the short term, pairs of children developed a repertoire of shared meanings (Brenner & Mueller, 1982) in the symbolic mode, which facilitated and enriched their interaction. As will be seen in the subsequent section, some of these shared meanings were most likely based on past common experience of dyad members, whereas others were jointly constructed during their play sessions.

RESULTS: STRUCTURAL PROPERTIES
OF EARLY SOCIODRAMATIC PLAY

Although we had planned a balanced analysis of the structural components of sociodramatic play as observed in our 3-year-old dyads, the data revealed the centrality of the role-play component in the children's organization of their play. Consequently, a major focus of our research effort was to devise a means of analyzing the pretend role play exhibited. We developed a two-dimensional system based on previous research for role content that presents, in addition, a converging analysis of social structure properties.

The thematic or scriptal component of social pretend play is integrally related to the role-play component, but is usually analyzed separately (e.g., Garvey & Berndt, 1977; Smilansky, 1968). In our data, a separate analysis of themes often added little information to that available from the role analysis. However, a few episodes exhibited an extended sequence of plotlike events with novel happenings, which were not sufficiently described by role-content analysis. These are discussed separately in a following section.

The remaining components (i.e., object substitution, pretend interaction, and metacommunication) were not subjected to detailed analysis, but their influence on the play can be seen in the role and theme descriptions. In a final section we will interpret the relationships among the structural components of sociodramatic play as revealed in this sample of 3-year-olds.

THE ROLE OF ROLES

Many of those who hold the view that engagement in sociodramatic play in the preschool years contributes in a causal way to the development of the child specify the role-playing aspect of this activity as the most critical factor. Support for this position is found among role theorists (e.g., Sarbin & Allen, 1968), particularly those who follow the views of George Herbert Mead (1934) and the symbolic interactionist tradition as well as in the results of more recent play-training studies reviewed by Saltz and Brodie (1982).

According to role theory, the construct of role is a social one referring to the organized cluster of behaviors that are identified with a particular status or position within a society and that are enacted when a person operates from that position. The enactment of roles always occurs in a social context and, by implication, requires a complementary role played by another, in either a "genuine or vicarious" mode (Sarbin & Allen, 1968, p. 545). The learning of roles was said to require the knowledge of both the role and its complement, referred to as the *role set*.

Mead (1934) designated the role-play that occurs in social pretend play as a major stage, which he called the *play stage* in his theory of the development of the self. The self was said to be social in origin and functioning, involving the integration of the reflected views of others toward oneself and resulting in the ability to act in a social manner toward oneself as one acted toward others. Children's pretend role-play contributes to the development of the self as a separate identity that is different from, but related to, others by allowing the child to "get outside himself and apprehend himself from some other perspective" (Stone, 1965/1971, p. 10). Because many identities are defined in terms of counteridentities (e.g., man–woman, parent–child, teacher–student), the experience of playing the role of these others provides a means for children to gain "a reflected view of their own identities from the perspective of those identities whose roles they perform"(Stone, 1965/1971, p. 10).

Contemporary definitions of pretend role-play emphasize the transformation of a single identity that occurs in pretending as a criterial feature (El'Konin, 1966; Garvey, 1979; Huttenlocher & Higgins, 1978; Smilansky, 1968). Those who have conducted detailed studies of sociodramatic play have recognized the importance of the complementarity issue in role assumption. Thus Smilansky implied the necessity of a partner in her description of the role categories "family and home," "professional," and "school-related." "Dramatization," her fourth category (which referred to re-playing experiences observed at the theatre, zoo, etc.), did not seem to require complementarity. Garvey and Berndt (1977) developed a more comprehensive system of categorization that was similar to Smilansky's findings concerning the content of children's roles. They also reported that certain role categories, once adopted by a child, led to adoption of a complementary role by another player or invention of the complement, using a doll or imaginary partner. In a more recent report, Garvey (1982) clarified her position with regard to complementarity of roles, indicating that traditional family roles (termed *relational*) require a role complement, which may be either a doll or another child.

The role content categories first described by Garvey and Berndt (1977) and then modified by Garvey (1982) are the following. *Functional* roles refer to unnamed roles represented by the actions of the players (e.g., driver–passenger, eater–cook). *Relational* roles include family roles (e.g., mommy, daddy, baby) as well as unidentified caretaker and pet. *Occupational* roles portray police officer, teacher, doctor, and so on, and *fantasy* roles derive from TV, stories, and imagination. Peripheral roles, those referred to by the children but not enacted, were identified by Garvey and Berndt (1977) but excluded from Garvey (1982).

TWO-DIMENSIONAL ANALYSIS OF CHILDREN'S PRETEND ROLES

The analysis described in the following section was developed to add the social role-structure dimension to the existing role-content categorization of play. As we examined the social pretend role-play of our 3-year-olds, we were confronted by a paradoxical phenomenon with respect to its relation to existing approaches to the study of young children's social and pretend role-play. On the one hand, the research on role content previously cited (e.g., Garvey, 1982, Garvey & Berndt, 1977) appeared quite compatible with the types of roles enacted by our subjects when these roles were analyzed for their content. In contrast, no existing system seemed to capture an aspect of the children's pretend play that we have termed *social role structure* (Garvey & Berndt, 1977; Iwanaga, 1973; Parten, 1932; Rubin, Maioni, & Hornung, 1976; Smilansky, 1968). The system presented here involves simultaneous consideration of the children's pretend roles and the forms of realistic social interaction taking place while one or both members of a dyad are pretending.

This two-dimensional analysis begins with role content assignment and subsequently evaluates the social structure of the dyad in relation to the content role(s) played by one or both. For a given play incident the role-content category for each child (i.e., functional, relational, occupational, fantasy) was first assigned individually and categorized by specific role content enacted. Thus specific role-content categories within the more general functional category might be grooming, cooking, or feeding. The dyadic social role structure was then derived, based on (1) comparison of the specific content roles of both players and (2) their social interaction.

SOCIAL ROLE STRUCTURE

In this section we describe the social role structure categories and report their proportional occurrence across dyads. Later, when role-content results are considered, the contribution of this analysis to an overall understanding of the children's social pretend becomes apparent.

The system for examining social role structure comprised two major categories, Solo Role-Play and Interactive Role-Play, which were each further divided into subcategories. Although our primary interest was in social-interactive play, it proved useful to consider the total corpus of pretending provided by the children. This distinction was (first) based entirely on child–child role relationships. The role of dolls was considered separately, and could be coded as nested within any Solo or Interactive subcategory.

In Solo Role-Play, only one of the play partners enacted a pretend role. Three categories were identified that varied in the degree of participation by the non-role-playing partner. Solo—Alone occurred when one child pretended—and the other appeared oblivious to the role enactment. Thus either one or both players could be engaged in Solo—Alone at the same point in time, as long as they were not attending to one another. In Solo—With Audience only one child enacted a role, with the partner observing but not interacting. This sometimes provided a prelude to Interactive Role-Play, as exemplified by L&A's separate but sequential cooking Solos described earlier. Solo—With Advisor refers to those occasions when the non-role-playing partner engaged in verbal interaction with the role-player, which usually consisted in directives or questions about the pretend role enactment. For example, L. frequently served as child-care advisor in response to A.'s statements that "my baby are still crying," usually with suggestions that the "baby" be fed or put to bed.

In Interactive Role-Play, the play partners each enacted a content role and both were involved in pretend interaction. Interactive Role-Play was coded as Shared Role-Play when both players adopted the same specific content role or as Differentiated Role-Play when different specific content roles were portrayed. An example of a shared role played by all of the dyads was the functional role of meal preparation, where each child would carry out different aspects of meal preparation (e.g., cooking, table setting, making toast), often with verbal planning and negotiation. The episode was often terminated prior to eating the meal, but on several occasions the players did eat together. In so doing, they jointly enacted a role set: first the functional role of meal preparation, followed by the functional role complement of eating the meal. Shared Role-Play involves parallel enactment of noncomplementary roles, although occasionally the children would, as described earlier, both engage in one Shared Role and then engage in the complement of that role. In this study Differentiated Role-Play was restricted to relatively simple complementary enactments, such as one child feeding another. The steps involved in the categorization process are illustrated in Table 2.

Child–Doll Role-Play

The children showed a more developed capacity to portray differentiated roles in their play with dolls and stuffed animals, which were often "cared for" as part of Solo events, or imbedded in interactive events involving the partner. However, inclusion of such play in the Differentiated role category would distort the children's sociodramatic control of this ability. Their complementary portrayal of "caregiver" and "baby" using dolls hardly presents the social or cognitive challenge of sharing representational meanings with an animate partner. Doll play itself represents a continuum of development. Such play is observed early in the second year, and probably begins as a representation of the global care-giving experience rather than portrayal of differentiated roles. When the dolls take on moods and experience desires, as they do in the hands of 3-year-olds, their status as highly compliant differentiated role partners becomes evident. Dolls may represent a transitional step to child–child Differentiated Role Play.

Table 2

Flowchart for Determining the Social Role Structure of a Pretend Episode

Criteria for determining codes	Social role structure codes
Determining Solo versus Interactive structure	
1. Is either child pretending?	
If *no* for both _____	No code
If *yes* for one, *no* for the other _____	Solo
If *yes* for both, consider:	
2. Is there social interaction *within* pretend?	
If *no* _____	Solo
If *yes*_____	Interactive
Determining social role structure	
Solo episodes	
3. Consider *nonpretend* social interaction in the episode.	
If *no* interaction (i.e., partner ignores or is unaware of Solo, or	
both children perform separate but simultaneous solos) _____	Solo—Alone
If nonpretender *observes* _____	Solo—With Audience
If nonpretender *verbalizes* concerning *pretend*_____	Solo—With Advisor
Interactive episodes	
4. Consider match of specific role content of players.	
If *match* _____	Interactive, Shared
If *nonmatch* _____	Interactive, Differentiated

Proportional Results

When the play sessions in this study were analyzed using the social role structure categories, individual differences were observed in the extent to which the
dyads enacted the various role types. Table 3 presents the proportion of the
pretend role-play in each of the three social role-structure categories (Solo,
Shared, Differentiated). In contrast to the interdyad variability, each dyad
showed consistency across the two sessions in the proportion of role-play in each
category.

All of the children engaged in Solo Role-Play despite the availability of a
partner. For dyads J.&K. and AA.&JJ., this was the favored type of role-play
in both sessions. L.&A., who were the most communicative and symbolically
inclined pair, showed proportionally less Solo play than the other dyads, and
engaged in Solo and Shared Role-Play with approximately equal frequency. An
analysis of the Solo subcategories, which is not given in Table 3, revealed that
both J.&K. and AA.&JJ. spent approximately half their time in the Alone and
Audience subcategories, with only one instance per session of Solo—with Ad-

Table 3

Proportions of Pretend in Social Role Structure Categories

Role category	Session I	Session II
AA&JJ		
Solo	0.66	0.58
Shared	0.22	0.25
Differentiated	0.11	0.16
	Solo ⪢ Shared > Differentiated	Solo ⪢ Shared > Differeniated
J&K		
Solo	0.64	0.51
Shared	0.21	0.26
Differentiated	0.15	0.23
	Solo ⪢ (Shared = Differentiated)	Solo ⪢ (Shared = Differentiated)
L&A		
Solo	0.38	0.40
Shared	0.39	0.40
Differentiated	0.23	0.19
	(Solo = Shared) > Differentiated	(Solo = Shared) > Differentiated

visor. The play of L.&A., on the other hand, was dominated by instances of the Audience and Advisor subcategories, with only rare instances of Solo—Alone enactments.

Within the Interactive Role-Play category, the proportion of Shared Role-Play exceeded that of Differentiated Role-Play for both L.&A. and AA.&JJ. J.&K.'s Interactive Role-Play was quite evenly divided between the two subcategories, as can be seen in Table 3. L.&A. engaged in substantially more Shared Role-Play than J.&K. and AA.&JJ., whose proportions of Shared episodes were quite similar. Shared Role-Play sequences tended to be relatively lengthier and to contain more complex interactions than Differentiated Role-Play for all three dyads. The content types most frequently enacted in Shared Role-Play were caretaking (of the dolls), cooking, and other aspects of meal preparation, tool use, grooming, and adorning with jewelry.

Entry into Shared Role-Play episodes was frequently initiated by one child, who was joined by the other after a very brief period; at other times Shared Role-Play was entered simultaneously, usually as the result of a suggestion or invitation by one of the children. In the former case, the initial actions of the second child could be called imitative. However, once Shared Role-Play was entered, it was no longer an imitative enactment by one of the children. Both pretended within the same specific role-content type (e.g., caretaking), but their actions were self-generated and individualistic.

The findings that Shared Role-Play was favored over Differentiated Role-Play and that more complex interactive sequences were enacted in the Shared social structure suggest that this form of social role-play may represent an early form of social pretending that, due to its relatively simple social structure (i.e., only one type of specific role content), facilitates the maintenance of pretend interactions.

Differentiated Role-Play was relatively infrequent in the pretend role-play of all dyads, as the low proportions in Table 3 indicate. Both AA.&JJ.'s and J.&K.'s Differentiated Role-Play was characterized by brief, complementary actions such as one child dressing, grooming, or adorning the other, often followed by role reversal. Other instances of Differentiated Role-Play enactments were the server–eater episodes of AA.&JJ. and J.&K.'s tea party with serving and drinking. The majority of L.&A.'s Differentiated Role-Play was accounted for by the driver–passenger sequences enacted on their trips. Two episodes of feeding–eating and a few brief instances of dressing and adorning were enacted.

A developmental interpretation of these results suggests that children may move from a predominance of Solo Role-Play (i.e., AA.&JJ., J.&K.), to increased Shared Role-Play (i.e., L.&A.), and finally to a predominance of Differentiated Role-Play, such as the "doctor" play of the mature role-players described at the opening of this chapter.

ROLE-CONTENT ANALYSIS

We also examined the role-play data from the perspective of the role-content categories of Garvey and Berndt (1977) and Garvey (1982). In this descriptive analysis we used four major categories: functional, relational (family), occupational, and fantasy roles, defined earlier in the chapter.

Functional and Relational

Despite substantial interdyad differences, the roles exhibited by these 3-year-olds were predominantly functional or relational in that order of frequency. For L.&A. and J.&K., the girl pairs, all relational role-play was child–doll role-play, in which the children enacted the roles of unnamed caretakers in both Solo and Interactive episodes. A balance between such relational role-play and functional role-play was shown by L.&A. in both sessions and by J.&K. in Session I. In J.&K.'s Session II play, child–doll role-play rarely occurred and functional role play predominated.

In contrast, the boys AA.&JJ. exhibited no child–doll role-play in either session, despite the availability of three dolls and an assortment of stuffed animals.

(When they did play with the panda bears it was not in a pretend manner.) These children were the only pair to engage in child–child relational role-play, although functional role-play strongly predominated in their pretend play. The relational role-play these children exhibited was largely motivated by JJ.'s desire (which became more explicit as the sessions progressed) to enact the role of "baby" or "little boy," and to assign the role of "caretaker-feeder" to A.A. Initially, AA. did not readily cooperate with this plan, partially because both immature articulation and lack of metacommunicative skill limited JJ.'s ability to convey his plan.

JJ.'s first mention of his role assumption occurred as he attempted to "sleep" in a small doll cradle in imitation of AA., who was in a child-size bed: "Mine, I gotta sleep here. I'ze a little boy." JJ. attempted to fit himself into this doll-size bed several times, even when AA. had abandoned the larger bed. Given JJ.'s real-life status as a little boy, his role intention remained ambiguous until he reported it to his mother outside the playroom at the end of Session I. He had concentrated throughout the session on persuading AA. to cook dinner for him. For example, as AA. engaged in manipulative play with the jewelry, such remarks as "It's for dinner?" (i.e., bracelets) and "For dinner, please" (i.e., pearls) failed to affect AA.'s behavior. JJ. finally succeeded in getting AA. to hold a baby bottle in his mouth, after which JJ. took it in hand and fed himself. He then exited the room and informed his mother that "It's a baby bottle, and I a baby boy."

From the outset of Session II, AA. showed that he understood his complementary role in JJ.'s plan, and alternated between cooperating by "making dinner" and "feeding" JJ. and thwarting this plan. Because interactive relational role-play was coded for this dyad only on the infrequent occasions when AA. cooperated, the frequency of functional role-play greatly exceeded that of relational. The high frequency of functional play exhibited by this dyad contributed disproportionally to the overall summary score.

Solo. Separate examination of the functional and relational role content of the structural category Solo Role-Play revealed that relational role-play predominated for L.&A. in both sessions and for J.&K. in their first session. Relational Solos were rare in J.&K.'s second session and in both sessions for AA.&JJ., where functional roles predominated. JJ. was credited with the "baby" role on several occasions when he drank from a baby bottle or sat in a doll-size high chair.

Interactive. Within the Interactive Role structure, the functional content category dominated across dyads. However, a sizable proportion of child–doll relational play was observed for L.&A., who frequently engaged in Shared Role-Play where both girls enacted caretaking roles to one or two dolls. J.&K.'s Interactive relational play was also Shared Role-Play but was infrequent and occurred only in Session I. All of AA.&JJ.'s relational role-play occurred when AA. cooperated as caregiver to JJ.'s "baby" role. Because this was child–child role-play it was considered in the Differentiated category.

Two unusual forms of relational role assignments to dolls, which were not subsequently developed to any degree, occurred in L.&A.'s sessions. Following a long debate over whether or not A. would accompany L. to a meeting or stay at home and "take care of the babies," L. designated a large doll as "the daddy" who could stay at home and babysit. When A. did not concur, L. abandoned her role assignment and designated the doll as "baby," but continued to refer to it as "he" in contrast to the other dolls.

A. also assigned non-"baby" roles to the dolls during what began as a Shared caretaking episode. She first designated two dolls as "one a boy and one a girl both"; there was no further development of this transformation until somewhat later when she told L. "Tomorrow, they're going to get married and they're both gonna live in this house forever and ever," to which L. responded "I know, they're married."

An additional role mention occurred when L.&A. were on the last of several searches for a "hose thing" to fix their car, which had run out of gas, and A. exclaimed, "We need a daddy." When L. responded with an incredulous look and said "What?", A. repeated her statement, then looked embarrassed, quickly grabbed a panda bear, and in an exaggerated voice said, "Daddy bear, Mommy bear, Daddy, bear."

Occupational and Fantasy

Role-play in the occupational and fantasy content categories occurred far less frequently than functional and relational roles. AA.&JJ. exhibited no clear instance of either type, although several elaborated role enactments (i.e., tool use, painting) approached occupational status, as when AA. accompanied his painting actions with the statement "I'm painting the house." J.&K. enacted only one occupational role, that of doctor, and no fantasy role in their sessions. The "doctor" role was first played by J., who used pieces of jewelry and a flashlight as medical tools. Among J.'s many attempts to persuade K. to play the "patient" role were questions in which she obliquely labeled her role, as she asked a silent, staring K. "Wanna get checked by the doctor?" When it was cleared that K. would not enact the complementary patient role, J. proceeded to "fix" the "sick" doll.

J. performed four Solo—With Audience doctor episodes with doll as "patient," which were followed by an episode of Shared Role-Play in which both girls played as "doctors," at first with a single doll "patient" and later each with her own. Following this, K. took her doll, a flashlight, and some jewelry to a corner of the room, where she enacted a Solo—Alone "doctor" episode.

L.&A.'s "doctor" play began when L. took the stethoscope, which A. had discovered hanging on a hook, and performed a Solo—with Audience, listening to the doll's heart (and other parts) quite thoroughly as A. watched. A. then engaged in similar "doctor" behavior in a Solo—With Advisor episode, as L. told her to "Check that baby." Other occupational roles played by L.&A. were an announced "carpenter" role by A. ("I'll be a carpenter. It's surely fun"), a rocket ship pilot by L. who used plastic bracelets as "fire things" to count down, ("10–9–1–2–9–rocket ship") and blast off (throwing bracelets), and a peripheral role (i.e., mentioned but not assumed) of "plumber," whom A. first identified as needed to fix a sink problem identified by L. ("no more water") and who apparently arrived surreptitiously during the session according to A. ("Now the plumber came. Now we'll have more water").

Fantasy characters were also mentioned and enacted by L.&A. in both sessions. A. assumed the roles of "bride" putting on a "marrying dress" and telling L. that she was getting married, identified herself as "like a stepmother" when she was dressed in a "beautiful veiled gown," and seemed to be enacting the role of "entertainer" as she pantomimed in front of a large mirror and repeated in an exaggerated voice "evening all"—all of this in Solo pretend.

L.&A. engaged in sustained Shared Role-Play sequences as "genies," which evolved into "genie ladies" in Session I and "genie meanies" in Session II. The exact nature of a "genie" was not apparent to the observers but was well understood by both girls. The role was introduced by L. who took a fringed adult-sized vest, put her head through an armhole, and told A., "You hafta be a genie. I'm a genie. Take this (a feather duster), and be a genie lady." As L. then leaped about the room, flapping her hands and the fringe, A. put on a filmy nightgown, said "Look what this genie put on!", and, with feather duster in hand, followed L. around the room. The "genies" worked magic (e.g., "bippety, boppity, boo"), had extended conversations about what "genies" like to do, with L. speaking in the first person (e.g., "I'm a genie, and I like to eat"), and A. referring to herself as "this genie" or "a genie." Additional fantasy roles, although not assumed by L.&A., were mentioned in discussion or invented. Thus a "tooth fairy" came "in a dark bedroom", "guests" were expected, and a "monster" hovered near the ceiling for a short period.

THEMES AT 3 YEARS OF AGE

As we began to compile a taxonomy of themes, it became clear that often the specific content of the role identified the theme. At this early age, it was only in rare cases, varying greatly across dyads, that the role structure remained relatively stable, and change was expressed through development of the theme. In general, little variation among dyads was shown in the content of the themes enacted, with most of them pertaining to home- and family-centered activities.

The most popular theme of both girl dyads was that of "adorning" (i.e., dressing up, putting on jewelry, grooming), which was also enacted by AA.&JJ. fairly often and occurred at every social-structure level. All dyads engaged in many sequences of meal preparation, which was the most frequent theme in AA.&JJ.'s play. These themes were closely followed in frequency of occurrence by the caretaking themes of feeding and bedding the dolls in the case of the girls, and the feeding of JJ. as "baby" in the boys' play. Other themes frequently enacted by all dyads were eating, fixing, cleaning, and dressing–undressing the dolls.

The best example of a social pretend play episode that required separate analyses of the role-play and theme components was an impressive dramatization by L.&A., which extended across 40 minutes of their first play session and was reinstated and enacted for shorter periods in Session II. We refer to the episode as "the fancy meeting" for reasons that will become apparent; however, its theme is more accurately described as traveling. During this lengthy episode, L.&A. were engaged in continuous social interaction dominated by social pretending and negotiations, which were thematically organized around the central event of traveling in a pretend car (the wooden apparatus in the stairs position).

In this episode, L.&A. implemented a complex social role structure consisting of the alternating use of functional Differentiated Role-Play (i.e., driver and passenger), which was in effect whenever the girls were in the car, and Shared Role-Play, which was used on the many occasions when travel-related activities were enacted. Relational (child–doll) role-play was sometimes embedded in the child–child role structure, and at other times (out of the car) caretaker roles were the primary specific content of Shared Role-Play sequences. Thus, in its most complex form, the role structure enacted by L.&A. involved the simultaneous enactment of the Differentiated Roles of "driver" and "passenger," the Shared relational roles of caretakers to the doll "babies," and additional assignment of a passenger role to the "babies."

Despite its complexity and its integral relation to the theme, the social role structure was relatively static when compared to the rapidly changing events that occurred in the development of the theme. Consequently, the theme of this social pretend play episode and others with similar complex and novel qualities could not be adequately summarized by a description of the role structure.

Our description of the theme development of the "fancy meeting" episode reflects the extent to which this lengthy span of sustained pretend interaction was guided by a shared knowledge of the event sequences involved in traveling in a car, and the contribution of other social and representational abilities.

The episode was instigated by A., who in response to L.'s inquiry if she wanted any popcorn said "No, we're going to a fancy meeting." L. then rejected this proposal (i.e., "No"), but several minutes later when A. suggested it a second time, L. (playing with the jewelry at the time) was interested: "Yeah, but you gotta take your jewelry." L.&A. immediately began to adorn themselves with jewelry, but did not embark on their trip until several minutes later when L. discovered the car keys. L. then stated that "We're going bye-bye," designated the wooden stairs as the car, and pantomimed unlocking and opening the door for A. as she entered the car. Once A. was seated in the car (on one side of the stairs), L. walked around to the other side and sat down with her back to A. These were the positions the two girls occupied throughout the episode, whenever they were in the car. From her front position, L. drove the car with an imaginary steering wheel and the keys, usually with a directive to A. such as "OK, we're going bye-bye now. Get in your seat!" L. also frequently invented car-related troubles such as running out of gas or crashes, which interrupted the trip and caused the two girls to leave the car in order to repair the current difficulty.

When A. was in the car, she consistently played the role of passenger, sat in the back-seat position facing L.'s back, and sometimes made passenger like comments such as "When are we gonna get there? We've been in the car so long." Whereas L.'s announced plans most frequently were concerned with car troubles, A.'s pronouncements were often concerned with the destination of the trip, which, in addition to the fancy meeting, included a fancy meeting at "Bubba" (Borough?) Hall, Arizona, Calizona (L's suggestion), a picnic, a fancy picnic, and a fancy picnic at Bubba Hall.

On several occasions, A. attempted to assume the role of driver with such actions as sitting on L.'s end of the stairs, picking up the car keys, and putting on a fur stole that L. wore when enacting the "driver" role. At such times, L. reclaimed her role by taking the prop from A. and by directing A. to sit in the passenger's seat (i.e., "Oops, you're still in my seat. I gotta sit here. You sit in back here"). Although A. never put forth a direct challenge to L. these incidents were shortly followed by A.'s refusal to go in the car, usually expressed within the pretend mode by way of the dolls. A's two favorite excuses for refusing to go on a trip were her need to care for her baby, who was either sick, crying, tired, or her baby's dislike of the idea (e.g., "This baby want to go to bed. She said she wanted to"). These refusals by A. usually resulted in L.&A. engaging in some form of caretaking activity, followed by lengthy negotiations in which L. attempted to persuade A. to get in the car and A. maintained the importance of staying home and not going to the meeting.

In addition to the car troubles, the trip was interrupted for the purposes of obtaining props, provisions, and accessories, and for providing for the needs of the "babies" and the "kids" who accompanied the players on some journeys (but on other occasions were left at home for a variety of reasons). These events occurred either as plans were being made to get into the car, as in the following excerpt, or while a trip was in progress, when one of the players would think of something that was urgently needed and the trip would stop while the need was fulfilled. As Session II began, L.&A. initiated a traveling episode in the following fairly articulate manner.

L. Get in the car.
A. Are we goin to the fancy meeting?
L. Yeah, but you havta get your fancy things.
A. My jewelry?
L. No. You havta get your brushes.
A. And my hat too? (Takes hat.)
L. No! That hat. (points to another hat) I havta put my hat on 'cause its raining.
    Quick it's raining. Open the doors, get in the car.

Then L.&A. climbed into the car with hats on, holding hair brushes, combs, and mirrors, and continued their journey, which functioned for the observers as our most fascinating sojourn into the private world of 3-year-old players.

INTEGRATING THE STRUCTURAL PROPERTIES

In contrast with mature sociodramatic participants, these 3-year-olds have been portrayed as "role-players" where role often defines theme, objects enhance roles, and communication in and out of pretend often strengthens roles, although on some occasions it moves thematic action forward. Role-playing itself often involved sharing the same role. This contrasts with the conventions observed in older children's play, in which each role is normally occupied by a single player. No doubt the infrequency of differentiated roles limited the children's ability to play out themes with which they were familiar. For example, both girl pairs played a "doctor" theme, sharing the role of "doctor," with the doll as "patient." In contrast, in the Smilansky example presented at the beginning of the chapter roles were sorted out and the order of play planned metacommunicatively prior to enactment.

The central role of objects in the children's play is apparent in the descriptive vignettes included in the chapter. However, remote object transformations were infrequent in these data, possibly due to the availability of many highly realistic props. The children did use substitute objects, playing with reality in interesting ways. Thus the feather duster was used as a wand and named the "feather-wander." In Session I, L. defined the sponge as a cake. When A. in Session II asked "Is this a cake?" L. replied, "No, it's a sponge."

Objects were used as essential props supporting both theme (e.g., the stairs as a car promoting the traveling theme) and roles. To be a "genie" one needed a fantastic garment; the dominant role of "driver" in the traveling theme was defined by ownership of the keys and the single fur piece available. Objects often suggested the content of play. For AA.&JJ. the play foods elicited a cooking scene, the paintbrushes the functional role of painter. The "fancy meeting" travel sequence actually began with L.'s taking the keys and announcing the theme with "Let's go bye-bye."

Communications within pretend served many functions. They represented events (such as L.&A.'s traveling disasters) that were never enacted. They also served in varying degrees to enhance role enactments. Their contribution to role enactment seemed to form a continuum: In functional roles the within-pretend statements had a descriptive quality (e.g., "I'm painting the house") and differentiated play with dolls involved empathic higher-pitched "mother" talk as the girls interacted with their "babies." In the "genie" episode, pretend language (e.g., "This genie likes . . . ") seemed to convert the pretend episode into an opportunity for the children to express some of their own personal preferences.

Most of the metacommunications of our 3-year-olds were implicit, and occurred both in and out of the pretend mode. For example, all functional role-play, which is defined as enacting an unnamed role, can be viewed as metacommunicative in the context of social pretending. Many instances of Solo—With Audience appeared to have metacommunicative properties in the sense that they seem to express the message "Let's pretend."

Explicit metacommunications occurred most frequently to announce pretend events or plans. They occurred rarely for roles, as the high frequency of functional role-play indicates. Explicit metacommunications were used effectively to announce object substitutions, but as we have already indicated, such transformations were performed infrequently.

All of the structural properties apparent in the sample of well-formed play presented earlier in the chapter were seen in primitive form in our young pretenders. Given greater familiarity, or a more mature partner, more advanced forms might be dramatized at age 3 years.

CONCLUSIONS

As represented by the children in this study, 3-year-olds appear competent in managing their social interactions in the play setting, both in moving from stranger status to acquaintanceship and in conveying to a partner the pretend meanings that they would like to share. These children were not yet mature sociodramatic players, like Smilansky's older subjects, despite the considerable skill they displayed. It may be that closely acquainted children would have presented more full-blown dramatic episodes. Alternatively, such familiars might reach social engagement earlier in a session and/or show more frequent socio-dramatic play of no greater maturity than observed in the present study. To what extent are the limitations observed in 3-year-olds such as those in this study reflective of social experience and the particular social context, and to what extent do they reflect a level of cognitive development less mature than that of the typical 4-year-old? The year between ages 3 and 4 is the target period for answering these questions with a more comprehensive research strategy.

ACKNOWLEDGMENTS

We would like to express appreciation to the mothers and children who participated in the study, to Barbara Glazewski and Sadie Julius of the Douglass College Speech Department who generously provided the furnished playroom in the Gatehouse Nursery for the study, and to our colleague Beth Lennon for her assistance with the videotaping. Special thanks are due to Inge Bretherton for her support and guidance during the writing of this chapter.

REFERENCES

Bateson, G. The message "this is play." In B. Schaffner (Ed.), *Group processes: Transactions of the second conference.* New York: Josiah Macy, Jr. Foundation, 1956.

Brenner, J., & Mueller, E. Shared meaning in boy toddlers' peer relations. *Child Development,* 1982, *53,* 380–391.

Doyle, A. B., Connolly, J., & Rivest, L. P. The effect of playmate familiarity on the social interactions of young children. *Child Development,* 1980, *51,* 217–223.

Elder, J. L., & Pederson, D. R. Preschool children's use of objects in symbolic play. *Child Development,* 1978, *49,* 500–504.

El'Konin, D. Symbolics and its functions in the play of children. *Soviet Education,* 1966, *8,* 35–41.

Fein, G. G. Play and the acquisition of symbols. In L. G. Katz (Ed.), *Current topics in early childhood education* (Vol. 11), Norwood, NJ: Ablex, 1979.

Fein, G. G. Pretend play in childhood: An integrative review. *Child Development,* 1981, *52,* 1095–1118.

Garvey, C. An approach to the study of children's role play. *The Quarterly Newsletter of the Laboratory of Comparative Human Cognition,* 1979, *1,* 69–73.

Garvey, C. Communication and the development of social role play. In D. Forbes & M. T. Greenberg (Eds.), *Children's planning strategies.* San Francisco: Jossey-Bass, 1982.

Garvey, C., & Berndt, R. The organization of pretend play. JSAS *Catalog of Selected Documents in Psychology,* 1977, *7.* (Ms. No. 1589)

Huttenlocher, J., & Higgins, E. T. Issues in the study of symbolic development. In W. A. Collins (Ed.), *Minnesota Symposia on Child Psychology* (Vol. 11). Hillsdale, NJ: Erlbaum, 1978.

Iwanaga, M. Development of interpersonal play structure in three, four, and five year-old children. *Journal of Research and Development in Education*, 1973, *6*, 71–82.

Jackowitz, E. R., & Watson, M. W. Development of object transformations in early pretend play. *Developmental Psychology*, 1980, *16*, 543–549.

Jeffers, V. W., & Lore, R. K. Let's play at my house: Effects of the home environment on the social behavior of children. *Child Development*, 1979, *50*, 837–841.

Lewis, M., Young, G., Brooks, J., & Michalson, L. The beginning of friendship. In M. Lewis & L. Rosenblum (Eds.), *The origins of behavior* (Vol. 4). *Friendship and Peer Relations*. New York: Wiley, 1975.

McCune-Nicolich, L., & Fenson, L. Methodological issues in studying early pretend play. In T. D. Yawkey & A. D. Pellgrini (Eds.), *Child's play: Developmental and applied*. Hillsdale, NJ: Erlbaum, 1983.

Matthews, W. S. Modes of transformation in the initiation of fantasy play. *Developmental Psychology*, 1977, *13*, 212–216.

Matthews, W. S., & Matthews, R. J. Eliminating operational definitions: A paradigm case approach to the study of fantasy play. In D. J. Pepler & K. Rubin (Eds.), *The play of children: Current theory and research*. Basel: Karger, 1982.

Mead, G. H. *Mind, self, and society*. Chicago: University of Chicago Press, 1934.

Nicolich, L. Beyond sensorimotor intelligence: Assessment of symbolic maturity through analysis of pretend play. *Merrill-Palmer Quarterly*, 1977, *23*, 89–99.

Parten, M. B. Social participation among pre-school children. *Journal of Abnormal and Social Psychology*, 1932, *27*, 243–269.

Piaget, J. *Play, dreams and imitation in childhood*. New York: Norton, 1962. (Originally published, 1946.)

Rubin, K. H., Fein, G. G., & Vandenberg, B. Play. In P. Mussen & E. M. Hetherington (Eds.), *Handbook of Child Psychology*, (4th ed.). *Socialization: Personality and social development* (Vol. 4) New York: Wiley, 1983.

Rubin, K. H., Maioni, T. L., & Hornung, M. Free play behaviors in middle- and lower-class preschoolers: Parten and Piaget revisited. *Child Development*, 1976, *47*, 414–419.

Saltz, E., & Brodie, J. Pretend play training in childhood: A review and critique. In D. J. Pepler & K. H. Rubin (Eds.), *The play of children: Current theory and research*. Basel: Karger, 1982.

Sarbin, T. R., & Allen, V. L. Role theory. In G. Lindzey & E. Aronson (Eds.), *The handbook of social psychology* (2nd ed., Vol. 1). Reading, MA: Addison-Wesley, 1968.

Schank, R. C., & Abelson, R. P. Scripts, plans, and knowledge. In P. N. Johnson-Laird & P. C. Wason (Eds.), *Thinking: Readings in cognitive science*. Cambridge: Cambridge University Press, 1977.

Schwartzman, H. B. *Transformations: The anthropology of children's play*. New York: Plenum Press, 1978.

Schwarz, J. C. Effect of peer familiarity on the behavior of preschoolers in novel situations. *Journal of Personality and Social Psychology*, 1972, *24*, 276–284.

Smilansky, S. *The effects of sociodramatic play on disadvantaged preschool children*. New York: Wiley, 1968.

Stone, G. P. The play of little children. In R. E. Herron & B. Sutton-Smith (Eds.), *Child's play*. New York: Wiley, 1971. (Originally published, 1965.)

Watson, M. W., & Fischer, K. W. Development of social roles in elicited and spontaneous behavior during the preschool years. *Developmental Psychology*, 1980, *16*, 483–494.

PART III

Symbolic Play with Toys and Words

CHAPTER 7

Agency and Experience: Actions and States in Play Narratives*

DENNIS PALMER WOLF
JAYNE RYGH
JENNIFER ALTSHULER

INTRODUCTION

Through the efforts of clinicians and cognitive developmentalists, we have come to understand how gradually young children realize that other people's actions, feelings, perceptions, and thoughts may differ from their own. For example, Mahler, Bergman, and Pine describe what they call the psychological birth of the human infant (1975) as a process of slow separation of the self from others in which infants slowly realize that other people are independent beings with distinct histories and agendas (Mahler *et al.*, 1975; Wolf, 1982). From quite a different vantage point, Piaget has argued a similar point:

*This paper was prepared using data originally collected in the Early Symbolization Project, a longitudinal study of early symbolic development funded by the Carnegie Corporation and the Spencer Foundation. The re-analysis described here has been funded by a grant from the Mailman Foundation.

> The child being ignorant of his own ego takes his own point of view as absolute and fails to establish between himself and the external world of things that reciprocity which alone would ensure objectivity [Piaget, 1926, p. 197].

However, the recognition of the distance that separates self from other is only one hemisphere of social understanding. Social cognition also demands an awareness of the *shared* dimensions of human behavior—or a knowledge of those behaviors and internal responses that make people alike despite differences in age, point of view, or roles. Even in very young children, we have implicit evidence for the early development of an appreciation for these shared dimensions. Children, as early as 2 years of age, adopt formats such as conversations and games in order to share plans and meanings with others (Garvey, 1977; Mueller, Bleir, Karkow, Hegedus, & Cournagen, 1977). Between the ages of 3 and 4 years, childrens' accounts of familiar events presume that their listeners share the same basic scripts for basic human routines (Schank & Abelson, 1977). Between ages 28 and 36 months, children begin to use their linguistic capacities to label and describe a basic set of experiential capacities in themselves and other human actors (Bretherton & Beeghly-Smith, 1982). In these same years, the ability to respond empathetically to the situations of other people (Zahn-Waxler, Radke-Yarrow, & King, 1979) also emerges.

Thus, the ability to understand others includes at least two conceptions: (1) Human beings are alike in basic ways. Like ourselves, other people are both *agents,* the performers of overt actions that cause observable events, and *experiencers,* hosts to internal but powerful events such as perception, sensation, emotion, and cognition. (2) Despite these shared capacities, as human agents we act independently and our own thoughts and feelings may not predict the internal states another person will experience in the same situation. Hence, understanding human behavior involves an appreciation of what is common to human actors as well as a sensitivity to the limits on that commonality. But although clinical and developmental research have left us with considerable understanding of children's knowledge of the differences between self and other, we have relatively little empirical or theoretical information about children's notions of what is common to human actors. Nevertheless, both children's own actions and their representations of human actions in speech and play contain considerable evidence for both the intrinsic importance and the rapidly changing nature of their concepts of others. Consider these instances of doll play, performed by the same child between the ages of 1 and 5 years, taken from our study, described here later.

J. (at 1:3) Picks up his large baby doll, stands up in a rocking chair and drops the doll into his crib. He throws his own favorite blanket in after the doll. Looking over the edge, he calls out "Ni—ni."

J. (at 2:0) Finds an enclosure made from blocks. He picks up a small figure with a wide-brimmed hat on: "Farmer want a bath. Gonna give farmer a bath." J. pretends to turn on imaginary faucets at one end of the enclosure. He swishes the figure around briefly, then says "Oh, no, soooooo hot. Gotta put some cold in." He makes the farmer figure get out and pretends to add some more water from the imaginary faucets. J. then puts the farmer back into the "bath." "Oh, no, sooooo hot, too hot. Ouch. Gotta put some cold in." He makes the figure hop out of the bath again.

J. (at 4:11) Is finishing a story in which a toy dragon takes a pond from the animals who live in a forest. He walks a group of large animals over to a group of small animals.

J. (speaks as the narrator). "The jungle (larger) animals lie to the small creatures."

J. (makes a large hippo speak to the small animals). "The pond is still here. It's just invisible."

J. (speaks as a small animal). "I will go and tell my friends."
He makes that small animal whisper to the other small animals.

J. (speaks as the narrator). "But the (large) animals lied. And the hippo goes like this." He makes the hippo act as if it were drinking from the spot where the pond once was. "So that the small creatures will think that the pond is still there."

In the first example the child represents only the routines that typically involve human actors. In the second example he portrays the focus and persistence that characterize human agency: The little farmer jumps into the bath, finds it uncomfortable, makes adjustments, tries again. In this same example the child also represents human activity as a mix of action and experience (e.g., taking a bath and feeling uncomfortable). In the third example, the narrow focus on physical sensations as a form of internal experience widens to a capacity for representing complex psychological experiences such as planning and deceit.

In this chapter, we are interested in filling out the picture of early social cognition by describing how children between the ages of 1 and 5 years construct an understanding of the fundamental and *common* dimensions of human behavior. As a first step, we discuss data from a longitudinal study of nine children's representations of human behavior in spontaneous and elicited play sessions. The data are analyzed in order to answer two basic sets of questions.

1. Outside of real-life situations in which people raise their voices, cry, or laugh, is there evidence that young children have any explicit knowledge of how other human beings are likely to act or experience the world? If so, how do children build up a repertoire of actions and states that can be attributed to others? What do such findings imply about the major steps through which children's concepts of others develop between late infancy and the age of 5 years?

2. Does this kind of social understanding develop in a regular fashion across individuals? Do some individuals progress more rapidly than others in this domain? Do individuals or groups exhibit differences in the way that they make use of their ability to comment on human behavior?

THE PROBLEMS OF ASSESSING CHILDREN'S CONCEPTS OF OTHERS

Many earlier assessments of children's knowledge of and responsiveness to others' experience depend heavily on overt behaviors such as bids for attention or offers of help. In part, this reliance on observable action derives from the realization that young children are still learning to represent their thoughts and thus what they *do* may be a more reliable test of their understanding than what they say. However, some research has documented changes in both the form and the content of children's symbolic productions that offer strong and potentially reliable indices of change in children's concepts of others. Thus, even during the preschool years children adapt their speech in response to the age and knowledge of their listeners, use language to share their thoughts and plans with others, and develop a vocabulary for describing internal states in themselves and other people (Bretherton & Beeghly-Smith, 1982; Bretherton, McNew, & Beeghly-Smith, 1981; Garvey, 1977; Giffin, 1983, Chapter 3, this volume; Sachs & Devin, 1976; Shatz & Gelman, 1973; Wolf & Pusch, in press). At as early as 1 year of age, children's play renditions of familiar events or scripts also provide us with a picture of their knowledge of the daily routines characteristic of men, women, babies, or children (Nelson, 1981; Nicolich, 1977; Schank & Abelson, 1977). Over time, these representations shift from imitations of characteristic actions to impersonations that include the speech and mannerisms of real-life or fantasy characters. And, as clinicians have long realized, some of the richest representations of human thought and activity occur once children are able to project what they know of human behavior onto small toys and dolls that serve as replicas for themselves and other people (Erikson, 1950, 1972; Freud, 1959; Klein, 1955; Lowe, 1965; Rubin & Wolf, 1979; Scarlett & Wolf, 1979; Winnicott, 1971).

REPLICA PLAY: A SOURCE OF KNOWLEDGE ABOUT CHILDREN'S CONCEPTS OF OTHERS

Virtually all normal children use toys to create and dramatize events provided that they have the materials and the familial or cultural permission to make-believe (Fein & Stork, 1981). However revealing replica-based narratives are to clinicians, they remain largely unexplored as a source of information about developmentally, rather than individually, founded conceptions of human actions, states, or motivations. This is unfortunate for a number of reasons.

1. Replica play is a naturally occurring instance of perspective taking in which children assume all the character roles because the figures or dolls do not speak (e.g., the child must, in turn, play both the "mother" trying to put a child to bed and the "child" who is resisting, despite where his or her sympathies and familiarity lie).

2. In replica play, children frequently also assume the stance of a narrator who comments on or explains the actions of the individual figures (e.g., "See, he doesn't know the dragon is hiding"; "That witch is mean, huh?"). Such comments cut beneath the surface of actions and dialogue to reveal something about plans, motivations, or feelings of the characters.

3. Replica play, as it is conducted by 2- to 5-year-olds, is usually a combination of manipulation, construction, gesture, and language. For instance, in putting a figure to bed, a child will walk the figure over to a block, lay it down, make yawning and stretching gestures, and say "She is very sleepy." Because of the fullness of the performance, it is often possible to have additional evidence suggesting how ritualistic or meaningful the child's descriptions of characters are.

Clearly, there are difficulties in using replica play to measure children's ability to understand the psychological lives of other people. As in assessing much of symbolic behavior, there is the problem of distinguishing imitations, rituals and parlor tricks from thoughtful behaviors (Huttenlocher & Smyth-Burke, 1981). Thus, for example, in the case of language development, it is difficult to know how to interpret the child's description of a figure as being "sad." *Sad* could be little more than a synonym for the verb *to cry* or a deliberately selected name for the experience of feeling unhappy. Finally, it is important not to confuse what children can ascribe to figures with what they can intuit about real people in actual situations. What replica play offers is a picture of the children's assumptions about the likely connections between situations and particular kinds of human experience, and not a picture of their ability to adjust those assumptions based on particular or novel information often provided by face-to-face interaction. In a sense, replica play offers information like that which emerges in the discussion of moral dilemmas among adolescents and adults. As with the work based on moral dilemmas, evidence drawn from replica play provides an index of the *categories* of human experience an individual realizes as relevant to a particular situation (Brown & Hernstein, 1975; Damon, 1977; Kohlberg, 1971).

BACKGROUND AND DESIGN OF THE STUDY

THE CHILDREN STUDIED

As a part of a larger study of early symbolic development, we collected observations of nine middle-SES children as they engaged in play with small replicas (e.g., small-scale figures and props). Both spontaneous and elicited instances
were collected. In this type of play, children use figures to act out character
roles while they take on the stance of narrator or stage manager, typically combining a linguistic narration with sound effects, motions, and constructions in
order to simulate the complexity of events and settings.

TASKS

To stimulate replica play, we often provided children with a set of props
suggesting a scene or situation (e.g., a large circle of green oilcloth, a toy dragon,
a group of small forest animals, several trees, bushes, and clumps of flowers).
Where we wanted to observe spontaneous play we only helped to take out and
set up the items. Where we wanted to test particular abilities we either performed whole narratives and asked children to replay them or we began a narrative and asked the child to complete it. When we presented the children
with short story starts, we described an interesting situation through a combination of figure movement, narration, and character speech. An example follows.

(The experimenter sets up a small stage with several trees; a small bear is perched
　　in one. The experimenter moves a group of three figures toward the trees).
EXPERIMENTER. One day a father went walking in the woods with his children,
　　a big girl, and a baby. The baby was tired and hot.
BABY. Daddy, when can we stop? I'm tired.
FATHER. Let's get over to the trees where we can rest.
BABY. It's so far . . .
FATHER. Just a little bit more.
(The figures are walked over to rest under the trees.)
EXPERIMENTER. They sat down under the trees but all at once, guess who came
　　along—a clown.
(The experimenter makes a clown figure somersault up to the family.)

(The experimenter then turns over the figures to the child, asking him or her to "show what happened.")

DATA COLLECTION

Children between the ages of 1 and 3 years were visited at home for several hours a week then biweekly when they were between the ages of 3 and 7 years. Spontaneous instances of replica play were recorded as frequently as they occurred and children were asked to engage in replica play on at least six occasions a year. These sessions were audiotaped and transcribed from the tape in combination with on-site observer notes. At intervals of approximately 6 months, sessions were videotaped and then transcribed. Transcriptions of both audio- and videotapes included the language of both observer and child (including remarks, sound effects, changes in voices, or other special effects); descriptions of the constructions and arrangements made by the child; and accounts of the manner in which props were made to move.

DATA ANALYSIS

Using previous research on children's ability to represent concepts of agency and experience (Bretherton & Beeghly-Smith, 1982; Rubin & Wolf, 1979; Watson & Fischer, 1977; Wolf, 1982) we developed the scoring system for assessing children's representations of others in replica play. This system was applied to both spontaneous and elicited instances of replica play. An abbreviated form of that scoring system is presented in Table 1.

All of the spontaneously occurring and elicited instances of replica play for nine children were scored for instances of the representation of human behavior. Each instance was scored in four ways: (1) *level of representation;* (2) *content* (e.g., Level 4 instances were broken down into emotions, elective social relations, and obligations); (3) *type of contextual evidence for the appropriateness of the ascription* (e.g., actions by the character, explanations by the child, additional character speech); and (4) *voice* (i.e., whether the child makes the ascription while speaking as a narrator or while speaking through the character). Beyond Level 1, a scorable instance had to include *both* a linguistic description of the figure's behavior and contextual evidence for the appropriateness of that description of the replica. Thus, to merit a Level 3 score, the child had to describe a character as having a sensation or perception and substantiate that remark with actions by

Table 1

Levels of Representation of Human Action in Replica Play [a]

Level	Description of behavior	Examples
Level 1	At this level the child treats the figure as if it were a representation of a human being, talking to it, feeding it, placing it in chairs or swings. However, the figure remains the passive recipient of the child's actions; the child makes no attempt to make the figure act as an independent agent.	C. wraps the figure up in a blanket and lays it in a box. C. sets a figure in sibling's baby swing, saying "Don't fall."
Level 2	At this level, the child describes the figure as an independent agent, ascribing speech and action to it. However, there is no evidence that the child ascribes any internal states to the figure.	C. walks figure over a pile of blocks, saying "She climbed up here." C. makes one figure face another, saying "Hi, want to go for a ride?"
Level 3	At this level the child ascribes sensations, perceptions, and physiological states to the figure.	C. puts figure in a toy bath, making it say "Ouch, too hot." C. plays with a dragon and a little duck, saying "Duck hears the dragon coming. He hides." C. makes figure climb up a table leg, then has it say "So tired, need a go a sleep."
Level 4	At this level the child ascribes emotions, obligations, simple moral judgements and elective social relations to the figure.	C. makes one figure take a toy bear from another, saying "She took the boy's bear and he's sad." C. makes a mother duck speak to a baby duck, saying "You are bad to run away. You have to come home right now." C. makes two figures fight and then face each other, saying "No, now let's be friends."
Level 5	At this level the child ascribes cognitions like thinking, planning, wondering, and knowing to the figure.	C. speaks for a pirate figure, saying "I think I know where to hide the gold so they can't get it." C. makes a figure hunt for other figures who have hidden, saying "He wonders where they went. He can't see them."

[a] In order for an utterance to be scorable in this system, it had to meet two criteria. (1) *Spontaneity:* It could not be an imitation of another speaker's comment or a repetition of an earlier utterance by the child. (2) *Situational Appropriateness:* It had to be accompanied by contextual evidence for the appropriateness of the ascription. This evidence could be drawn from surrounding utterances or from accompanying actions that the child made the figure perform.

the figure or further remarks about what the character experienced. For example, the child might remark "Hey, I hear someone coming" and then make the figure hunt about as if looking for another character.

LONGITUDINAL FINDINGS

As a first step in picturing the development of representations of human behavior, we established the *age of onset* for each of the levels described in Table 1. The age of onset was defined as the second occasion on which a child made a figure exhibit a particular type of human behavior. (If two such performances occurred within a single session, the two had to ascribe two *different* instances of that particular type of behavior.) Table 2 presents the ages of onset for Levels 1–5 for each of the nine children.

As the data indicate, seven of the nine children followed the hypothesized order; the other two children each invert two adjacent levels. These results are significant at the $p < .01$ level, using the binomial test (Phelps, in preparation). Although the ranges of ages of onset are similar through Levels 1–3 (24, 26, and 24 weeks between the appearance of a level in the first and the last child, respectively), the ranges of ages of onset for later levels grow wider (38 weeks range for Level 4, 78 weeks for Level 5). However, even as the range widens, the children showed no consistency in the rate at which they moved through the five levels. In other words, among the children we observed there were no

Table 2
Age in Weeks of Onset for Levels of Representing Human Action[a]

| | Subjects | | | | | | | | |
| | Boys | | | Girls | | | | | |
Levels	1	2	3	1	2	3	4	5	6
Level 1: Passive agency	76	70	84	76	69	90	68	66	68
Level 2: Independent agency	105	112	98	113	116	111	124	123	112
Level 3: Perception and sensation	113	112	137	121	132	111	124	114	112
Level 4: Emotion, obligation, social relation	133	112	137	132	121	142	142	121	150
Level 5: Cognition	210	184	184	132	197	202	158	154	162

[a] Ages of onset are presented in terms of weeks in order to give a clearer picture of the ordinal nature of this development.

individuals who consistently lagged behind or raced ahead in their ability to formulate complex representations of human behavior.

If we were to examine the data on a molecular or session-by-session level, factors like fatigue, interruptions, or new props would result in fluctuating levels of performance. However, when we group transcripts into half-year blocks, the broadly available and progressive growth curve of this type of social cognition becomes clear. Between the ages of 1 and 5 years, children either conserve or enhance their representations of human activity. The robustness of this development is indexed in Table 3, which presents the highest level in the scale used by each child in each successive half-year of data collection. Of the nine children, only two showed any regressions at all. Even for those two individuals, their highest scores fall back from a previously attained level in only one out of eight half-years.

Finally, if we examine the range of representations used by each child in each half-year of the study, we gain additional insight into the nature of this kind of social cognition. Table 4 lists all of the levels used by each child in each half-year up to age 5 years. Although Level 1 (the representation of passive agency) may disappear from their repertoires, once any other level is acquired, children continue to make active use of it. (There is one exception to this statement: In the final half-year, G4 drops Level 5 in the period 3–3½.)

These changes in social cognition occur in a different pattern than that proposed for other types of social cognition—such as moral judgment or perspective taking (Kohlberg, 1971), where it has been hypothesized that later, more powerful or inclusive levels of thinking gradually supplant earlier acquired modes of reasoning. In the case at hand, children are building a vocabulary of repre-

Table 3
Highest Level of the Representation of Human Behavior
in Each Half-Year between 1 and 5 Years

	$1-1\frac{1}{2}$	$1\frac{1}{2}-2$	$2-2\frac{1}{2}$	$2\frac{1}{2}-3$	$3-3\frac{1}{2}$	$3\frac{1}{2}-4$	$4-4\frac{1}{2}$	$4\frac{1}{2}-5$
B.1	1	1	3	4	4	4	5	5
B.2	1	1	4	4	4	5	5	5
B.3	0	2	4	4	4	5	5	5
.G.1	1	1	4	4	4	5	5	5
G.2	1	1	4	4	4	5	5	5
G.3	—[a]	2	3	4	4	5	5	5
G.4	1	1	4	4	4	5	5	5
G.5	1	1	4	5	4	5	5	5
G.6	1	1	3	4	5	—[a]	5	5

[a] Insufficient data.   B = Boy.   G = Girl.

Table 4
Levels of Representations of Human Behavior
Used by Individual Children in Successive Half-Years

	$1-1\frac{1}{2}$	$1\frac{1}{2}-2$	$2-2\frac{1}{2}$	$2\frac{1}{2}-3$	$3-3\frac{1}{2}$	$3\frac{1}{2}-4$	$4-4\frac{1}{2}$	$4\frac{1}{2}-5$
B.1	1	1	1, 2, 3	1, 2, 3, 4	1, 2, 3, 4	1, 2, 3, 4	1, 2, 3, 4, 5	1, 2, 3, 4, 5
B.2	1	1	1, 2, 3, 4	2, 3, 4	1, 2, 3, 4, 5	1, 2, 3, 4, 5	1, 2, 3, 4, 5	1, 2, 3, 4, 5
B.3	0	1, 2	1, 2, 3, 4	1, 2, 3, 4	1, 2, 3, 4	1, 2, 3, 4, 5	1, 2, 3, 4, 5	1, 2, 3, 4, 5
G.1	1	1	1, 2, 3, 4	1, 2, 3, 4, 5	2, 3, 4	1, 2, 3, 4	1, 2, 3, 4, 5	1, 2, 3, 4, 5
G.2	1	1	1, 2, 3, 4	1, 2, 3, 4	2, 3, 4, 5	1, 2, 3, 4, 5	1, 2, 3, 4, 5	2, 3, 4, 5
G.3	$-^a$	1, 2	1, 2, 3	1, 2, 3, 4	2, 3, 4	2, 3, 4, 5	2, 3, 4, 5	1, 2, 3, 4, 5
G.4	1	1	1, 2, 3, 4	1, 2, 3, 4, 5	1, 2, 3, 4	1, 2, 3, 4, 5	1, 2, 3, 4, 5	1, 2, 3, 4, 5
G.5	1	1	1, 2, 3, 4	1, 2, 3, 4, 5	1, 2, 3, 4	1, 2, 3, 4, 5	2, 3, 4, 5	2, 3, 4, 5
G.6	1	1	1, 2, 3	1, 2, 3, 4	1, 2, 3, 4, 5	$-^a$	1, 2, 3, 4, 5	1, 2, 3, 4, 5

^{a} Insufficient data.   B = Boy.   G = Girl.

sentations of human behavior, and thus, this type of social-cognitive development is better conceptualized in terms of the range of available levels rather than the modal or highest level used. Additionally, in this (and similar) domains it is important to analyze the comparative richness with which children use any particular level by describing the range of different descriptors they possess (Brown, 1973) or by inventing ways of judging the aptness of their ascriptions.

TOWARD A DEVELOPMENTAL MODEL
FOR UNDERSTANDING OTHERS

In part because of Piaget's stress on egocentrism and psychoanalytic emphasis on the gradual and difficult nature of separation from the caretaker, we have presumed that young children's major form of social development inheres in developing a gradual understanding of the differences between self and other. However, the research just presented suggests that between the ages of 1 and 5 years, children begin to represent two aspects of human behavior. First in action and then through representational behaviors, children begin to apprehend themselves and others as independent agents. In a parallel fashion, children recognize that, beyond performing actions, human actors also undergo internal experiences. The data just presented argue for the surprisingly early onset of these two concepts in children's replica play. However, other research suggests that these findings are not peculiar to the nine children we observed.

UNDERSTANDING HUMAN AGENCY

It appears that infants have a primitive concept of *agency,* which is evident in their ability to recognize the locus of action or the prime mover in an event. Infants grow distressed if a ball of one color rolls behind a screen and a ball of another color emerges from the far side (Bower, 1974) and they exhibit surprise if a figure that has been acting as the agent is, at last, acted upon (Golinkoff, 1975). Toward the close of the first year, as both motoric and planning skills develop, infants exhibit a strong sense of personal agency, which is evident in their willingness to overcome obstacles to get what they want and the determined way in which they use other people as "tools" to secure their goals (Bates, Begnini, Bretherton, Camaioni, & Volterra, 1979; Uzgiris & Hunt, 1975).

Possibly because caregivers do not always comply or comprehend, infants gradually recognize other people as separate or independent agents. Between 9 and 15 months, many children exhibit separation anxieties as well as simple strategies for recovering other people, which range from seeking and following behavior to early conversational skills or even to substituting a favorite blanket or toy for a missing caregiver (Ainsworth & Bell, 1970; Bowlby, 1969; Mahler et al., 1975; McDevitt, 1972; Winnicott, 1971). Also as a part of coping with the autonomy of self and other, children between the ages of 12 and 24 months may invent strategies for gaining the attention of others, engaging and holding partners in interactive games, and sharing information (Bruner & Sherwood, 1976; Mueller et al., 1977; Sander, 1969; Trevarthen & Hubley, 1979). In the later preschool years, children begin to comment on and seek to harness the potential independence of human agents. Nowhere is this as evident as in play, where 3- and 4-year-olds begin to direct how other participants are to interpret their literal surroundings and play out dramatic roles (Garvey, 1974; Giffin, Chapter 3, this volume; Wolf, 1982; Wolf & Pusch, in press).

UNDERSTANDING HUMAN EXPERIENCE

Throughout this same period, children build up at least an implicit understanding of the internal experiences common to human actors. Brazelton, Koslowski, and Main (1974) have demonstrated that infants alter their behaviors in interactions with toys and human partners. Incipient in the 18-month-old's use of language and play to contact others is the understanding that people—unlike objects—attend, hear, and see. Children close to a year of age begin to engage in intentional communicative acts in which they vary their bids for attention in order to secure and maintain the attention of other people (Bates et al., 1979). In their second year, children exhibit social referencing behaviors in which they check the reactions of others as a part of deciding how to react to a strange display (Campos & Stenberg, 1981). There is also evidence that children between 1 and 2 years extrapolate from their own internal experience, making empathetic offers of comfort and interest to others (Zahn-Waxler *et al.*, 1979). In the ensuing 2 years, children's awareness of internal experience becomes increasingly articulate. Even in novel and experimental tasks children demonstrate their knowledge of how perception and sensation work (Masangkay, McCluskey, McIntyre, Sims-Knight, Vaugh, & Flavell, 1974) and what different individuals know and understand (Sachs & Devin, 1976; Shatz & Gelman, 1973).

REPRESENTING THE COMPLEXITY
OF HUMAN BEHAVIOR

As finely tuned as the conception of human beings appears to be in early behavior, the continued articulation of these concepts appears to depend, in part, on their representation in various symbolic forms. For example, observations of children's symbolic behavior during the second and third years indicate how language and play activity amplify understandings about agency. Children making the transition from single to multiword utterances can encode the differences in situational roles played by individual actors. Whereas the 15-month-old might only describe a fight by saying "Hurt," a 2-year-old could describe the same event with the utterance "She hurt me." In dramatic play, children also portray the distinct activities of familiar dyads such as parent and child, doctor and patient. As the data presented here indicate, 12-month-olds are likely to address a doll only as a replica of a human, 18-month-olds can treat figures as passive agents, and between 18 and 24 months, children make figures act as if they were the locus of intention and independent action (Scarlett, 1983; Watson & Fischer, 1977; Wolf, 1982).

It is following the early representations of human agency that children begin to acquire the linguistic terms to represent and communicate symbolically about different types of internal states in themselves and others. For instance, Bretherton and Beeghly-Smith (1982) found that by 28 months, children could label and provide simple causal explanations for internal states both in themselves and others. In the fourth year, Borke (1973) found that children could apply terms like *happy* and *sad* to pictures of children in situations likely to provoke those states. The data presented herein provide strong longitudinal evidence that children first develop the capacity to ascribe perceptions or sensations, then emotions, and finally, cognitions to figures in replica play.

Taken together these separate findings suggest two phases in the early development of children's concepts of human behavior. In a first phase, children exhibit an implicit understanding of agency and experience in themselves and others. With the onset of symbolic capacities, both of these concepts can be made explicit through language, gesture, and their combined use in play. During this second phase, children first represent the agency of different actors. Subsequently, they begin to represent, explain, and reflect on internal experiences as a part of the human repertoire. The data from replica play discussed here demonstrate that, by age 4 years, even in the hypothetical situations of replica play, the children we studied were able to attribute sensations, perceptions, emotions, obligations, and cognitions to figures.

INDIVIDUAL DIFFERENCES
IN THE USE OF SOCIAL KNOWLEDGE

Over time both the complexity and the richness of the descriptions of human characters increase in all children's play. Despite these shared patterns of change, there are at least two noticeable contrasts in the way children make use of their ability to comment on human behavior. The first of these differences concerns the proportions of utterances about characters that describe *agency* as compared to *experience*. The second difference shows up in the kinds of internal states individual children emphasize.

DIFFERENCES IN EMPHASIS
ON AGENCY OR EXPERIENCE

The following excerpts are each performed by 4-year-olds who both have a repertoire including Levels 1–5 (although there is no evidence of Level 5 ascriptions in these transcripts). In both excerpts the child plays out a scene in which two sets of characters resolve a fight over the same spot in a jungle. Although both excerpts are taken from the same narrative-completion task, the first child concentrates on setting to rights the internal or psychological worlds of the figures whereas the second child describes a lively sequence of character actions that resolve the situation.

G.2 (as narrator). I know, when they (characters from first set) come out, they *see* he's (character from second set) dancing and they *liked* him.
G.2 (as mother and baby figures). Look mommy, look, look. Baby look, (he's) dancing. (She rushes the child figure over and makes it kiss the dancing

figure. She makes the mother and child and additional figures join in, all dancing, humming, and jumping.)

G.2 (as narrator speaking to figures). And you can rest in the pond. (She puts figures into a plastic bag.) Into the pond with you and and you and you.

G.2 (speaking to the observer). I'm really putting it away . . . (He) goes into the pond, because he *likes* ponds.

G.2 (speaking as that figure). I just *love* resting in ponds.

B.1 (positions one set of characters behind some trees watching the other set. As narrator). They peek out.

B.1 (moves a figure from the other set across the pond). Swimmy, swimmy, swimmy.

B.1 (moves a second figure up to pond). Walking, walking, walking.

B.1 (makes the two last figures collide, with loud cries).

B.1 (as narrator). They all fall down.

B.1 (makes a third figure walk around the clearing of trees he had set up earlier. The figure knocks them down). Bop.

B.1 (as narrator). The forest comes down, because he doesn't *want* any trees. Then they don't fight over them.

However, in attempting to isolate such differences it is critical to separate developmentally based differences (e.g., differences occasioned by individuals' level of skill within a particular domain) from differences occasioned by other factors, such as cognitive style, culture, or gender (Wolf & Grollman, 1982). To accomplish this, each child's data was divided into bands, based on the highest level of human representation exhibited in each transcript. Thus each child had five bands of transcripts: The first had an upper bound of Level 1 representations; the second had an upper bound of Level 2, and so on. Particularly with respect to Levels 3, 4, and 5, this matching by upper bound helps to control for possible differences in children's acquisition of linguistic terms referring to sensations, feelings, or thoughts. Having created five bands of level-matched data, we examined how individuals made use of the abilities commonly held by all the children. As the clearest findings derive from examining the data from transcripts with an upper bound (Upbd) of Levels, 3, 4, 5, we will concentrate on these.

In order to test for differences in children's emphasis on action or internal experience, individuals were rank ordered for the relative prominence of utterances concerned with *experience* for all three bands of data where they had the capacity to ascribe internal states to characters (i.e., those with an upper bound of Level 3, Level 4, and Level 5). Kendall tau correlations indicate that individuals are remarkably stable with respect to their inclusion of this kind of information about characters. Children's ranks correlate strongly even as their repertoires increase: Across the first band of data (Upbd 3 scripts, where the repertoire includes only Levles 1, 2, and 3) and the second band (Upbd 4 scripts, where Levels 1, 2, 3, and 4 are available) the correlation is .89, which is significant at the .001 level. Between the second and third band (Upbd 5 scripts, where Levels 1, 2, 3, 4, and 5 are used), children's rank orders for prominence of internal experience descriptions are correlated .82, which is again significant at the .001 level. The rank-order correlations between the first and third bands of data is .82, also significant at the .001 level.

Mann–Whitney tests indicate that it is girls who either see the relevance of psychological information or feel comfortable discussing internal states. Their story narrations typically include more ascriptions of experience or internal states than do boys' sessions of replica play. For transcripts with an upper bound of Level 3, girls exceed boys with $p < .02$; for transcripts with an upper bound of Level 4, girls exceed boys with $p < .02$; for transcripts with an upper bound of Level 5, girls exceed boys with $p < .04$. Therefore, girls, as compared to boys, refer to the psychological aspects of events throughout the period when both boys and girls are regularly acquiring the ability to describe internal states in their characters. Given that the pool of utterances is composed largely of descriptions of agency or internal experience, this implies that, relative to girls, boys emphasize descriptions of how characters act: where they go, what they say, what they accomplish, how they cope with obstacles.

Despite these strong and apparently stable gender differences, several facts modify the simplistic interpretation that boys talk about agency and girls describe experience. All the children studied were capable of describing their characters as agents *and* experiencers from their third year on. Thus, what is measured here is the "outright" quality of girls' attributions of internal states. The boy in the preceding example may be alluding to pain when he makes two characters collide and cry or he may be representing friendship when he says "Then they don't fight anymore." What distinguishes boys' and girls' character representations is the tendency of girls to describe internal states frequently and explicitly. Thus, as early as the third year, individual children expose what may be either their view of how important psychological information is to the understanding of events or the ease with which they talk about internal events in front of an audience.

DIFFERENCES IN DESCRIPTIONS OF EXPERIENCE

A second difference in children's representations of human characters concerns the types of internal experiences that individuals elect to use from their available repertoire. At each of the three bands of data, children were rank ordered for the percentage of Level 3, 4, and 5 utterances in the descriptions of characters' internal experiences. The correlations performed on these ranks are presented in Table 5.

As already indicated, early in the development of the capacity to ascribe internal states to figures, some individuals show a greater interest in combining attributions of perception, sensation, and physical ability (Level 3) with descriptions of character's speech and action. As their repertoire develops to include affective and social characterization (Level 4), these same children move on to emphasize emotions, relations, and obligations in their play. Correspondingly, those children who initially make less use of their capacity to describe perceptions and physical states in figures elect to emphasize these attributes, rather than describing feelings or relationships once their repertoires include both possibilities.

The third band of data provides a situation in which to ask whether the patterns of preference evident in the previous band are stable, even as children's repertoire of internal states becomes broader. When comparing patterns of use across Upbd 4 and Upbd 5 data, we find that children's use of Level 3 correlates strongly across these two bodies of transcripts (.63, $p < .01$). Children's use of Level 4 ascriptions in Upbd 4 transcripts also correlates positively with their use of Level 4 in Upbd 5 transcripts (.59, $p < .01$). Neither children's previous usage of Level 3 or 4 has any predictive value for their use of Level 5 in the final band of data. Therefore, what appears to stabilize is a relative preference in one group of children for emphasizing the perceptions, physical abilities, and sensations of characters. This contrasts to a second group of children who emphasize the affective and social attributes of human behavior. Additional Mann–Whitney tests for group differences suggest that the individuals emphasizing affective and social states in the two later bands of data are more likely to be girls. For Upbd 4 transcripts, $p \leq .01$; $p \leq .07$ for in Upbd 5 transcripts (which can only be regarded as suggestive).

GENDER DIFFERENCES IN THE USE
OF SOCIAL UNDERSTANDING

These differences in the relative prominence of *agency* and *experience*, or the types of internal experience children attribute to characters, may be part of a larger, subtler constellation of gender differences in the comprehension and representation of human behavior. The gender differences just discussed are frequently accompanied by additional contrasts in boys' and girls' representation of human behavior in replica play. As can be seen in the two jungle stories excerpted earlier, although boys and girls may recognize the same situations as

Table 5
Significant Kendall Tau Correlations for Types of Internal State Descriptions
in Upperbound (Upbd) 3, 4, and 5 Transcripts[a]

Use of Level 3, Upbd 3 data × Use of Level 3, Upbd 4 data = $-.80, p \leq .002$
Use of Level 3, Upbd 3 data × Use of Level 4, Upbd 4 data = $.63, p \leq .01$
Use of Level 3, Upbd 4 data × Use of Level 3, Upbd 5 data = $.63, p \leq .01$
Use of Level 4, Upbd 4 data × Use of Level 4, Upbd 5 data = $.59, p \leq .01$

[a] All other correlations not significant.

conflictual, they resolve those conflicts in quite different ways (Forbes & Dan-aher, 1982). In the instances cited, the girl made the two sets of characters see each other in a new light and the boy made one of the characters remove the objects that had caused the fight in the first place. In addition, there is evidence that girls and boys show distinct patterns of affiliation with the characters they create. From the third year on, individuals show a stable preference for an in-timacy with, or a distance from, their characters. When children exhibit inti-macy with play characters, they frequently speak through the figures to create a first-person conversational narrative (e.g., "Oh, I ate too much, I feel like I'm sick"). A child assuming greater distance from the characters speaks about the figures as an outside observer, using a third-person narration. The data suggest that girls are more likely to adopt the intimate, conversational strategy, whereas boys are more likely to speak about their characters from the vantage point of an observing narrator.

Given the small sample and the uneven numbers of boys and girls, these findings on gender differences must be treated as preliminary. There is, how-ever, a great deal of information on gender differences in social behavior that suggests the essential correctness of the descriptions. In other symbolic tasks, such as verbal stories (Pitcher & Prelinger, 1963; Sutton-Smith, Botvin, & Ma-hony, 1973), toy preference (Goodenough, 1957), and doll play (Bach, 1945; Erikson, 1950; Sears, Rau, & Alpert, 1965), girls have been observed to under-score what characters experience and boys to emphasize what characters say and do.

However, this data also suggests two ways in which we could deepen our understanding of what may, by now, be a presumed type of gender difference. First, this data indicates that in homogeneous populations the order and *rate* of acquisition of these categories is no different across boys and girls. Significantly, this is the same conclusion reached by a number of other investigations of gen-der differences in social knowledge or insight (Borke, 1971; Gitter, Mostofsky, & Quincy, 1971; Maccoby & Jacklin, 1974; Savitsky & Izard, 1970). Thus, the noticeable variance in the relative place given to *agency* and *experience* in human behavior is not based on differential ability, but on distinctive patterns for using

the same core concepts. Such differences may derive from different constructions of what is important or relevant in representing events. Alternatively, boys
may feel less comfortable than girls when engaging in behavior that is highly
subjective or expressive. Both Matthews (1977) and Lever (1976) have observed
that girls engage in ideational games that depend on the mutual sharing of make-
believe, whereas boys engage in material forms of play that center on object use.
Whatever the specific root of these contrasts in play may be, such patterns clearly
prefigure some of the differences in emphasis that are evident when adult men
and women report or reflect on human events (Carlson, 1972; Gilligan, 1982).

CONCLUSIONS

Years ago, Freud briefly focused his interest on reading between the lines of
behavior in a child's symbolic play. Watching from a distance, Freud observed
a small boy become absorbed in playing hide-and-seek, lose-and-find games with
a stick and spool, just after he had "found" his mother in a hug and then "lost"
her to her own activities. Since those first observations, we have become accustomed to the idea that play provides a window into the otherwise invisible
inner worlds of children. However, that same window can be looked through
in two directions. As much as it provides a view of the psychological contours
of children's private lives, it also reveals what children understand about the
behavior of other people: their actions, sensations, perceptions, feelings, and
thoughts.

In the context of doll play, children elaborate their concepts of other people
in a regular manner. Once they are able to describe the agency or independent
actions of figures, children begin to ascribe internal experiences to the figures:
perceptions, sensations, and physical abilities, then feelings and social relations,
and, finally, cognitions. This development is not only ordinal but relatively
even: There is no evidence that such understandings develop more rapidly or
more gradually in particular individuals among the nine children we studied.
Clearly, the apparent ordinality and evenness of this development could be the
by-product of a small, homogeneous, and well-trained group of children. However, cross-sectional investigation indicates that at least the transitions from Levels 1 to 2 and from 2 to 3 appear in the same order in a much larger and more
diverse group of subjects (Scarlett, 1983). Earlier studies of communicative abilities and interactional skills have forced us to correct earlier notions of 1-year-
olds as symbiotic or asocial. Similarly, the complexity of children's play char-
acterizations should prompt us to revise descriptions of preschoolers as likely
to view human behavior simply in terms of overt actions.

In fact, between the ages of 2 and 5 years, young children's knowledge of human behavior is already articulate enough that it begins to show considerable variation across individuals. As early as the third year, individuals exhibit stable preferences for including or ignoring psychological information in their representations of human actions. Despite a common pool of understandings about others, individual children emphasize distinct sets of internal states in their descriptions of characters. Not surprisingly, those individuals who emphasize internal experience, particularly emotions and social relations, are girls. This suggests how early factors like gender begin to interact with raw social knowledge to produce what may be different styles of social perception, variations in willingness to share subjective experience, or even contrasting views of what matters most about human behavior.

ACKNOWLEDGMENTS

Sharon Grollman, Pat McKernon, Shelley Rubin, Jennifer Shotwell, and Ann Smith helped to collect, transcribe, and analyze these children's play narratives. A number of people have commented on and helped in the revision of earlier drafts of this chapter. They include Inge Bretherton, Howard Gardner, and Sharon Grollman.

REFERENCES

Ainsworth, M. D. S., & Bell, S. M. Attachment, exploration, and separation: Illustrated by the behavior of one-year-olds in a strange situation. *Child Development,* 1970, *41,* 49–67.

Bach, G. R. Young children's play fantasies. *Psychological Monographs,* 1945, *59,* (No. 2).

Bates, E., Begnini, L., Bretherton, I., Camioni, L., & Volterra, V. *The emergence of symbols: Cognition and communication in infancy.* New York: Academic Press, 1979.

Borke, H. Interpersonal perception of young children. *Developmental Psychology,* 1971, *5,* 263–269.

Borke, H. The development of empathy in Chinese and American children between three and six years of age. *Developmental Psychology,* 1973, *9,* 102–108.

Bower, T. G. R. *Development in infancy.* San Francisco: Freeman, 1974.

Bowlby, J. *Attachment and loss* (Vol. 1). *Attachment.* New York: Basic Books, 1969.

Brazelton, T. B., Koslowski, B., & Main, M. The origins of reciprocity: The early mother-infant interaction. In M. Lewis and L. A. Rosenblum (Eds.), *The effect of the infant on the caregiver.* New York: Wiley, 1974.

Bretherton, I., & Beeghly-Smith, M. (1982). Talking about internal states: The acquisition of an explicit theory of mind. *Developmental Psychology,* 1982, *18,* (6), 906–921.

Bretherton, I., McNew, S., & Beeghly-Smith, M. Early person knowledge as expressed in gestural and verbal communication: When do infants acquire a "theory of mind." M. E. Lamb and L. R. Sherrod (Eds.) *Infant social cognition.* Hillsdale, NJ: Erlbaum, 1981.

Brown, R. *A first language.* Cambridge, MA: Harvard University Press, 1973.

Brown, R., & Hernstein, R. *Psychology.* Boston: Little, Brown, 1975.

Bruner, J. S., and Sherwood, V. Early rule structure: The case of peek-a-boo. In J. S. Bruner, A. Jolly, and K. Sylva (Eds.), *Play: Its role in development and evolution.* London: Penguin, 1976.

Campos, J., & Stenberg, C. R. Perception, appraisal and emotion: The onset of social referencing. In M. Lamb & L. R. Sherrod (Eds.), *Infant social cognition* Hillsdale, NJ: Erlbaum, 1981.

Carlson, R. Understanding women: Implications for personality theory and research. *Journal of Social Issues,* 1972, *28,* 17–32.

Damon, W. *The social world of the child,* San Francisco: Jossey-Bass, 1977.

Erikson, E. *Childhood and society.* New York: Norton, 1950.

Erikson, E. Play and actuality. In M. W. Piers (Ed.), *Play and development* New York: Norton, 1972.

Fein, G., & Stork, L. Sociodramatic play: Social class effects in an integrated classroom. *Journal of Applied Developmental Psychology,* 1981, *2,* 267–279.

Forbes, D., & Danaher, D. *Sex differences in children's conflict behavior: Conflict resolution versus conflict mitigation.* Unpublished paper, Peer Interaction Project, Harvard Graduate School of Education, 1982.

Freud, S. Creative writers and daydreaming. In J. Strachey (Ed.), *The standard edition of the complete psychological works of Sigmund Freud* (Vol. IX). London: Hogarth, 1959.

Garvey, C. Some properties of social play. *Merrill-Palmer Quarterly, 20*(3), 1974, 164–180.

Garvey, C. The contingent query: A dependent act in conversation. In M. Lewis and L. A. Rosenblum (Eds.), *Interaction, conversation and the development of language.* New York: Wiley, 1977.

Giffin, H. *Young children's metacommunications in play.* Paper presented at the Biennial Meeting of the Society for Research in Child Development, Detroit, April 1983.

Gilligan, C. *In a different voice.* Cambridge, MA: Harvard University Press, 1982.

Gitter, A. G., Mostofsky, D. & Quincy, A. J. Race and sex differences in the child's perception of emotion. *Child Development, 42,* 1971, 2071–2075.

Golinkoff, R. Semantic development in infants: The concepts of agent and recipient. *Merrill-Palmer Quarterly,* 1975, *21,* 181–193.

Goodenough, E. W. Interest in persons as an aspect of sex differences in the early years. *Genetic Psychology Monographs,* 1957, *55,* 287–323.

Huttenlocher, J., & Smyth-Burke, T. *Event encoding in infancy.* Cognitive Science Technical Report Series 47). University of Chicago, 1981.

Klein, M. The psychoanalytic play technique. *American Journal of Orthopsychiatry,* 1955, *25,* 223–237.

Kohlberg, L. From is to ought: How to commit the naturalistic falacy and get away with it in the study of moral development. In T. Mischel (Ed.), *Cognitive development and genetic epistemology.* New York: Academic Press, 1971.

Lever, J. Sex differences in the games children play. *Social Problems,* 1976, *23,* 478–487.

Lowe, M. Trends in the development of representational play in infants from one to three years: An observational study. *Journal of Child Psychology and Psychiatry,* 1965, *16,* 33–47.

Maccoby, E., & Jacklin, C. N. *The psychology of sex differences.* Stanford, CA: Stanford University Press, 1974.

Mahler, M., Bergman, A., & Pine, F. *The psychological birth of the human infant.* New York: Basic Books, 1975.

Masangkay, Z., McCluskey, K., MacIntrye, C., Sims-Knight, J., Vaughn, B., & Flavell, J. The early development of inferences about the visual percepts of others. *Child Development,* 1974, *45,* 357–366.

Matthews, W. S. Modes of transformation in the initiation of fantasy play. *Developmental Psychology,* 1977, *13,* 212–216.

McDevitt, J. V. *Separation-individuation and object constancy.* Paper presented at the New York Psychoanalytic Society, 1972.

Mueller, E., Bleir, M., Krakow, J., Hegedus, K., & Cournagen, P. The development of peer verbal interaction among two-year-old boys. *Child Development,* 48(1), 1977, 284–287.

Nelson, K. Social cognition in a script framework. In J. Flavell and L. Ross (Eds.), *Social cognitive development,* Cambridge: Cambridge University Press, 1981.

Nicolich, L. Beyond sensorimotor intelligence: Assessment of symbolic maturity through analysis of pretend play. *Merrill-Palmer Quarterly, 23*(2), 1977, 89–101.

Phelps, E. Methods of analysis for ordinal data. In D. Wolf and H. Gardner, (Eds.) *The making of meanings.* Manuscript submitted for publication, in preparation.

Piaget, J. *Language and thought of the child.* London: Routledge & Kegan Paul, 1926.

Pitcher, E., & Prelinger, E. *Children tell stories.* New York: International Universities Press, 1963.

Rubin, S., & Wolf, D. The development of maybe: The evolution of social roles into narrative roles. *New Directions for Child Development,* 1979, *6,* 15–28.

Sachs, J., & Devin, J. Young children's use of age-appropriate speech styles in social interaction and role-playing. *Journal of Child Language, 3,* 1976, 81–98.

Sander, L. The longitudinal course of early mother–child interaction: Cross-case comparison in a sample of mother–child pairs. In B. Foss (Ed.) *The determinants of infant behavior* (Vol. 4). London: Metheun, 1969.

Savitsky, J. C., & Izard, C. E. Developmental changes in the use of emotion cues in concept formation task. *Developmental Psychology,* 1970, *3,* 350–357.

Scarlett, W. G. The development of children's concept of story. Paper presented at the Biennial Meetings of the Society for Research in Child Development, Detroit, April 1983.

Scarlett, W. G., & Wolf, D. When it's only make-believe: The construction of a boundary between fantasy and reality. In D. Wolf (Ed.), *Early Symbolization, New Directions for Child Development 3,* 1979, 29–40.

Schank, R. C., & Abelson, R. P. *Scripts, plans, goals and understanding.* Hillsdale, NJ: Erlbaum, 1977.

Sears, R. R., Rau, L., & Alpert, R. *Identification and child rearing.* Stanford, CA: Stanford University Press, 1965.

Shatz, M., & Gelman, R. The development of communication skills: Modifications in the speech of young children as a function of the listener. *Monographs of the Society for Research in Child Development,* 1973, *38,*(5, Serial No. 152).

Sutton-Smith, B., Botvin, G., & Mahony, D. Developmental structures in fantasy narratives. *Human Development,* 1973, *9,* 1–3.

Trevarthen, C., & Hubley, P. Secondary intersubjectivity: Confidence, confiding and acts of meaning in the first year. In A. Lock (Ed.), *Action, gesture and symbol.* New York: Academic Press, 1979.

Uzgiris, I., & Hunt, J. McV. *Assessment in infancy.* Urbana: University of Illinois Press, 1975.

Watson, M., & Fischer, K. W. A developmental sequence of agent use in late infancy. *Child Development,* 1977, *48,* 828–836.

Winnicott, D. W. *Playing and reality.* New York: Basic Books, 1971.

Wolf, D. Understanding others: A longitudinal case study of the concept of independent agency. In G. Forman (Ed.), *Action and thought,* New York: Academic Press, 1982.

Wolf, D., & Grollman, S. Ways of playing: Individual differences in imaginative play. In K. Rubin & D. Pepler (Eds.), *The play of children: Current theory and research.* New York: Karger, 1982.

Wolf, D., & Pusch, J. Pretend that didn't happen: Children's responses to interruptions in play. In J. Johnson & L. Galda (Eds.), *Play and narrative.* City name: Alblex, In press.

Zahn-Waxler, C., Radke-Yarrow, M., & King, R. Child-rearing and children's prosocial initiations toward victims of distress. *Child Development,* 1979, *50,* 319–330.

CHAPTER 8

Waiting for the Birth of a Sibling: The Verbal Fantasies of a 2-Year-Old Boy

VIRGINIA VOLTERRA

Surely there must be a possibility of observing in children at first hand and in all the freshness of life the sexual impulses and wishes which we dig out so laboriously in adults from among their own débris—especially as it is also our belief that they are the common property of all men, a part of the human constitution, and merely exaggerated or distorted in the case of neurotics.

Freud, 1909 p. 6

INTRODUCTION

The material reported in this work is the product of a fortunate chance occurrence. As part of my research in child development, I was following a little boy, Francesco, for nearly 2 years—from the age of 1 year 4 months (1:4) to the age of 3:4. I would go to his home every 2 weeks, and audiotape 2-hour sessions that I then transcribed verbatim. My objective was to study one of the most impressive phenomena of early childhood: The child who at 1 year is still barely communicating with either gestures and/or at most with isolated words, and who reaches age 3 years in near perfect command of his or her mother tongue.

The analysis of Francesco's language production has, in fact, enabled us to identify a series of actual phases or stages and certain fundamental processes through which language acquisition is carried out. These more strictly linguistic results have long since been published and discussed and, by and large, confirmed by other researchers (Bates, 1976; Parisi & Antinucci, 1974; Volterra, 1972, 1976; Volterra & Antinucci, 1979).

By a fortunate coincidence, in the course of the data collection Francesco acquired a baby sister, and this event permitted us to gather indirectly some extremely interesting though quite unexpected data reported in the present chapter—data that have been totally ignored in previous linguistic-oriented accounts.

During the sessions held in the spring and summer of 1971, while Francesco's mother was expecting her second child, we began to note in him significant changes and a keen interest in the arrival of the new baby, but we did not attribute any particular importance to them. It was only several months following the birth of Francesco's sister Chiara that we had the complete transcriptions in front of us and realized that from the material contained in those tapes we could reconstruct just how Francesco had experienced the entire period of waiting for the new baby, in particular the fantasies that his mother's pregnancy had prompted.

While analyzing the data we were struck by a very strong analogy between Francesco's fantasies and those Freud (1909) described in "Analysis of a phobia in a five-year-old boy," more popularly known as "little Hans." Just as Freud related that the great event in Hans's life was the birth of his little sister Hanna when the child was exactly 3:6, we too can claim that the big event in the life of Francesco was the birth of his baby sister Chiara when he was precisely 2:9. The only notable difference appears to be that although Freud—or rather, the father of little Hans—could reconstruct only a posteriori all of the pertinent jealousies and fantasies that the child had evidently experienced throughout the entire pregnancy, we were able to follow, step by step, the formation and evolution of these very fantasies in Francesco; as we shall see shortly, they came through with extreme clarity in his everyday speech. It was the similarity between the two accounts that induced us to publish the present work; it seemed to us that it might prove useful to compare and test some psychoanalytical opinions on early child language with material that came out of typical linguistic research and not an analytical setting.

The problem of early child language is addressed by classic psychoanalysis— and by *classic* we mean here Sigmund Freud and Melanie Klein in particular— in an extremely fragmented and in some ways contradictory manner. On one side is the view that the unconscious in children is still in close contact with the conscious and from that it follows that early child language is capable of expressing in a direct way the unconscious desires and fantasies. The other view is that early child language is basically inadequate—inadequate to permit the unconscious to come through and therefore insufficient for traditional analysis. And in the works of Freud and Klein we find several passages that clearly express both the first and the second views.

For example, in his work on little Hans, Freud (1909) constantly stressed the importance and richness of early child language. Having attentively followed his language up to age 3 years, Hans's parents became aware that because the child was allowed to express himself without fear, those same sexual impulses and desires appeared that, as Freud states, "we dig out so laboriously in adults from among their own débris" (Freud, 1909, p. 6).

In fact, in the case of little Hans we find one of Freud's most resolute claims in support of what we have called the first position.

> I do not share the view which is at present fashionable that assertions made by children are invariably arbitrary and untrustworthy. The arbitrary has no existence in mental life. The untrustworthiness of the assertions of children is due to the predominance of their imagination, just as the untrustworthiness of the assertions of grown-up people is due to the predominance of their prejudices [Freud, pp. 102–103].

But in the introduction to the same work, acknowledging the undoubted merits of Hans's father–analyst, Freud raised serious doubts as to the possibility of adopting the analytical method as a rule with children because of their inadequate linguistic abilities.

> But his services go further than this. No one else, in my opinion, could possibly have prevailed on the child to make any such avowals; the special knowledge by means of which he was able to interpret the remarks made by his five-year-old son was indispensable, and without it the technical difficulties in the way of conducting a psycho-analysis upon so young a child would have been insuperable. [1909, p. 5].

Although convinced that analysis of child neuroses could prove to be of great theoretical importance, Freud remained skeptical of any possible application of the psychoanalytic technique to children, and he expressed these same doubts more explicitly at the beginning of *From the History of an Infantile Neurosis.*

> An analysis which is conducted upon a neurotic child itself must, as a matter of course, appear to be more trustworthy, but it cannot be very rich in material; too many words and thoughts have to be lent to the child, and even so the deepest strata may turn out to be impenetrable to consciousness [Freud, 1918, pp. 8–9].

Later on, Freud (1933) explicitly recognized the usefulness and the importance of child analysis although he kept stressing the difficulty of applying the same verbal technique used with adults.

> We had no misgivings over applying analytic treatment to children who either exhibited unambiguous neurotic symptoms or who were on the road to an unfavourable development of character. . . . The technique of treatment worked out for adults must, of course, be largely altered for children. A child is psychologically a different object from an adult. As yet he possesses no super-ego, the method of free association does not carry far with

him, transference (since the real parents are still on the spot) plays a different part [p. 148].

The writings of Melanie Klein reflect a substantially analogous attitude toward child language, or rather a tendency to carry both of these positions to their extremes. Using Freud's doubts over the use of psychoanalysis with children as a springboard, Klein (1932/1975) advocated a child analysis based on the play technique rather than the verbal technique used with adults.

> If we do this we shall succeed in making speech—as far as the child is already able to speak—an instrument of its analysis. The reason why we have to do without verbal associations for long periods of their analysis is not only because small children cannot speak with ease but because the acute anxiety they suffer from only permits them to employ a less direct form of representation. Since the primary archaic mode of representation by means of toys and of action is an essential medium of expression for the child, we could certainly never carry out a deep analysis of a child by means of speech alone. Nevertheless, I believe that no analysis of a child, whatever its age, can be said to be really terminated unless the child has employed speech in analysis to its full capacity, for language constitutes the bridge to reality [p. 14, note].

At the same time, it seems clear that Klein (1932/1975) believed that the child's unconscious is much more transparent than the adult's.

> But if we take into consideration how the child's psychology differs from that of the adult—the fact that its unconscious is as yet in close contact with its conscious and that its most primitive impulses are at work alongside of highly complicated mental processes—and if we correctly grasp the child's mode of expression, then all these drawbacks and disadvantages vanish and we find that we may expect to make as deep and extensive an analysis of the child as of the adult. More so in fact. In child analysis we are able to get back to experiences and fixations which in the analysis of adults can often only be reconstructed, whereas the child shows them to us as immediate representations [p.9].

In the final analysis it would appear that Klein, and implicitly Freud himself, acknowledged that what children say often directly reflects their unconscious, but felt that adopting the verbal technique used with adults would be of little benefit in child analysis. In the first place, they judged the language of children, especially very young ones, to be basically inadequate. In second place, they held that the excessive anxiety children suffer from makes a thorough verbalization on their part impossible. In short, Klein and Freud held that this verbalization, although indispensable, is very difficult to achieve.

The material at our disposal on the language of a very young child outside of an analytic setting shows that this verbalization is carried on continually by the child and with great immediacy and spontaneity—even if, as Klein claimed, it seems possible only early on when the child has not yet experienced excessive anxiety.

In the present work, we want to reassert the claim made by Freud and Klein on the predominance of child imagination and the very close contact that exists between the unconscious and the conscious. However, we also want to counter the opinion that there is insufficient language ability in very small children and claim instead that before "the acute anxiety they suffer from" prevents them from translating their unconscious fantasies into words, these very fantasies continually and explicitly come through in their language.

ANALYSIS OF THE DATA

It may be useful to describe briefly the methodology we adopted. Our main objective was to collect the child's spontaneous language in the most natural situation possible; therefore, we went to Francesco's house approximately every 2 weeks and usually stayed all afternoon. The child was allowed to play freely and interact with whomever he pleased, usually in his playroom, sometimes in the garden or in other rooms of the house where he chose to play. In addition to the two observers (Paola Tieri and myself) the mother was present at every session, the father less frequently, and other relatives and acquaintances sporadically. The tape recorder we used was equipped with a powerful microphone capable of recording everything uttered by Francesco and other speakers. The recorder was placed in a corner of the room next to the father's audio equipment (the father often taped classical music, so the presence of a tape recorder in that spot in no way disturbed Francesco) and it remained on for about 2 hours. The content of the tapes and the additional explanatory comments on the situation were always transcribed in their entirety within a few days after each session.

The sessions began in May, 1970 when Francesco was 1:4. The present work is based on the transcriptions of Sessions 20–33, covering the period from March, 1971—the onset of the pregnancy—to October, 1971—the birth of the little sister Chiara.

All those sentences that seemed particularly significant are presented in the following pages. Between sessions we have inserted comments that, we want to stress, are purely explanatory in nature and in no way presume to offer psychoanalytical interpretations, which we neither wish nor are trained to do.

It is also important to add that in Francesco's family the new birth was discussed openly from the beginning. The transcriptions enabled us to reconstruct and evaluate both the attitudes of the family members and our own attitudes as observers.

By Session 20, at the very beginning of his mother's pregnancy, Francesco suddenly shows aggression toward his dolls as is evident in several of his sentences—a behavior that he had not exhibited in the preceding 19 sessions:

Session 20: 12 March 1971[1]

(He throws a doll on the floor and hits it)

V. Why are you hitting it?
Francesco, why?

20-31 'cause she's bad, bad

V. She's bad? Well, what did she
do?

20-32 smacks (noun)

20-33 Francesco throws it out

(On a napkin is a doll playing a drum and he says she is bad. Maybe he's told it to his grandmother)

M. Francesco, tell Virginia which
one is the bad girl.

V. Why is she bad?

20-34 . . . bad girl.

20-35 she has a stick.

M. What is she doing with the
stick?

20-36 da da da.

M. To who?

V. No she is playing the drum.

M. You see she is good, she is
playing the drum.

(He steps on a doll)

V. Take the doll.

M. Now she wasn't bad, I don't
believe it.

* * *

20-207 made peepee in her pants,
peepee in her pants.

V. She didn't make peepee in her
pants, she's dry.

In Session 21, Francesco refers to an episode that occurred the day before; the aggression he has already displayed against the dolls is now directed at chil-

---

[1]20 = number of session; 31 = 31st utterance made by the child in the course of that session. The child's sentences appear on the left hand side of the page. V = Virginia (called "Inni" by the child); M = Mother; P = Paola; Pd = Father. Comments appear in parentheses. Asterisks separate the excerpts where segments of the dialogue have been omitted here. The transcription was not phonetic, but respected the modifications the child made on words. In part this baby talk was lost in the translation from Italian into English. The complete original text, however, is in the author's possession.

dren smaller than him. He also speaks of *pancia* ("belly") and *ettellino* "little brother"), and for the first time a mysterious *bimbo mio* ("my child") is mentioned.

Session 21: March 1971

21-94 The little girl.	V. No, don't hit the little girl . . .
21-95 Ahr ahr.	V. Who goes like that?
21-96 The little girl.	M. Yesterday he went to Alessandra's party. And he behaved aggressively toward a 1-year-old girl.
21-97 Bad that little girl.	M. But that's not true that she was bad. When you wanted her tricycle she gave it to you right away.
21-98 Go away . . . go away.	V. Why did you send her away?
	M. What did the little girl want?
21-99 The tricycle.	M. The tricycle. Whose? The one that belongs to . . .?
21-100 Lalla (his name for his little cousin Alessandra)	
	M. And so he sent her away saying that she was ugly. What did Mommy say to you . . .
21-101 This little girl naughty.	V. What game did you play with her?
21-102 The belly. . . .	
21-103 Smack . . . then I smack go away.	
	V. Why did you say to her "away, little girl"?
21-104 Little brother is coming home. Little brother is coming.	
	V. What does he have at home?
	M. He's coming?
21-105 Little brother.	V. Who is coming? The little bird?

21-106 I said, "Away! You don't
       touch belly there, it's little
       girl"

          M. You don't touch the belly of the
             little girl? But who wanted to
             touch the belly of the little girl?

21-107 I did.

          M. Oh! you. Then who has told you
             that you don't touch the little
             girl's belly? Who is it who comes
             to tell you?

21-108 The little girl, my child.

          M. Your child? 'Cause you have a
             child?

21-109 A teeny, teeny one.

          M. Ah! You have a teeny teeny one?

          V. And where do you have it?

21-110 At my house.

          V. At your house?

21-111 At Tullio's (the child of the
       housekeeper).

          V. At Tullio's? You have a little
             brother at Tullio's.

21-112 Teeny teeny.

          V. Ah! You have a teeny teeny child
             of yours at Tullio's. And why do
             you keep it at Tullio's?

21-113 He speaks, this child, he   V. He speaks?
       speaks.

21-114 Bang bang (changing the
       subject).

          M. Francesco in the morning always
             leaves over a little of his food.
             Who do you leave it for,
             Francesco?

21-115 The little boy.   M. Which little boy?

21-116 Tiny little bottle, my bottle.

It is important to analyze briefly the episode that gave rise to this long sequence. The preceding day, Francesco had gone to his little cousin Alessandra's party, he had quarreled with a little girl, younger then he, and he had hit her on her belly. The words he uses, "Away! you don't touch belly there, it's little girl," were in fact uttered by Francesco's mother, who had been startled by this sudden aggression. As for the "little brother" that is mentioned, we can only offer hypotheses. Given that it really means "little brother" and not "little bird" (he says *ettellino*, which could be interpreted as *fratellino*, "little brother," or *uccellino*, "little bird"), as the observer seems to interpret it, it can refer either to his cousin Alessandra's little brother who was at the party, or it can be a little brother that someone has evidently begun to speak about to him. The interesting point here is that this *ettellino* is immediately linked to the belly of the little girl–mommy. As for the "my child" and "teeny teeny," we need only stress here that (verbally) he moves it immediately from his house to Tullio's. Finally, as to the "food" that he takes care to leave over (in reality, it is for the little birds in the garden who are always given leftovers and crumbs) we want to stress the role of the parent Francesco has up to now been assuming with this child–boy. Let us examine more data.

Session 22: 14 April 1971

22–68 I pushed Paolo.	M. You pushed Paolo. Tell Virginia why you pushed Paolo.
22–69 Little, not big, Paolo, little.	
	V. He's little, he's not big, I know. But it's not his fault, is it? And why did you . . .
22–70 He has the pacifier.	V. And you, what do you have when you go to bed?
22–71 . . . Pacifier.	V. So you are little too if you have a pacifier?
	M. Today he made a whole speech about a little baby.

* * *

(He had put the little brush in his mother's eye)

	M. What did you do to Mommy's eye the other morning?
22–108 Went da da and it hit . . . here.	
	M. I got hurt, yes I did, and then what did Mommy put on it?
22–110 Band-aid.	M. The Band-Aid and the ointment.

In Session 22, the aggression now appears to be directed at his little cousin Paolo, and in part toward his mother. Here it is important to recall one of

Klein's (1927/1975) views, which is fundamental to our understanding of Francesco's problems and difficulties in this period, particularly this aggressive behavior against his mother and her belly.

> There is another relation which plays a fundamental role. This is the relation to brothers and sisters; every analysis proves that all children suffer great jealousy of younger sisters and brothers as well as of older ones. Even the quite small child, which seemingly knows nothing about birth, has a very distinct unconscious knowledge of the fact that children grow in the mother's womb. A great hate is directed against this child in the mother's womb for reasons of jealousy, and—as typical of the phantasies of a child during the mother's expectancy of another one—we find desires to mutilate the mother's womb and to deface the child in it by biting and cutting it [p. 173].

Confirming this unconscious awareness of children regarding their mother's pregnancy, a sentence of Francesco's mother appearing in Session 22 informs us that Francesco already speaks often of a "little child," a figure that will be frequently named in subsequent sessions.

Session 23: 27 April 1971

| | M. And where do you keep the teeny teeny child? |
| 23-97 In my pocket. | M. Show it to Inni and Paola. |

(He pretends to take something out of his pocket.)

| | V. How small he is. But does he *eat*? |
| 23-98 No. | M. And what is the name of the little child? |

23-99 Francesco.

As to the "place" where this mysterious "teeny teeny child" is kept—that is, in Francesco's pocket-belly—it should be noted that already by Session 21 (as evidenced in its complete transcription) the child often talks about things he has in his pocket, such as tissues or keys, and in Session 22 he discovers with delight a piece from a game in his pocket. The other important piece of information in this session is that he calls the child "Francesco." This means that for some reason Francesco indentifies with this child of his; this identification will be reconfirmed later.

The sentences transcribed here from Session 24 seem to have little to do with all the others; they appear rather to be closely connected to the subsequent session, so it seems opportune to examine both sessions jointly. The transgressions that he attributes to the little bear and the monkey are attributed immediately thereafter to "my child," with Francesco assuming the role of the wise old parent toward all three.

Session 24: 12 May 1971

24-115 . . . Little bear has a booboo.

V. How beautiful this bear is!

24-116 There's booboo here.

V. This bear has a booboo?

24-117 Yes.

V. How did he get the booboo?

24-118 Like this bang with a screwdriver.

V. With the screwdriver?

24-119 Yes.

V. But why was he playing with the screwdriver, that little bear?

24-120 He went over there. . . .

24-121 He took Daddy's hammer.

V. Well, I'll bet he hurt himself; why, little bears can't use hammers and screwdrivers, if they do, they'll hurt themselves.

* * *

24-146 You see monkey.

V. *La scimmia* ("the monkey," f), not *scimmio* (m), *scimmia*.

24-147 *Scimmio* (repeats error by using the masculine gender.)

V. What a lively checkered outfit he has on.

24-148 Those pants, he made peepee in it (facing monkey).

V. He made in his pants?

24-149 Yes.

24-150 Take this off? (the safety pin that holds up the monkey's suspenders).

V. No, why do you want to undress him?

24-151 Because he made peepee in his pants.

Session 25: 29 May 1971

25-8 I have the big belly, I have (pulling up his pants that are too wide for him).

P. But it's not that they're too wide, it means that you've gotten thinner.

* * *

V. Be careful with those pliers . . .
Once I saw a child pick up pliers
like these and hurt himself.

(Referring indirectly to an episode where Francesco had disobeyed)

P. Did you see that child Francesco?

25-52 My child got that booboo on
his finger. He picked up the
pliers.

P. He picked up the pliers.

25-54 My child.

V. Your child picked up the pliers
and what did he do?

25-55 A booboo on his finger.

* * *

25-77 (Closing the front door of the
house) That's so the ugly boy
doesn't come in.

These sentences, like many others that we have examined or are about to
examine, seem to confirm fully the observations made at the Tavistock Clinic
of Child Psychology on children who go through the same experience as Francesco (Harris, 1969). These children, too, shift from playing child to playing
mother, as is evident from statements like "my child," "I have a baby in my
belly," "I have a baby in my Mommy's belly," and "my child is born."

The subsequent session shows how these statements are comparable to Francesco's production. Let us examine them in turn.

Session 26: 12 June 1971

M. Listen . . . did you tell Paola
about the cannon.

26-24 My baby got scared.

P. Why did he get scared? Where is
your baby?

26-25 There.

(The cannon that goes off to signal noon-time is described.)

M. And then what happens? Your
child, what did he do?

26-26 He cried, then he cried.

* * *

26-34 Bam! I close the door of the
car (he pretends; laughs).

M. You close it well now! Did you
put on the steering wheel block?

26-35 . . . I do it this way . . .
I'm going to see my wife.

V. You're going to see who?

P. Your wife . . .

V. Who went da! da! to him?

* * *

26-112 I went "pic."

V. You went "pic" because he was a
bad boy? What had he done?

26-113 He touched the little pot
(the monkey; it was really
Francesco who several days
before turned over the little
pot).

26-122 (Addressing the monkey
with a loud voice) . . . Why
did you touch the little pot?

P. What did he say?

26-123 He said yes, he touched the
little pot.

M. Ah! He touched the little pot?
And you, what did you do to
him?

26-124 It all fell here and hurt him.

* * *

V. But I'm not in the least bit afraid
of thunder. Only teeny teeny
children are afraid of thunder.

26-163 Why are there teeny teeny
teeny children?

V. Because there are. Why, don't
you like them?

26-164 No.

V. And why not?

26-165 Pi . . . pipo paapo (a little
game he plays with his
father).

V. They go pipo-papo, the little
children?

(He throws something on the floor)

*   *   *

26-170 Goes "boom"!   P. It sounded like the cannon at
                                             noon.

26-171 Why does the cannon go
"boom"?

                                          P. So that everyone can hear that it's
                                             noon.
26-172 No!   V. Are you afraid of the cannon?
26-173 So much, and then, I . . .
(goes "boom" and bangs
at the same time).

                                          V. Huh?

26-174 The cannon goes "boom."
                                          V. Oh, the cannon.
26-175 This is the Gianicolo (the   P. The Gianicolo is here?
hill in Rome from which the
noonday cannon is fired).
26-176 I brought my baby to the
Gianicolo.

                                          V. And your baby, what did he say?
                                             Was he frightened?

(He does not answer)

                                          V. Where is your baby now?
26-177 Asleep.   P. Listen, is your baby teeny teeny?
                                             Do you like your baby?

26-178 He's behind here (behind the
bicycle).

                                          V. Does he like to ride the bike?

26-179 . . . he likes it!? (He
changes the subject)

*   *   *

26–212 (Shouts) my wife is singing!	V. What is your wife doing, singing?
26–213 Yes.	V. But where is your wife?
(Unintelligible).	V. Sleeping? And what is your wife's name? So I can call her.
26–214 (He calls her, shouting.) My wife!	V. What is your wife's name?
26–215 I'll go get her. . . .	V. Oh, you'll go get her, good. We'll wait for her.
26–216 Here she is. (He pretends to bring her.)	V. Hi, Francesco's wife!

In reality, "my baby" is, on one hand, none other than Francesco himself who gets frightened at the sound of the Gianicolo cannon and cries; on the other hand, Francesco is also identifying with the father–husband who closes the car door and goes home to his "wife"; not only that, but on another occasion he even goes to get this wife of his to introduce her to us! But when he scolds the monkey for having "touched the little pot," he is playing the mother who does not want Francesco to go near the stove while she is cooking. Finally, when he lets his defenses down and asks "Why are there teeny teeny teeny children" and openly admits that he does not like these teeny teeny children at all, he is not assuming here any particular role other than Francesco at 2:5, who is afraid of the arrival of a little baby who will probably be allowed to do all those things (cry because he's afraid of thunder, urinate in his pants, etc.) for which he is scolded because "he's a big boy now." This complex network of identifications continues and becomes richer in new details in the subsequent session.

Session 27: 6 July 1971

(Francesco has succeeded in unbuttoning his mother's dress, pretending to take out the "little baby"; following his mother's questioning "Where is the little baby?" he shows it to Virginia; Virginia asks "But where will you put it?" and "Did you get his bed ready for him?" Francesco looks around and then his mother says "Let's put him in Francesco's room.")

(He leaves in the car, waving)

	M. Who are you waving at?
27–77 My wife.	V. Is your wife still around?
27–78 Yes, still.	V. I thought you had gotten divorced.
	M. Where is your wife?
27–79 She's playing.	M. Playing, is she?

27-80 With my baby.

M. What is her name?

V. The baby too, but then you go to work if you have a wife and a baby?

27-81 This came out (a small piece of a keychain).

M. What is your wife's name?

V. Is her name Virginia? Is her name Paola?

27-82 Yes now . . . now . . . now is your daughter's name?

V. My daughter? She's not named anything because I don't have one.

M. Virginia doesn't have a daughter.

V. I don't have one, do you?

(He answers yes with a nod of his head)

V. Where is your daughter?

27-83 She's over there.

V. There where? What is your daughter's name?

27-84 Daniela, Daniela.

M. Daniela? Is your wife?

27-85 She's little.

M. She is little!

27-86 My little baby.

M. Your baby is little! Yes, I know that your baby is teeny teeny.

27-87 Virginia is little too.

V. But which is the little baby? Whose little baby is this?

27-88 Mine.

27-89 Ciao!

V. What is this baby of yours like? Is he good or bad?

27-90 No!

M. What do you mean "no."

27-91 Vroom, the car is here.

M. It's here.

27-92 I take for a ride?

M. Take it for a ride.

27-93 I am going to buy a little a little bit of milk.

M. What are you going to buy?

27-94 Milk.

M. A little milk?

27-95 Af . . . after . . . this is my baby.

V. Oh, a little milk for your baby?

27-96 Where are they here?

V. Where are what?

27-97 Vroom vroom ciao!

(He goes away in the car)

M and V. Ciao!

27-98 Good morning.

(He comes back).

V. Where is the milk? Did he buy it?

M. Where is the milk?

M. Oh, somewhere else, I see.

27-99 It's somewhere else. It's in the car.

27-100 In the car.

M. And aren't you going to take it out of the car. Aren't you going to get it?

27-101 Should I take it from here?

M. Sure.

27-102 Here we are.

V. And who are you going to give it to now?

27-103 To my baby.

V. Does your baby like milk?

27-104 You give it.

V. Let's give it to Riccardo (a stuffed animal).

27-105 I'll buy another one for Riccardo.

V. Oh, it wasn't for Riccardo?

27-106 . . . My baby . . . .

V. And where do you keep this baby?

27-107 (Annoyed) He's home.

V. But where do you live?

27-108 Somewhere else.

* * *

(Virginia shows Francesco the photograph on her driver's license taken when she had long hair)

V. Do you know who this is?

(Francesco is perplexed)

M. Who is it, Francesco?

27-127 It's your daughter.

V. No, it's not my daughter; it's me with long hair. I had it cut after that.

27-140 (To his mother who has
       come back into the room
       after having answered the
       telephone.)   M. What's the matter with Renato?

                                      V. No, he called.

27-141 Do you have Renato too?   V. Huh?
       (Francesco's father's name is
       Renato).

27-142 You do, or where is your   V. It's near the University.
       house?

27-143 You have . . . your little   V. What do I have at my house?
       friends.

27-144 Your little friends.

                                *   *   *

                                      M. You already did some damage
                                         today? What did you do today?

(The mother tells Virginia that he fell with a bottle in his hand)

                                      M. Augusta told me that you hurt
                                         your knee, is that true? And that
                                         it bled?

27-185 . . . here . . .   V. What were you doing with a
                                         bottle in your hand?

27-186 Do you know it fell?   V. But what were you doing with
                                         the bottle in your hand? Where
                                         did you want to bring it? Huh?

27-187 It fell!   M. Yes, but where did you want to
                                         bring it, huh?

27-188 Down!   M. But you don't touch bottles or
                                         any other thing made of glass;
                                         Mommy told you that.

27-189 They all (fell) even my little
       baby dropped a whole
       bottle.

                                      M. Oh, your baby dropped the
                                         bottle.

27-190 He took (it) boom . . . touch M. And what did you do to your
       . . . I take it.   baby?

27-191 (Severely) a . . . spanking.   M. A spanking.

27-192 Here he is, he's naughty.

It seems that we now have sufficient material to make a more analytical comparison of Francesco's and little Hans's fantasies. At 4:9, Hans began to display a series of fears and was caught up in anxiety attacks that practically kept him from leaving the house. At that point, the father, a follower of Professor Freud who for 2 years had been taking notes on the behavior and development of his son, tried to practice real analysis on Hans in an attempt to unblock the situation. This analysis came to a successful conclusion 5 months later, revealing that the birth of his little sister Hanna a year and a half before had indirectly played an important role in the evolution of the neurosis. In particular, and of greatest interest to us, the fact emerges that even though no one had spoken with him about the child in his mother's belly, Hans had taken notice of his mother's pregnancy and was just as aware that Hanna was with them even before she was born. Freud comments

> And at this point Hans gave us a surprise, for which we were not in the very least prepared. He had noticed his mother's pregnancy, which had ended with the birth of his little sister when he was three and a half years old, and had, at any rate after the confinement, pieced the facts of the case together—without telling anyone, it is true, and perhaps without being able to tell any one. All that could be seen at the time was that immediately after the delivery he had taken up an extremely skeptical attitude towards everything that might be supposed to point to the presence of the stork.[2] *But that—in complete contradiction to his official speeches—he knew in his unconscious where the baby came from and where it had been before*, is proved beyond a shadow of doubt by the present analysis; indeed, this is perhaps its most unassailable feature.

> The most cogent evidence of this is furnished by the fantasy (which he persisted in with so much obstinacy, and embellished with such a wealth of detail) of how Hanna had been with them at Gmunden the summer before her birth, of how she had travelled there with them, and of how she had been able to do far more then than she had a year later, after she had been born [1909, p. 129].

And so the analogy with the fantasies about the forthcoming child begins to take form—an analogy that appears even more evident if we examine some of the sentences of Hans himself. Just like Francesco, Hans attributes forbidden actions to his unborn sister, actions that he himself would like to perform but that at the same time disturb and frighten him.

> Hanna travelled to Gmunden in the big box, and Mummy travelled in the luggage train with the box; and then when we got to Gmunden Mummy and I lifted Hanna out and

---

[2] It is astonishing to us that Hans's parents, although extremely progressive in most respects, trying to be clear and explicit on nearly every subject, never spoke to their child about the pregnancy and persisted in telling the tale of the stork. Only 2 years after Hanna's birth, at the end of analysis, did they decide to describe the way things really are. Evidently in those times it was totally unthinkable to tell young children how babies are born.

put her on the horse. The coachman sat up in front, and Hanna had the old whip [the whip he had last year] and whipped the horse and kept on saying "Gee-up," and it was such fun [p. 75].

There is no doubt that we are dealing here with actions he wished to perform but that frightened him.

HANS. When you're cross with them you tease them and when you shout "Gee-up!" (Hans has often been very much terrified when drivers beat their horses and shout "Gee-up."
I. Have you ever teased horses?
HANS. Yes, quite often. I'm *afraid* I shall do it, but I don't *really* [p. 79].

In addition, Hans, like Francesco, imagined that he himself is "making" babies, or rather a baby that by some strange coincidence is also named Hans!

At Gmunden I lay down in the grass—no, I knelt down—and the children didn't look on at me, and all at once in the morning I said: "Look for it, children; I laid an egg yesterday." And all at once they looked, and all at once they saw an egg, and out of it there came a little Hans [p. 85].

And just as Francesco treats the children with love and concern,

"I had them to sleep with me, the girls and the boys. . . . When I couldn't get all the children into the bed, I put some of the children on the sofa, and some in the pram, and if there were still some left over I took them up to the attic and put them in the box, and if there were any more I put them in the other box [p. 94].

The father comments on this: "I have already noticed in earlier records that since Hans's return from Gmunden he has constantly been having phantasies about 'his children,' has carried on conversations with them, and so on" (p. 93).

Finally, Hans, like Francesco, imagined that he has a wife and "In his triumphant final phantasy . . . he was married to his beautiful mother and had innumerable children whom he could look after in his own way" (p. 114).

We could go on, but instead of a meticulous analysis that only psychoanalysts could and perhaps will do, we are more interested in convincing the reader that we are in no way dealing with a purely chance similarity. This similarity is of extreme interest, for at least two reasons. First, it is significant that the fantasies of Hans, who was told the tale of the stork, are similar to Francesco's, although Francesco was explicitly told that the baby was in his mother's belly. Second, as we already hinted at the beginning. Hans's fantasies about his mother's pregnancy appeared a posteriori, at the time of the analysis, but Francesco's fantasies appeared during the pregnancy itself.

We also want to point out that it is this very difference that makes Francesco's data particularly valuable, in our opinion, because it permits us to follow the first appearance, the development, and the consequent relative disappearance of these fantasies about "my baby," "my wife," and all the others. We can actually say that in the last session we examined, Session 27, when Francesco's mother is in her 6th month, these fantasies reach their peak in the sense that they appear more frequently and are richer in detail than at any other time. By Session 28, although the content is closely tied to the preceding sessions, there is much less richness of material.

Session 28: 23 July 1971

28-69 He breaks everything, boy!
my baby breaks everything.

V. What does he break?

28-70 My toy.

V. He broke your toy? Which toy did your baby break? Where is your baby?

* * *

(We are outside in the garden by a small pool)

P. What about you, aren't you going in for a swim?

28-94 Tomorrow.

P. Oh, tommorow! And today, who's going in?

28-95 My baby.

P. Oh, your baby today? Did you undress your baby?

28-96 Yes.

P. Then take him in for a swim.

(But he is the one who actually goes in for the swim)

* * *

28-112 (Pointing to the painter who has been painting the house for several days) Who is he?

P. He is the man who is fixing up the house.

28-113 Michele

P. Michele?

28-114 He has a baby. . .

P. What is his name?

28-115 Gianni.

P. Gianni is his baby's name? Is he little like you? Is he bigger?

28-116 He is bigger (turning to Michele).
Is your baby bigger?

As is evident in this session just as in the others, "my baby" gets into trouble, on one hand, and on the other does things that Francesco is afraid to do himself: He breaks toys, but he also goes in the pool for a swim that he was a bit afraid to take at the beginning. Furthermore, in this session we find great interest in other people's children. In this period, having established a relationship with an adult, Francesco sets about at once to find out if he or she has any children and he repeatedly asks about them. In the case of the observer, as we saw in the preceding sessions, he persists in his questioning about a possible "daughter" and "little friends" she might have and whose existence he evidently fears. Perhaps he is also afraid that other adults, like his mother, may betray him with other little babies.

In any event, Session 28, for the most part rather poor in material, appears to bring an important period to a close. From this point on, in the five subsequent sessions that also precede the birth of his sister, we will find only a fleeting reference to "my wife" and an even more fleeting one to "my baby." Francesco, as we will see, became more and more evasive and not very willing to express his fantasies about the forthcoming arrival freely. His words reveal merely the echo of the adult participation; when asked persistently about his little brother, he responded hurriedly and rather mechanically, demonstrating that he has passively internalized the adults' explanations.

Session 29: 14 August 1971

	V. Tell me, has your little brother arrived yet?
29-51 I'm going to get my little brother.	V. Good, go get him.
29-52 Where is he? Where is he? Where is my little brother?	
	V. Oh, I don't know where he is? Is he here?
29-53 He's with Jesus (an explanation that is habitually given him by his grandmother) [3].	M. Where is he?
29-54 With Jesus.	P. This is a new one on me!
29-55 Far far away.	V. But what is it?
29-56 Let's go outside and play, Virginia.	

[3]Unlike his parents, Francesco's grandmother and probably other adults continue to tell the traditional tale whereby the little brother or sister will be brought by the baby Jesus or by the stork.

* * *

(He has just been told the story of Goldilocks)

	V. Tell me what your room is like. Is there a crib?
	M. A big bed.
	V. And whose big bed is it?
29-118 Mine . . .	M. And who are we putting in your room?
29-119 The little child.	M. The little child.

Session 30: 27 August 1971

	M. Whose puppy is that?
30-57 It's my wife's.	P. It's your wife's?
30-58 Yes!	P. You mean, you have a wife? Where is she? Let me see her.
30-59 She's in the car.	P. Oh, you left her there.
	M. What is your little brother bringing you when he arrives?
30-60 a car just like it . . . vroom . . . vroom . . . (just like Maurilio's, a friend of his. His parents have promised that his little brother is bringing a new car)	

(Francesco is very excited about the idea and he goes on for a bit about Maurilio's car.)

	P. But I didn't know that little brothers bring things like that. Well, then, how many brothers and sisters do you want? So many?
30-64 Yes, I do, so many . . .	
30-65 I shut the motor off vroom vroom (getting into his old car).	
30-66 Why are you getting up?	P. If I don't, you'll run me over.

30–67 Vroom vroom.	P. You sure do need a new car because this one's a little old. Let's hope you little brother hurries up and gets here . . . no?
30–68 No, I this . . . this is not old.	P. No, it's not old, but, well, it is a bit small.
	M. Where should we put your little brother? Tell Paola where you're going to put him?
30–69 In the crib.	M. Where? In (whose) room?
30–70 Mine . . .	

If we attempt to explain this unmistakable change that has appeared in our data, it is important to recall once again that the material we are examining here is essentially linguistic in nature, and therefore our evaluation is valid only at this level. The fact that Francesco does not speak more explicitly about his fears and desires regarding his little brother does in no way mean that these fantasies of his no longer exist. Rather, it is probable that as the pregnancy progresses his anxiety will increase. This claim should be confirmed by other extralinguistic data that could show that Francesco's anxiety really increased as the pregnancy advanced, but as our research had other objectives, we did not gather data on all aspects of his behavior. The only thing we are able to affirm is that throughout that entire period, Francesco did not tolerate being apart from his mother and consequently he became much naughtier.

At this point we can directly apply Klein's statement on children (1932/1975, p. 14, note) in which she affirms that "the acute anxiety they suffer from" makes their use of language difficult and "permits them to employ a less direct form of representation . . . primary and archaic" by means of toys and action. In Francesco's case it would appear that precisely when this so fantasy-filled and dreaded event drew near, the child no longer wished to speak of it or was no longer able to do so.

In Session 31, we were not able to find even the remotest hint of the event. In Session 32 Francesco repeats the words of the adults, and tell about a little girl in nursery school who cries because she wants her mother (something that Francesco does regularly); he pretends to revert to infancy, making believe he does not know how to talk.

Session 32: 27 September 1971

(The topic of conversation is the car that his little brother is bringing as a gift)

M. But she (Paola) doesn't know who is going to bring it to you.

32-81 My little brother, that's who!
If you cry at school: nothing.

    P. If you cry at school: nothing.
Your little brother already told
you that?

    M. No, it's not that he's not
bringing him anything; he's
bringing that for little children,
because only little children cry.
They don't understand that their
mommy is coming back.

*   *   *

32-142 O . . . betto

    M. And who is Roberto?

32-143 He's the one at school.

    P. But then you *do* have little
friends in school!

32-144 Little girl, teeny teeny.

    P. There's a teeny teeny girl

32-145 She's really crying, that little
girl.

32-146 She wants her mommy, her
mommy wasn't there.

    P. And you, what do you say to that
little girl?

32-147 Don't cry because your
mommy's coming; don't cry

    P. That's right. Tell her "play with
me."

32-148 (turning over a chair,
speaking in nonsense)
Gagga, gagga

    V. What a silly child!

    M. Every once in a while he gets
small again.

32-149 Baba, gaga.

    P. Well, where is this little girl who
is so small that she speaks so
stupidly!?

32-150 There she is.

    P. Little girl, it's okay that you are
small, but learn to speak well!

32-151 Gr gr ah.

    V. Hey, what are you, a lion? It's no
fun playing with someone who
talks like that; we're leaving!

Finally, in the last session before the mother goes to the hospital to deliver, and after a fleeting reference to "my baby" who at this point lives alone in another house, we are witness to a pathetic, extreme attempt by Francesco dressed as a traffic police officer trying to kick out the bad child who is virtually on the doorstep.

Session 33: 13 October 1971

33–24 Wait, I'll go buy ice cream
without the car.

                    V. You're walking there?

33–25 Yes.   P. You buy it and we'll wait.

33–26 I'm going near my baby's
house.

                    V. Near your baby's house?

33–27 Yes . . .   V. Why doesn't your baby live here
                                  any more? Has she moved?

33–28 Yes (and he runs off).

* * *

(The day before returning by car from downtown we got into a terrible traffic jam)

33–34 Tomorrow there was too
much traffic of cars

                    M. Tomorrow there was too much
                              traffic?

33–35 I did like this: I kicked them
(out).

(Paola shows him the photograph of the traffic jam in the newspaper)

                    V. But was it tomorrow or yesterday
                              that there was so much traffic? I
                              think it was yesterday.

33–36 No.   V. Oh, it really was tomorrow?

33–37 . . . He was too naughty, and
I kicked him out like this . . .
out like this, tomorrow I have
my hat, I kill.

                    V. You don't have any hat!

P. Tomorrow what are you going to
do with your hat? Kill someone?

(He goes into the kitchen and comes back with a pair of goggles on. He also puts a basket on his head pretending that it is a policeman's cap)

V. A policeman with goggles is
coming; who knows who sent
him? Good day, Mr. Policeman.

33–38 Come on. Come on!
(directs traffic).

P. How hard it is to be a traffic
policeman.

33–39 When a child breaks his car I
kick him out like this.

V. Who is it that's breaking his car?

33–40 A bad boy.

Now that all of the sessions have been examined, it seems opportune to summarize and outline the more salient aspects of each session:

Session 20: 12 March 1971—age 2:1;15
Aggression toward his dolls
Session 21: 28 March 1971—age 2:2;1
Aggression toward children smaller than he is
He begins to speak of "my child" "teeny" (who is at Tullio's)
Session 22: 14 April 1971—age 2:2;17
Aggression toward his cousin Paolo who is "teeny"
Aggression toward his mother
His mother informs us that he is talking about his "teeny baby"
Session 23: 27 April 1971—age 2:3;0
He keeps the little baby in his pocket, he shows it; its name is Francesco
Session 24: 12 May 1971—age 2:3;15
The little bear hurt himself because he picked up Daddy's screwdriver and
hammer
The monkey made peepee in his pants
Francesco is the wise parent
Session 25: 29 May 1971—age 2:4;2
The big belly is discussed
"My child"hurt himself because he picked up Daddy's pliers (a threat made
to Francesco)
Session 26: 12 June 1971—age 2:4;15
The monkey turned over the little pot that was on the stove (Francesco had
actually done it)

"My baby" is afraid of the cannon and he cries (Francesco was afraid of it and he cried)

"My wife" appears on the scene

Session 27: 6 July 1971—age 2:5;9

A scene, not on tape: the "teeny baby" is in the mother's belly, he takes it out and shows it to Virginia, the observer

Francesco has a wife and child; he goes out to buy milk for this little child–baby

"My baby" dropped a bottle (Francesco had actually done it), he was very stern and gave it a spanking

Virginia is asked about her child (that she does not have) and he talks of "tiny little friends" that are at Virginia's house

Session 28: 23 July 1971—age 2:5;26

"My baby" breaks everything: "my toy"

"My baby" takes a swim in the pool

He asks about Michele's babies

Session 29: 14 August 1971—age 2:6;17

His little brother is with Jesus (Grandma's doing!)

He has found out that his room will also be inhabited by a "little child"

Session 30: 27 August 1971—age2:7;0

His little brother, when he comes, will bring a big new car

He replies in monosyllables to any questions regarding his "little brother"; he will put him in the "crib" in his room

Session 31

Nothing of any significance

Session 32: 27 September 1971—age 2:8;0

His little brother will bring him a big car as a present

He pretends he's the little child who doesn't know how to talk

Session 33: 13 October 1971—age 2:8;16

"Near my baby's house"; the baby has moved

Dressed as a traffic police officer he gets angry with a "bad boy" and kicks him out

21 October 1971

Chiara is born

FINAL REMARKS

We would like to suggest here some more general considerations that may be drawn from the present work.

Developmental psycholinguists now have available to them some extremely interesting material, but they analyze only certain aspects, and from a linguistic point of view; other important topics are either treated superficially or totally ignored. In this chapter I have tried to present some data that are particularly relevant, in my view, to psychologists, therapists, and other professional groups working in the field of child development.

The limitations of this work are evident: It is always difficult when dealing with a topic that is outside one's own field of research. As a psycholinguist I have analyzed and compared data probably more suited to a psychoanalyst. This fact may have led to a certain degree of naiveté and/or possible misinterpretations of the material I have examined. On the other hand, this work is based on data gathered outside the analytical setting and it gave us the unique opportunity of verifying Freud's and Klein's opinions on child language.

Our data confirm Freud's and Klein's claims about the close contact between the unconscious and the conscious in children and about the freshness of their impulses and desires: Francesco's examples show that children are able to let their unconscious desires and fantasies come through their language in a direct manner.

However, our data go beyond Freud's and Klein's expectations. The fact that at the age of two Francesco is already letting his fantasies come through in his language with such a degree of immediacy and spontaneity dissipates Freuds's and Klein's fears that language in very small children may be insufficient and inadequate.

Once again, it appears that very small children are both able and willing to speak, but more often than not it is the adults who are not able and not willing to listen.

ACKNOWLEDGMENTS

I wish to thank Fiorella Bassan for her advice, criticism, and suggestions, and Elizabeth Bates for having encouraged me repeatedly to publish this material. I want to thank Paola Tieri who participated with me in the data collection and transcription.

REFERENCES

Bates, E. *Language and context: Acquisition of pragmatics.* New York: Academic Press, 1976.
Freud, S. [Analysis of a phobia in a five-year-old boy.] In James Strachey (Ed. and trans.) The standard edition of the complete psychological works of Sigmund Freud. (Vol. 10). London: The Hogarth Press, 1909.

Freud, S. [From the history of an infantile neurosis.] In James Strachey (Ed. and trans.) The standard edition of the complete psychological works of Sigmund Freud. (Vol. 17.) London: The Hogarth Press, 1918.

Freud, S. [New introductory lectures on psycho-analysis.]In James Strachey (Ed. and trans.) The standard edition of the complete psychological works of Sigmund Freud. (Vol. 22). London: The Hogarth Press, 1933.

Harris, M. *On Understanding Infants.* London: Dickens Press, 1969.

Klein, M. [Criminal tendencies in Normal children.] In *Love, guilt and reparation and other works—1921-1945.* New York: Delacorte Press—Seymour Lawrence, 1975. (Originally published, 1927).

Klein, M. *The psycho-analysis of children.* New York: Delacorte Press—Seymour Lawrence, 1975. (Originally published, 1932.)

Parisi, D., & Antinucci, F. Early Language development: A second stage. In *Current Problems in Psycholinguistics.* Paris: Éditions du Centre National de la Recherche Scientifique, 1974.

Volterra, V. Il "no". Prime fasi di sviluppo della negazione nel linguaggio infantile. *Archivio di Psicologia, Neurologia e Psichiatria,* 1972, *33,* 16-53.

Volterra, V. A few remarks on the use of the past participle in child language. In *Italian linguistics.* Lisse: The Peter de Ridder Press, 1976.

Volterra, V., & Antinucci, F. Negation in child language: A pragmatic study. In E. Ochs Keenan & B. Schiefflin (Eds.), *Developmental Pragmatics.* New York: Academic Press, 1979.

CHAPTER 9

Developmental
Trends for Action
and Speech
in Pretend Play*

LARRY FENSON

INTRODUCTION

Pretend play and language are perhaps the two most dramatic early expressions of the young child's developing symbolic competencies, and considerable research has been published since the mid-seventies detailing developments in each domain (see Bloom & Lahey, 1978, for a review of early language development; and see Fein, 1981, and Rubin, Fein & Vandenberg, 1982, for reviews of pretend play). Some researchers have charted developments in both domains and have attempted to identify structural similarities in the symbolic skills expressed in the two mediums (for reviews, see Bates, Benigni, Bretherton, Camaioni, & Volterra, 1979; Bates & Snyder, in press; Fein, 1979; Fischer &

*Portions of this study were presented at the International Conference of Infancy Studies, Austin, Texas, March 1982. The research was facilitated by a faculty research grant from the San Diego State University Foundation.

Corrigan, in press; McCune-Nicolich, 1981). Rather than examining developments in each domain independently, the present research examined the relative roles of action and speech in pretend play per se across a period of major changes in symbolic capacities—20 to 31 months. Specifically, information was sought on sequential developments in pretend action and speech and on the ways in which the relative roles of these modes of expression change between late infancy and toddlerhood.

The growth of pretend action can be characterized by three trends: decentration, decontextualization, and integration. *Decentration* refers to the child's increasing tendency to incorporate players other than self into play activities (Piaget, 1946/1962). The child's first attempts at pretense are directed toward the self. These acts are followed a few months later by decentered acts directed toward both animate and inanimate recipients (Fein & Apfel, 1979; Fenson & Ramsay, 1980; Inhelder, 1971; Lowe, 1975; Nicolich, 1977; Sinclair, 1970). Subsequently, animate objects are endowed with independent action potential (Corrigan, 1982; Largo & Howard, 1979; Lowe, 1975; Shimada, Sano, & Peng, 1979; Watson & Fischer, 1977), reflecting a further distancing from self.

Decontextualization refers to the child's decreasing reliance on prototypicality for the identification and use of objects in play activities (Werner & Kaplan, 1963), and is most clearly reflected by object substitution and the creation of imaginary objects (Belsky & Most, 1981; Elder & Pederson, 1978; Fein, 1975; Jackowitz & Watson, 1980; Jeffree & McConkey, 1976; Overton & Jackson, 1973; Pederson, Rook-Green, & Elder, 1981; Ungerer, Zelazo, Kearsley, & O'Leary, 1981).

Integration refers to the child's increasing ability to combine separate actions into coordinated behavior sequences. The first sequences to appear are likely to involve variations on a single theme (Belsky & Most, 1981; Fenson & Ramsay, 1980; Nicolich, 1977) and are followed within a few months by integration of different themes (Fenson & Ramsay, 1980; McCall, Parke, & Kavanaugh, 1977; Nicolich, 1977; Rummer, 1981; Shimada, Kai, & Sano, 1981).

These trends describe the child's pretend actions. Far less information is available concerning developmental features of pretend language during play. Ungerer *et al.* (1981) argued that linguistic expressions of pretense should be included in the analysis of pretend play in that verbal metaphors form an integral part of symbolic play and, like actions, appear to reflect the child's ability to generate symbols. Yet little information exists. Garvey (1979) and Garvey and Berndt (1977) have described certain thematic and linguistic features of pretend games in dyadic interactions. Indirect evidence (based on data gathered outside the play context) suggests that the developmental shift in children's play from self-referenced actions to actions directed toward other animate objects and inanimate objects might also occur for language (Bowerman, 1976; Leonard,

1976; Sachs, 1980; Volterra, Bates, Benigni, Bretherton, & Camaioni, 1979). Corrigan (1981), in a longitudinal sample of three children, observed this shift from self to others as recipients, and then to others as agents. Little or no information exists concerning decontextualization in speech. We do not know the extent to which language is used to designate substitute or imaginary objects at various ages. Information regarding integration in language exists, of course, in a broad sense, in the form of data on the growth of syntax. However, with the possible exception of mean length of utterance (MLU), variables have not been defined that permit evaluation of the comparability of the growth of integration in pretend action and speech. Thus, insufficient evidence exists to conclude whether developmental changes in the use of pretend language broadly parallel those for pretend action.

The problem is further confounded by the practice of using language as a sufficient or even a necessary criterion for designation of actions as symbolic (e.g., Ungerer *et al.*, 1981). Although this strategy is a reasonable one for ensuring that only symbolic acts are so coded, it confounds language and action measures and biases scoring in favor of older or more verbal children. In order to examine the separate contributions of action and speech to symbolic play, categories of pretend action and speech were defined using comparable criteria but coded separately in the present study.

Another objective of this study was to assess the relative roles of action and speech in play and how these roles change with age. Several possibilities exist.

1. Language and action might serve parallel functions; that is, both might be used individually or in combination to depict substitute objects, active agents, and other pretend elements.
2. Speech and action might serve complementary roles; that is, certain forms of pretense may be more likely to be expressed verbally, others by action.
3. Language might gradually take over as the primary mode for expression of pretense.

Evaluation of these alternative possibilities should be facilitated by separate analyses of action and speech.

The 1-year period from age 20 to 31 months was selected as the study interval for two reasons. First, interest focused on the composition and role of language in play across a period of dramatic changes in linguistic competence. At 20 months, most children are on the threshold of a surge in language acquisition, which results in impressive gains in both semantic and syntactic development over the next year (Brown, 1973). Second, this interval was of interest with respect to developments in action-based play. As described earlier, information is available on developmental transitions in action-based play up to age 24 months or beyond. However, few studies have traced developments in play across this entire age span using all major levels of pretend play. In particular, data were sought that would permit estimates of the time of emergence of more advanced forms of action-based play, which have seldom been cast within a developmental framework.

Many prior studies have restricted observations to spontaneous play. However, several studies (Corrigan, 1982; Fenson & Ramsay, 1981; McCall *et al.*, 1977; Watson & Fischer, 1977) have demonstrated that modeling and/or prompting are effective ways of eliciting emergent behaviors, which are often infrequent in spontaneous play but are of particular importance in studying new forms of symbolic competence. Even so, in some cases modeling studies have elicited performance levels that fell short of maximal symbolic ability levels by modeling acts that were either not sufficiently challenging or used too narrow a range of actions, or both. In this study a wide range of actions, organized around everyday themes, were modeled in an attempt to challenge even the oldest age group tests. To ensure further that children's performances reflected their maximum competence, following a postmodeling play period each child was prompted with specific requests to perform selected difficult previously modeled acts.

In sum, the purposes of this study were (1) to track developments in action-based and linguistically based pretense across a 1-year period beginning at age 20 months and (2) to study possible changes in the ways gestures and speech complement each other in pretend play across this period. To encourage expression of a wide range and complexity of pretend acts, both modeling and prompting techniques were employed.

METHOD

SUBJECTS

The sample included 72 children, 24 at each of three ages: 20 months ($M = $ 20 months, 18 days), 26 months ($M = $ 26 months, 4 days), and 31 months ($M = $ 31 months, 1 day), ± 3 weeks at each age. There were an equal number of males and females at each age. Four additional children were excluded from the final sample (3 of age 20 months and 1 of age 26 months) due to fussiness or refusal to stay in the playroom. The children were all from middle-SES backgrounds.

PROCEDURE

Following a 3-minute free-play period in the presence of the mother, an adult model entered and enacted a pretend scene incorporating a wide range of play acts while the child watched (typically with great interest). The model described each action as it was performed. The model then invited the child to resume play with the toys and departed. Following 3 additional minutes of play time, the model reentered the room and requested that the child perform a subset of previously modeled acts. This four-part episode—consisting of a premodeling play period, modeling, a post modeling play period, and prompting of specific target behaviors—was repeated with three different toy sets and modeled scenes. No break occurred between episodes except for the time required to exchange toys. The duration of the entire session was approximately 30 minutes.

The three modeled episodes, depicting making breakfast for a doll, giving a doll a bath, and taking a doll to the doctor, are described in Table 1. The scripts were designed to include a variety of actions representing all the major play categories of interest. A separate set of child and doll-sized objects was provided

Table 1
Descriptions of the Three Modeled Scenes[a]

Scene 1. Preparing breakfast

The E pours from an empty cereal box into a bowl, cuts a plastic banana over the bowl using a cylindrical rod as a knife, and slices some "apple" into the bowl, a scouring pad serving as the apple. E adds some imaginary raisins from another bowl, transferring them one at a time, adds some imaginary milk from a pitcher, stirs the contents of the bowl, and feeds the contents to a doll with a small spoon. E then pours "milk" from the pitcher to a cup and gives the doll a drink from the cup. Each time the pitcher is used, it is put back into a cardboard box serving as a refrigerator.

Scene 2. Bathing a doll

The E draws a bath by turning on imaginary water faucets over a box serving as a tub, places a doll in the tub, adds a toy boat and imaginary duck "for the doll to play with," rubs "soap" (a block) on a sponge and washes the doll, pours imaginary shampoo over her head, rinses the doll's hair with a cup of imaginary water from the faucet, dries her with a paper towel, combs her hair with an imaginary comb, and lets the doll look in the mirror "to see how pretty she is."

Scene 3. A visit to the doctor

The E feels the "baby's" forehead, says she is sick and that she needs to see the doctor. She is put in a wagon and covered with a blanket. E explains that he is "driving the baby to the doctor" as he pulls the wagon. E then says "here we are," takes the "baby" out of the "car," where she is approached by a teddy bear (the "doctor") wearing a stethoscope. The "doctor" listens to the "baby's" chest, looks in her eyes and ears with his "light" (a wooden stick), pours imaginary medicine from a bottle to a spoon and feeds it to the doll, and then sends her home in the "car" where she is put in bed and covered with a blanket.

[a] Scenes were accompanied by a running commentary by the experimenter (E) explaining his actions.

for each of the three episodes. Some modeled actions called for the use of miniature replicas and some for substitute objects; for still others, imaginary objects sufficed.

The prompted actions represented forms of pretense considered to be among the most difficult of those modeled (e.g., making a bear, which served as a "doctor," give the doll, which served as a "baby," some "medicine." If the child balked at the standard requests, the model requested several simpler actions (e.g., "Put the boat in the bathtub") including at least one action that the child had already displayed either spontaneously or imitatively. The alternate requests were made to distinguish noncompliance from lack of comprehension. All children so tested responded affirmatively to at least one alternate request.

The mother was asked not to prompt or direct her child's play, but was encouraged to respond to any specific requests her child made(e.g, "Can you pour me some milk"). She was provided with a tablet and pen and asked to record all her child's verbalizations during the play episodes. The experimenter watched the session from an adjacent room through one-way glass. The entire session was videotaped.

DATA CODING

A coding scheme was adapted from prior studies, which permitted separate but parallel scoring of action-based and linguistically based expressions of pretense. The first measure of action reflected a lack of decentering. *Self-directed acts* were gestures centering on the self (e.g., child combs own hair). The next three action measures tapped aspects of decentration. Gestures directed toward animate or lifelike objects other than self (e.g., child combs doll's hair) were termed *passive other-directed acts*. Play acts directed toward or centered about inanimate objects were termed *object-directed acts* (e.g., child pours from a pot to a cup). Play acts in which independent agency or action potential was attributed to animate or lifelike objects other than self were termed *active other-directed acts* (e.g., child makes a doll pour a cup of milk). The next two measures reflected aspects of decontextualization. *Substitutive acts* were scored when a child used an object for a purpose not typically associated with it (e.g., child "cuts" toy banana with a wooden rod). Gestures implying that a pretend element had been created in the absence of an object representing or containing that element were termed *inventive acts*. Inventivelike actions supported by a greater degree of structural support were classified as object- or other-directed acts, depending upon the target. Thus, if a child pretended to take a drink from an apparent imaginary cup held in his or her hand, the action was classified as inventive. If the child took a pretend drink from a real cup, the strong structural support for the invented liquid disqualified the act as inventive; in this case, it would have been scored as a self-directed act, based on the self as the target. Finally, two measures tapped the child's integrative skills. *Single-scheme combinations* were credited when the same play-act was directed toward two or more different recipients (e.g., child combs doll's hair, then combs own hair). *Multischeme combinations* were defined as the commission of two or more different play-acts in a logical or ecologically valid order (e.g., child places doll in bed, then covers doll with blanket).

Language, of course, has many functions during play. Interest here focused on the ways in which children used speech to express pretense. Accordingly, language categories were defined that paralleled the eight measures of action-based pretense. *Self-directed utterances* were coded when a child described actual or hypothetical play acts directed toward the self (e.g., "I comb my hair") or made a descriptive reference to self (e.g., "Me dirty"). *Passive other-directed utterances* were coded when the child described an act applied to an animate or lifelike object other than self (e.g., "I comb her hair") or described some feature of a doll or similar object (e.g., "Baby's clean now"). *Object-directed utterances* depicted actions applied to or descriptions of inanimate objects (e.g., "Cut this"; "That's hot"). *Active other-directed utterances* were scored when a child attributed action potential, needs, wants, or feelings to animate or lifelike objects other than self (e.g., "Baby's crying"). Verbal transformation of an object into something else was termed *substitution*. References to pretend substances or objects in the absence of physical support for the created element were termed *invention* (e.g., "There's a tiger over there"). Single-scheme utterances were credited when two successive statements reflected variations on the same theme (e.g., "Put the doll to bed, now the bear"). *Multischeme utterances* were scored when two consecutive statements by the child showed a logical relationship (e.g., "Be careful. You will hurt yourself").

To develop a more complete picture of language use during play, two additional language categories were coded. *Other play-related* speech included all play-related langue without direct pretend references. This category contained six subtypes: (1) Identifies or names objects (e.g., "This is a block"); (2) Specifies ownership ("That's mine"); (3) Seeks information (What's that thing"); (4) Describes nonpretend actions ("I get doll"); (5) Nonpretend comments ("Boat's on the table"); (6) Accents or exclamations ("All done"; "there"; "OK"). *Nonplay-related* speech included all verbalizations not relating to play context (e.g., "I want to go now").

Scoring was done from transcriptions of the tapes. These transcripts indicated each action and each utterance in serial form, actions on the left side and utterances on the right side of the records. Utterances that coincided with actions were listed on the same line. Actions and utterances were coded at different times. Coders were free to examine utterances while scoring actions and vice versa, but it was necessary to do so only in a limited number of situations, particularly in cases involving decontextualized references or action. Suppose, for example, that a child said "This is a bed." Knowing that the child was holding a box rather than an actual bed would enable the utterance to be properly scored as substitutive. Coders were *not* permitted to use the code assigned to an utterance as the basis for coding an accompanying action or vice versa. Thus it was possible for concurrent actions and utterances to be coded differently; for example, if a child said "Close your eyes baby" while placing a doll in a bed, the action was coded as passive other-directed and the utterance was coded as active other-directed. Alternatively, the child might make the doll walk to the bed (an active other-directed act) while saying "Put her to bed" (a passive other-directed reference). That is, the child's verbal specification of an active doll did not influence the code assigned to the play act and vice versa.

With the exception of substitution and invention, only a single code was assigned to each action or utterance. Substitutive and inventive acts usually occurred in conjunction with another action; for example, child, treating a block as soap, rubs it on the "baby." In such cases, the child was credited with substitution as well as with a passive other-directed act. To disallow one or the other would have presented a distorted account of the child's play.Similarly, the separate components of linguistic and action-based multischemes were credited to their respective appropriate categories as well. Each multischeme combination was counted only once, regardless of its length.

The mother's record of her child's utterances was used only as an aid to intelligibility for verbalizations appearing on the audio record. Utterances appearing in the mother's account but not on tape were disregarded. To assess reliability, half the records were scored by two coders. The ratio of agreements:total instances exceeded 90% for all categories of action and language. Attaining these levels, however, required considerable training of each coder.

RESULTS

Both the proportion of children demonstrating a given form of behavior and frequency of occurrence proved to be useful measures, serving different purposes. Proportion scores indicated the age of emergence of each type of action and verbalization, whereas frequency scores were used to determine the prevalence of the various forms of gestural and linguistic pretense.

PROPORTION DATA FOR THE ACTION MEASURES

Developmental Trends

Table 2 shows the proportion of children at each age who demonstrated one or more instances of each type of action-based pretense in the pre- and post-modeling phases. To test for age differences, separate 3×2 chi-square (χ^2) tests were applied to the pre- and postmodeling values. Significant effects were followed by $2 \times 2 \chi^2$ tests, with experiment wise error rate controlled by use of Ryan's procedure (Linton & Gallo, 1975, pp. 301–304). Significant pairwise contrasts are also indicated in Table 2.

It is apparent from inspection of Table 2 that the various measures of action do not appear at the same time. Four measures (self-directed acts, passive other-directed acts, object-directed acts, and substitutive acts) were already present in the spontaneous play of most children at 20 months and remained so thereafter.

Two forms of play (active other-directed acts and inventive acts) were rare or absent in spontaneous play at all ages. These categories were also infrequent following modeling at 20 months; they were demonstrated by a minority of children at 26 months and by a majority of children at 31 months.

Of the two types of integration, multischeme combinations showed a more regular incremental pattern in spontaneous play. Following modeling, proportions for this measure approached or attained maximal levels at all three ages.[1] Single-scheme combinations were demonstrated by half or more of the children in each age group, but did not show age-related changes either prior to or following modeling.

Effects of Modeling

Modeling had no measurable effect on the earlier appearing measures because the proportion of children demonstrating these actions already approached maximal levels prior to modeling; an exception was substitution, which did show a significant pre- to postmodeling increase at 26 months ($p < .05$ by McNemar's test for change in related proportions; Siegel, 1956, pp. 63–67). Proportional increases also occurred following modeling at 31 months for active other-directed

---

[1]In the present study, the number of children demonstrating multischemes at 20 months (50%) is double the proportion reported for 19-month-olds in an earlier study at the same laboratory (Fenson & Ramsay, 1980). The difference is probably attributable to the greater range of possible multischemes afforded by the wider range of toys in the present study as well as by the slightly older mean age.

Table 2

Proportion of Children Showing Each Type of Action-Based Play

Action measure	Premodeling phase (age in months)			Postmodeling phase (age in months)			Significant pairwise comparisons[a]	
	20	26	31	20	26	31	Pre-	Post-
Self-directed	.88	.79	.88	.75	.67	.67	—	—
Passive other-directed	.83	.96	1.00	.96	1.00	1.00	—	—
Object-directed	1.00	.92	1.00	.96	1.00	1.00	—	—
Active other-directed	.04	.08	.17	.13	.29	.58	—	2
Substitution	.71	.46	.83	.88	1.00	1.00	3	—
Invention	.00	.25	.13	.08	.42	.63	—	1, 2
Single scheme combinations	.58	.50	.54	.63	.79	.54	—	—
Multischeme combinations	.50	.79	.83	.92	1.00	1.00	2	—

[a] The numbers 1, 2, and 3 designate significant contrasts between age levels ($p < .05$ or better) for the 20-26, 20-31, and 26-31-month comparisons, respectively. Blanks indicate the absence of any significant comparisons.

acts and invention ($p < .05$ or better by McNemar's test). These latter results provide strong support for the effectiveness of modeling; that is, at 31 months most children were capable of demonstrating these advanced actions, but did not do so spontaneously. Younger children, even when encouraged with modeling, did not imitate these actions.

Effects of Prompting

The effects of prompting, like modeling, were related to developmental level. Prompting was significantly more effective in boosting proportional representation for older as opposed to younger children for the later-appearing measures (active other-directed acts and inventive acts). The proportions of children of the three ages who responded appropriately to a request for active other-directed acts were .00, .22, and .67 at 20, 26, and 31 months, respectively. For inventive acts, these proportions were .22, .61, and .94, respectively. In each case, the 20-26 month contrast was significant by χ^2 tests executed as described earlier ($p < .05$). For active other-directed acts, the 26-31 month contrast was also significant ($p < .05$). Prompting was equally effective at the three ages in eliciting simpler acts, with proportions approaching or reaching 1.00 in most cases.

FREQUENCY DATA FOR THE ACTION MEASURES

Developmental Trends

Table 3 shows the pre-and postmodeling mean frequencies for the eight action measures and summarizes statistical results for age. Variables exhibiting sufficiently high mean frequencies were submitted to analyses of variance (ANOVAs), with age and sex as between-subjects factors and modeling (pre-versus postmodeling phase) as a within-subjects factor. For each measure, pairwise age differences were evaluated by means of Newman–Kuels tests when the overall ANOVA indicated a significant age effect. Alpha was set at $p < .05$ for all pairwise tests. An extension of the median test for k groups (Siegel, 1956, pp. 179–184) was used to evaluate age differences for the less frequently occurring variables, active other-directed acts and inventive acts. Pairwise differences for these two measures were evaluated with Ryan's test, with alpha (α) set at $p < .05$.

The age trends for the frequency data are generally in accord with the picture portrayed by the proportion data, but add further information on the composition of play at the various ages. Decentered acts (passive other-directed acts and object-directed acts) remained the most common form of action-based pretense at all three ages in both spontaneous and elicited play, and were joined increasingly as age advanced by decontextualized acts (substitution and invention) and by multischeme combinations. Pairwise differences between successive ages were far more common following modeling, once again highlighting the ability of modeling to magnify differences in competence not detected in spontaneous play (particularly between 20 and 26 months).

Effects of Modeling

The ANOVAs performed on the action measures yielded strong pre-post effects ($p < .001$) for four measures (passive other-directed acts, object-directed acts, substitution, and multischeme combinations). These forms of play were more frequent following modeling. Possible pre–post increases in frequency were evaluated separately at each age for the two later appearing variables by Wilcoxon tests. For both active other-directed acts and inventive acts, a significant

Table 3
Frequencies for the Action-Based Measures

Action measure	Premodeling phase (age in months)			Postmodeling phase (age in months)			Test value for age effect	p level	Significant pairwise comparisons[a]	
	20	26	31	20	26	31			Pre-	Post-
Self-directed	2.50	3.00	3.58	2.50	2.75	2.13	$F(2, 66) = 0.17$	—[c]	—	—
Passive other-directed	5.04	5.00	8.63	9.83	15.88	17.92	$F(2, 66) = 5.70$	$< .01$	2, 3	1, 2
Object-directed	5.13	7.38	10.71	9.54	14.71	17.50	$F(2, 66) = 7.17$	$< .01$	2	1, 2
Active other-directed	0.04	0.08	0.21	0.13	0.38	0.83	$\chi^2(2) = 19.66$[b]	$< .01$	—	—
Substitution	1.58	1.33	3.21	2.58	6.29	8.25	$F(2, 66) = 18.43$	$< .001$	2, 3	1, 2, 3
Invention	0.00	0.38	0.13	0.08	1.08	2.38	$\chi^2(2) = 15.29$[b]	$< .01$	—	—
Single-scheme combinations	1.04	1.08	1.13	1.38	1.75	0.79	$F(2, 66) = 1.50$	—[c]	—	—
Multischeme combinations	2.00	2.83	5.54	4.92	8.33	10.71	$F(2, 66) = 6.03$	$< .05$	2	1, 2

[a] The numbers 1, 2, and 3 designate significant contrasts between age levels ($p < .05$ or better) for the 20–26-, 20–31-, and 26–31-month comparisons, respectively. Blanks indicate the absence of any significant comparisons.
[b] Based on postmodeling phase only.
[c] Not significant.

increase in frequency occurred from pre- to postmodeling only at 31 months (p < .05 and .01, respectively).

Sex Effects

A main effect of sex occurred for only one variable, multischeme combinations, $F(1, 66) = 6.03$, $p < .05$, the mean being higher for girls than for boys. This effect replicates an earlier finding from the same laboratory (Fenson & Ramsay, 1980). A difference favoring girls for multischeme combinations was also found by Largo and Howard (1979) for 24-, 27-, and 30-month-old children.

PROPORTION DATA
FOR THE LANGUAGE MEASURES

Developmental Trends

Table 4 shows the proportion of children at each age credited with at least one instance of each type of linguistic expression, prior to and following modeling, and indicates the results of statistical analysis pertaining to age. Proportional increases with age were evaluated by means of the same procedures applied to the action measures shown in Table 3, that is, 3 × 2 χ^2 tests followed by Ryan's procedure.

Each of the six single-unit measures of linguistic pretense registered an age-related increase prior to and/or following modeling. With only one exception (passive other-directed acts), these increases occurred between 20 and 26 months or between 20 and 31 months, but not between 26 and 31 months.

The types of expression occurring in gestural form at 20 months (self-directed acts, passive other-directed acts, object-directed acts, and substitutive acts) appeared more slowly in linguistic form, approaching or attaining majority status only at 26 or 31 months. The two variables showing a later onset in the gestural mode (active other-directed acts and inventive acts) showed differing patterns in language. One (invention) followed a similar course in the two domains, appearing later than the other forms of play in each mode, but was less common before and after modeling in language. Inventive utterances were demonstrated by a substantial number of children only at 31 months, in the postmodeling phase. Attribution of independent agency, on the other hand, emerged earlier in language than in action, appearing even prior to modeling in a significant number of 20-month-olds. Nonetheless, the proportion of children credited with active other-directed language increased significantly from 20 to 26 months, both prior to and following modeling.

Table 4
Proportion of Children Showing Each Type of Linguistic Expression

	Premodeling phase (age in months)			Postmodeling phase (age in months)			Significant pairwise comparisons[a]	
Language measure	20	26	31	20	26	31	Pre-	Post-
Self-directed	.00	.38	.29	.08	.21	.42	1, 2	2
Passive other-directed	.08	.25	.75	.38	.71	.88	2, 3	2
Object-directed	.29	.71	.75	.21	.75	.92	1, 2	1, 2
Active other-directed	.33	.88	.92	.42	.79	.88	1, 2	1, 2
Substitution	.21	.54	.50	.08	.67	.75	1	1, 2
Invention	.00	.08	.13	.00	.25	.46	2, 3	2
Single-scheme combinations	.04	.08	.17	.04	.25	.17	—	—
Multischeme combinations	.38	.50	.96	.33	.67	.92	—	2

[a] Numbers 1, 2, and 3 designate significant contrasts between age levels ($p < .05$ or better) for the 20–26-, 20–31-, and 26–31-month comparisons, respectively. Blanks indicate the absence of any significant comparisons.

Of the two measures of integration, only multischeme combinations increased in proportion with age. Single-scheme combinations were uncommon at all ages in language.

Effects of Modeling

Three language measures showed pre- to postmodeling increments, by McNemar's test. Increases occurred for passive other-directed acts at 20 and 26 months ($p < .01$ in each case), for substitution at 31 months ($p < .01$), and for invention at 31 months ($p < .01$).

FREQUENCY DATA
FOR THE LANGUAGE MEASURES

Developmental Trends

Table 5 presents mean frequencies for the language categories, by age, prior to and following modeling, and indicates statistical results for age effects. Sta-

Table 5
Frequencies for the Language Measures

Language measure	Premodeling phase (age in months)			Postmodeling phase (age in months)			Test value for age effect	p level	Significant pairwise comparisons[a]	
	20	26	31	20	26	31			Pre-	Post-
Pretend										
Self-directed	0.00	1.00	0.63	0.21	0.50	0.71	Not done	—	—	—
Passive other-directed	0.17	1.17	3.08	0.58	4.33	3.33	$F(2, 66) = 7.16$	< .01	2, 3	1, 2
Object-directed	0.63	2.08	3.08	0.67	5.42	4.46	$F(2, 66) = 7.34$	< .01	2	1, 2
Active other-directed	1.13	4.88	5.21	1.08	7.63	7.13	$F(2, 66) = 7.78$	< .001	1, 2	1, 2, 3
Substitution	0.58	1.17	1.42	0.25	2.21	2.54	$F(2, 66) = 4.41$	< .05	—	1, 2
Invention	0.00	0.33	0.13	0.00	0.55	0.88	$\chi^2(2) = 14.19$[b]	< .01	—	2
Σ										
Pretend	2.50	10.63	13.55	2.79	20.63	19.05	Not done	—	—	—
Other play-related	7.29	20.55	16.54	3.54	14.17	9.92	$F(2, 66) = 9.91$	< .001	1, 2, 3	1, 2
Nonplay-related	1.04	4.75	6.08	2.00	3.08	5.50	$F(2, 66) = 7.98$	< .001	1, 2	2
Single-scheme combinations	0.04	0.08	0.17	0.04	0.29	0.17	Not done	—	—	—
Multischeme combinations	0.71	3.67	5.50	0.46	3.96	5.40	$F(2, 66) = 12.35$	< .001	1, 2, 3	1, 2, 3

[a] The numbers 1, 2, and 3 designate significant contrasts between age levels ($p < .05$ or better) for the 20–26-, 20–31-, and 26–31-month comparisons, respectively. Blanks indicate the absence of any significant comparisons.
[b] Based on postmodeling phase only.

tistical procedures paralleled those used to evaluate the frequency data for the action measures.

In order to compare pretend verbalizations to other play-related language and to nonpretend language, the six single-unit measures of linguistic pretense were summed (see row labeled Σ, Pretend in Table 5). Taken together, Σ, Pretend; Σ, Other play-related; and Σ, Nonplay-related language provide a complete account of all intelligible utterances recorded during the play episodes.

At 20 months, linguistic expressions of pretense both prior to and following modeling were relatively infrequent, averaging 2.50 and 2.79, respectively. The comparable values for gestural pretense, derived by summing the first six categories in Table 3, were 14.29 and 24.66. From 20 to 26 months, linguistic expression of pretense increased more than fourfold prior to modeling and more than seven times after modeling. An additional modest increase occurred from 26 to 31 months prior to modeling, whereas a slight decrease occurred following modeling.

Most individual measures of linguistic pretense also exhibited age-related increases in frequency. Increases between successive ages were more often significant following modeling than prior to modeling, and more often significant between the two extreme ages or between 20 and 26 months than between 26 and 31 months.

Attributions of independent agency comprised the most frequently occurring individual category of linguistic pretense. Passive other-directed and object-directed utterances represented the next most frequent categories, followed by substitution. Inventive and self-directed utterances were rare at all ages. Multischeme utterances increased between adjacent ages both prior to and following modeling. Single-scheme combinations did not vary with age and were rarely exhibited.

Effects of Modeling

The overall ANOVAs indicated significant pre- to postmodeling increments in frequency for the following language measures: passive other-directed, object-directed, active other-directed, and substitutive utterances. A modeling effect also occurred for inventive utterances at 31 months ($p < .01$) as determined by Wilcoxon test.

Sex Effects

There were no main effects of sex for any of the language measures and only a lone interaction of no interest.

CONTRIBUTIONS OF ACTION AND LANGUAGE TO PRETEND PLAY

One of the purposes of this study was to chart age-related changes in the extent to which children relied on action, gestures, or a combination of the two to express pretense. For this purpose, a tabulation was made for each child of the number of instances when a pretend action occurred unaccompanied by language, when a pretend utterance occurred unaccompanied by action, and when a pretend action and a related utterance co-occurred.[2] At 20 months, actions unaccompanied by language accounted for 83% of all expressions of pretense. Unaccompanied utterances accounted for 8% and action accompanied by language totaled 9%. The picture was substantially different at 26 months. Action alone dropped to 45% of the total, language alone increased to 28%, and action and speech together increased to 27% of the total. The corresponding values at 31 months were 53% for action alone, 23% for speech alone, and 24% for action and speech together.

These data illustrate the increasing prominence of speech (alone or in conjunction with action) in children's pretend activities. However, these data also establish that unaccompanied action remains a common mode for the expression of pretense, at least through the middle of the third year.[3]

DISCUSSION

The present research examined gestural and linguistic features of pretend play during the period of rapid growth in symbolic skills that marks the transition from infancy to early childhood. By defining separate but parallel measures of gestural and linguistic pretense, it was possible to examine the extent to which developments in each domain are characterized by the same developmental trends.

---

[2]The co-occurrence of action and language does not necessarily imply that the same measure was coded in each domain, but only that an action was accompanied by an utterance supporting the action in some way.

[3]The percentage of pretend actions unaccompanied by language in the present study is much higher than the 5% figure reported by Ungerer, Zelazo, Kearsley, and O'Leary (1981) in their sample of 18–34-month-olds (p. 190). The difference may be due to the fact that Ungerer, Zelazo, Kearsley, and O'Leary designated passive other-directed acts as functional rather than symbolic play. This form of action contributed heavily to the "action alone" category in the present study.

Consistent with prior research on action-based play, gestural depiction of passive agents and objects emerged prior to depiction of active agents. This sequence for decentration did not hold for language, where attribution of active agents was as common as passive characterization, even at 20 months. Many 20-month-olds verbally characterize agents as being active; this also suggests that measures of action underestimate this skill. That is, it may be that children of this age may often regard agents as active but may not express this view in their actions due to difficulties in manipulating dolls so they appear active (Wolf, 1981). It should also be noted that verbal attribution of active agency often referred not to actions but to internal states. The ability of children as young as 20 months to reference internal states and motives verbally is also convincingly demonstrated by Bretherton and Beeghly (1982). Language is clearly more suited for these purposes than are gestures. Perhaps this is one of the spurs for invoking language in these contexts.

Decontextualization in play has typically been indexed by the ability to use substitute objects. The ability to create imaginary objects has been employed infrequently in play studies. Both of these competencies evidenced growth between 20 and 31 months in both verbal and gestural form, each emerging more slowly in language than in action. Though the results seem to suggest that substitution precedes invention developmentally, caution must be exercised here. Like invention, substitution varies with degree of physical support (Ungerer *et al.*, 1981). Most of the substitutions modeled in the present study relied on physically similar objects with ambiguous functions (e.g., blocks, sticks) and hence were easy substitutions. Use of dissimilar objects or objects with opposing functions may have proved more challenging and narrowed the developmental difference between the time of appearance of substitution and invention. Nonetheless, the early appearance of substitution in the present case is consistent with findings from other studies relying on relatively prototypic materials (e.g., Jackowitz & Watson, 1980).

A steady increase in integrative skills was also registered in both expressive modes, as reflected by multischeme combinations. Though several prior studies have charted the growth of action-based combinations, this study was the first to score single- and multischeme combinations in language. Linguistic multischemes proved to be an effective index of linguistic integration, which may find application outside of the pretend-play context as well. Comparisons between this measure and MLU are worth pursuing. Single-scheme combinations were demonstrated only infrequently in action and even less frequently in speech. Production of single schemes in both domains may have been limited in the present study by the absence of duplicate or similar copies of play items, which seem to facilitate their occurrence, at least in gestural form (McCune-Nicolich & Fenson, in press).

By the midpoint of the third year, then, the child's pretend play is multi-faceted. Spontaneous play is characterized by frequent display of pretend gestures directed toward both animate and inanimate recipients and by occasional display of object substitution. Verbally, children of this age frequently make reference to active as well as passive agents. Integrated sequences occur with some frequency in both gestural and linguistic form. The addition of modeling and prompting procedures not only boosts the frequency of the forms of gestural and verbal pretense seen in spontaneous play, but also reveals an additional competency in both domains—the ability to depict imaginary objects.

Only a few studies have scored invention. Two reports (Elder & Pederson, 1978; Overton & Jackson, 1973) demonstrated ability to use an imaginary object in the youngest age groups tested (2.5 and 3.0 years, respectively), in response to a verbal request. Jackowitz and Watson (1980, found that none in their sample of 16-months-olds imitated a model's inventive acts (no-object condition,) but 38% of their 23-month sample did so. These studies, together with the present results, suggest that the capacity to create imaginary objects is not achieved by a majority of children until well after the second birthday.

The ability to invent imaginary objects, whether depicted verbally or by action, is an impressive new skill that bears closer examination. Ungerer et al. (1981) distinguished between two levels of invention, one dependent on physical support, the other occurring with minimal props. In the present study, invention with physical support was implied in almost all actions directed toward the self or toward others or objects (e,g., in pouring and feeding) as well as in associated verbal references. These responses in each domain were scored as self-directed acts or decentered acts, depending upon the recipient. Clearly, invention without physical support is a more difficult, later-appearing form of pretense, as expressed in action or speech. Proportional representation for this measure approached or exceeded majority status in both gestural and verbal form only in the 31-month group. These results differ from those of Ungerer et al. (1981), who found little or no invention without physical support, even in their oldest group of 34 months. The higher incidence of invention without support in the present study may be attributable to two factors. First, four different inventive acts were modeled within the context of an organized pretend scene. Second, invention was scored separately for action and language, rather than requiring language alone or in conjunction with action as a criterion. Ungerer et al. may have limited the opportunity to observe invention too severely by modeling only one instance and by requiring language as a prerequisite for coding this form of play.

In an interesting study, Overton and Jackson (1973) asked 3-, 4-, 7-, and 8-year-old children to perform selected pretend actions such as brushing their teeth, combing their hair, hammering a nail, and cutting paper, in the absence of any objects. The younger children typically used a body part to represent the missing object (e.g., a finger as a toothbrush or a fist as a hammer), whereas older children generally pretended to be holding the missing object. Though coders in the present study were not asked to make this distinction when crediting a child with invention, in many cases children did appear to pretend to hold the absent object. On the other hand, in the prompting phase children often responded to a request requiring invention with a substitutive response (e.g., a block for a duck). These interesting phenomena merit further systematic study.

A final topic concerns the relative contributions of gesture and language to pretend play. Three different ways in which the respective roles of action and speech might vary with age were outlined. Each of these proved to be in part correct. First, to an extent action and language served parallel functions; each mode was used to depict passive agents, substitute objects, and the like. Second, action and language served complementary roles in that certain forms of pretense were more likely to be expressed verbally, others by action. Language served as the primary mode for the depiction of active agents, whereas action was more commonly used to denote imaginary objects. Third, it was suggested that language might gradually take over as the primary mode for the expression of pretense. In fact a dramatic increase did occur between 20 and 26 months in the use of language to convey pretense, either alone or in conjunctin with action, with a corresponding drop in the use of unaccompanied action. However, gesture did not always give way to language for the expression of higher forms of pretense. Both actions and verbalizations were represented among simpler and more advanced forms of pretense. Whether gestures or language was used depended in part on the child's purposes. A child may be able to depict a hungry doll more readily through words than through actions, but actions are more appropriate than words for feeding a doll. Thus it may be nonsensical to expect language to replace gesture in play completely. The uses of gesture and language are somctimes parallel, sometimes complementary, and sometimes mutually exclusive.

ACKNOWLEDGMENTS

Diane Barnett, Debra Duvall, Carole Rosen, and Jeff Farris ably assisted in the development of the coding scheme and scored the data. Elizabeth Bates and Lorraine McCune-Nicolich contributed highly constructive reviews of an earlier draft.

REFERENCES

Bates, E., Benigni, L., Bretherton, I., Camaioni, L., & Volterra, J. *The emergence of symbols: communication and cognition in infancy.* New York: Academic Press, 1979.

Bates, E., & Snyder, L. S. The cognitive hypothesis in language development. In I. Uzgiris & J. McV. Hunt (Eds.), *Research with scales of psychological development in infancy.* Champaign-Urbana: University of Illinois Press, in press.

Belsky, J., & Most, R. K. From exploration to play: A cross-sectional study of infant free play behavior. *Developmental Psychology*, 1981, *17*, 630–639.

Bloom, L., & Lahey, M. *Language development and language disorders.* New York: Wiley, 1978.

Bowerman, M. Semantic factors in the acquisition of rules for word use and sentence construction. In D. M. Morehead & A. E. Morehead (Eds.), *Normal and deficient child language.* Baltimore: University Park Press, 1976.

Bretherton, I., & Beeghly, M. Talking about internal states: The acquisition of an explicit theory of mind. *Developmental Psychology*, 1982, *18*, 906–921.

Brown, R. *A first language: The early stages.* Cambridge, MA: Harvard University Press, 1973.

Corrigan, R. The control of actor-recipient relations in pretend play and language. Paper presented at the Society for Research in Child Development, Boston, April 1981.

Corrigan, R. The control of animate and inanimate components in pretend play and language. *Child Development*, 1982, *53*, 1343–1353.

Elder, J. L., & Pederson, D. R. Preschool children's use of objects in symbolic play. *Child Development*, 1978, *49*, 500–504.

Fein, G. G. A transformational analysis of pretending. *Developmental Psychology*, 1975, *11*, 291–296.

Fein, G. G. Echoes from the nursery: Piaget, Vygotsky, and the relationship between language and play. *New Directions in Child Development*, 1979, *6*, 1–14.

Fein, G. G. Pretend play in childhood: An integrative review. *Child Development*, 1981, *52*, 1095–1118.

Fein, G. G., & Apfel, N. Some preliminary observations on knowing and pretending. In M. Smith & M. B. Franklin (Eds.), *Symbolic functioning in childhood.* Hillsdale, NJ: Erlbaum, 1979.

Fenson, L., & Ramsay, D. S. Decentration and integration of play in the second year of life. *Child Development*, 1980, *51*, 171–178.

Fenson, L., & Ramsay, D. S. Effects of modeling action sequences on the play of twelve-, fifteen-, and nineteen-month-old children. *Child Development*, 1981, *52*, 1028–1036.

Fischer, K., & Corrigan, R. A skill approach to language development. In R. Stark (Ed.), *Language behavior in infancy and early childhood.* Amsterdam, Holland: Elsevier—North Holland, in press.

Garvey, C. An approach to the study of children's role play. *Quarterly Newsletter of the Laboratory of Comparative Human Cognition*, October 1979, Vol. 1, *44*, 69–73.

Garvey, C., & Berndt, R. Organization of pretend play. JSAS *Catalog of Selected Documents in Psychology*, 1977, *7*, 1589. (Ms. No. 1589)

Inhelder, B. The sensory-motor origins of knowledge. In D. Walcher & D. L. Peters (Eds.), *Early childhood: The development of self-regulatory mechanisms.* New York: Academic Press, 1971.

Jackowitz, E. R., & Watson, M. W. The development of object transformations in early pretend play. *Developmental Psychology*, 1980, *16*, 543–549.

Jeffree, D., & McConkey, R. An observation scheme for recording children's imaginative doll play. *Journal of Child Psychology and Psychiatry*, 1976, *17*, 189–197.

Largo, R. H., & Howard, J. Developmental progression in play behavior of children between nine and thirty months. I. Spontaneous play and imitation. *Developmental Medicine and Child Neurology*, 1979, *21*, 299–310.

Leonard, L. *Meaning in child language*. New York: Grune & Stratton, 1976.

Linton, M., & Gallo, P. S., Jr. *The practical statistician*. Monterey, CA: Brooks/Cole, 1975.

Lowe, M. Trends in the development of representational play in infants from one to three years: An observational study. *Journal of Child Psychology and Psychiatry*, 1975, *16*, 33–47.

McCall, R. B., Parke, R. D., & Kavanaugh, R. D. Imitation of live and televised models by children one to three years of age. *Monographs of the Society for Research in Child Development*, 1977, *42*(5, Serial No. 173).

McCune-Nicolich, L. Toward symbolic functioning: Structure of early pretend games and potential parallels with language. *Child Development*, 1981, *52*, 785–797.

McCune-Nicolich, L., & Fenson, L. Methodological issues in studying early pretend play. In T. D. Yawkey and A. D. Pellegrini (Eds.), *Child's play: Developmental and applied*. Hillsdale, NJ: Erlbaum, in press.

Nicolich, L. Beyond sensorimotor intelligence: Assessment of symbolic maturity through analysis of pretend play. *Merrill-Palmer Quarterly*, 1977, *23*, 89–99.

Overton, W. F., & Jackson, J. P. The representation of imagined objects in action sequences: a developmental study. *Child Development*, 1973, *44*, 309–314.

Pederson, D. R., Rook-Green, A., & Elder, J. L. The role of action in the development of pretend play in young children. *Developmental Psychology*, 1981, *17*, 756–759.

Piaget, J. *Play, dreams, and imitation in childhood*. New York: Norton, 1962. (Original French edition, 1946.)

Rubin, K. H., Fein, G. G., & Vandenberg, B. Play. In E. M. Hetherington (Ed.), *Charmichael's manual of child psychology: Social development*. New York: Wiley, 1983.

Rummer, C. A. *The effects of modeling and behavioral guidance on immediate and deferred imitation by 15- and 19-month-olds*. Unpublished doctoral dissertation, University of Hawaii, 1981.

Sachs, J. The role of adult-child play in language development. In K. Rubin (Ed.), *Children's play*. San Francisco: Jossey-Bass, 1980.

Shimada, S., Kai, Y., & Sano, R. Development of symbolic play in late infancy. *Bulletin of the Research Institute for the Education of Exceptional Children*, Tokyo Gakugei University, Tokyo, October 1981, 17.

Shimada, S., Sano, R., & Peng, F. A longitudinal study of symbolic play in the second year of life. *Bulletin of the Research Institute for the Education of Exceptional Children*, Tokyo Gakugei University, Tokyo, December 1979, 12.

Siegel, S. *Nonparametric statistics for the behavioral sciences*. New York: McGraw-Hill, 1956.

Sinclair, H. The transition from sensory motor behavior to symbolic activity. *Interchange*, 1970, *1*, 119–129.

Ungerer, J. A., Zelazo, P. R., Kearsley, R. B., & O'Leary, K. Developmental changes in the representation of objects in symbolic play from 18 to 34 months of age. *Child Development*, 1981, *52*, 186–195.

Volterra, V. Bates, E., Benigni, L., Bretherton, I., & Camaioni, L. First words in language and action: A qualitative look. In E. Bates (Ed.), *The emergence of symbols: Cognition and communication in infancy*. New York: Academic Press, 1979.

Watson, M. W., & Fischer, K. W. A developmental sequence of agent use in late infancy. *Child Development*, 1977, *48*, 828–836.

Werner, H., & Kaplan, B. *Symbol formation*. New York: Wiley, 1963.

Wolf, D. *How to speak a story: The emergence of narrative language*. Paper presented at the Jean Piaget Society, Philadelphia, May 1981.

CHAPTER 10

The Effect of Contextual Variation on Symbolic Play Development from 20 to 28 Months*

INGE BRETHERTON
BARBARA O'CONNELL
CECILIA SHORE
ELIZABETH BATES

INTRODUCTION

Studies of early symbolic play inspired by the work of Jean Piaget (1946/1962) have singled out four areas of development (Fein, 1981): (1) the capacity to act "as if" or perform actions outside their usual context, (2) the capacity to use a placeholder as stand-in for a realistic object; (3) the ability to represent roles other than one's own, and (4) the ability to combine pretend schemes into meaningful, ordered sequences.

*This study was funded by a grant from the Spencer Foundation to Elizabeth Bates and Inge Bretherton.

Piaget (1946/1962), viewed the onset of symbolic play, together with language and deferred imitation, as simultaneous manifestations of one underlying semiotic function. From this standpoint the ability to act "as if" or to simulate real-world behavior indexes an emerging representational ability. The capacity to let a placeholder stand for a realistic object signals the infant's readiness to acquire arbitrary symbol systems (arbitrary in the sense that the symbol does not have to resemble the object for which it stands). A growing ability to pretend at the actions of others and not just one's own is taken as evidence for decentration, which implies understanding that the world is made up of objects and agents that are independent of the self. Finally, the enactment of pretend sequences (not just single actions) exemplifies one aspect of a more general combinatorial ability, which also surfaces in the production of multiwork utterances and other relational activities. These points have been addressed in studies by, among others, Bates, Benigni, Bretherton, Camaioni, and Volterra, 1979; Corrigan, 1982; Fein, 1975; Golomb, 1977; Fenson, Chapter 9, present volume; Fenson and Ramsay, 1980, 1981; Killen and Uzgiris, 1981; Lowe, 1975; McCune-Nicolich 1981; Shore, 1981; Shore, O'Connell, and Bates, in press; and Watson and Fischer, 1977.

Another approach is to examine pretense as it relates to the development of social understanding. Especially useful in this regard is the work on scripts or event schemata by Mandler (1977) and Nelson (1981). These authors suggest that representation, at the most basic level, may be organized in terms of *scripts* (a term coined by Schank & Abelson, 1977), which are defined as skeletal frameworks of events containing information about who, to whom, what, where, when, why, and how. Links between the elements of scripts or event schemata are temporo-causal, in contrast to the links between members of a classification hierarchies that are based on similarity.

That even infants acquire *implicit* script knowledge of routine events such as eating, going to bed, having a bath, or going to the store is evident when they protest alterations in habitual routines. The ability to represent everyday scripts *explicitly* and outside their normal context emerges in rudimentary form in symbolic play at the end of the first year (Bates *et al.*, 1979; Volterra, Bates, Benigni, Bretherton, & Camaioni, 1979). In this chapter we are concerned with two developing aspects or dimensions of event representation in pretend play (roles and actions) as these are affected by a variety of contextual manipulations.

The ability to represent make-believe roles proceeds from single roles (e.g., self-representation) to the representatin of entire role networks. The ability to represent actions proceeds from single schemes to multischeme sequences. The literature concerning this development is more thoroughly reviewed in Bretherton (Chapter 1, this volume). It will be briefly illustrated here by reference to Nicolich's (1977) systematic replication of Piaget's (1946/1962) observations of Jacqueline, Lucienne, and Laurent. Nicolich studied the spontaneous symbolic play of five infants in their homes at monthly intervals during the second year. On the basis of these observations, a developmental sequence consisting of 5 levels was identified (see Table 1). Because her objective was the creation of a general scale, Nicolich did not treat role and action representation separately. Scales for these two distinct dimensions can, however, be derived from her findings. (Nicolich's Level 1 will not be of concern here because the recognitory gestures that define this level do not seem to be accompanied by a clear awareness of their nonliteral quality.)

In terms of roles, infants begin by re-enacting their own behavior out of its usual context (Nicolich's Level 2). They simulate eating, drinking, or sleeping, signaling awareness or pretense by "knowing" smiles and sound effects that accompany the various actions. This is followed by two concurrent developments (both classed as Level 3). Infants project their own role onto passive recipients (people or dolls) or enact the behavior or roles of others ("mopping" the floor or "reading" the newspaper in emulation of the parents). Nicolich's

Table 1
Development of Symbolic Play[a]

Nicolich levels and criteria	Examples
Sensorimotor period	
1. Presymbolic Scheme: The child shows: understanding of object use or meaning by brief recognitory gestures. No pretending. Properties of present object are the stimulus. Child appears serious rather than playful.	The child picks up a comb, touches it to his hair, drops it. The child picks up the telephone receiver, puts it into ritual conversation position, sets it aside. The child gives the mop a swish on the floor.
2. Autosymbolic scheme: The child pretends at self-related activities. Pretending Symbolism is directly involved with the child's body. Child appears playful, seems aware of pretending.	The child simulates drinking from a toy baby bottle. The child eats from an empty spoon. The child closes his eyes, pretending to sleep.
Symbolic Stage I	
3. Single-scheme symbolic games Child extends symbolism beyond his own actions by:	
A. Including other actors or receivers of action, such as doll or mother.	Child feeds mother or doll Child grooms mother or doll.
B. Pretending at activities of other people or objects such as dogs, trucks, trains, and so on.	Child pretends to read a book. Child pretends to mop floor. Child moves a toy car with appropriate sounds of vehicle.

(continued)

Table 1 (*Continued*)

Nicolich levels and criteria	Examples
4. Combinatorial symbolic games	
4.1. Single-scheme combinations: One pretend scheme is related to several actors or receivers of action.	Child combs own, then mother's hair. Child drinks from the bottle, feeds doll from bottle. Child puts an empty cup to mother's mouth, then experimenter, and self
4.2 Multischeme combinations: Several schemes are related to one another in sequence.	Child holds phone to ear, dials. Child kisses doll, puts it to bed, puts spoon to its mouth. Child stirs in the pot, feeds doll, pours food into dish
5. Planned symbolic games: Child indicates verbally or nonverbally that pretend acts are planned before being executed.	Child finds the iron, sets it down, searches for the cloth, tossing aside several objects. When cloth is found, she irons it.
5.1 Planned single-scheme symbolic acts Transitional Type: Activities from Levels 2–3 that are planned. A. Symbolic identification of one object with another. B. Symbolic identification of the child's body with some other person or object.	Child picks up play screw-driver, says "toothbrush" and makes the motions of toothbrushing.
5.2 Combinations with planned elements: These are constructed of activities from Levels 2–5.1, but always include some planned element. They tend toward realistic scenes.	Child picks up the bottle, says "baby," then feeds the doll and covers it with a cloth Child puts play foods in a pot, stirs them. Then says "soup" or "mommy" before feeding the mother. She waits, then says "more?" offering the spoon to the mother.

[a] Sequence of symbolic levels, according to Nicolich, 1977.

Level 4 is characterized by the ability to enact two similar roles in parallel (the child brushes her own hair, then the mother's) without pretending at a true *interaction*. Next infants master the use of a doll as agent. This behavior (beyond Nicolich's Level 5) was first pointed out by Inhelder, Lézine, Sinclair, and Stambak (1972). When infants treat a doll as agent the doll becomes a source of independent action (e.g., a mirror is placed in its hand so it can look at itself). Subsequent developments in which children produce interactions between several dolls or animals have been described by Wolf (1982; personal communication, May 1982) as well as Watson and Fischer (1980).

Nicolich's work (Table 1) also documents the development of action representation. An infant's first symbolic acts are limited to one scheme at a time: "drinking" from an empty cup *or* "stirring" with a spoon *or* "wiping" the mouth with a cloth (Level 2). Later in the second year (Level 4) infants combine previously disconnected single-scheme miniscripts into meaningful sequences of two or three schemes (stirring, then drinking, then wiping the mouth). During Level 5 we begin to see evidence for planned sequences. Such planning can take the form of behavioral or verbal search for objects needed to implement a script. An even later development, beyond Nicolich's (1977) outline, is the performance of several episodes (dinnertime, bathtime), each composed of its own ordered action sequences. According to Inhelder, Lézine, Sinclair, and Stambak (1972) such multi-episode play becomes common during the third year; it has yet to be systematically studied (see McCune-Nicolich & Fenson, in press, for a discussion of the same point).

Detailed observations of spontaneous play have been useful in delineating the chronological order in which enactive symbolic capacities generally emerge. It may be a mistake, however, to think of the levels described by Nicolich in absolute terms—that is, as levels a child either has or has not attained. The degree of perceptual support offered by the verisimilitude, size, and organization of the props or by the temporo-dynamic support of modeling (where familiar scripts are, as it were, recalled *for* the child) all seem to have a bearing on the level at which a child plays.

Contextual support can be manipulated so as to *enhance* or *depress* the quality of play. The presentation of organized toy sets that suggest a particular scenario (such as bedtime) appears to facilitate the production of scheme sequences (McCune-Nicolich & Fenson, in press). Likewise, modeling has been consistently shown to lead to an increase in the quantity and/or quality of ensuing symbolic play when compared with premodeling performance (e.g., Fenson, Chapter 9, this volume; Fenson & Ramsay, 1981; Kagan, 1981; Largo & Howard, 1979; Watson & Fischer, 1977).

When modeling is used in conjunction with realistic and substitute objects, the quantity and/or quality of symbolic schemes tends to be significantly affected by prop characteristics. Infants appear to be more willing to imitate schemes modeled with prototypical rather than nonprototypical objects (e.g., Fein, 1975; Jackowitz & Watson, 1980; Kagan 1981; Killen & Uzgiris, 1981; Largo & Howard, 1979; Watson & Fischer, 1980; Ungerer, Zelazo, Kearsley, & O'Leary, 1981). This is not suprising because substitution of nonprototypical objects always involves a reduction in contextual support (the appearance of the object cannot be used to call up the appropriate scheme). However, some forms of substitution seem to be more difficult than others. With a counterconventional object (comb equals spoon) the object's appearance is not only unhelpful, but actually misleading. Hence, it makes sense that object substitution seems hardest to elicit when it involves a counterconventional object (comb equals spoon), as opposed to a placeholder that has no strong object-associated schemes (stick equals spoon) (see Ungerer *et al.*, 1981).

In addition, modeling as an eliciting technique has interesting properties that go beyond those of play facilitation. An infant's level of role and action representation in imitative play does not, it appears, invariably correspond to the level at which the behavior is demonstrated by the model. One-year-olds often simplify a putting-the-doll-to-bed scenario by substituting themselves for the doll, which is left to one side as infants try to climb into the tiny doll bed themselves or cover their own stomach with the doll blanket (personal observation). Rubin and Wolf (1979) made similar observations in a case study of a 2-year-old boy. This child simplified a modeled interaction between two toy agents by reducing reciprocal roles to parallel ones. When re-enacting a scenario where a lion growled at and chased a boy-figure, this 2-year-old made both lion and boy-figure growl and run. Along somewhat similar lines, Fenson (Chapter 9, this volume) noted that children who were verbally prompted to engage in empty-handed miming often picked up a substitute object to perform the requested scheme. According to Elder and Pederson (1978), use of a placeholder is easier than empty-handed miming. These sporadic observations suggest that enhancement of symbolic play through modeling may have its upper limits, a finding in accord with Piaget's (1946/1962) theory in which imitation is linked to the child's level of conceptual development. Constraints on imitation set by the child's spontaneous level of performance have also been documented in studies of language imitation (e.g., Slobin & Welsh, 1973).

In sum, there is ample evidence for an orderly acquisition of symbolic abilities with respect to roles and actions when repeated observations of spontaneous play with the same toys are used as the basis of assessment. On the other hand there is equally ample evidence that manipulations of contextual support (of the perceptual and temporal variety) can exercise enhancing or dampening effects on play, albeit within certain constraints imposed by the child's level of conceptual development.

In the short-term longitudinal study reported here, we tested the effect of contextual variations (modeling in conjunction with realistic toys and two kinds of object substitution) against spontaneous play within the same sample of children at 20 and 28 months of age. Three scenarios were demonstrated after giving the child an opportunity to engage in free play with each of the toy sets. The modeled scenarios contained an approximately equal number of schemes or actions, but the level of role representation was designed to become increasingly difficult, beginning with self as agent, followed by doll as active recipient in the second scenario and doll as agent vis-à-vis another doll in the third scenario. All three scenarios were demonstrated with a set of realistic toys and two types of object substitution (nonmeaningful placeholder and counterconventional object).

In addition to examining the contextual effects of modeling and object substitution, we conducted a detailed qualitative analysis of (1) the divergence of modeled and reproduced levels of play, (2) the integration language and action in play, and (3) the significance of verbal and behavioral protest to modeled object substitution. We had noticed such protest in a previous study with 13-month-olds (Bates, Bretherton, Snyder, Shore, & Volterra, 1980), but had not systematically analyzed it in terms of its possible relationships to spontaneous and postmodeling play. All analyses were carried out on the 20- and 28-months data. Finally, we looked at the longitudinal stability of individual differences, a topic about which very little information is available in the literature.

METHOD

SAMPLE

The sample consisted of 15 boys and 15 girls who participated in a longitudinal study of symbol development. Of these children, 27 had also been seen at 10 and 13 months; 3 were recruited at 20 months after several children of the earlier longitudinal sample had moved away. We obtained parent's names through birth announcements in the local newspaper. Written invitations were followed by a telephone call. Of the families thus contacted, 72% agreed to participate. For purposes of the present study children were seen at 20 and 28 months. A home observation followed by a laboratory session were scheduled at each age. The data reported here were obtained during the laboratory sessions at 20 and 28 months.

SETTING

Each session took place in a 3- by 5-m carpeted laboratory playroom with two one-way mirrors. Child, mother, and experimenter were seated on three beanbag chairs around a very low table. The session was recorded with the aid of two videocameras. A special-effects generator was used to select the better of the two views. A microphone hung directly above the table to pick up speech.

PROCEDURE

Two experimenters were trained to model scenarios at each of the two ages. Each experimenter played with an equal number of boys and girls. A warm-up session and comprehension task (reported in Bretherton, Bates, McNew, Shore, Williamson, & Beeghly-Smith, 1981) always preceded the first and second scenario presentation. The third scenario followed after a free-play session (see O'Connell & Bretherton, Chapter 12, this volume) and language testing. If the child invited an adult to participate in the scenario the adult was encouraged to join in; otherwise, both adults were asked to remain passive during the post-modeling period.

For each of the three scenarios the experimenter first gave the child an opportunity to play with the relevant toys spontaneously. Modeling started after the child sat back or engaged in perseverative play (usually after 2 minutes or so). The experimenter demonstrated a scenario three times, encouraging the child to play with the toys after each modeling period. During the second and third demonstration a placeholder or counterconventional object was substituted for the instrument (Scenario 1) or recipient of action (Scenarios 2 and 3). Criteria for ending the postmodeling sessions were similar to those for terminating the spontaneous play episode, except that children often spontaneously signalled "all done." The props, script, substitute objects, and postmodeling play invitation for each scenario are listed in Table 2.

As Table 2 indicates the first scenario (eating breakfast) was modeled with the self as agent, the second scenario (giving a doll a bath and ride) involved a doll as active recipient (like Nicolich's Level 3, but treating the doll as a sentient being by talking to it; see Bretherton, Chapter 1, this volume). The third scenario (a mother bear puts a baby bear to bed) represented an interaction between an active and a passive toy animal. The first and second scenarios were modeled with six schemes; the third scenario contained five schemes.

Because the data were collected as part of a large correlational study of symbol development, the order in which the scenarios and the object substitution conditions were modeled was not varied. Instead, the task was treated as a test with presentation of items arranged in ascending order of difficulty. The order of scenarios was determined by the level of role complexity, with the easiest scenario (breakfast) always followed by middle-level scenario (bathtime) with the most difficult scenario (teddy bears) last. Within each scenario, toys were first presented for spontaneous play, followed by modeling of the realistic, placeholder, and counterconventional conditions. The counterconventional condition was modeled after the placeholder condition because it was held to be most difficult on the basis of work by Ungerer et al. (1981).

We judged this procedure justifiable because a comparison of random and ordered scenario presentations in a previous study with 13-month-olds yielded equivalent results for both (Shore, 1979).

DATA REDUCTION

The videotaped sessions were transcribed onto coding sheets with two columns. In the first column, modeled and nonmodeled symbolic schemes, search for prototypical objects, nonverbal refusal of nonprototypical objects, and non-

Table 2

Props, Enactment, Object Substitutions, and Postmodeling Invitations

	Scenario		
	Breakfast (self-referenced)	Bathime (other-referenced)	Bedtime (other agent–patient)
Props	Pitcher, spoon, cup, bowl, napkin	Doll, tub, towel, bunting, stroller	Big bear, small bear, bed, pillow, blanket
Script	*Let's have some breakfast. Stir the orange juice.*	*This is my baby.*	*This is momma bear* (low voice), *and this is baby bear* (high voice showing bears).
	(Stir in pitcher with spoon.)	(hold doll, looking at it.)	*Poor baby's so sleepy.*
	Pour the juice in the cup.	*What a dirty baby. You need a bath.*	(Hold small bear against big bear, use big bear's arm to pat small bear.)
	(Pour pitcher to cup)	(Put doll in tub.)	*Poor baby's so sleepy.*
	Slurp while drinking from cup.)	*Wash the baby.*	(Repeat same action.)
	Mm, good juice.	(Making washing motions.)	*Momma bear is going to put baby bear to bed*
	Now let's have some cereal.	*Got to dry it off.*	(Hold small bear against big bear, tip both over bed, leave small bear in bed.)
	(Scrape spoon in bowl, eat with spoon.)	(Take doll out of tub and dry with towel.)	*Cover him up.*
	Mm, good cereal.	*Now let's get dressed.*	(Hold blanket against big bear, tip over bed and leave blanket on baby bear; readjust blanket if necessary.)
	(Scrape spoon in bowl, eat with spoon.)	(Wrap doll in bunting.)	*Night-night baby bear.*
	Mm, good cereal.	*And go for a ride in the stroller.*	(Make big bear kiss small bear with smacks.)
	All done.	(Put doll in stroller.)	*Night-night baby bear.*
	Got to wipe my mouth.	*Go for a Rüide.*	(Repeat above action.)
	(Wipe mouth with napkin two or three times without actually touching mouth.)	(Push stroller with doll forward.)	*Go to sleep.*
Postmodeling invitation	*Would you like to have breakfast?*	*Can you take care of the baby?*	*Can you make momma bear put baby bear to bed?*
Object substitution	4-inch wooden cylinder, comb substituted for spoon	4-inch wooden cylinder, shoe substituted for doll	4-inch cylinder, small van substituted for small bear

task behaviors such as climbing on the table or handing toys to the experimenter were described in sequence. Intercoder agreement for schemes and behavioral protest at 20 and 28 months (calculated on the basis of three complete independently transcribed cases at each age) was 88% and 91% respectively. Sound effects and verbal utterances were transcribed in the second column of the coding sheet. Intercoder agreement for vocalizations and speech (based on five complete cases at 20 months and three cases at 28 months) was 84% for both ages. All calculations were based on point-to-point comparisons of transcripts, not totals.

The following measures were derived from the completed transcripts and tabulated separately for each scenario and for each condition within scenarios (spontaneous, realistic, placeholder, counterconventional).

1. *Scheme frequency*: The frequency of modeled and nonmodeled scenario-relevant schemes. Modeled schemes were those listed in Table 2. Nonmodeled schemes included meaningful actions such as wiping the cup with the napkin, rocking the doll, and making the teddybear dance. Nonrelevant schemes were actions such as banging on the table, pointing to posters in the room, or stacking the stroller in the bathtub.

2. *Scheme diversity*: as for scheme frequency, but excluding repititions.

3. *Modeled scheme diversity*: only counted as schemes actually performed by the experimenter (see Table 2).

4. *Meaningful sequences*: tallied as meaningfully ordered, unbroken sequences (which included modeled and nonmodeled schemes) of two or more actions. The longest meaningful sequence within each scenario condition was also noted. At 28 months only, we also calculated high-level sequences (sequences of three or more schemes). An example of nonmeaningful sequence, by our criteria, would be putting the doll in the stroller and the stroller in the bathtub. A more complete description is provided in the appendix.

5. *Descriptive utterances*: tallied as utterances referring to or describing a scenario-related action or prop (e.g., "bear," "put it in," "roll it").

6. *Pretend utterances*: utterances referring to a make-believe action, substance, state, or location (*"wash* the *dirty* baby," *"drink juice,"* "he's *tired,"* "go to *work"*). At 28 months a further distinction was made between the description of pretense ("I *pour orange juice"*) and verbal role-play that included talking to or for an agent or recipient ("that was *good breakfast"*, "go to *sleep,* baby"). Naming of the baby or bear counted as a pretend utterance only when it was applied to the substitute objects.

For the sequence and language measures, we also calculated second-level intercoder agreements, based on point-to-point comparisons of the transcripts. These were 90% for meaningful sequences (based on 18 complete transcripts) and 84% for descriptive–pretend language (based on 19 complete transcripts). An approximately equal number of transcripts from both ages were included in these computations.

7. *Protest*: Behavioral or verbal protest against placeholder and counterconventional substitution during postmodeling sessions, taking one of three different forms: search for the vanished prototypical or realistic object, rejection of the substitute, and conventional use or naming of the placeholder or counterconventional object (breaking the pretend illusion). All three categories of protest could be behavioral and/or verbal (e.g., actual search for the doll versus asking, "where's de odder baby"; tossing the substitute block away versus protesting, "dat's not a baby" or simply saying "no"; conventional use of the shoe substituted for the doll versus claiming "dat's a shoe"). The three categories of protest were combined into a behavioral and a verbal protest score at each age.

RESULTS

The data were subjected to four types of analysis. First, we performed age (2) × gender (2) × contextual conditions (3) analysis of variance (ANOVAs) on all play and language variables, with age and contextual conditions as within-subjects factors. Our purpose was to test hypotheses regarding age and gender differences in conjunction with experimental variations of contextual support. Second, we conducted a very detailed qualitative analysis in order to compare the level of postmodeling play and language with the level at which scenarios had been demonstrated by the experimenter. These qualitative analyses were carried out separately for each scenario at both ages. Third, we examined the relationship of verbal behavioral protest during the two object-substitution conditions to the other play and language measures. Finally, we assessed the stability of individual differences across all four contextual conditions, both within and across age.

AGE, GENDER, AND CONDITION EFFECTS

Age

Scheme frequency and descriptive utterances were the only variables unaffected by age. We found no interactions of age with other independent variables. Scheme diversity, sequenced schemes, and longest sequence increased significantly from 20 to 28 months across all four contextual conditions (see Table 3).

Table 3
Mean Performance on Play and Play Language Variables by Age (in months) and Condition[a]

Variables	Premodeling Spontaneous (SP) 20	28	Postmodeling Realistic (RL) 20	28	Placeholder (PH) 20	28	Counter-conventional (CC) 20	28	Age $F(1, 28)$	$p <$	Condition $F(3, 84)$	$p <$
Scheme frequency	10.2	12.2	14.2	15.9	10.6	11.9	10.4	9.9	—[b]		8.6	.0001
Scheme diversity	6.8	9.0	9.3	12.4	7.5	9.2	6.3	8.1	15.9	.001	12.4	.00001
Sequenced schemes	4.2	6.2	6.1	9.1	5.3	7.4	4.5	6.1	10.7	.003	4.4	.01
Longest sequence	2.5	2.9	2.6	3.6	2.4	3.2	2.2	3.1	17.4	.0001	—[b]	
Descriptive utterances	3.7	4.4	2.9	3.5	1.7	1.7	1.3	1.4	—[b]		13.4	.00001
Pretend utterances	1.2	4.9	2.1	7.9	1.4	6.1	1.3	5.2	32.5	.0001	3.5	.002

[a] Tukey's Honestly Significant Difference tests ($p < .05$) showed the following post hoc differences for condition:

  Total schemes: RL > SP, PH, CC
  Total different schemes: RL > SP, PH, CC
  Total sequenced schemes: RL > SP, CC
  Descriptive language: SP > RL > PH, CC
  Pretend Language: RL > SP, CC

[b] Not significant.

Overall, scheme diversity increased by 33% and sequenced schemes by 45% from 20 to 28 months. The finding of no increase in scheme frequency accompanied by a significant increase in scheme diversity indicates that the play of the 20-month-olds was more repetitive. The most striking development occurred in pretend utterances, which rose fourfold overall (corroborating Fenson, Chapter 9, this volume). The impression of greatly increased sophistication in the play of the 28-month-olds largely derived, we believe, from the clarifying and amplifying aspects of pretend language. For example, the same little girl who said "wrap it" as she attempted to dress the doll in a bunting at 20 months remarked "I'm going to put dis on her for to keep her warm" as she performed the same action at 28 months. At 20 months she merely described her own behavior; at 28 months she attributed sensations to the doll (see Wolf, Rygh, & Altshuler, Chapter 7, this volume, for similar findings).

Gender

No significant gender effects or interactions with gender were obtained in this study. There was a tendency for girls to engage in more spontaneous play with the doll during the second scenario, but this was not pronounced enough to yield overall gender differences.

Contextual Conditions

The four contexts used in this study were spontaneous free play and three postmodeling conditions (realistic, placeholder, and counterconventional). As already noted, the same basic toy set was used for all four conditions during each scenario presentation, except that the most central prop was replaced with a placeholder or counterconventional object during the second and third modeling.

As hypothesized, we observed a significant *increase* in most measures when spontaneous performance was compared with realistic postmodeling behavior (summed across all three scenarios). As Table 3 indicates, scheme frequency, scheme diversity, sequenced schemes, and pretend language all rose significantly after modeling with the realistic objects. There were only two exceptions. The longest sequence did not increase after realistic modeling and descriptive utterances were actually more frequent during the spontaneous condition, which elicited a lot of initial labeling as the toys were set out.

Comparison of the realistic and substitution conditions yielded the expected *decrease* in performance after modeling with the placeholder and the counterconventional objects (see Table 3). This was true for all measures except longest sequence. Significant declines were observed for scheme frequency, scheme di-

I. BRETHERTON, B. O'CONNELL, C. SHORE, AND E. BATES

versity, and sequenced schemes as well as for pretend and descriptive utterances. However, post hoc tests (see Table 3) showed that for sequenced schemes and pretend utterances, only the realistic versus counterconventional differences were significant. For no variable did we obtain significant differences between the two object-substitution conditions, although the counterconventional means were consistently lower (see Table 3). We can only speculate as to the reasons for this. Unlike Ungerer *et al.*, (1981), we always presented the counterconventional substitute after the placeholder. Moreover, our substitute object was always accompanied by a set of realistic "anchor" toys.

As previously indicated, the analysis of contextual effects was carried out with the data summed across scenarios. Separate ANOVAs for contextual effects within scenarios were not appropriate because of too many zero scores for some conditions at 20 months. Nevertheless, we did observe the expected contextual fluctuations in the means for the separate scenarios except for the breakfast scenario at 20 months. Our findings, then, are not due to the children's performance during only one of the three scenarios.

To sum up, the results reported so far replicate, within one sample and with testlike presentation, the results of several earlier studies in which similar manipulations were carried out separately, cross-sectionally, and with counterbalanced order of presentation. The data thus provide encouraging support for researchers wishing to develop systematic tests of symbolic play abilities, whether to assess general symbolic skills or social understanding. It is also noteworthy that, for the most part, play and play-related language were similarly affected by the contextual manipulations.

A QUALITATIVE ANALYSIS OF MODELED AND REPRODUCED LEVEL OF SYMBOLIC PLAY

As we pointed out earlier, modeling as an eliciting technique is interesting not merely because of its facilitating effects on subsequent play, but also because there is suggestive, but so far largely anecdotal, evidence that children reduce the level of complexity when modeled play greatly exceeds their spontaneous ability. The converse phenomenon, that they expand or enhance complexity when modeled play is very easy, has not been previously documented, but we decided to examine our data for such evidence. The findings presented below are based on comparisons of modeled and reproduced play and play-related language at both ages, with judgements of complexity frequently based on joint assessment of the two types of measures. For the most part, data are reported across all postmodeling conditions rather than for each contextual condition separately.

Roles

Breakfast. The breakfast scenario was modeled with the self as agent, that is, at the lowest level of role representation. However, because mother and experimenter were present and permitted to respond to overtures, children had the opportunity to involve one of the adults as passive recipient or as agent, thereby enhancing the modeled level of role complexity. This is what they did, but in substantial numbers only at 28 months. Seven of the 20-month-olds and 20 of the 28-month-olds included one or both adults in their play with the breakfast implements (sign test, $p = .002$). Of the 7 20-month-olds, 3 treated one or both adults as passive recipient (e.g., holding a cup to her mouth) and 4 invited her to participate as agent (e.g., by giving her a cup and inviting her to drink). At 28 months, 15 children involved an adult as agent and 5 children included an adult as passive recipient. Note that giving a cup to an adult in this context is ambiguous and was not considered an invitation to enter play as agent unless accompanied by the appropriate language.

Bath. This scenario was modeled with a doll as active recipient (see Bretherton, Chapter 1, this volume, for a definition). Almost all (29) children engaged in some care-giving behavior toward the doll at both ages. However, at 20 months only 3 children treated the doll as active recipient by talking to it or imputing sensations to it. Seventeen other children talked about their own action toward the doll ("dry it," "put in"). By contrast 18 28-month-olds assigned the doll an active recipient role (sign test, $p = .001$). Note that the judgment of active recipient is difficult to make on the basis of motor behavior alone. In this study, assignment to this category was made on the basis of verbal behavior, although behavioral criteria, such as careful positioning of the doll in the tub or stroller, could perhaps be developed in the future. Five of the 28-month-olds used the doll as agent (e.g., sat it in the tub and told it to take a bath). Only three children involved an adult as agent at 28 months. The lesser use of an adult during the second scenario was probably due to the presence of a doll as potential partner.

Even though the word *dirty* was in the vocabulary of many 20-month-olds, only 1 of the children mentioned the make-believe dirtiness of the doll. At 28 months, 11 children did so (sign test, $p = .001$).

To sum up, the role structure of the bath scenario was generally enacted slightly below the role level at which it was modeled at 20 months. At 28 months, a majority of children reproduced the modeled level and a very few enhanced it.

Bears. The third scenario was demonstrated with one figure in an agent role (mother bear) vis-à-vis the other in an active recipient role (baby bear). Striking age changes occurred. Altogether, 27 of the 20-month-olds did put one or both bears to bed. However, only 1 of the 20-month-old children used one bear as recipient of the other bear's action (by making mother bear kiss the baby bear).

Of the remaining 26 children, 17 reduced the reciprocal roles to parallel ones, as expected on the basis of the findings of Rubin and Wolf (1979). These children put the large and the small bear (or substitute) to bed sequentially or together during at least one of the postmodeling conditions. The 9 remaining children used only one bear (or bear substitute). Altogether, 16 of the 20-month-olds treated one or both bears as active recipients of their own care-giving actions and the other 10 used one or both bears exclusively as passive recipients (they did not talk to the bears or attribute sensations to them). Contrary to our expectations children did not simplify the substitution conditions by conspicuously avoiding the baby bear substitutes. The realistic (mother) and substitute (baby) bears received equal use during the placeholder and counterconventional conditions, and this was true at both ages.

At 28 months, the level of role complexity changed dramatically. All children played with both bears during at least one postmodeling condition. Twenty-four children (compared to one at 20 months) enacted the scenario with mother bear as agent vis-à-vis baby bear as patient, making mother bear kiss and/or wish "night-night" to the baby bear (sign test, $p < .001$). Twenty-one children enacted both behaviors, thus treating the baby bear as *active* recipient of the mother bear's care. The remaining six children simplified the modeled role structure by putting both bears to bed, treating them as active recipients of their own action. We should emphasize, however, that no single child made the large bear act out the complete sequence of care-taking behavior the experimenter had demonstrated. Only three children made the mother bear hug as well as kiss the baby bear. The modal level of role representation at 28 months could thus be described as mixed, with the child putting the baby bear (or substitute) to bed and/or covering it with a blanket him- or herself, followed by use of mother bear as agent to kiss and talk to the baby bear.

Pretend states ("sleepy," "go to sleep," "night-night," "wake up") were commonly mentioned when talking to or about the bears. Sleep-related terms were used by 13 20-month-olds and 26 28-month-olds (sign test, $p = .003$) in talking to or about the bears.

Actions

That action complexity was reduced for all scenarios is evident from inspection of the longest sequence measure (see Table 3). The means were consistently below the number of modeled schemes even at 28 months (overall $M = 3.2$). Scheme frequency and diversity did differ by scenario, however, with the intermediate (bath) scenario generating most schemes at both ages, $F(2, 56) = 18.1$ and 13.5 respectively, $p < .001$.

Two of the scenarios had two subepisodes. Breakfast consisted of drinking juice and eating cereal; during the bath scenario the doll was washed, then taken for a ride. This two-part structure of the first two scenarios enabled us to check whether the increased scheme diversity at 28 months was primarily due to further elaboration of two-episode scripts, enacted in simplified form at 20 months, or whether 20-month-olds were prone to produce primarily one-part, and 28-month-olds more two-part, scripts. The latter hypothesis was confirmed. At 20 months 6 children performed an eating–drinking sequence during the breakfast scenario, whereas 16 did so at 28 months (sign test, $p < .01$). For those children who reproduced both subepisodes at either age there was no significant difference in the order (drinking–eating versus eating–drinking). Overall, eating was much more common than drinking. The favorite activity at 28 months actually consisted of "pouring" from one container to the other. With regard to the bath–ride sequence of the second scenario, 11 children enacted both subepisodes in sequence at 20 months. This increased to 23 children at 28 months (sign test, $p < .001$). At 28 months (but not 20 months), input order tended to be preserved during the realistic condition, 15 of 17 children, chi- square (X^2) (1) = 9.9, $p < .01$ and the placeholder condition, 11 of 14 children, X^2 (1) = 4.6, $p < .05$. This finding did not hold for the counterconventional condition, during which the two subepisodes were enacted by only 4 children, in any case. There was, of course, no logical reason why drinking–eating during the breakfast scenario should be performed in that order, but the same was true for the bath–ride sequence during the second scenario in which children did tend to reproduce the input sequence. Unfortunately, the structure of our scenarios did not allow us to test whether reproduction of input order could be improved by causal as opposed to purely temporal links between episodes, as suggested by findings from the storytelling literature (Nelson & Gruendel, 1981; Stein, 1978).

The meaning of actions was clarified and amplified by language in many instances, but much more strikingly so at 28 than at 20 months. Even though we had independent evidence that all 20-month-olds had some food and drink words in their vocabulary, only 10 20-month-olds referred to make-believe food during the breakfast scenario. At 28 months, 22 of the children did so (sign test $p < .004$). In many cases the substances named by the children differed from those modeled by the experimenter and included milk, coffee, tea, beer, cheese, and applesauce. With regard to the bathtime and teddy bear scripts, most pretend utterances referred to internal states of the replicas discussed earlier in the section "Roles." However, at 28 months 5 children also talked about imaginary substances (water, soap) and imaginary destinations for the doll's ride (school, work, store) during the bath scenario. These verbal inventions (see also Fenson, Chapter 9, this volume) added greatly to the richness of play at 28 months.

PROTEST TO OBJECT SUBSTITUTION
AND ITS RELATION TO PLAY

Despite the significant increase in play over age during the placeholder and counterconventional conditions (see Table 3), verbal protest to object substitution also rose significantly ($M = 1.1$ versus 3.5, $t(28) = 5.0, p < .001$) whereas behavioral protest remained stable over age ($M = 1.7$ versus 2.0). We had expected protest to decline from 20 to 28 months, because object substitution is generally believed to become easier as children acquire the ability to do with less contextual support in the use of symbols (decontextualization). Piaget (1946/1962) and others (e.g., Werner & Kaplan, 1963) have suggested that the capacity for decontextualization improves with age. We were hence somewhat surprised by our findings (but see Golomb, 1977).

Systematic correlations of protest and play measures emerged only at 28 months. At this age those children who showed the highest quantity and quality of *spontaneous* play and play-related language in response to presentation of the realistic toy set tended to protest *most* during the later *substitution* conditions (see Table 4). In addition, performance during the substitution conditions was negatively related to protest.

In a few cases the child's resistance to the modeled object substitution was quite passionate ("I don't want to play this game"; "I'm going to stomp on it, I'm going to squish it"). Only one child in the sample seemed to accept the imposition of a placeholder or counterconventional object in a truly playful spirit: After we had offered him a comb as stand-in for a spoon, he pointed to the cup, asking "Is that a cup?" However, play and protest were not mutually exclusive. The majority of children displayed both behaviors.

STABILITY OF INDIVIDUAL DIFFERENCES
WITHIN AND ACROSS AGE

Within Conditions

The different play measures (scheme frequency and diversity, sequenced schemes) shared much variance at both ages. For example, when scheme frequency for each contextual condition was correlated with the diversity and sequence measures for the same condition at each age, the obtained correlations ranged from .80 to .93 ($p < .001$). In other words, in this paradigm quantitative and qualitative measures (within each of the four conditions) yielded largely similar information with respect to individual differences. An exception was the

Table 4
Play and Play Language Behaviors Correlated
with Pretest Measures at 28 Months

Play measures	r (28) Two-tailed
Placeholder scheme frequency × verbal protest	− .43**
Placeholder scheme diversity × verbal protest	− .58****
Counterconventional scheme diversity × verbal protest	− .39**
Sequenced placeholder schemes × verbal protest	− .46***
Counterconventional pretend utterances × verbal protest	− .39**
Spontaneous scheme frequency × behavioral protest	.58****
Spontaneous scheme diversity × behavioral protest	.38**
Sequenced spontaneous schemes × behavioral protest	.50***
Realistic descriptive utterances × verbal protest	.41**
Spontaneous descriptive utterances × behavioral protest	.41**
Spontaneous descriptive utterances × verbal protest	.33*

$*p < .10. **p < .05. ***p < .01. ****p < .001.$

longest sequence measure, for which correlations with other measures were lower but still highly significant. Pretend utterances were consistently related to their corresponding play measures only at 28 months (range .38 −.76, $p < .05$). Descriptive utterances were less consistently correlated with corresponding play measures and will not be further discussed here.

Across Conditions Within Age

The strongest intercondition relationships between equivalent measures occurred for the two substitution conditions (placeholder and counterconventional). They ranged from .41−.84 ($p < .05$) at 20 months to .43−.68 ($p < .05$) at 28 months. At 20 months, corresponding variables for the spontaneous and counterconventional conditions were also significantly related (range .46−.52, $p < .05$). At 28 months, correlations between realistic and object substitution conditions fell just short of two-tailed significance.

Across Age

Only measures for the spontaneous condition were significantly correlated from 20 to 28 months (range .38−.44, $p < .05$). No significant longitudinal correlations were found for the three postmodeling conditions (realistic, placeholder, counterconventional).

Table 5
Correlations of Play and Play
Language at 20 Months with
High-Level Sequenced Schemes
(Three or More Schemes per
Sequence at 28 Months)

20-Month measures	r (28) Two-tailed
Scheme frequency	.43*
Scheme diversity	.52**
Sequenced schemes	.46**
Descriptive language	.46**
Pretend language	.74***

*$p < .05.$ **$p < .01.$ ***$p < .001.$

Longitudinal correlations for general measures (summed across the four conditions) were also examined. Only one general measure at 28 months, high-level sequenced schemes (comprising all meaningful sequences of three or more schemes), was significantly associated with general measures at 20 months (see Table 5). The best predictor of high-level sequenced schemes at 28 months turned out to be pretend language at 20 months.

DISCUSSION

The major findings of this study can be summarized in terms of group differences and individual differences.

GROUP DIFFERENCES

Age

A significant developmental improvement was observed in the ability to reproduce modeled scenarios based on breakfast, bath, and bedtime scripts. This was true for all three postmodeling conditions as well as for spontaneous play. Pretend utterances showed the most dramatic rise over age, contributing to the sophistication of role and action representation at 28 months. Action representation was enhanced and clarified by language when children labeled imagined actions, substances, and locations. Role representation was enhanced by language whenever children spoke to or attributed internal states to a figure, thus treating it as active rather than passive recipient. This finding parallels our data regarding the acquisition of internal state language in everyday contexts by the same children (Bretherton & Beeghly, 1982). Only at 28 months, however, were a majority of children able to reproduce a script in which two toy figures engaged in reciprocal interaction.

Pre- and Postmodeling Play with Realistic Objects

At both ages the quality and quantity of script enactment improved after modeling with realistic objects. Exceptions were two qualitative measures (longest sequence and descriptive utterances). Apparently children could not use the temporal support of modeling to increase the *maximum length* of their meaningful action sequences, although modeling did affect the *number* of such sequences produced. Descriptive utterances were most frequent during spontaneous play due to a tendency to label the toys on presentation by the experimenter.

Postmodeling Play with Realistic and Substitute Objects

At both ages we noticed a significant deterioration in script reproduction after modeled object substitution, although for some variables only the differences between realistic and counterconventional conditions were statistically significant. Object substitution appeared to influence action and language in similar and predictable ways, but the increase in protest at 28 months was unexpected. Piaget (1946/1962) viewed early object substitution as assimilation of a substitute to the (imagined) realistic object. It is as if the child, needing tangible support for his or her schema, used the substitute because nothing better was at hand. During the preschool years, however, some children actually relish the use of substitutes (Wolf & Grollmann, 1982). They appear to enjoy the contradiction between the actual and imagined function of the object. Our 28-month-olds, by contrast, may have been at a transitional stage at which they became very aware of the "correct" object required by the script and were hence offended rather than amused by our "toying" with a reality they had just begun to master. Alternatively, we may have been seeing more lasting style differences of the kind pointed out by Wolf and Grollmann (1982). We will return to this topic shortly.

Level of Modeled and Reproduced Play

At 20 months only a few children re-enacted the breakfast scenario by inviting adult participation, thus increasing the level of role complexity on reproduction of the script. During the bath scenario most 20-month-olds used the doll as passive rather than active recipient (i.e., they reduced the modeled role complexity slightly). Most striking was the 20-month-olds' inability to reproduce the teddy bear scenario as modeled. The modal behavior was to simplify the role structure and treat both bears in the same fashion. Action structure was also simplified.

At 28 months, by contrast, a majority of children invited an adult to participate in the breakfast scenario, whereas the bath scenario tended to be enacted at the modeled level with the doll as active recipient. Longitudinal change was most dramatic for the teddy bear interaction of the third scenario, which was at least partially mastered by the great majority of 28-month-old children. In addition, a larger number of children imitated the central acts of both subepisodes of the breakfast and bathtime scenarios at 28 months.

Content

The bath scenario elicited consistently more play than the other two scenarios. Content saliency, order effects, or level of role complexity (the scenario was neither too easy nor too difficult) may be responsible for these findings. We cannot choose between these alternatives at present.

INDIVIDUAL DIFFERENCES

Correlations Within Contextual Condition

Within conditions the different quantitative and qualitative measures gave very similar information with respect to individual differences. Pretend language was also related to play schemes during the same condition, but only 28 months.

Correlations Across Contextual Conditions

The children's performance during the two object-substitution conditions was consistent at both ages. By contrast, realistic postmodeling play was not correlated with the substitution conditions at 20 months and only marginally at 28 months. Counterconventional and spontaneous play showed significant relationships at 20 but not at 28 months. Thus, the stability of individual differences over conditions was not especially impressive but did exceed chance expectations.

Correlations With Protest

Only at 28 months did we obtain significant associations of play with protest. Correlations with spontaneous play were positive and those with substitution performance were negative. In other words, children who showed the highest quality of spontaneous play also tended to resist the imposition of a placeholder, and—not suprisingly—engaged in significantly less play during the substitution conditions. At 20 months, on the other hand, more protest did not mean less play.

Correlations Across Age

Only individual differences in *spontaneous* play were consistent across age. No reliable longitudinal correlations emerged for the three postmodeling conditions. Even though the two substitution conditions were intercorrelated at each of the two ages, these measures showed no developmental stability. Verbal and behavioral protest were also not correlated from 20 to 28 months. Only one general 28-months measure (high-level sequences) was predictable from a number of general measures at 20 months. To find longitudinal stability of individual differences for spontaneous but not reproduced play was unexpected, in view of Piaget's hypothesis that imitation is related to a child's level of conceptual development (Piaget, 1946/1962).

IMPLICATIONS

This study differs from others in that a test format instead of random (or counterbalanced) presentation of items was used. Yet the results are in line with those from other studies (cited earlier) that also found that modeling enhances and object substitution depresses performance. Our fear that repeated demonstration of the scenarios might produce a training effect strong enough to counteract the effects of substitution proved to be unwarranted. Repeated demonstration might also have induced boredom. However, the findings concerning protest to placeholder and counterconventional objects indicate that the children were alerted, not bored, by our substitutions. The fact that the longest sequence did not change across conditions also argues against a fatigue effect.

Several investigators are attempting to develop standardized assessments of symbolic play, whether to measure the child's level of symbolic skills (e.g., McCune-Nicolich & Fenson, in press) or the child's level of social understanding (e.g., Bretherton, Chapter 1, this volume). Our group data give encouraging support to such efforts, although we suggest that more fine-grained levels of role representation and deliberate trade-offs between action and role complexity might usefully be incorporated into such instruments. We suspect, for example, that representation of an interaction between two doll or animal figures may be possible for a specific child, provided the modeled action sequence is very simple. The same child may not be able to show this ability in conjunction with a complex action sequence. The aim of a test or assessment of spontaneous or elicited symbolic play should, in our view, be to bracket a child's level of role and action representation by specifying which level is possible under which conditions of contextual support (for other types of contextual variation see Fenson, Chapter 9, this volume). In other words, we do not believe that a child's level of performance is absolute, but that it varies within certain limits depending on the degree of temporal and perceptual support offered. It is therefore more interesting to discover the range of a child's ability under different contextual conditions than to attempt to establish whether he or she has the ability in an absolute sense.

Although the group data suggest that the creation of standardized symbolic play tests is feasible and useful, the individual difference data point to obstacles in the way of that goal, especially if such tests were to use modeling. It is puzzling that children who did well in free play did not do *correspondingly* better after realistic modeling. Some investigators (Fischer, personal communication, June 1982) propose that postmodeling behavior may be more reliable because it measures competence or what the child *can* do, whereas spontaneous play assesses only what the child *will* do (motivation). This speculation is not in accord with our data showing that postmodeling play *was* affected by motivational factors (modeled object substitution engendered protest). Things are further complicated by the fact that realistic and substitution postmodeling play were not correlated at 20 months and only weakly at 28 months. Hence, we suggest that the significance of object substitution may need to be rethought. If it is true that some children are more resistant to "toying" with reality, one ought to find that they have a general tendency to resist reproduction of any modeled distortion of play or language. Such distortions could include reversed roles, reversed sequence, or—in language—implausible commands and agrammatical utterances. This topic deserves further study because somewhat analogous effects were noted by Wolf and Grollman (1982). They identified object-dependent children who preferred "good" substitutes (a red bead equals a red cherry) and object-independent children whose construction of a play reality was not tied to the availability of specific props. Another possibility is that protest to modeling of noncanonical events is likely to be pronounced when an ability has just been mastered, but not when it has become firmly established.

That individual differences were not strikingly stable across age even for spontaneous play may be due to the relatively short observation period. Kagan (1981) found that when he increased the sample of behavior for each child (averaging symbolic play over four or more adjacent monthly sessions), impressive longitudinal stability of individual differences did emerge. If a test is to be useful for relating individual differences in symbolic play to individual differences in language or social cognition (see Bretherton & Bates, in press) we need to know how often and/or how long a child must be observed to obtain a representative sample of behavior.

The fact that we can predict and understand direction but not relative magnitude of behavioral change in response to experimental manipulations of symbolic play may delay the construction of a standardized assessment instrument. In the meantime, merely knowing that play can be reliably enhanced or depressed by contextual variations (without knowing how much) can be helpful in educational and clinical settings. Some of the experimental manipulations we have described in this study (as well as those presented by Fenson, Chapter 9, this volume) could serve to explore an individual child's play systematically. Manipulations of the action and role complexity of modeled scripts together with built-in opportunities for enhancement or simplification of the level of modeled play would give additional flexibility both in initial diagnosis and for intervention. Educators could use our contextual variations to challenge a child who is delayed in symbolic play to reach higher levels of script representation. Knowledge of common scripts is, after all, necessary for engaging in cooperative pretending with other children (see Nelson & Seidman, Chapter 2, this volume). Similarly, a clinician might be interested in the meaning of play with several small figures. Before attributing deep emotional significance to a child's play with a mother and baby figure in parallel roles, however, it is vital to discover whether parallel roles merely represent that child's highest level in play with replicas.

In short, modeling in conjunction with individually tailored variations in contextual support and event complexity can be a creative tool for assessment of and intervention with individual children, even though we need further research before we can use the same manipulations in a standardized symbolic play test.

APPENDIX

SEMANTIC SEQUENCING FOR
SCENARIOS AT 20 AND 28 MONTHS

The purpose is to determine how many bits of the modeled scenario the child can string together in a logical way.

In order to be counted, the sequence must be planful in some way (there is a reason for stirring before eating, for instance). Although this is hard to operationalize, the sequence should not be just random actions strung together.

Actions may be counted *whether or not* they were actually modeled, provided they are related to the scenario in an obvious way (e.g., feeding mother or experimenter with a spoon).

Only actions in one unbroken sequence may be counted in a string. Once an illogical action occurs, the sequence is considered ended.

Because very few children actually reproduced all aspects of the modeled scenario, logical sequences will be counted very "locally." This means that any sequence of behavior that accomplishes dressing the doll and putting her into the stroller, for example, can be given credit even though the bathing sequence was modeled first.

The point is to get some measure of the child's comprehension of the scenario and his or her ability to demonstrate that comprehension by reproducing the sequence of events.

ACKNOWLEDGMENTS

We would like to thank the 30 children and their mothers who made this project possible. Marjorie Beeghly, Andrew Garrison, Kim Kirschenfeld, Sandra McNew, and Carol Williamson deserve acknowledgment for their unstinting and conscientious help in data collection and transcription. Special thanks are due to Lorraine McCune-Nicolich for making detailed comments on a prior version of this chapter.

REFERENCES

Bates, E., Benigni, L., Bretherton, I., Camaioni, L. and Volterra, V. *The emergence of symbols: Cognition and communication in infancy.* New York: Academic Press, 1979.

Bates, E., Bretherton, I., Snyder, L. Shore, C., & Volterra, V. Gestural and vocal symbols at 13 months. *Merrill-Palmer Quarterly,* 1980, *26,* 407–423.

Bretherton, I., & Bates, E. *The development of representation from 10 to 28 months: Differential stabililty of language and symbolic play.* In R. N. Emde & R. Harmon (Eds.), *Continuities and discontinuities in development.* New York: Plenum, in press.

Bretherton, I., & Beeghly, M. Talking about internal states: The acquisition of an explicit theory of mind. *Developmental Psychology,* 1982, *18,* 906–921.

Bretherton, I., Bales, E., McNew, S., Shore, C., Williamson, C., & Beeghly-Smith, M. Comprehension and production of symbols in infancy: An experimental study. *Developmental Psychology,* 1981, *17,* 728–736.

Corrigan, R. The control of animate and inanimate components in pretend play and language. *Child Development,* 1982, *53,* 1343–1353.

Elder, J. L., & Pederson, D. R. Preschool children's use of objects in symbolic play. *Child Development,* 1978, *49,* 500–504.

Fein, G. A transformational analysis of pretending. *Developmental Psychology,* 1975, *11,* 291–296.

Fein, G. Pretend play in childhood: An integrative review. *Child Development,* 1981, *52,* 1095–1118.

Fenson, L., & Ramsay, D. Decentration and integration of the child's play in the second year. *Child Development,* 1980, *51,* 171–178.

Fenson, L., & Ramsay, D. Effects of modeling action sequences on the play of twelve-, fifteen-, and nineteen-month-old children. *Child Development,* 1981, *52,* 1028–1036.

Golomb, C. Symbolic play: The role of substitutions in pretence and puzzle games. *British Journal of Educational Psychology,* 1977, *47,* 175–186.

Inhelder, B., Lézine, I., Sinclair, H., & Stambak, G. Les débuts de la fonction symbolique. *Archives de Psychologie,* 1972, *41,* 187–243.

Jackowitz, E. R., & Watson, M. W. Development of object transformation in early pretend play. *Developmental Psychology,* 1980, *16,* 543–549.

Kagan, J. *The second year: The emergence of self-awareness.* Cambridge, MA: Harvard University Press, 1981.

Killen, M., & Uzgiris, I. Imitation of actions with objects. *Journal of Genetic Psychology,* 1981, *138,* 219–229.

Largo, R., & Howard J. Developmental progression in play behavior in children between 9 and 30 months. *Developmental Medicine and Child Neurology,* 1979, *21,* 299–310.

Lowe, H. Trends in the development of representational play in infants from one to three years: An observational study. *Journal of Child Psychology and Psychiatry,* 1975, *16,* 33–47.

McCune-Nicolich, L. Toward symbolic functioning: Structure of early pretend games and potential parallels with language. *Child Development,* 1981, *52,* 785–797.

McCune-Nicolich, L., & Fenson, L. Methodological issues in studying early pretend play. In T. Yawkey & A. D. Pellegrini (Eds.), *Child's play: Developmental and applied.* Hillsdale, NJ: Erlbaum, in press.

Mandler, J. H. Categorical and schematic organization in memory. In C. R. Puff (Ed.), *Memory organization and structure.* New York: Academic Press, 1979.

Nelson, K. Social cognition in a script framework. In J. H. Flavell & L. Ross (Eds.), *Social cognitive development*. Cambridge: Cambridge University Press, 1981.

Nelson, K., & Gruendel, J. Generalized event representations: Basic building blocks of cognitive development. In A. Brown & M. Lamb (Eds.), *Advances in developmental psychology* (Vol. 1). Hillsdale, NJ: Erlbaum, 1981.

Nicolich, L. M. Beyond sensorimotor intelligence: Assessment of symbolic maturity through analysis of pretend play. *Merrill-Palmer Quarterly*, 1977, *23*, 89–99.

Piaget, J. *Play, dreams, and imitation in childhood*. New York: Norton, 1962. (Original French edition, 1946.)

Rubin, S., & Wolf, D. The development of maybe: The evolution of social roles into narrative roles. *New Directions for Child Development*, 1979, *6*, 15–28.

Schank, R. C., & Abelson, R. P. *Scripts, plans, goals and understanding*. Hillsdale, NJ: Erlbaum, 1977.

Shore, C. *Assessing decontextualization in symbolic play: A methodological study*. Unpublished master's thesis, University of Colorado, Boulder, 1979.

Shore, C. *Getting it together*. Unpublished doctoral dissertation, University of Colorado, Boulder, 1981.

Shore, C., O'Connell, B., & Bates, E. First sentences in language and symbolic play. *Developmental Psychology*, in press.

Slobin, D., & Welsh, C. Elicited imitation as a research tool in developmental psycholinguistics. In C. Ferguson & D. Slobin (Eds.), *Studies in child language development*. New York: Holt, Rinehart & Winston, 1973.

Stein, N. L. The comprehension and appreciation of stories: A developmental analysis. In S. Madeja (Ed.), *The arts and cognition* (Vol. 2). St. Louis: Cemrel, 1978.

Ungerer, J. A., Zelazo, P. R., Kearsley, R. B., & O'Leary, K. Developmental changes in the representation of objects from 18–34 months of age. *Child Development*, 1981, *52*, 186–195.

Volterra, V., Bates, E., Benigni, L., Bretherton, I., & Camaioni, L. First words in language and action: A qualitative look. In E. Bates, L. Benigni, L. Bretherton, L. Camaioni, & V. Volterra. *The emergence of symbols: Cognition and communication in infancy*. New York: Academic Press, 1979.

Watson, M. W., & Fischer, K. W. A development sequence of agent use in late infancy. *Child Development*, 1977, *48*, 828–836.

Watson, M. W., & Fischer, K. W. Development of social roles in elicited and spontaneous behavior during the preschool years. *Developmental Psychology*, 1980, *16*, 483–494.

Werner, H ., & Kaplan, B. *Symbol formation*. New York: Wiley, 1963.

Wolf, D. Understanding others: A longitudinal case study of the concept of independent agency. In G. Forman (Ed.), *Action and thought: From sensorimotor schemes to symbol use*. New York: Academic Press, 1982.

Wolf, D., & Grollman, S. Ways of playing: Individual differences in imaginative play. In K. Rubin & D. Pepler (Eds.), *The play of children: Current theory and research*. New York: Karger, 1982.

CHAPTER 11

Conceptual Organization in the Play of Preschool Children: Effects of Meaning, Context, and Mother–Child Interaction

MARIA KREYE

INTRODUCTION: THEORETICAL CONSIDERATIONS

Until comparatively recently, little was known about the conceptual abilities of preschoolers. Most studies of concept formation in young children concluded that children under 4 years of age are lacking in concept-formation skills (Nelson, 1974). A variety of inadequacies have been noted—young children have a mediation deficiency (Kendler, 1972), they fail to differentiate perceptual dimensions (L. B. Smith & Kemler, 1978, 1977; Tighe & Tighe, 1972), they use inappropriate strategies (Gollin & Schadler, 1972), or they may show a production deficiency in classification tasks (Flavell, 1970). If children create groups of objects, they shift from one criterion to another, they form alignments with objects that are selected at random, they build towers or designs. If they begin to use criteria more consistently, they may select objects that all differ or share one aspect, but their grouping indicates conceptual instability. Perceptual discriminations appear to be unstable, as well as the mode of sorting (N. W. Denney, 1972; Flavell, 1970; House, Brown & Scott, 1974; Inhelder & Piaget, 1964; Markman, & Machida, 1981; Vygotsky, 1962). Concept-formation ability in children under 4 years of age is therefore often described in the research literature in negative terms (Damon, 1981; Nelson, 1974; Nielson & Dockrell, 1982).

The evidence that young children's conceptual organization is unstable comes from both of the traditional theoretical frameworks within which children's concept formation has been investigated, that is, the Piagetian as well as the behaviorist schools of thought. In either case, inferences about a child's conceptual skills are made on the basis of outcomes of abstract logical or scientific tasks, which the child is required to solve by acting on materials in certain predetermined ways. An analysis of the theoretical models shows that they follow the assumptions underlying abstraction theory in the methodologies they employ.

Abstraction theory assumes that concepts are formed by a process of feature abstraction. Similar features are noted in the environment and related according to a conceptual rule (Bourne, Ekstrand, & Dominowski, 1971). Furthermore, it is assumed that similarity is a property of stimulation emanating from the environment (Gibson, 1969). Both assumptions have been challenged on various grounds. From an organismic perspective (Weiss, 1941) it can be argued that what is perceived as similar changes across situations. Depending on internal state, current context, and past experience, similarity may be perceived now where it was not in the past, and vice versa. Tversky (1977) noted that similarity is a judgment on the part of the perceiver and like other judgments depends upon context and frame of reference.

Yet most traditional studies of child concept formation implicitly follow the assumptions underlying the abstraction theory model of concept formation. Within a behaviorist framework, perceptual learning studies are most often employed. They are designed to demonstrate how children acquire specific concepts, such as reversal or oddity (e.g., House et al., 1974). In these experiments, children are required to discriminate particular perceptual dimensions such as color, form, or size across a series of displays. They are reinforced for "correct" choices—those that indicate the child has learned a conceptual rule that serves as a criterion for object selection. For example, in an oddity experiment the child is reinforced when selecting the single object that differs from the other objects in the display. A selection of the odd object across trials indicates that the child has learned a conceptual rule, namely oddity (e.g., Gollin, Saravo, & Salten, 1967).

In Piagetian research, free classification studies are most often used to investigate concept formation in young children. Children are required to select from an array those objects that go together, such as those that have the same color or the same shape. The groupings the child selects are judged on the basis of the perceptual dimensions that appear to serve as criteria for the child's selections.

From either experimental approach, results indicate that children under 4 years of age have great difficulty in concept-formation tasks and children under 3 years are usually unable to do these tasks at all. It is also generally reported that young children fail to cooperate in these experiments.

There appear to be two aspects to the problem. One is that neither the behaviorist nor the Piagetian theory focuses on the age range under consideration. For behaviorists, preschoolers are not able to form concepts because they have not yet developed the prerequisite skills of perceptual discrimination assumed to be necessary for concept formation. Children of this age range are described more in terms of what they lack in comparison to older children rather than in terms of possible modes of conceptualization they might possess.

In Piagetian theory, the preschool age falls between the end of the well-explained sensorimotor period and the beginnings of logical thought, with little explanation offered as to how this transition might occur. (Toulmin, 1977). Both theories lack explanatory power in their account of concept formation in the preschool child.

The second problem is related to the first: The weakness in the theoretical frameworks is related to the inappropriate use of a methodology that appears to be suitable for older children and adults, but not necessarily for young children. Failure to demonstrate concept formation in young children, however, is most often ascribed to children's inability rather than to a methodology that may not be able to access what young children can do (S. D. Smith & Gollin, in preparation). For example, if child concepts are based on meaning, rather than on abstraction of perceptual dimensions, experimental materials such as geometric forms that differ in color, size, or form are not likely to tap organizing strategies the child might possess. Meaningful items such as cups and spoons may elicit the child's conceptual skills; they may be able to access it.

Nelson (1981) and Mandler (1979) have proposed a script model of knowledge acquisition that used Schank and Abelson's (1977) work as a starting point and offered a far more informative framework of early conceptual development than either of the traditional models achieve. The script model in essence proposed that knowledge is acquired within a participatory framework, in social interaction. Young children come to represent recurring experiences through event schemata. Event schemata in turn form the basis for the creation of taxonomic categories because they allow substitution of similar objects in particular slots of their structure (Mandler, 1979).

The script model of knowledge acquisition draws attention to two important aspects of concept formation that have not been a focal interest in traditional theory or methodology: (1) the social interactive aspect, and (2) the content of knowledge acquisition, namely the specific experiences of the child.

A comparison of the abstraction-theory model and the script model makes it apparent that they deal with concept formation at different levels of analysis. Event schemata, as conceived in the script model, are akin to concepts as traditionally defined; they also represent collections of similars, they are generalizations. Their function is the same, as well; they are distillations of past experience that allow the prediction of future events (Bolton, 1977).

Toulmin (1973), in a discussion of levels of rationality in human behavior, pointed out that the more inclusive level logically determines what can be asked at a more reductionist level, but not the other way around. It follows that the more comprehensive level in concept formation as described in the script model should precede the level of elements that abstraction theory describes and that most studies of child concept formation address, apparently with little success.

Weiss (1967) in a discussion of organic systems was concerned with the fact that most scientific endeavors tend toward an absolute reductionism. But as phenomena are isolated into their component parts, a great deal of information about the interrelationship among the parts while they were still united is lost. When we observe phenomena, we tend to move "back and forth between telescopic and microscopic vision." As we move down the scale, we "gain precision," but "lose perspective." Moving upward we recognize new patterns we could not see before. The novel patterns reflect properties of the global arrays whose units we saw at a more molecular level. If we work at the level of the element we may not find any hint of what the total structure looks like, nor can the pattern of the whole be predicted from a simple upward projection of elemental properties (Weiss, 1967, pp. 802, 806).

Mandler (1979), in accord with Weiss's statement, had proposed that event schemata, derived from experience, may form the basis for the construction of taxonomic categories. But event schemata most likely cannot be reconstructed from knowledge of organizational rules pertaining to taxonomic categories, and event organization may follow principles that are different from the principles that are used in the creation of taxonomic classes. Rules of organization may differ at different levels of analysis as well as across levels of analysis.

Donaldson's influential work (1978) criticized Piagetian concept-formation experiments because they were disembedded from meaningful contexts. Once such contexts were provided, problems could be solved at much younger ages than had previously been supposed. Hence, if we want to learn more about the conceptual rules by which young children organize their environment we may thus have to pay attention to whether the task has meaning for the child.

Event schemata represent meaning in context. For present purposes, an *event schema* will be defined as a behavioral sequence organized on the basis of meaning. *Meaning* in turn can be defined as the significance of an event in terms of an earlier experience. The meaning of an event may be based on species experience (*phylogenetic* in origin) or on individual experience (*ontogenetic* in origin).

Some meanings in human development appear to be of the "wired-in" phylogenetic kind. For instance, optical flow patterns have meaning for young children, which is apparent from their reactions to rapidly approaching objects (Pick, 1977). Moving eyes are prepotent attention-getters that elicit smiling and bring infants into facial contact with a care giver who has meaing for their survival (Hess, 1970). Gibson (1969) has proposed that there is a fit between the perceptual system of an organism and the ecological niche in which it evolved. The way the system is organized reflects what is meaninful in the species sense— what aids in its survival. From research on visual physiology (Grobstein & Chow, 1975; Pettigrew, 1976; cortical organization (Hubel, 1976), and infant perception (Bower, 1974; Salapatek, 1977), it is apparent that human infants are born with capabilities that are the result of phylogenetic experience.

But human development is also characterized by a long period of immaturity, which allows a further, more fine-grained adaptation to very specific environmental conditions (Bruner, 1972). Human survival depends as much on ontogenetic experience as on species experience. A mechanism for the retention of individual experience is therefore essential. William James (1901) speculated that what is retained of experience is a "sense of sameness" across events, which he thought was at the heart of concept formation. He called it the principle of constancy in the mind's meanings. This experience of sameness organizes past events and renders future encounters in a variable environment more predictable, hence makes events meaningful.

From Brazelton, Tronick, Adamson, Als, & Weise (1975) and Trevarthen's (1982) work, it is apparent that meaning is established and expressed from birth within the mother-child relationship. Mothers and infants develop a mutual causal relationship with clear expectancies of particular responses by both members of the dyad. As Bruner (1975a, b) has proposed, the child's experience becomes structured by way of well-practiced caretaking and play routines. These routines have meaning for the child. They allow him or her to predict what will happen in the couse of some future encounters. They appear to form the basis of early conceptual organizations (Mandler, 1979).

Organization of experience within the context of social interaction allows parents to structure environmental stimulation to the child's capabilities. The mother often provides directive or provides what Bruner called scaffolding for activities that expand children's experience beyond what they would be able to do on their own or even beyond what is currently meaningful to them. Mandler observed that in many parent–child routines, the meaning or purpose of a behavioral sequence may not be clear to the child participant. It is also possible that the child's meaning differs from adult meaning in these circumstances. From the diary literature on children's first word use, it appears that early words or concepts often have idiosyncratic meanings. They summarize a child's experience in a way that is different from adult organization. It seems that the interaction between mother and child affords children an opportunity to align their own meanings with the socially accepted meaning of a word or a concept.

Children's comprehension in early years relies heavily on context. Context permits the mother, as well as the child, to interpret what the other is saying (Huttenlocher, 1974; Ryan, 1974). It appears that for young children meaning is entailed in context and context is an integral part of the structure of language (Bates, 1976), as it well may be of the structure of concepts.

The acquisition of knowledge appears to be as much motivated by the child as by the mother's directive. Trevarthen (1982) concluded from his studies on infants that they actively use human companions to gain knowledge from the time their minds recognize objects of knowledge, even before they can effectively manipulate things. Through mental partnership with the caretaker, they may have the effect of acting when direct action is impossible for them.

Mother–child interaction, as an adaptive mechanism, appears to be a very efficient means for achieving a fine tuning between a new offspring and a variable environment while laying the groundwork for conceptual organization that will alllow the adult to function on his own on the basis of knowledge acquired from experience.

The study presented in this chapter was an attempt to find out more about young children's conceptual skills by addressing them at a level of function that seemed appropriate to their developmental status. In particular, it seemed likely that early concepts would be learned within the everyday experiential context of children's lives. Early concepts were thought to reflect that experience in their content and be based on the meaning events have for the child rather than on abstraction of perceptual features as such. An object sorting experiment was designed with materials that let the child act out his experience in spontaneous play. At the same time it afforded the investigator an opportunity to see if and how the experimental context in general and the meaning context in particular affected the object groupings the child created.

The purpose of presenting this study in a volume on symbolic play is to show how children's play can be used by investigators of early cognitive development to elicit conceptual skills that may be elusive in other experimental situations. Play can be used as a methodological tool in experiments in the same sense that it is used in play therapy (Erikson, 1963): to reveal children's thoughts by actions on objects of their experience.

AN EXPERIMENT INVESTIGATING CONCEPTUAL
SKILLS IN PRESCHOOL CHILDREN:
METHODOLOGICAL CONSIDERATIONS

One objective of this study was to investigate the following issues in child concept formation.

1. Are young children able to form stable conceptual organizations of several types if contextual conditions support concept formation?
2. Is it likely that children form concepts on the basis of meaning rather than feature abstraction?
3. Are contextual effects different at different levels of development?

Specifically, it was hypothesized that for young children conceptual organization is an integral part of the structure of context. Young children use conceptual organizations that fit the meaning of the context. If contextually supported, the young child's concepts may follow the same principles as the older child's and show the same degree of stability. It was expected that the younger the child, the more context dependent his or her concepts would be.

A second aim of the study was to generate heuristic information from naturalistic observation that would become a guide to future research in an area about which little is known at present (Damon, 1981; Nielson & Dockrell, 1982). It was hoped that information about how children go about organizing objects would provide as much information as whether they do it.

PLAY AS A METHODOLOGICAL TOOL

Bruner (1972) suggested that observational learning and play are important mechanisms in primate adaptation. Play is meaningful in terms of species survival. Observations of children between 2 and 7 years of age show that a substantial part of their waking hours is devoted to play (Schell & Hall, 1979). In play, the child spontaneously organizes objects and people. Play activity thus appears to be highly suited to accessing a young child's conceptual ability. Play is based on the child's experience; it is meaningful and purposeful; it is a mode of organization 2- and 3-year-old children have used for some time; they are skilled in it and devote much of their time to it. It may in fact be their primary mode of conceptual organization. Play can demonstrate what children of this age range *can* do in terms of conceptual strategies employed and conceptual groupings created. Children also *like* play, thus eliminating some problems of motivation and cooperation that frequently are obstacles in experiments with young children, often making it impossible to access conceptual abilities at all. Furthermore, it eliminates the need for experimental instructions, whose meaning the child may not be able to grasp. Ricciutti (1965) observed, in studies attempting to develop appropriate instructions for 3-year-olds, that children who may not have grouped objects during an experimental session started to play with them spontaneously afterwards and organized them quite systematically. Ricciutti's observations demonstrate that a considerable degree of organizing behavior occurs if young children are simply presented with test materials without any instructions.

In the present study, a free-play format was therefore used, where children's natural inclination to play was utilized for a demonstration of their conceptual organizing ability, which may not be accessible in any other way. By systematic variation of experimental conditions, the effect of such conditions on children's organizing strategies was observed and measured. The type and potency of context was manipulated and the relative effect of context was observed in how the children organized objects as they played.

SYSTEMATIC VARIATION OF CONTEXT

In a free-play situation there can be no direct control of the child's concept formation strategies, but indirect control can be achieved by altering the environment in predictable ways and measuring the relative effects on spontaneous strategies (Bitterman, 1960).

Because it was proposed that children's conceptual rules are embedded in context, different aspects of context were conceptualized and manipulated. The *physical–perceptual context* was singled out as exerting an influence on concept formation, and so was the *social–verbal* or interactive context between mother and child. It was also proposed that child concepts are based on meaning. In order to demonstrate this, the *meaning context* was varied systematically as well.

Physical–Perceptual Context

Perceptual learning studies show that young children may be able to solve a difficult problem in the context of a particular perceptual dimension but be unable to transfer it to another dimension (Gollin & Schadler, 1972; Schadler, 1973; Tighe & Tighe, 1972). The perceptual or task context appears to be crucial to what is singled out for attention by the child, how it is processed, what conceptual rule is learned, and whether it can be transferred to a new context.

There are indications that the physical–perceptual context may be an integral part of the structure of early concepts. It was therefore one of the aspects of context that was manipulated in this experiment.

Social–Verbal Context

Vygotsky (1962) proposed that children learn concepts in social interaction. As soon as children can communicate their early idiosyncratic concepts, which are based on subjective experience, these concepts become modified in social use. Several studies have shown that even 3- and 4-year-olds are capable of organizing stimuli in certain ways if instructed to do so (e.g., Schadler, 1973; L. B. Smith & Kemler, 1977; Tighe & Tighe, 1972). One of the methodological difficulties when working with young children is precisely that their performance is highly dependent on their comprehension or interpretation of instructions used by the experimenter (N. W. Denney, 1972; Ricciutti, 1965). The social–verbal aspects of context appear to be particularly potent in early concept formation and were therefore included as a second condition in this experiment.

Meaning Context

Donaldson's (1978) work has demonstrated that the meaning of a context influences whether the child can solve a concept-formation task or not. Because child meaning and adult meaning are not necessarily congruent at young ages and meaning in absolute terms is difficult to define, the meaning context can be varied systematically. If such variation produces predicted effects and control conditions do not, it can be concluded that whatever the absolute meaning may be for child or experimenter, there is some shared reference that determines the kind of conceptual organization produced. Furthermore, if conceptual organization changes as the meaning of a context changes, it is reasonable to assume that young children form concepts on the basis of meaning. Contextual meaning was therefore included as a third experimental condition in this study.

MEASURES OF CONCEPTUAL ORGANIZATION

In a play situation, an experimental task is not specified as such. The outcome of a presentation of materials may be any manner of grouping. Nevertheless, particular aspects of grouping activity can be measured and can yield different kinds of information about children's conceptual skills.

Size and Amount of Groups Created

In this experiment, the size of a group was used to indicate the relative stability of the ordering principle over time, the same way it is used in traditional free-classification studies. In those studies, a shift in apparent criterion of selection is inferred if the child is shifting from objects similar in one aspect to objects that share another aspect. The more objects are grouped that belong together in terms of a specific criterion, the more stable conceptual grouping is judged to be. Furthermore, the amount of groupings of a particular kind serve as an index of stability when a particular type of conceptual organization is considered. In Piagetian research, a progression from resemblance sorting to consistent sorting to exhaustive sorting is reported, when the child learns to group two things because they look alike, then extends the scope of the sort to more than two until he or she can sort all the objects that can be considered equivalent (Kofsky, 1966). The amount of grouping shows how systematic the child's conceputal organization is and how exhaustive and thus how robust is the organizing principle that is used.

Types of Conceptual Groupings

Free-classification studies report that there is a progression of different ordering strategies as the child's cognitive abilities expand (Kofsky, 1966). Young children's object grouping often proceeds from random groupings or graphic arrays to groups where members share some attribute or differ in certain respects to groupings that show some consistency in ordering criteria used (N. W. Denney, 1972; Inhelder & Piaget, 1964; Vygotsky, 1962). Ordering strategies described in the perceptual learning literature include position perseverance (Gollin & Schadler, 1972) extradimensional or reversal shift strategies (Tighe & Tighe, 1972).

Some experiments on children's concept formation used meaningful material in their investigations when they employed nominal classes instead of perceptual dimensions as vehicles for studying conceptual skills (D. R. Denney & Moulton, 1976; N. W. Denney, 1974). In these cases, younger children tended to group in terms of complementarity, older children in terms of similarity relationships. Complementary relationships are those in which members of a group are selected on the basis of sharing a context or theme (e.g., rabbit–carrot). Similarity relationships are those based on taxonomic ordering (e.g., rabbit–cat). The literature on the *syntagmatic-paradigmatic* shift (Mandler, 1979; Nelson, 1981) indicates that there is a developmental shift from the predominant use of syntagmatic or figurative relationships (Piaget, 1963) to the use of taxonomic categories, although both strategies are available to children at young ages.

Because both ordering strategies appear to be available to young children, an attempt was made in this experiment to elicit them differentially by contextual manipulation. Meaning contexts were designed that conveyed either a complementarity or a similarity structure. This allowed a test of the proposition that young children use conceptual organizations that fit the meaning of a context. If they do, complementarity grouping should predominate in a complementarity context, similarity grouping in a similarity context. Graphic arrays were thought to occur with a *lack* of meaningful context.

For this experiment it was desirable to define complementarity and similarity in different terms than is usually the case. Nominal similarity as used in the paradigmatic–syntagmatic literature appeared to be a relatively advanced form of categorization. It was thought that basic-level object categorization would be more appropriate in an experiment with very young children. Rosch (1977) reported that basic chunking of experience occurs at a basic object level, at which objects share a maximum of cues. For example, a rabbit's perceptual appearance and motion is more likely to be noted as similar to another rabbit's than to those of a horse. The grouping of rabbit–rabbit (basic level category) should precede the grouping of rabbit–horse (nominal category). It was expected that for young children, basic-level object classes would be more appropriate as vehicles for a demonstration of ordering capacities than more complex nominal classes (Mervis & Crisafi, 1982). Similarity relationships were therefore defined in terms of similar basic-level objects. Complementarity relationships were seen as involving objects from different basic-level object classes.

EXPERIMENTAL MATERIALS: INTEREST, FAMILIARITY, AND MEANING

The methodological strategy using spontaneous play relies heavily on experimental materials and their interest value to the child. Ricciutti's (1965) study showed that there were clear task-content preferences in children at very young ages. Certain stimuli induced more congitive activity than others. Strong differential object preference was associated with more frequent cognitive manipulative structuring in the infants. It is therefore necessary to offer a range of task materials if we have to rely on their intrinsic appeal to elicit organizing strategies in the child.

If children's concepts are based on meaning and meaning is derived from experience, materials have to be used with which the child is familiar. To measure context effects, grouping objects should have meaning in and of themselves, apart from context. Some objects acquire contexts independent meanings early. Fenson, Kagan, Kearsley, and Zelazo (1976) reported that at 7 months, babies mouth, chew, or bang a cup. By 13 months, they may pretend to drink from it, thus demonstrating that the object has acquired intrinsic meaning for the child and furthermore that this meaning is congruent with social use. From Nelson's (1981) and Mandler's (1979) work, it would appear that the more familiar the child is with an object that recurs in many different events, the earlier its intrinsic meaning should be established.

Sorting Objects

The sorting objects used in this study were toys with which all the children were familiar: dishes, furniture, clothes, and vehicles. They all lent themselves to being organized in terms of a child's experience, in terms of a script in Nelson's (1981) sense. The toys were selected to give the child's play structure through their content. Furthermore they came from different domains of experience and represented different themes. At the same time they could be organized either figuratively (e.g., a plate and a cup) or taxonomically (e.g., plate–plate).

Contexutal Props

In addition to sorting objects, large organizer toys were used as contextual props. They suggested different scripts in Nelson's sense, although at the time the experiment was designed they were simply provided to serve as a perceptual context. Two such props were given for each set of play materials. For example, a table was provided along with the dishes at one time, a dishrack was presented with the dishes another time. The organizer toy was used to elicit a script that either accessed complementary–figurative grouping (table) or classificatory–similarity grouping (dishrack). The props were used to suggest a different meaning context to the child.

METHOD

Subjects

Participating in this study were 96 children (48 boys, 48 girls). Their ages ranged from 24 to 48 months; they were divided into three age groups, 28, 36, and 44 months. The children were recruited individually through babysitting cooperatives and through mother referrals. Most of them came from upper-middle-SES families. All except one child lived with both parents. Approximately 10% of the mothers worked outside the home. In the oldest age group (40–48 months), 12 out of 32 children went to preschool, usually twice a week. In the middle age group (32–40 months), 6 out of 32 went to preschool. In the youngest age group (24–32 months), none did.

Experimental Design

A 2 × 2 × 3 × 2 mixed factorial design was employed with three between-subject variables and one within-subject variable. Between-subject variables were (1) physical–perceptual context: presence or absence, (2) social–verbal context: presence or absence; (3) age: 28, 36, or 44 months. The within-subject variable was contextual meaning: complementarity or similarity.

Materials

Some of the materials used in this study were commercially available, some were homemade. They were the two kinds of toys described earlier; sorting objects that lent themselves to be grouped in some way, such as dishes, and larger ones that could be used in organizing the smaller ones, such as a table or a dishrack. The toys were comparatively large, so even the youngest children could organize items although their fine motor movements were not as precise as those of the older children. A toy plate, for instance, was 5 1/2 inches in diameter. A wooden table that could be used with the dishes measured 16 inches by 10 inches and was 8 inches high. Care was taken to ensure that the objects to be grouped as well as the organizer toy were of approximately the same size within tasks and across tasks. The size of the toys was held constant so as not to prejudice the selection of particular toys that might be perceptually more salient because of their size alone.

Four sets of sorting objects were used: dishes, clothes, furniture, vehicles. Each of these was composed of four kinds of objects that represented a basic level object class. For example the set of dishes consisted of four plates, four cups, four spoons, and four forks. Clothes consisted of four hats, four sweaters, four pairs of pants, and four coats. Furniture consisted of four tables, four chairs, four cupboards, and four beds. Vehicles consisted of four cars, four airplanes, four boats and four traincars.

In addition, four sets of organizer toys were used in conjunction with the four sorting sets. They served as contextual props for the physical–perceptual condition. For the social–verbal condition four sets of cue cards were used in conjunction with the four sorting sets. The two organizer toys or cue cards for each sorting set suggested a context or script. For example, in the physical-perceptual context dishes were presented to the child with a table or dishrack; in the social–verbal condition, the dishes were presented with cue cards for the mother than read either "Let's play setting the table" or "let's play washing the dishes." For the clothes set the organizer toys were either four dolls or a wardrobe. The cue cards read "Let's play dressing the babies" or "Let's put the clothes away after washing them." For the furniture set the organizer toys were either a dollhouse or a U-Haul truck. The cue cards read "Let's play house" or "Let's play moving to another house." For the vehicle set the organizer toys were four dolls or a landscape board. The cue cards read "Let's play sharing toys" or "Let's play the road, lake and airport game."

Procedure

The children were visited individually in their homes by two observers at a time when the mother, but no siblings, were present. They were observed during morning hours between 8 and 12 a.m., when mothers reported they would be most alert.

At the beginning of the session, the observers asked the mother for a suitable room in the house where no toys other than the experimental ones would be visible. The child was given a music box as a warm-up toy. Ten to 20 minutes were spent on establishing rapport with the mother and the child. During that time, the experimenter explained to the mother what her role would be in a particular contextual setting. If experimental conditions called for social–verbal interaction, the mother was shown the cue cards and instructed how to use them. If conditions did not require a social–verbal context, the mother was asked to stay with the child in the room, be supportive and responsive, but remain uninvolved in the child's activities.

The procedures followed in the presentation of task materials were similar to the procedures developed for infant testing with the Bayley Scales of Infant Development (Bayley, 1969), with which the primary observer was experienced. Task materials were presented one set at a time. Materials not in use were put in a trunk which contained the toys or out of the child's view. Tasks were presented in a predetermined balanced random order, so that no one task appeared more than once in the same position in a given experimental condition. In keeping with the Bayley procedures, however, if a task was refused on a first presentation, it was re-introduced again at a later time, when and if the flow of the session appeared to be opportune for a second presentation.

Presentation of Materials. The children generally preferred to play on the floor. The mother and the experimenter sat on the floor with them. The other observer usually sat on a nearby chair or sofa. At the beginning of a presentation, the experimenter first arranged the contextual conditions of the task by setting up the organizer toy (table) and/or giving the mother the appropriate cue card ("let's play setting the table"). The children played with the toys under one of four contextual conditions: (1) physical–perceptual context, in which a large toy such as a table suggested a context: (2) social–verbal context, in which the mother conversed with the child: "let's play set the table"; (3) physical *and* social context, and (4) no context. In addition, the same objects were presented twice to each child, once each under a different meaning condition (e.g., table/dishrack).

Presentation of Task. The experimenter opened a box with the small toys (e.g., dishes) and arranged them in a random array on the floor. She then said, "See these? You can play with them any way you like. When you are finished, you can tell me."

If verbal comments were to be made by the mother, she was instructed to begin creating a context before the child started to play. In all conditions, the mother was asked not to name any of the grouping objects nor to point to them so as not to prejudice what the child would pay attention to. Within the social–verbal context, mothers conversed with the children until they got the impression that the children understood the meaning of a context and how they might play with the objects. For example, mothers might say "Show me how you set the table. What do we usually need for breakfast? Let's pretend we are having dinner. Daddy is coming home, too. What else do you need?" Mothers were instructed to support the child's ordering verbally, without being specifically directive.

Once the materials were presented, the observers recorded all the child's actions with the toys and noted symbolic expressions involving grouping objects. When the child indicated that he or she was finished playing with the particular materials they were put away and a new set was introduced until all eight presentations were completed.

Data Recording and Reduction

Behavior Recording. The two observers recorded the order in which objects were selected, the kind of object chosen, its placement, and spatial groupings.[1] From the observer protocols, two independent raters transcribed behavior segments for scoring. A behavior segment consisted of a child's action that involved contact with an object and/or placement of an object. If there was discrepant information from the two protocols on a given behavior segment, that segment was not included in the subsequent analysis. Discrepant information was discarded in order to establish a consistent basis for the assessment of rater reliability in scoring of segments. Observer agreement was calculated at .94 on the

[1]Sequential and spatial groupings (Ricauitti, 1965; Starkey, 1981) were not treated separately.

basis of transcribed segments that were in agreement versus the total number recorded.

Scoring. The transcribed behavior segments were scored by the two raters in terms of (1) size of groups (two, three, or four members) and (2) type of conceptual organization (complementarity, similarity, or graphic array). The frequency with which a particular type of grouping was used by a particular child was calculated across tasks in a given meaning condition. The composite score on a specific dependent measure was the basic datum for all subsequent analyses. Rater reliability ranged from .90 to .94.

Each dependent variable was analyzed separately by a 2 × 2 × 3 × 2 multivariate analysis of variance (MANOVA). Effects were investigated in terms of the between–subject factors: presence or absence of perceptual context; presence or absence or verbal context and age (28, 36, or 44 months). The within–subject factor was meaning: complementarity or similarity of context structure.

RESULTS

Accessing Conceptual Skills through Play

All children played with the materials. They all organized toys into complementarity as well as similarity groups. The extent to which they participated, however, varied with contextual conditions. Table 1 shows how contextual conditions affected the child's play. When the mother was involved and the child had an organizer toy to play with, all children across ages became involved in play. When no script was suggested by an organizer toy or by the mother's suggestion, about one-fourth of the children refused to play with the toys at one time or another. The effect of context on play was most notable in the youngest age group. When the youngest children had only an organizer toy to suggest a script, almost a third of them refused to play with materials at some time. When they had only their mother to suggest a context, the majority of children refused to play at one time or another.

Table 2 shows how the provision of a context or script influenced children's participation in the sorting tasks. It is apparent that the simple presentation of materials for play was an effective strategy to induce children's object manipulation across conditions. Without contextual support, there was a high degree of object manipulation but conceptual grouping, particularly the creation of large three- and four-member groups was impaired. When children had both an organizer toy and the mother's conversation to suggest a script the highest degree of conceptual organization was obtained. With partial support, only two-thirds of the tasks led to large conceptual groups in the youngest children. The

Table 1
Percentage of Subjects that Participated in All Tasks under Different
Contextual Support Conditions

Age in months	Perceptual–verbal	Perceptual	Verbal	Control
Mean	(%)	(%)	(%)	(%)
28	100	63	38	75
36	100	100	100	87
44	100	100	100	75

results indicate that it is possible to access young children's conceptual organizing skills by a free-play technique that employs meaningful materials such as those selected in this experiment, but that accessing is more effective if contextual support is provided.

Conceptual Stability

The robustness of conceptual organization was measured in terms of the frequency with which three- and four-member groups were created (Figure 1). There were significant main effects of age, $F(2,84) = 18.0$, $p < .000$; percep-

Table 2
Task Participation under Different Contextual Conditions

Age in months	Perceptual–verbal (%)	Perceptual (%)	Verbal (%)	Control (%)
Tasks leading to *object manipulation* under different contextual support conditions				
28	100	93	90	96
36	100	100	100	95
44	100	100	100	96
Tasks leading to *conceptual groupings* under different contextual conditions				
28	100	84	81	68
36	98	95	92	79
44	96	100	96	93
Tasks leading to *large conceptual groups*				
28	93	68	62	53
36	92	83	71	65
44	92	89	93	89

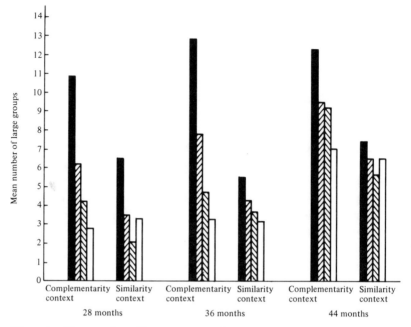

Figure 1. Mean number of large groups as a function of age × meaning × perceptual × verbal support. Solid bar refers to perceptual–verbal; top right to bottom left diagonal hatching refers to perceptual alone; top left to bottom right refers to verbal alone; open bar refers to control group.

tual support, $F(1, 84) = 47.7$, $p < .000$; verbal support, $F(1, 84) = 14.8$, $p < .000$; and meaning, $F(1, 1) = 18.6$, $p < .050$. The findings indicated that stable conceptual groupings increased with age. The provision of a perceptual context aided substantially in the formation of stable groupings. Verbal context had a similar effect but it was less pronounced. Across ages, more large groups were created in a complementarity context than in a similarity context. A significant interaction between perceptual and verbal support, $F(1, 84) = 4.3$, $p < .040$, showed that, at all ages, children created large groups more frequently if they had both a perceptual *and* verbal context. Under this combined effect, younger children performed similarly to older ones. A significant interaction between age and perceptual context condition, $F(2, 84) = 3.6$, $p < .032$, indicated that without perceptual support, 28- and 36-month-olds created few large groups but 44-month-olds made many.

The results of the analysis of the occurrence of large groups supported the hypothesis that children as young as 2 and 3 years of age show stable conceptual organization. The hypothesis that the stability of conceptual organization depends on contextual support and that the younger the child the more context-dependent his ordering would be was supported as well.

Conceptual Meaning

The proposition that children's concepts are based on meaning and that the child uses conceptual organizations that fit the meaning of a context was assessed by measuring context appropriate grouping.

Complementarity Grouping. As expected, complementarity grouping was high in a complementarity context and low in a similarity context, $F(1, 1) = 26.7$; $p < .035$ (Figure 2). It increased with age, $F(2, 84) = 11.2$, $p < .000$; perceptual support, $F(1, 84) = 53.2$, $p < .000$, and verbal support, $F(1, 84) = 17.3$, $p < .000$. Complementarity grouping was highest under the combined perceptual and verbal condition, $F(1, 84) = 7.9$, $p < .006$. In this case, the youngest children created as many groups as the older ones. A significant age $\times$ perceptual context interaction, $F(2, 84) = 6.3$, $p < .003$, indicated that

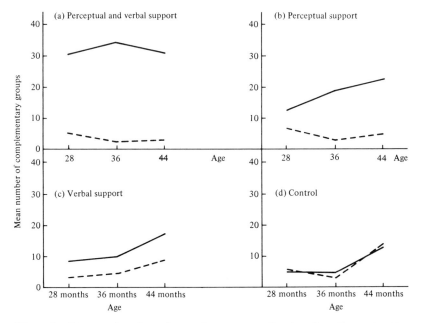

Figure 2. Mean number of complementarity groups as a function of age $\times$ meaning $\times$ perceptual $\times$ verbal support conditions. Solid line refers to complementarity context; broken line refers to similarity context.

without perceptual support 28-month-olds made far fewer complementarity groups than the older children.

Similarity Grouping. Similarity grouping was more frequent in a similarity context than in a complementarity context, but contrary to expectations the effect was not significant, $F(1, 1) = 4.9, p < .157$. Similarity grouping increased as a function of age, $F(2, 84) = 5.6, p < .005$; perceptual context, $F(1, 84) = 13.6, p < .000$; and verbal context, $F(1, 84) = 9.1, p < .003$. There was no significant perceptual–verbal interaction, $F(1, 84) = 1.5, p < .220$, although the effect was in the predicted direction. (Figure 3). Similarity grouping occurred comparatively frequently in a complementarity context. Children often picked up similar objects such as four plates, *in order* to make complementarity groups such as table settings.

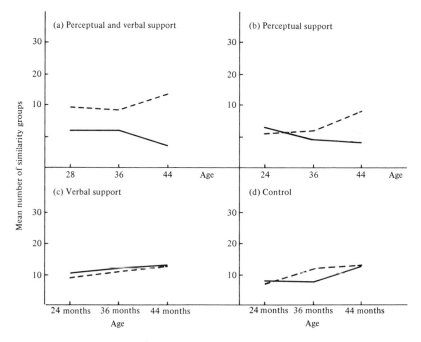

Figure 3. Mean number of similarity groups as a function of age × meaning × perceptual × verbal support conditions. Solid line refers to complementarity context, broken line refers to similarity context.

Meaning Shift in Conceptual Organization. Because the contextual effects of meaning were not symmetrical, it was of interest to know if the *difference* between complementarity and similarity grouping was significant in the two meaning contexts (Table 3). It was found that indeed complementarity exceeded

Table 3
Differences between Complementarity and Similarity Grouping under Specific Conditions of Meaning and Contextual Support

	Complementarity context		Similarity context	
Age in months	Complementarity grouping	Similarity grouping	Complementarity grouping	Similarity grouping
Perceptual–verbal				
28	30.625	12.125	5.375	19.500
36	34.125	11.125	2.500	18.125
44	31.875	7.250	3.250	23.458
Perceptual				
28	12.500	13.375	6.500	10.250
36	19.125	8.875	3.625	12.125
44	22.875	8.375	5.250	18.375
Verbal				
28	8.625	10.250	3.875	8.500
36	10.125	12.125	4.500	11.250
44	17.375	13.875	8.875	13.625
Control				
28	5.250	8.125	6.125	7.875
36	5.000	8.125	2.875	12.125
44	13.250	12.000	14.250	13.250

similarity grouping in a complementarity context and similarity exceeded complementarity grouping in a similarity context, $F(1, 1) = 276.1, p < .038$. The results supported the hypothesis that children used conceptual organizations that fit the meaning of a context.

Developmental Trends. A significant main effect of perceptual context, $F(1, 84) = 18.1, p < .000$, but not of verbal context, $F(1, 84) = 2.5, p < .116$, indicated that across conditions children grouped in a context-appropriate way if a perceptual context was present, but not in a verbal context. When the effects of meaning and age were examined within each contextual condition, a developmental trend became apparent. When both an organizer toy and the mother's suggestion was provided, all children, regardless of age, shifted from complementarity grouping in a complementary context to similarity grouping in a similarity context, $F(1, 1) = 448.1, p < .030$. When only an organizer toy was given, a meaning $\times$ age interaction, $F(2, 1) = 16.9, p < .000$, indicated that this was not sufficient to understand the meaning of the context for 28-month-olds, but adequate for 36- and 44-month-olds. Figure 4 indicates that the social–verbal context alone was beginning to convey meaning to 44-month-olds but not to the younger age groups.

Graphic Arrays

The results on conceptual stability and meaning were indirectly supported by the results obtained on the use of graphic arrays (building with objects, making designs and lines). Graphic arrays increased with a *lack* of context, particularly perceptual context, $F(1,84) = 30.3$, $p < .000$. This type of grouping appeared most frequently in situations where the meaning of a context did not seem clear to the child, in a verbal context or under no-context conditions.

DISCUSSION

The results of the experiment indicated that young children's concepts are not unstable as such; rather, concept formation on the basis of abstraction of dimensions alone may be unstable at young ages. Younger and older children used the same principles of organization, although similarity grouping appeared to be a more basic mode of organization. Similarity grouping was used more context-independently than complementarity grouping. This information can be reconciled with findings from the syntagmatic–paradigmatic-shift literature (Nelson, 1982) if we think of concept formation as a process of differentiation and integration where basic level object classes are established prior to their selective integration into nominal classes (see Kreye, in preparation).

The results of this experiment demonstrated that child concepts are based on meaning and embedded in context. Meaning was best conveyed to children when mothers talked to them about the physical array in view. It was surprising to find that the perceptual context conveyed meaning earlier and more effectively than the verbal context. (However, it should be noted that mothers were instructed not to name any of the grouping objects.) The less meaning a context provided, the less conceptual organization occurred.

Once the meaning of a context was established, the youngest children did not differ from the oldest children in the kind of conceptual rule they used or in the extent of their conceptual organization and the degree of the shift under different contextual conditions. When the meaning was clear and the purpose established, the appropriate rule was applied exhaustively no matter what the developmental age of the child. Developmental differences therefore have to be ascribed more to differences in context embeddedness of meaning and conceptual rule than to differences in conceptual stability, comprehension of meaning, or even to availability of different conceptual organizations as such. Children at different developmental levels appear to differ above all in their context dependency.

The change in theoretical perspective seemed indeed to provide a more ad-

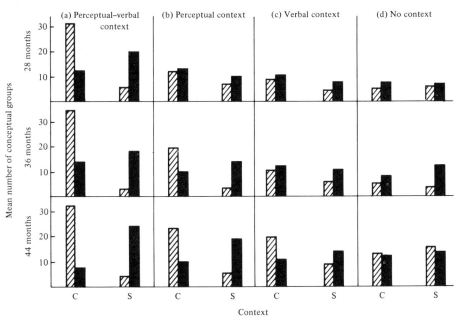

Figure 4. Mean number of conceptual groups as a function of age × meaning × perceptual × verbal support conditions. Hatched bar refers to complementarity grouping; solid bar refers to similarity grouping. C refers to complementarity context, S refers to similarity context.

quate framework for the investigation of young children's concept formation. The methodological approach that included consideration of meaning and context was effective in accessing the conceptual skills of children between 2 and 4 years of age.

The purpose of this investigation was not only to test particular predictions about children's conceptual skills but also to generate heuristic information about the circumstances of their application. Conceptual organization differed in different contextual settings, but it is not apparent from the results of the study why this might have happened and how. The following discussion offers some insights and suggests some possibilities.

Differential Effects of Perceptual and Verbal Contexts
on Conceptual Organization

Across ages, the combined perceptual–verbal context was most effective in establishing the meaning of the situation. When only one kind of context was available, the perceptual context was more effective than the verbal context. This probably can best be explained by young children's prevalent use of a sensorimotor mode of conceptual organization. As Langer (1980) pointed out, the pragmatic actions of young children are not yet based on the use of symbols, which language represents. The child of 2 or 3 years of age is more experienced in the medium of concrete perceptual objects than in the medium of symbols. From birth, children order their surround in terms of perceptual differences (Salapatek, 1977). Earliest concepts are often idiosyncratic and based on physical–perceptual aspects of objects and events (Bowerman, 1977). The evidence seems to indicate that the child is able to generate a conceptual rule early in life based on a concrete, physical–perceptual context.

Studies that demonstrate how effective rule instruction is (Schadler, 1973; L. B. Smith & Kemler, 1977; Tighe & Tighe, 1972) for perceptual learning and concept formation at young ages provide, in fact, both a perceptual and a conversational context. The child is shown how he can organize materials that are in view. The experimenter talks about the here and now. Such procedures are more like our present full contextual condition than the verbal condition as conceptualized in this experiment. In our verbal condition, conversation was restricted. The naming of objects was avoided so as not to prejudge object selection. No direct relationship was established between conversation and grouping materials. The child had to generate a conceptual rule solely on the basis of the mental representations the conversation addressed. It is, therefore, not surprising that the verbal context was less effective than the perceptual context in promoting the generation of context-appropriate grouping and conceptual stability.

At 2 and 3 years, children are still comparatively inexperienced in an abstract mode of cognitive organization. Piaget put the transition from a sensorimotor mode to one in which actions are mentally represented at about 18 months of age. The results of the differential effects of perceptual and verbal contextual support can thus be explained in terms of the limited skill in mental representation young children have versus their considerable experience of ordering in sensorimotor terms. A conversational context alone was not able to access the younger children's conceptual skills as effectively as a perceptual context. It is striking, however, how effective conversation was when used with perceptual support. It appeared to focus children's activity in a mode they were experienced with, in a way similar to what Vygotsky (1962) described when he spoke of how scientific concepts are taught by focusing the attention of the child on particular dimensions of the concept.

Incidental observations from this investigation offer some clues *how* the different contexts affected child organizing strategies.

Perceptual Context. Observations indicate that the perceptual context provided a spatial frame of reference for organizing materials, much as a puzzle game provides for missing pieces. S. Sugarman (1979) noted, in her investigation of classification in 1–3-year-olds that children at these ages are intrigued by spatial containment. Markman *et al.* (1981) similarly found that 3-and 4-year-olds are influenced in their object sorting by the salience of the spatial arrangements of objects as such. From observations made in the present experiment, it seemed that the perceptual context provided the child with a particular space or locality into which objects could be fitted. Weiss (1941) suggested that the environment must initially appear to a new organism as a cohesive continuum and that out of this continuum discrete fragments are attended to in order to find regularities in the flow of phenomena. For the young child, grouping objects may appear as such fragments that belong into particular places in the larger framework of the natural surround. The perceptual context in this study provided particular spaces for fitting objects, thus giving direction to the child's ordering activity by promoting some ways of organization and constraining others. For instance, a dishrack promotes ordering plates in rows and silverware in a basket. It would be difficult to make a table setting within its topographical arrangement.

The importance of locality as a criterion by which to order objects is apparent from several different types of observations. Moore & Clark (1975), in studies of the acquisition of object permanence, found that for an infant two different objects may be judged to be the same object if they appear in the same locality. Location may be a criterion as well in the concept formation of 2- and 3-year-olds. Children in the present study sometimes practiced what can be termed dislocation. Children might create a group consisting of a table and four chairs around it. Then, one chair would be taken away and put in a different spot, then brought back to the table. This would be repeated and the child would gradually transfer the whole group to the new spot, then it would be brought back to the old place as if to assure the child of its identity regardless of locality. This happened often enough that it suggested to observers that a conceptual grouping may be partly defined by the young child in terms of *where* it belongs in a particular context. Studies on the acquisition of the oddity concept in young children (Gollin & Schadler, 1972) have indicated that 3-year-olds often use position perseverance as a strategy in selecting objects in such a task. Here again, the child may use locality as a criterion by which to compare one object to another.

Observations from the present experiment, furthermore, suggest that the criterion of locality may develop from an undifferentiated "dishes belong on the table" to a more specific spatial concept of "a spoon belongs next to a plate." Very young children would often put handfuls of dishes on the table or stuffed clothes into the wardrobe. They knew where these objects belonged, but not yet in terms of specific spaces for them. The importance of a bounded space as a requirement for conceptual organization was also demonstrated by a 33-month-old in the control group who went to get plastic container lids in order to group furniture. He said that he could not do it without them. Most children could not order clothes without a doll or a wardrobe that provided spaces for doing so.

A further indication that specific spaces were used as a help in conceptual organization came from observations on marking. Children often would mark a space with a particular object, a second space with another one, and so on. Then they would proceed to put the remaining objects in the appropriate spaces. For instance, a child might put a hat on the top shelf of the wardrobe, a sweater on the second, and pants on the third shelf. The child then would pick up items randomly, but match them with the ones that marked the shelf. If the child picked up a pair of pants it would go on the third shelf, a sweater would be put on the second shelf, and so on until all items were sorted.

Some observations indicated that for some children, particular motor movements were used in conjunction with particular localities in producing certain object groupings. For example, a 28-month-old requested that the toy wardrobe should be put on a chest in her house, so that she could order the toy clothes by using her arms in the same way she did when putting away her real clothes. Another child regularly put a doll's arms behind its back in order to put its coat on. That movement was apparently tied to the placement of the garment for that child. Some children used the same motions in removing objects from organizer toys when their play was finished as they had in placing them initially. Repetition in organization may be a relatively effective means for reproducing an outcome that was judged to be appropriate at one time. It would insure a similar outcome with a relatively low cognitive load until the child has mastered a novel organization. This strategy would allow the child to become more flexible without increasing the memory load beyond his or her ability.

Sugarman (1979) noted in a study of classification and correspondence in 12- to 36-month-olds that children's procedures for producing class-consistent products mapped directly onto the outcomes they produced. Classes were grouped in space only if they were organized that way first in action. Between-class correspondences were produced simply by repetition of the same act of combination that resulted in a series of identical subunits. By 30 months, children could construct correspondences and classes in different ways. Action patterns and spatial groupings were no longer closely tied. Organizing objects had become more flexible.

Piaget proposed that concepts arise out of action. From present observations, it also seemed that such actions were often intimately tied to a particular perceptual context and have to be understood in terms of the context within which they occur. This point is well illustrated by a phenomenon that was occasionally observed: A child was presented with 16 items of clothing and 4 dolls. The child would systematically put pants on all four dolls, then begin to dress them in sweaters, but would forget one of them. Next the child would dress them all in coats, then hats. The forgotten sweater was left over. The child might look at all the dolls, but would be unable to place that sweater, although one of the doll's upper torso was naked, which the child clearly saw. The perceptual discriminations the child made and the resultant groupings appeared to be part of the behavioral sequence observed.

Social-Conversational Context. The verbal context appeared to exert its effects primarily by the establishment of a link between the objects in view and the experiences of the child with similar objects in the past. The youngest children often did not spontaneously use the perceptual context in organizing grouping objects. In the perceptual–verbal condition, the mother's conversation appeared to link the present situation to the child's experience of a similar situation in the past and thus allow access to conceptual skills by pointing out the analoguous contextual relationships. This, in turn, made it possible for the child to apply familiar rules of organization to the novel setting. For the younger children, the mother seemed almost to act as a mediator between the unfamiliar situation and their own experience so that they could bring it to bear on the task. For example, the mother would say "How do we set the table when daddy comes home? What do we need?" Many children would apply their experience in a literal sense. They would set the table only for family members and leave the rest of the dishes. They would give their parents setting a spoon and fork, but said that they only needed a spoon for themselves as in real life. Once they had set the table, they would sit down to eat. Because they were the sole diners, they proceeded to eat from their own plates first, then eat from the other plates until nothing was left. The rules of organization were not only completely embedded in the experimental context but they were re-enacted in terms of a series of behavioral sequences appropriate to a given situation. These children had a "dinner script" in Nelson's (1981) sense but it did not exist in isolation. The dinner script was tied to the washing up script and so forth as if children had a whole string of such scripts to help them organize their day. For example, in a context of "washing up," some children said "You have to eat first," then proceeded to eat from the dishes, stack them, and then wash them up. "Washing up" appeared to be embedded in the larger event of preparing food, cooking, eating, and cleaning up.

In the younger age group, organization of objects often occurred by embedding them in a sequence of events and repeating these events, thus creating groups of similar objects as would be predicted from Mandler's (1979) model of category formation. For instance, a relatively common way of playing with the landscape board included driving a car from the house to the airport. The child then picked up a plane, flew around with it, landed, and let the grandmother disembark. The child then drove her home in the car. The sequence was repeated with different cars and different airplanes, transporting different people. In this way, the game ended with a group of cars next to the house and a group of airplanes at the airport. This again is similar to what Sugarman (1981) reported.

The young children appeared to order their experiences in terms of a time and event sequence as well as in terms of spatial relations. Furthermore, it appeared that temporal ordering was an earlier mode of organizing than ordering in spatial terms, in the same sense that temporal grouping preceded spatial grouping in Riciutti's (1965) and in Starkey's (1982) research. Under control conditions, the youngest subjects used ordering in terms of narrative extensively. This mode declined with age, as an analysis of the frequency of symbolic expression showed. The preoccupation with spatial containment that D. Sugarman (1979) observed and Markman et al. (1981) reported in 3-year-olds may reflect the relative recency of the acquisition of organizing skills in spatial terms.

When children were given verbal support alone, the mother's guidance ceased to be effective for the youngest group and was only partially successful for the older children. Because the verbal context did not allow naming of grouping objects by the mother, her success in establishing a link with the child's experience rested on her ability to access it in terms of mental representation alone. It appears that the youngest children could not use the mothers' suggestions without the presence of perceptual cues. For instance, one child responded to the mother's comment "Let's pretend we are dressing a baby" by saying "But there is no baby, feel the floor, there is no baby." He was apparently unable to create that context by mental representation alone.

As a group, 36-month-olds in the verbal condition responded more to the mothers' suggestions than any other group. They appeared to realize that the mother was referring to past events of their experience, but sometimes no link to analogous experiences could be established. Instead, they responded by long narratives that contained experiences, but were not germane to the task. For instance, in the context of ordering vehicles, the child would pick up a car, recall that they went to get gas, that the man took the credit card, and the father bought bubble gum. The child responded in terms of mental representation and its characteristic mode of organization into behavioral sequences but not appropriately to the context the mother tried to create. Typically, 44-month-olds understood the mothers' comments fairly well, but often were more interested in grouping objects in their own way than following the mother's conversational framework, although they were now able to do so. They used narrative much less as a way of organizing objects. Like Markman et al.'s (1981) subjects, they were preoccupied by creating spatial arrangements, such as alignments, designs, and other types of graphic arrays with the objects in view.

Absence of Context. The control conditions were interesting in several respects. Often children simply identified objects ("That is a table," "That is a chest") or they involved the mother and asked "What is this?" "What is that?"

as they picked up items. Sometimes they would answer the question themselves. They would pick up a car, then ask "What is this?" and answer "A car," and then go on to the next object. The youngest children would, many times, indicate an object's use or function by trying to use it in a real sense. They would lay their heads on toy beds, try to sit on toy chairs, or force dolls' pants on their feet. It seemed as if the child could not yet distinguish between these small objects, which were in a sense symbols, and real objects. Bretherton, Bates, McNew, Shore, Williamson, and Beeghly-Smith (1981) have suggested that these types of actions may be equivalent to labeling an item. The observations from the present study indicate that this is a likely explanation, because older children in the same situation characteristically identified them.

In older children, identification of objects often led to similarity grouping. Children tended to pick out similar objects sequentially from the array confronting them in the sense Sugarman (1981) described it in the study cited earlier. A child would select a car, then say "Here is another one," and proceed until all cars were assembled. There would be a focus on one particular class at a time. This way of creating similarity classes was more characteristic of controls than of contextually supported children. The provision of a spatial context appeared to facilitate a more flexible way of ordering such as occurred when children marked spaces, selected different objects sequentially, but were still able to put them into appropriate places. The single-class mode of organization related to identification was to a great extent responsible for the finding that controls grouped significantly more often in terms of similarity than complementarity.

Controls did a great deal of repetititve object manipulation. For example, one child picked up a car, put his finger in its door, closed the door, and tried the same thing on the other side. He repeated this well over a dozen times. Children would open and close cabinet doors in the same repetititve way, pull out wheels on an airplane, and push them in again. They appeared to examine the objects as such more closely than children that had contextual support. They tried to bend them, take off parts, and put them back. They were interested in how objects were constituted and what they could do with them.

Mother–Child Interaction

The combined physical–perceptual and social–conversational context was clearly representative of the natural conditions under which young children learn about their environment. The typical situation was much as Huttenlocher (1974) and Ryan (1974) described it; mothers and children talked about objects that were present, that could be seen and manipulated. But mothers as well as children also referred to past experience with the type of object that was the focus of attention, which in turn led to object interaction in terms of that experience. The mother often appeared to function as the child's "auxiliary ego" (Renée Spitz, as discussed by E. Freud, 1981) in the same sense that Trevarthen (1982) speaks of the child as actively using human companions to gain knowledge.

Mothers, in turn, had a strong tendency to direct their children's activity, particularly the young child's activity. They often provided a kind of scaffolding in Bruner's sense, by not only marshaling the children's experiental knowledge, but also structuring it in a way that allowed them to expand on that structure. For example, the mother might say "Remember how we set the table when daddy comes home? What do we need for drinking?" "What do you need to do when Grandma comes to eat with us?" For many mothers, it was an effort to restrain the inclination to structure the children's play and leave the intitiative to the children, specifically when their organization differed from what the mothers thought was appropriate ordering. Children, in turn, sought out the mother's guidance and directed much of their activity toward her. They showed her experimental objects, told her what they would do with them, and asked for guidance if they were not sure of a way to play with them.

There was a reciprocal interaction between mother and child, much as Brazelton et al. (1975) described it for his much younger infants. It was also evident that the joint reference of mother and child in attention to the same object that Bruner associated with the origins of communication and language was an integral part of the mother–child interplay. The meaning of an object often appeared to become clear to the child within that social interaction.

Mother–child interactions under partial contextual support differed to a large extent from those under full contextual support conditions. Furthermore, the effects of partial support were different for younger and older children.

Perceptual Context. If given a perceptual context only, 28-month-olds spent a great deal of their time trying to involve the mother in their play. Many times they would plead with her to tell them what to do, or they would try to involve her by playing on her body. They might fly an airplane on her head, run a car up her leg, or try to put an item of clothing on her fingers. The younger children clearly expected the mother to introduce them to a way of approaching experimental materials. They sometimes played either with the organizer toy or the grouping objects, but did not relate them to each other spontaneously. They appeared to know that the two were related because they involved both in their play. For example, a child might pick up a doll, open and shut its eyes, then put it down. The child then might pick up a hat and say "dolly's hat," but make no attempt to organize the clothes in terms of the doll. Their interest in the materials tended to decline fairly rapidly and often they would retreat into their mother's lap or leave the field entirely. The situation appeared to be stressful for them. Mothers often could not understand why the child would not relate the grouping objects and the organizer toy. They seemed unaware to what extent they normally provided directive to the children that allowed them to do so.

Typically, 36-month-olds still tried to involve the mother, but adjusted better to the situation than 28-month-olds. As a rule, they used the organizer toy as a means for grouping objects. Mothers watched with interest but often said they thought the child "could do better," indicating that under normal circumstances they would suggest ways of playing with materials. In contrast to the younger child's difficulty with the perceptual support condition, 44-month-olds thrived on it. For older children, it was the most popular of experimental conditions, partly *because* there was no mother directive. The 44-month-olds "performed" for their mothers and the observers, and often told her "I know what to do." They tended to accompany their ordering by their own verbal directives such as "now I put the table in the kitchen." At this age, mothers seldom expressed a desire to help the child; most were confident that children would be able to work on their own.

Social–Conversational Context. In the verbal condition the normal mother–child interaction was left intact, but it was hampered by the lack of perceptual context. The child usually did not understand the mother's conversation very well. For some mother–child pairs this did not pose a problem. When the child started to play, the mother responded to the child's utterances and guided the child in his or her terms, whatever they were. There was an object-related interaction, but it did not necessarily reflect the contextual meaning the mother had tried to impart. Children created their own meaning and often played at great length under these conditions. As a rule, the verbal-context-only condition was the most difficult for both mothers and children, particularly in the youngest age group. Many mothers tried hard to convey a contextual meaning and were astonished and sometimes dismayed that the child did not respond to their directives. They expected the children to understand much more of their conversation than they did. Mothers appeared unaware to what extent children relied on the perceptual context for their understanding of the mother's speech.

Children at different ages reacted differently to the situation; 28-month-olds seemed to interpret their mother's conversational comments as directives or commands, but if they could not understand them without perceptual context, they tended to retreat from materials into their mother's lap. Sometimes they sucked their thumbs and appeared confused and frustrated. They played least of any group observed. In contrast, 36-month-olds often responded in one of two ways: They might take an isolated word that they understood, such as in, and proceed to put objects "into" each other. In both younger age groups, children often tried to create their own perceptual context. If the mother suggested to play "washing up" with the dishes, children carried the dishes to the kitchen sink. Many attempted to get a doll for clothes, put dishes on the dining table to create a setting, or tried to get their own dollhouse or garage.

The oldest children understood more of the conversational context, but like their counterparts in the perceptual context condition they preferred to play by their own rules rather than by the mother's directive. This was sometimes the case because the conversation was not clear to the children, so that it was simpler for them to follow the rules they could generate on their own. But even if the meaning of the context appeared to be understood, the children at times would say to the mothers, "Don't tell me what to do," and follow their own organizational designs. The 44-month-olds gave the impression of relative independence of their conceptual organization from the mothers' initiative and guidance.

No Context. In contrast to the partial contextual support conditions, the control condition was seldom problematical for the mother–child pair. Mothers watched what children did with materials but they did not convey any particular expectations. Children typically showed objects to the mother, brought them into her vicinity, or gave her objects to hold. They tried to get their own organizer toys, such as dolls or trucks. There was an attempt to involve the mother as well as to generate the perceptual context within which they normally would play. The control condition differed from partial contextual support conditions in that there were no aspects of the situation likely to cause apprehension, such as an organizer toy the child did not know what to do with or a mother's directive that could not be understood.

In general, it appeared that the younger the child, the greater the attempt to generate a full context if none or only a part of it was provided. Partial support conditions elicited a greater effort at establishing full support conditions than was the case with controls. Older children seemed to generate their own rules and these could often be applied in a flexible manner. This was demonstrated by a 44-month-old in the control condition who asked the experimenter "Do you want me to do it this way or that way?" She then proceeded to sort dishes into groups of four plates, four cups, four spoons, and four forks, then shifted to making four place settings consisting of one plate, cup, spoon, and fork each.

Meaning and Purpose of a Task

The experimental evidence showed that young children shift their conceptual grouping in accordance with the meaning of a context. Incidental observations showed that a presentation of objects for play was usually interpreted as a task by the child. Older children would often preface their play by saying, "Now let me see." They would sit still for a while, then proceed to order objects systematically. Their ordering reflected the meaning of the context, it was planned and had a purpose. Children often corrected themselves, implying and sometimes saying "I made a mistake," further indicating that they had a plan of action.

The apprehension occasionally created in the partial support condition, but not in the control condition, indicated the child was aware that the context conveyed a purpose for ordering yet was not able to discern it. Controls generated their own rules for organization and rarely showed such apprehension. Under control conditions, the two meaning conditions were indentical because no context was provided. When objects were presented for the first time, the children would play at length, often terminating a sessin by saying "I'm finished." They indicated that they had done the task, however they had defined it for themselves. When materials were presented a second time, children would often say "I did this one already." They were then asked to try once more. Often they played an abbreviated version of their previous session, showing that their play had a structure that could be re-enacted; this in turn implied some kind of purposeful organization. Under contextually supported conditions, where each context conveyed a different meaning and purpose, this happened far less frequently.

Sometimes a child's organizing had a purpose that was not readily apparent to an observer. For example, one child put clothes into the wardrobe in a random fashion, which was recorded by the observers. After the experiment was over, her mother suggested she do it "right" and showed her how. The child replied that she wanted to do it her own way and proceeded to create a similar "random" arrangement to the one she had produced the first time. There had been a purpose to her ordering even if it was not apparent to the observers. Children of all ages formed some stable conceptual grouping without contextual support. The youngest ones created only a few; the older ones performed almost as well as contextually supported children. The 44-month-olds demonstrated a robustness in their conceptual organization that was not expected. The developmental trend can be explained in terms of context embeddedness of meaning. Grouping materials used in this study were selected on the basis of being meaningful to the child, that is, for their significance in terms of children's experience. Furthermore, they were selected for their relative context independence as far as meaning was concerned.

Under control conditions, the youngest children created few stable conceptual groupings. It is possible that for younger children, few objects were meaningful outside of a context. If concepts were based on meaning, yet few groupings objects had meaning of themselves, far fewer groups would be expected without contextual support, which indeed was the case. It was often observed that control children created stable groups with a limited variety of materials. For instance, a child might create concepual groups with dishes, but not with clothes. The child could form a plate–cup–spoon group without a table, but was not able to relate a hat, a coat, and pants without a doll. Dishes had acquired meaning independent of context, but clothes appeared to have only meaning within a context. Some objects related to a child's experience, others did not.

For older control children, more of the grouping objects had acquired meaning in and of themselves. Developmental differences could therefore be less a matter of conceptual skill as such than a reflection of the more limited experience a younger child has had in this world.

CONCLUSION

The results of this study clearly show the validity of the proposition that a change in theoretical perspective from an abstractionist to a pragmatic viewpoint could provide a more adequate framework within which to investigate young children's concept formation. It also became evident that an inquiry into conceptual skills at an early age requires a methodology that can access such skills.

The script model of concept formation (Mandler, 1979; Nelson, 1981) appears to be able to focus on early phases of cognitive development and to explain how children organize their experience in a theoretically much more informative way than the traditional models do. Proper accessing of small children's cognitive skills is more likely within this framework, and can therefore allow a greater in-depth analysis of developmental phenomena. It will allow an exploration of children's organizing capabilities in terms of their skills rather than deficiencies, which will be more fruitful in generating ideas and investigations. From Kuhn's (1970) analysis of theoretical paradigms these are general criteria by which any theory should be evaluated.

The results of the experiment showed that a free-play format is an effective methodological approach to experimentation with small children. In free play, children organize objects as they do in everyday life. There are few constraints on their strategies other than those imposed by experimental materials. The variation in the content of materials offers the investigator the opportunity to elicit differential strategies in children's organizing and to see what they are in different task contexts.

One of the most striking effects observed in this study was that the youngest children's organizing did not differ from that of the oldest children, provided they had full contextual support, specifically the mothers's verbal suggestion of a context and a perceptual array into which objects could be fitted. For the youngest children, the mother's structuring of the context was essential in accessing their conceptual abilities. Future research should explore this aspect of young children's organizing more extensively in order to understand the acquisition of concept-formation skills more fully.

In general, the experiment made it clear that children as young as 2 and 3 years old form stable conceptual organizations. They were surprisingly able concept formers. But it was also clear that their concepts were embedded in specific contexts and that the younger the children, the more context-dependent their organizations were.

The interpretation of young children's performance given in many early classification studies needs to be qualified in the light of the present evidence. It cannot be said that young children's concepts are unstable as such; rather, concept formation on the basis of dimensional abstraction may be unstable at young ages. The present evidence indicated that children organized objects on the basis of the meaning of a context, rather than in terms of abstraction of specific features, and that their concept formation was stable if they understood the meaning of a context.

For this investigation *meaning* was defined as the significance of an event in terms of past experience. A distinction was made between meaning in a phylogenetic sense and meaning in an ontogenetic sense. The proposition that children organize their experience on the basis of meaning is less concerned with *how* they organize it, as the script model is, but *why* experience gets organized the way it does, an issue that the script model does not deal with as such.

From the present perspective, concept formation is a process of adaptation to particular environmental conditions. Recurring events become meaningful and predictable on the basis of past experience and allow the individual to respond to events in a more fine-tuned fashion.

What is meaningful to the child at birth is probably largely a reflection of species adaptations. Some experiences, such as nursing, may be more salient in terms of species propensities and therefore become organized earlier than others. Early meanings therefore may be similar across cultures. There is some evidence in support of this view from studies of language acquisition. Early child utterances from different languages appear to express the same limited set of meaning structures (Bates, 1976; Brown, Cazden, & Bellugi, 1973; Slobin, 1970).

If conceptual rules are more or less content-specific in early cognitive development, we need to know what the domains of experience are that contain them. Flavell (1982) has recently suggested that conceptual skills may develop independently in different areas of experience and may not assist each other's development. Cognitive development may be more heterogeneous and less homogeneous or stagelike than was supposed. Knowledge of the content of organized experience rather than of the syntax of organization alone may be able to clarify some of these current issues in early cognitive development.

ACKNOWLEDGMENTS

The research reported in this chapter is based on a doctoral dissertation completed in 1981 at the University of Colorado in Boulder. The author is particularly indebted to E. Gollin and E. Bates for their inspiration and guidance on that thesis. Special thanks go to I. Bretherton for her assistance in revising an earlier version of this chapter.

The author gratefully acknowledges the help of P. Brown, M. Trask, A. Berendes, and G. Kantor in data collection and processing. R. Kliegl's expertise and help in computer analysis was invaluable. Special appreciation is expressed to the mothers and children who made this study possible.

REFERENCES

Bates, E. Pragmatics and sociolinguistics in child language. In D. Morehead and A. Morehead (Eds.), *Normal and deficient child language*. Baltimore: University Park Press, 1976.

Bayley, N. *Manual for the Bayley scales of infant development*. New York: Psychological Corporation, 1969.

Bitterman, M. E. Toward a comparative psychology of learning. *American Psychologist*, 1960, *15*, 704–712.

Bolton, N. *Concept formation*. New York: Pergamon Press, 1977.

Bourne, L. E., Jr., Ekstrand, B. R., & Dominowski, R. L. *The psychology of thinking*. Englewood Cliffs, NJ: Prentice-Hall, 1971.

Bower, T. G. R. *Development in infancy*. San Francisco: Freeman, 1974.

Bowerman, M. The acquisition of word meaning: An investigation of some current conflicts. In N. Waterson and C. Snow (Eds.), *Proceedings of the Third International Child Language Symposium*. New York: Wiley, 1977.

Brazelton, T. B., Tronick, E., Adamson, L., Als, H., & Weise, H. Early mother-infant reciprocity. In *Parent–infant–interaction* (CIBA Foundation Symposium 33). Amsterdam, Holland: Elsevier, 1975.

Bretherton, I., Bates, E., McNew, S., Shore, C., Williamson, C., & Beeghly-Smith, M. Comprehension and production of symbols in infancy: An experimental study. *Developmental Psychology*, 1981, *17*(6), 728–736.

Brown, R., Cazden, C., & Bellugi, U. The child's grammar from one to three. In C. A. Ferguson and D. L. Slobin (Eds.), *Studies of child language development*. New York: Holt, Rinehart & Winston, 1973.

Bruner, J. S. Nature and uses of immaturity. *American Psychologist*, 1972, *27*, 687–708.

Bruner, J. From communication to language: A psychological perspective. *Cognition*, 1975, *3*, 255–287. (a)

Bruner, J. The ontogenesis of speech acts. *Journal of Child Language*, 1975, *2*, 1–19. (b)

Damon, W. Exploring children's social cognition on two fronts. In J. H. Flavell and L. Ross (Eds.), *Social cognitive development: Frontiers and possible futures*. New York: Cambridge University Press, 1981.

Denney, D. R., & Moulton, P. A. Conceptual preferences among preschool children. *Developmental Psychology*, 1976, *12*(6), 509–513.

Denney, N. W. A developmental study of free classification in children. *Child Development*, 1972, *43*, 221–232.

Denney, N. W. Evidence for developmental changes in categorization criteria for children and adults. *Human Development*, 1974, *17*, 41–53.

Donaldson, M. *Children's minds*. New York: Norton, 1978.

Erikson, E. H. *Childhood and society*. New York: Norton, 1963.

Flavell, J. H. Developmental studies of mediated memory. In H. W. Reese & L. P. Lipsitt (Eds.), *Advances in child development and behavior* (Vol. 5). New York: Academic Press, 1970.

Flavell, J. H. On cognitive development. *Child Development*, 1982, *53*, 1–10.

Fenson, L., Kagan, J., Kearsley, R. B., & Zelazo, P. R. The developmental progression of manipulative play in the first two years. *Child Development*, 1976, *47*, 232–236.

Freud, E. Developmental Psychobiology Research Group Seminar, University of Colorado Health Sciences Center, Denver, 1981.

Gibson, E. J. *Principles of perceptual learning and development*. New York: Appleton-Century-Crofts, 1969.

Gollin, E. S. Saravo, A., & Salten, C. Perceptual distinctiveness and oddity-problem solving in children. *Journal of Experimental Child Psychology*, 1967, *5*, 586–596.

Gollin, E. S., & Schadler, M. Relational learning and transfer by young children. *Journal of Experimental Child Psychology*, 1972, *14*, 219–232.

Grobstein, P., & Chow, K. L. Receptive field development and individual experience. *Science*, 1975, *190*, 352–358.

Hess, E. H. Ethology and developmental psychology. In P. H. Mussen (Ed.), *Carmichael's manual of child psychology*. New York: Wiley, 1970.

House, B. J., Brown, A. L., & Scott, M. S. Children's discrimination learning, based on identity or difference. In *Advances in child development and behavior (Vol. 9)*. New York: Academic Press, 1974.

Hubel, D. H. The visual cortex of the brain. In *Readings from Scientific American*. San Francisco: 1976.

Huttenlocher, J. The origins of language comprehension. In R. L. Solso (Ed.), *Theories in cognitive psychology* (The Loyola Symposium). Potomac, MD: Erlbaum Press, 1974.

Inhelder, B., & Piaget, J. *The early growth of logic in the child*. New York: Harper & Row, 1964.

James, W. *Principles of psychology*. New York: Holt, 1901.

Kendler, T. S. An ontogeny of mediational deficiency. *Child Development*, 1972, *43*, 1–19.

Kofsky, E. A. A scalogram study of classifcatory development. *Child Development*, 1966, *37*, 191–204.

Kreye, M. W. Context and concept: The use of conceptual organization by two and three year old children. In preparation.

Kuhn, T. S. *The structure of scientific revolutions*. Chicago: University of Chicago Press, 1970.

Langer, J. *The origins of logic: Six to twelve months*. New York: Academic Press, 1980.

Mandler, S. M. Categorical and schematic organization in memory. In C. R. Puff (Ed.), *Memory, organization and structure*. New York: Academic Press, 1979.

Markman, E. M., Cox, B., & Machida, S. The standard object sorting task as a measure of conceptual organization. *Developmental Psychology*, 1981, *17*(1), 115–117.

Mervis, C. B & Crisafi, M. A. Order of acquisition of subordinate, basic and superordinate level categories. *Child Development*, 1982, *53*(1), 258–266.

Moore, M. K., & Clark, D. *Piaget's stage IV error*. Paper presented at the Society for Research in Child Development, Denver, April, 1975.

Nelson, K. Concept, word and sentence: Interrelations in acquisition and development. *Psychological Review*, 1974, *81*, 267–285.

Nelson, K. The syntagmatics and paradigmatics of conceptual development. In S. Kuczaj (Ed.), *Language, cognition and culture*. Hillsdale, NJ: Erlbaum, 1981.

Nielson, I., & Dockrell, J. Cognitive tasks as interactional settings. In G. Butterworth & P. Light (Eds.), *Social cognition. Studies of the development of understanding*. Chicago: The University of Chicago Press, 1982.

Pettigrew, J. D. The neurophysiology of binocular vision. In *Readings from Scientific American*. San Francisco: Freeman, 1976.

Piaget, J. *The origins of intelligence in children*. New York: Norton, 1963.

Pick, H. L. Lecture: Developmental plasticity seminar. University of Colorado, January 1977.

Ricciutti, H. N. Object grouping and selective ordering behavior in infants 12 to 24 months olds. *Merrill-Palmer Quarterly*, 1965, *11*, 129–148.

Rosch, E. Principles of categorization. In E. Rosch and B. B. Lloyd (Eds.), *Cognition and categortization*. Potomac, MD: Erlbaum Press, 1977.

Ryan, J. Early language: Towards a communicational analysis. In P. M. Richards (Eds.), *The integration of a child into a social world*. Cambridge, England: Cambridge University Press, 1974.

Salapatek, P. Pattern perception in early infancy. In L. B. Cohen & P. Salapatek (Eds.), *Infant perception* (Vol. 1). *Basic visual processes*. New York: Academic Press, 1977.

Schadler, M. Development of relational learning: Effects of instruction and delay of transfer. *Journal of Experimental Child Psychology*, 1973, *16*, 459–471.

Schank, R. C., & Abelson, R. R. *Scripts, plans, goals, and understanding.* Hillsdale, NJ: Erlbaum, 1977.

Schell, R. E., & Hall, E. *Developmental psychology today.* New York: Random House, 1979.

Slobin, D. I. Universals of grammatical development in children. In G. B. Flores d' Arcais & W. J. M. Levelt (Eds.) *Advances in psycholinguistics.* New York: American Elsevier, 1970.

Smith, L. B., & Kemler, D. G. Developmental trends in free classification. Evidence for a new conceptualization of perceptual development. *Journal of Experimental Child Psychology*, 1977, *24*, 279–298.

Smith, L. B. & Kemler, D. G. Is there a developmental trend from integrality to separability in perception? *Journal of Experimental Child Psychology*, 1978, *26*, 498–507.

Smith, S. D., & Gollin, E. S. Accessing cognitive organizations: A developmental analysis. In preparation.

Starkey, D. The origins of concept formation: Object sorting and object preference in early infancy. *Child Development*, 1981, *52*, 489–497.

Sugarman, S. *The development of classification and correspondence from 12 to 36 months: From action to representation.* Paper presented at the biennial meeting, Society for Research in Child Development, San Francisco, March 1979.

Sugarman, S. The cognitive basis of classification in very young children: An analysis of object ordering trends. *Child Development*, 1981, *52*(4), 1172–1178.

Tighe, T. J., & Tighe, L. S. Stimulus control in children's learning. In A. Pick (Ed.), *Minnesota Symposia on Child Psychology* (Vol. 6). Minneapolis: University of Minnesota Press, 1972.

Toulmin, S. Rules and their relevance to human behavior. In T. Mischel (Ed.), *Understanding other persons.* Totowa, NJ: Rowman and Littlefield, 1974.

Toulmin, S. Lecture: Developmental plasticity seminar. University of Colorado, April 1977.

Trevarthen, C. The primary motives for cooperative understanding. In G. Butterworth & P. Light (Eds.), *Social cognition. Studies of the development of understanding.* Chicago: The University of Chicago Press, 1982.

Tversky, A. Features of similarity. *Psychological Review*, 1977, *84*(4), 327–352.

Vygotsky, L. S. *Thought and language.* Cambridge, MA: MIT Press, 1962.

Weiss, P. 1 + 1 ≠ 2 (one plus one does not equal two). In C. G. Quarton, T. Melnechuk, & F. O. Schmitt (Eds.), *The neurosciences.* New York: Rockefeller University Press, 1967.

Weiss, P. Self-differentiation of the basic patterns of coordination. *Comparative Psychology Monographs*, 1941, *17*, 1–96.

CHAPTER 12

Toddler's Play, Alone and With Mother: The Role of Maternal Guidance*

BARBARA O'CONNELL
INGE BRETHERTON

INTRODUCTION

THEORETICAL FRAMEWORK

The theories of Piaget (1962) and Vygotsky (1962, 1978) have motivated much of the research in developmental psychology during recent years. Even research-ers who have made a departure from the frameworks of these two thinkers have incorporated many of their ideas (e.g., Case & Khanna, in press, Fischer, 1980). These two theorists provide rather different perspectives on the process of de-velopment. Indeed, they are often characterized as representing opposing view-points, but, in fact, they complement one another more than they diverge.

*Support for this project was provided to the senior author by a National Science Foundation graduate fellowship and to the second author by the Spencer Foundation.

The primary difference between the two theories is their localization of the "site" of the construction of knowledge. According to Piaget, the child is the architect of his or her knowledge about the world. More specifically, the child's action in and on the world structures this cognitive organization. It is not that this knowledge resides in the child, but rather it is created by the child as a consequence of his or her commerce with the world. The cognitive structures described by Piaget are, in some way, an emergent property of the interface of the child's existing cognitive organization and constructive processes with the organization and structure of the world.

Vygotsky's position shifts the emphasis from the child-as-architect and instead attributes primary importance to the social context in the process of cognitive development. The child is embedded in and reflects the social milieu (e.g., Wertsch, in press & 1983, Zukow, 1980). All the child's knowledge is first encountered in the social realm and later becomes internalized and incorporated into the child's cognitive organization; functions are first interpsychological and later become intrapsychological (Vygotsky, 1978, p. 57). To understand the child's cognitive organization, one must first understand the structure and content of the child's social world.

In the process of pointing out the differences between these two theorists, some authors exaggerate their positions. Piaget is seen as ignoring, or at best minimizing, the influence of the social context (Fischer, 1980); Vygotsky is seen as emphasizing the social aspects of development more than the cognitive organization with which the child comes equipped. In fact, the differences are not nearly so glaring. Cole, Hood, and McDermott (1979), in a comparison of laboratory and naturalistic observation, assert that "cognition resides neither "in the head" nor in the environment. It refers to the principles organizing interactions between individuals and their environment" (p. 14). Neither Piaget nor Vygotsky would take issue with such a claim, although they would disagree as to where most of the "work" was being done—inside the child or outside in the social world.

Our purpose here is not to present a detailed account of the theories of Piaget and Vygotsky. Nor do we intend to describe *the* critical experiment that will determine who was more correct—such an experiment could never be designed. Rather, we would like to suggest that the processes involved in cognitive development, as described by these two theorists, can be woven together in a way that could make developmental research a more fruitful enterprise.

Piaget suggested that the child must reach a state of disequilibrium—a mismatch between his or her current formulations of the world and new problems with which she or he is confronted—before further cognitive reorganization can occur. Until this transition state is achieved, the child's cognitive structures are impermeable to reorganization. The manner in which the child detects this mismatch is not made explicit; why does the child reorganize (accommodate) instead of continuing to assimilate new information to existing structures? (See Brown,1982, for a discussion of the problem of invoking a homeostatic mechanism, *equilibration*, as a means of inducing change.) Nevertheless, the reorganization of the child's cognitive structures is not a random process but, instead, an orderly progression that is constrained by the information available in the world and the child's existing cognitive structures. The information that triggers reorganization must be only slightly more difficult than that which the child is currently able to assimilate; only then will a state of disequilibrium result and in this state of readiness new formulations are generated.

Vygotsky, too, claimed that the child must achieve some specified level of functioning before he or she is able to incorporate anything more from the social environment. He went further and proposed a *zone of proximal development*, which he defined as the distance between what the child can do on his or her own and what the child can do with assistance. Because the social world is the source of all the child's knowledge, instruction is clearly important (Wertsch, in press-a) but only insofar as it proceeds just ahead of development, that is, affecting those skills in the zone of proximal development. Vygotsky stated quite clearly that every psychological function in the child's development appears twice—first between people and only later inside the child.

Throughout the course of development, the match between the child's current state of cognitive organization and the information impinging on this organization will be just discrepant enough to force a change in structure. Piaget then turns the controls over to the child, who begins the task of restructuring, whereas Vygotsky sets the wheels of social interaction into motion and allows the child to reorganize his or her knowledge as an individual embedded in a social context, only later incorporating the solution into his or her own cognitive organization.

The present study examines the role of social interaction in structuring knowledge for the child and considers the contribution of the child's readiness to this process. We look only at a brief moment in time but this may permit us to draw at least some conclusions. We have chosen a play setting as the context for this observation—a setting familiar to both child and mother. We set the stage for this investigation by considering some important issues in the field of play research.

DEFINING AND CATEGORIZING PLAY

Although play in children and animals has long been a topic of research and discussion, there is no consensus as to either its function or the behaviors that are encompassed by the term. Fagen (1981) reviewed, in some detail, the definitional offerings of a number of theorists and investigators. These definitions range from those like Bolwig's, which attempts to delimit the behaviors that can be considered playful: "[Play is] any action which is performed as an outlet for surplus energy which is not required by the animal for its immediate vital activities such as collecting food, eating, mating, nursing and other activities which further its own survival and that of its species" (as cited in Fagen, 1981, p. 501), to those like Eibl-Eibesfeldt's, which is so broad as to admit almost any behavior: "We may consider play as an experimental dialogue with the environment" (as cited in Fagen, 1981, p. 501).

The resolution of this definitional issue need not concern us here; our goal is not to explicate the nature of play but rather to use play as a means of studying the child. In keeping with the position of other investigators involved in such study, we can safely consider the child's activities with toys as a form of play behavior.

In the study to be discussed here, children were permitted to play alone and with their mothers in a relatively unconstrained setting. Toys were selected to encourage a variety of activities and to prevent biasing the child toward a particular type of play. There is sufficient evidence to suggest that the play activites in which children engage depend on their developmental level, the toys with which they are provided, the particulars of the play setting, and a variety of other factors. A brief review of some of the literature will serve as a starting point for the construction of a coding scheme that captures the child's biases and propensities in a play setting such as this. The review is organized around three variables that are important for the present study: (1) the categories of play behavior under investigation, (2) spontaneous versus elicited play behavior, and (3) solitary versus collaborative play settings.

CATEGORIZATION OF PLAY BEHAVIORS

In a review of the research on play in young children, Nicolich (1978), pointed out the problems arising from the use of varying methodologies across studies. Comparability is limited and the generalization of findings is difficult. Despite these problems, this brief review illustrates that most investigators have focused on similar features of the child's play activity.

Most investigations of the young child's play have been concerned with symbolic play. This emphasis derives from the Piagetian idea that both language and symbolic play are manifestations of a more general, underlying ability—the capacity to use symbols (R. Corrigan, personal communication, July 1981; Fein, 1975; Fein & Apfel, 1979; Franklin, 1973; Jeffree & McConkey, 1976; Lowe,

1975; McCune-Nicolich, 1980, 1981; Overton & Jackson, 1973; Watson & Fischer, 1977). Because the present study attempts to assess the effect of social interaction on a wide range of play behaviors, those studies that considered a broader spectrum of play categories will be described in greater detail.

Largo and Howard (1979) observed 9- to 30-month-old children and mapped the progression from the early forms of play to symbolic play. They described three categories of play behaviors: (1) exploratory play (9 months), which involved visual exploration, mouthing, and manipulation of toys: (2) spatial play (15–24 months), which consisted of activities such as stacking objects, putting objects into containers, and forming spatial arrangements with objects; (3) representational play (15–30 months) included (a) conventional uses of objects (e.g., brushing with a hairbrush) directed toward the self, to others, or to a doll, (b) object substitutions (using a block as a hairbrush), and (c) acting out a pretend sequence (putting a doll to bed).

In a longitudinal study with children from 10 to 40 months, Lezine (1973) described four levels of play. The first of these (9–12 months) included the application of simple motor schemes to all objects within reach (e.g., banging with several different toys). From 12 to 17 months, children applied a conventional action (brushing with a hairbrush) to a variety of objects, some of which were inappropriate recipients of the action (brushing a bottle or a mirror). Around 18 months of age these conventional activities occurred in longer sequences and more closely approximated conventional uses of the objects involved (e.g., brushing mother's hair, the doll's hair, and a teddy bear's fur). Finally, the children combined actions into a thematic sequence such as feeding a doll, wiping her mouth, and putting her to bed.

In their study of manipulative play during the first 2 years of life, Fenson, Kagan, Kearsley, and Zelazo (1976) categorized play behaviors into three classes. The first, relational acts, consisted of relating two objects appropiately (putting a lid on a pot), inappropriately (touching a spoon to the bottom of a pot), or by grouping (putting two cups together). "Pretend" behaviors comprised the second class, symbolic activities—eating, drinking, or pouring. The third class included two types of activities, performing two identical actions in sequence (putting two cups on saucers) and combining two different but thematically related acts into a sequence (stirring in pot and then in a pitcher).

At the beginning of this review, the problem of the lack of comparability of these studies was raised. Most investigators use different sets of toys, although Lowe and Costello (1976) have proposed a standardized set of objects that could be used in studies of this type. Often it seems that investigators select similar sorts of objects for use in experimental settings but these may vary in color, size, or other dimensions. It has been suggested that toy size alone may have a dramatic effect, not only on the sorts of play behaviors one observes but also on the age of emergence of those behaviors (Bretherton, O'Connell, Shore, & Bates, Chapter 10, this volume). Toy selection may bias the child toward a particular type of activity and preclude the performance of others; consequently, the nature of the play behaviors observed may change from study to study (J. Shube, personal communication, July 1981). Another difficulty is that a single activity, banging a block for instance, is considered to lie at one end of a continuum that extends up to the sequencing of symbolic play acts. It seems instead that the nature of the play activity and whether or not these activities occur singly or in sequences are orthogonal dimensions; a child can combine acts into sequences or not regardless of the nature of the activity. Finally, it should be clear from the preceding review that the number and content of the play categories used by different investigators varies considerably. Lezine (1973) does not even distinguish types of play but rather focuses her categorization scheme on the number and type of objects to which actions are applied.

There appears to be an orderly progression in the play skills demonstrated by young children despite these problems; undifferentiated exploration is followed by stacking and grouping objects by similar shape or function; finally, symbolic play with its various levels of sophistication is observed. This progression provides the framework for the coding scheme used in the present study as it seems to capture the range of activities children demonstrate with the typical experimental toys (e.g., blocks, dolls, pots, and pans).

ELICITED VERSUS SPONTANEOUS PLAY

Only a few studies of play have been directed at the child's spontaneous play with toys. Fenson *et al.* (1976) and Nicolich (1977) presented children with a set of toys and permitted them to play while the experimenter observed the children's behavior. Zelazo and Kearsley (1980) allowed children to play with any one of an array of toys while the mothers sat nearby reading. Shimada, Sano, and Peng (1979) followed a similar procedure. With these exceptions, all other investigations of play behavior have employed a variety of elicitation procedures, such as verbally suggesting activities to the child during play (Fein & Apfel, 1979; Largo & Howard, 1979), modeling activities with toys that the child was to imitate (Fenson & Ramsey, 1980; Watson & Fischer, 1977), or calling the child's attention to a particular toy or set of toys (Sinclair, 1970). In a study of 12- to 18-month-olds, Belsky and Hrncir (1981) observed children playing spontaneously with a set of toys and subsequently with an experimenter who suggested specific activities. These investigators were interested in developing a measure of motivation, however, and were not concerned with the play behaviors per se.

An explanation for this emphasis on structured play may lie (Chapter 9, present volume) calls the relatively infrequent spo rence of many of the behaviors of interest, particularly those which are just emerging. In his study of 12- to 19-month-olds, he found that play following modeling was significantly more complex than spontaneous play with the same objects (see also Bretherton *et al.*, Chapter 10, this volume). In addition, this propensity (or ability) to imitate increased with age. In the same vein, Largo and Howard (1979) found that developmental changes were more obvious in structured than in free play. K. Fischer (personal communication, 1981) observed children playing spontaneously with a set of toys following an elicited imitation task using the same toys and found no difference between the two situations. The spontaneous play was more akin to delayed imitation than to free play, however, as it followed a modeling session.

The significant differences in the children's performance in spontaneous and elicited play situations lends some support to Vygotsky's argument that activities conducted with the assistance of capable collaborators enable children to achieve more than they might on their own. Because neither particular play behaviors nor their age of emergence were the focus of the present study, a free-play setting that permitted spontaneous activity was considered to be best for observing the mother–child interaction. Further, a comparison between elicited and spontaneous techniques is permitted by the collaborative play session in that the components of the child's play that are the direct consequence of mother's suggestions (elicited) are considered separately from those that are spontaneous initiated by the child.

INDEPENDENT VERSUS COLLABORATIVE PLAY

Typically, play studies are structured so that the child's mother or caretaker, although present in the experimental room, is not an active participant in the play situation. She may sit by and observe or read but is usually instructed to respond minimally to the child's questions and to resist the child's overtures for assistance or participation. Her role is one of providing emotional support for the child and interactions are intended to occur only between child and experimenter.

A few studies, however, have permitted the child's mother to take an active role. Nicolich (1977) allowed mothers to play with their children but they were instructed to engage only in activities initiated by the child and were not permitted to initiate activities themselves. Dunn and Wooding (1977) observed 18- to 24-month-olds in their homes under two different conditions—while mother was relaxing and while she was doing housework. These investigators were not interested in directly comparing the collaborative play with the child's spontaneous play; instead they focused on variables such as length of play bouts and toy selection. Shimada *et al* (1979) permitted both mother and experimenter to respond to and play with the child but only in activities that the child had previously demonstrated on his or her own.

The purpose of the present study was to assess the nature of the mother–child interaction in the context of two play situations: one in which the mother plays a passive role and one in which she is an active participant. In the collaborative situation, the mother's behavior was not constrained in any way and she could both initiate activities and respond to the child's initiatives.

To summarize, the present study differs from previous investigations of play in young children not only in its intent, which is to observe any changes in the child's play that may be induced by a more sophisticated play partner, but in its method: it considers a broad range of play categories and allows for spontaneous play rather than experimenter-elicited play in both an independent and a collaborative play situation.

CATEGORIES OF PLAY USED
IN THE PRESENT STUDY

The categories used in this study are similar to, but broader in scope than, those employed by other researchers. The distinctions between play types are not as fine-grained as they are in some investigations (e.g., McCune-Nicolich, 1980) but we thought it best to assess whether there are any gross changes in the child's play behavior when mother participates before proceeding to more detailed analyses of the nature of those changes.

Four categories of play were used to describe the child's behavior. Exploratory play, considered the least sophisticated, consisted of manipulating and examining toys. Combinatorial play included instances of putting toys together— for example, inserting blocks into the shape box or stacking toys. A symbolic play category encompassed all activities that could be described as pretense play or "acting as if". The final category, ambiguous play, is more of a methodological necessity than a behavioral category of interest; it included all play behaviors that could not be clearly classified as one of the three previous types. These categories are discussed in some detail in "Play Categories."

METHOD

SUBJECTS

Subjects were 15 boys and 15 girls who participated in a longitudinal study of symbol formation at 10–28 months of age (Bates, Bretherton, Shore, & McNew, 1983; Bretherton, McNew, Snyder & Bates, 1983). Children were observed in the present study at 20 months ($\overline{X}$ = 20 months, 1 week; range = 19 months, 2 weeks to 21 months, 1 week) and 28 months ($\overline{X}$ = 28 months, 1 week; range = 27 months, 3 weeks to 29 months, 2 weeks). Names were obtained from local birth announcements and all children with birthweights under 5.5 pounds were excluded. Parents were contacted by letter and follow-up phone call with an acceptance rate of 70%.

MATERIALS

Children were presented with a standard set of toys during each observational period. The toy set consisted of 13 plastic colored nesting cups, a Creative Playthings wooden shape box with 18 colored wooden blocks of 6 shapes; a Plexiglas doll house with 2 rooms, movable doors, windows, and a removable roof; Fischer-Price furniture, peg people, and a toy jeep. All toys except the house and the shape box were of approximately equal size.

PROCEDURE

Subjects were observed in two conditions at both ages: a 15-minute independent play session in the child's home and, 2 or 3 days later, a 5-minute laboratory play session with the child and his or her mother. All sessions were videotaped.

There is a confound between the sequencing and the location of the play sessions. The collaborative play session in the laboratory always followed the solitary play session in the home. These sessions were only small segments of a lengthy series of tasks in which the children participated. The sequence of task presentation was fixed to minimize any order effects that may have interfered with or complicated correlational analyses carried out on the data. Although this is a serious methodological flaw for our purposes here, evidence will be presented suggesting that practice effects alone do not account for the results.

Home Session

In the home play session, the experimenter placed the toy set on the floor in front of the child and, if necessary, drew the child's attention to the toys. Although there was no standard presentation arrangement, all toys were visible to the child. In most cases children readily began playing with the toys, but when a child appeared reluctant the mother played with the child for 1 or 2 minutes until the child seemed content to continue playing on his or her own. During the 15-minute play session the mother, sitting nearby, was interviewed about her child's language by an experimenter. It should be noted that mothers were always in the same room as the child and were usually seated only a few feet away; consequently, the home and laboratory sessions are approximately equivalent in terms of mother's proximity to the child. The difference between the 2 sessions lies in the fact that mother's attention was directed toward the interviewer in this situation rather than toward the child. Mothers were instructed to respond minimally to their child's overtures for assistance or attention. Portable video equipment was used to record this session.

Laboratory Session

The laboratory was a large, carpeted room at the University of Colorado furnished with beanbag chairs and a table. Between other experimental procedures (part of the longitudinal study) an experimenter brought in the toy set and placed it on the floor near the mother and child. Toys were arranged as described earlier. The experimenter instructed the mother to play with the child and show him or her how to use the toys and left the room. Mother and child were permitted to play together for 5 minutes. The entire laboratory session was videotaped from behind a one-way mirror and from a second camera concealed in the playroom.

DATA ANALYSIS

Videotapes of all play sesssions were transcribed by independent coders. All language and play were transcribed. Interrater agreement for transcriptions was based on point-to-point comparisons of six different interactions (1 minute each) involving children of both sexes from random locations on the videotapes. Reliabilities were calculated separately for mother and child vocalizations as well as for nonverbal behavior; the percent interrater agreement ranged from 83% for the child's vocalizations at 20 months to 98% for the child's nonverbal behavior at 20 months. Interrater agreement for all play measures (described here later) was calculated on a point-to-point basis from 1-minute segments randomly selected from four transcripts at each age (2 boys and 2 girls). In this case, percent interrater agreement ranged from 86% for the 28-month-olds' exploratory play to 100% for combinatorial play at 28 months. Interrater agreement for mothers' instructions was calculated from 1-minute segments randomly selected from four transcripts at each age (2 boys and 2 girls) and ranged from 93% for symbolic gestural suggestions to 97% for combinatorial verbal suggestions.

PLAY CATEGORIES

Initially, the play behavior observed during the two sessions was categorized according to a hierarchical system. Although exploratory play consisted of only one level, both combinatorial and symbolic play contained four levels of play activity. These were collapsed within each play category because only one of the levels usually accounted for the majority of the child's behavior and instances of the other levels were comparatively infrequent.

The final coding scheme consisted of four play categories. Each category includes a number of different types of activity and the following descriptions include all the play behaviors that were counted as instances of a category.

Exploratory Play

This type of play consists of all manipulative behaviors, such as handling, throwing, banging, or mouthing objects or touching one toy to another. Exploratory play was not counted if the child was in the process of searching through the toys for a particular object but only when objects the child picked up were subjected to examination.

Combinatorial Play

This category includes putting things together. Instances of combinatorial play are: putting one object into another, both fine-fitting and gross insertions (e.g., putting shape blocks into the shape box or toys into the house); stacking objects on top of one another; making spatial configurations with toys such as aligning blocks or arranging furniture in some spatial array; classification or grouping objects by function or shape (e.g., putting all the chairs together or separating the blocks into groups of identical shapes). Each addition to a configurational or classificatory group counts as one instance of combinatorial play;

for example, a child who makes a pile of four balls, adding new ones in succession, receives a score of 3:1 for the initial group of two balls and 1 each for the two additional balls. Blocks of different shapes were counted as different combinatorial acts when inserted into the shape box. Some children discovered only one block–hole combination and repeated it whereas others managed to insert all six shapes correctly; this method of counting was an attempt to capture this difference.

Symbolic Play

The fact that this type of play is called *symbolic* implies that the child uses the toys as symbols to stand for or represent other objects or activities. In this context, the question arises as to whether the children are treating the figures as if they stood for people or whether they are simply engaging in play that they have learned is appropriate with miniature toys of this sort. Although this issue has some bearing on research directed at the relationship between play and language, it is not critical in the present study because the purpose here is not to investigate symbol systems per se. (This issue is raised again in "The Concept of Readiness.") The symbolic play category consists of all instances of pretense play or "acting as if." It includes conventional or functional uses of objects such as pushing the toy car. These sorts of activities have been described as recognitory gestures that "identify" the object for the child (Nicolich, 1977). Despite their infrequent occurrence in this sample (pushing the toy car with no passengers was the only possible instance) they were included in an attempt to classify as much of the child's behavior as possible. Also included in this category are instances of object substitution (using a block for a bed) and the use of an independent agent (making the peg people walk or talk). This category also encompasses general pretend activities such as seating people in chairs around the table or taking people for a ride in the toy car.

Ambiguous Play

The inclusion of this category is the consequence of a problem that confronts all workers involved in play research—what counts as an instance of a category? One can pose this question in regard to configurational or classificatory acts (see Langer, 1980; Sugarman, 1979), but most have addressed this issue in the context of analyzing symbolic play (Dunn & Wooding, 1977). For example, if a child makes a long line of blocks, it is not clear whether the child is simply putting together things that look alike or constructing a train (combinatorial versus symbolic play in the current classification system). Unless the child names the object constructed or uses the line of blocks as if it were a train, it is impossible to discriminate between these two possibilities. If a child puts four peg people into the car but does not push the car, is the child pretending that the people are preparing to go for a ride or putting pegs into holes in which they fit? Again, the answer must be equivocal.

This play category was designed to include all the child's play activities that were of this ambiguous nature. This is a conservative coding strategy in that any play behavior that could have been classified as symbolic but was less than clear in its execution was coded as ambiguous play. Any play activity that might have been symbolic (e.g., block–train example) but could clearly be classified as combinatorial was coded as combinatorial play; that is, children were given combinatorial play credit for clear combinatorial acts even if the child had intended that the act be symbolic. Borderline symbolic activities (e.g., putting people in the car) were coded as ambiguous play. More often than not, when children made combinatorial groups they identified them as such (e.g., saying "cups" while pointing at a line of cups). This coding strategy gives the children maximum credit for activities they perform clearly but does not give them credit for seemingly sophisticated behaviors they may not have intended and whose classification as symbolic play would represent an inference on the part of the observer.

None of the child's play behaviors was coded under two categories (i.e., doubly represented). This coding scheme captures the bulk of the activities these children demonstrated with the toys used in this study.

CODING

The 15-minute independent play session was divided into three 5-minute segments to permit a comparison of the child's activity over blocks of time equal to the duration of the collaborative play session. The first 5-minute segment of independent play was used for comparison with the 5-minute collaborative session. The last 5-minute segment of the independent play session was used for the assessment of practice effects.

Frequency and Diversity Measures

A frequency count was used as a measure of the child's activity within each play category. The number of different activities performed within each category served as a measure of play diversity. This latter measure excludes repetitions.

Responses and Imitations

Mother's influence on the child's play may be considered to be either indirect (in the sense that her presence alone and/or her ability to respond naturally might enhance the child's play) or direct (to the extent that she actively and purposefully guides the child's play behavior). In order to evaluate the latter effect systematically, an additional measure was recorded from the collaborative play session: the child's responses to the mother's verbal and gestural directives as well as the child's imitations of the mother's activities. Child responses were coded whenever the child performed an activity that the mother had suggested either verbally (e.g., "Take the man for a ride in the car"), gesturally (e.g., pointing to the correct hole in the shape box for the block the child is holding), or through a verbal–gestural combination. Imitations were coded whenever mother demonstrated an activity and the child, with no intervening activity, successfully duplicated her action. Unsuccessful attempts by the child to respond to mother's directives or to imitate her demonstrations were not coded.

Analysis of variance (ANOVA) was used to analyze these data. All reported F ratios were significant at $p = .05$ or less unless stated otherwise. Tests after ANOVA (Newman–Keuls) were applied to significant main effects and interactions. Data were tested for normality by a chi-square for goodness of fit (Siegel, 1956).

Number of Maternal Suggestions

The number of times mothers verbally suggested, demonstrated, or gesturally indicated an activity, as well as the use of any combination of these strategies, was recorded for each of three play categories—exploratory, combinatorial, and symbolic—from the collaborative play session. Examples of scorable maternal directives included pointing to the next nesting cup in the sequence if the child was stacking nesting cups (gestural only, combinatorial play), saying "This one next" while pointing (verbal and gestural, combinatorial play), saying "Can you make the people eat dinner at the table like this?" while seating people at the table (verbal and demonstration, symbolic play).

Ambiguous play was not included as a play category in this analysis. Ambiguous play consisted of the child's borderline symbolic acts and was included as a play category because children engaged in activity that could not be coded as symbolic either due to the observer's inability to determine the child's intentions or execution of the act suggested that the child had little understanding of the activity (e.g., putting people in the car facing backwards). The ambiguous play category was designed to capture the child's behavior but has little relevance for the description of maternal behavior. However, children sometimes responded to a symbolic play suggestion by their mothers with one of these ambiguous acts. To prevent inflation of the maternal success measure in the symbolic play category by counting ambiguous responses by the child as successful symbolic acts, one symbolic play suggestion was deducted from each mother's total symbolic play suggestion score for every suggestion that elicited an ambiguous act. Although this procedure entails some information loss, it has the advantage of not attributing success to the mother when the child executed a less than satisfactory response to a suggestion for symbolic play.

These data were analyzed by ANOVA with the same constraints discussed earlier.

Maternal Success Rate

In addition to recording the frequency of maternal suggestions, a success rate was calculated for each mother in each play category. The success rate was the percentage of maternal suggestions in each play category to which the child successfully responded.

In order for a maternal suggestion to be coded, the child had to be attending to the mother. Maternal suggestions were not counted if the child was playing with another toy or was oriented away from the mother. In general, however, mothers verbally directed their child's attention to their activity before offering suggestions.

RESULTS

The presentation of the results begins with an evaluation of session duration on the child's play behavior based on analyses of the independent play session. Following this, a comparison of the two conditions, independent versus collaborative play, will be presented. These analyses were designed to determine whether or not the collaborative play setting altered the play behavior of the children from the sort of play observed during the independent session. Next, an assessment of practice effects will be presented. As we will see, there were differences between the two play sessions that can be attributed to the influence of mother as a play partner. The final section presents results from an analysis of the maternal variables, which was an attempt to assess the manner in which mothers try to influence the course of the collaborative play session.

Two of the videotapes (2 boys at 20 months, collaborative play session) had no sound due to equipment failure and hence could not be used. Analyses of variance were executed with gender as a between-subjects factor; the missing data were replaced by cell means and the appropriate number of degrees of freedom were subtracted from the error terms. There was no significant main effect of gender in any analysis nor did this variable interact with other factors in any analysis. On the basis of these results, the two boys with missing data were excluded from the sample and data were collapsed across gender. The sample to be discussed henceforth, then, consisted of 28 children—15 girls and 13 boys.

INDEPENDENT PLAY: ASSESSMENT OF SESSION DURATION ON PLAY BEHAVIOR

The home session was longer than the laboratory session (15 versus 5 minutes) and the analyses described subsequently provided a means of determining if children altered the number or variety of activities they engaged in as a function of time. It is possible that, with time, children become more familiar with the toys and engage in play behaviors late in a session that were not observed earlier. If this were the case, any observed differences between the two play sessions might be the consequence of increased familiarity and practice. This is a possibility we should investigate before proceeding any further.

The independent play session was divided into three 5-minute blocks. Timing began once the child had touched a toy after being left to play alone by both mother and experimenter. Frequency and diversity scores for the four play categories were recored for each 5-minute block. Separate ANOVAs were performed on frequency and diversity data with time blocks (three 5-minute segments), age (20 and 28 months), and play type (exploratory, combinatorial, symbolic, and ambiguous) as within-subjects factors.

There were significant main effects of age and play type but because these effects are more relevant to later discussion, their consideration will be postponed. The variable of interest in these analyses was time blocks. Although there was no main effect of time in the frequency analysis, $F(2, 54) = 0.09$, there was a time block $\times$ play type interaction, $F(6, 162) = 2.89$. Tests after ANOVA indicated that the number of exploratory play activities decreased from the first 5 minutes to the last 5 minutes whereas the amount of combinatorial play increased over the same time span. There were no changes in either symbolic or ambiguous play. There was no main effect of time blocks in the analysis of play diversity, $F(2, 54) = 1.18$, $p < .32$, but again there was a significant time block $\times$ play type interaction, $F(6, 62) = 2.78$; the diversity of exploratory play decreased with time but there were no changes in the other three play types. It is interesting to note that, although the *number* of combinatorial activities increased over time, the diversity of combinatorial play did not change. There were quite a few children who repeated an activity they were able to execute successfully for the duration of a time block rather than experimenting with a novel activity. This was particularly true in combinatorial play when children discovered the correct hole for a block in the shape box. For example, one child who performed 36 combinatorial acts during one 5-minute segment had a repertoire consisting of three behaviors. This sort of repetitive behavior was not at all rare and consequently, the diversity measure may be superior to the frequency measure for capturing the quality of the child's play; the frequency measure may simply be an index of the child's willingness to do anything at all.

In light of these findings, we have chosen to discuss only the analyses of play diversity in the remainder of this section. Although ANOVAs were performed on both frequency and diversity measures, presentation of the results from both would be something of a burden for the reader.[1] In every case, results from analyses of play frequency paralleled those of play diversity. The authors will be glad to provide interested readers with these results upon request. A discussion of the potential superiority of diversity measures is presented in "Some Qualitative Consideration."

In summary, the frequency and diversity of exploratory play decreased over time; the number of combinatorial activities increased as a function of time, although the diversity of combinatorial play was unaffected. Neither the frequency nor the diversity of the remaining two play types, symbolic and ambiguous play, changed significantly over the course of the 15-minute session. It appears that children initially investigate the toys and, having explored them sufficiently, they become involved in more structured play. To make the two play sessions comparable in terms of this initial burst of exploration, the first 5 minutes of the independent play session were used for comparison with the 5-minute collaborative play session.

COMPARISON OF CONDITIONS:
INDEPENDENT VERSUS COLLABORATIVE PLAY

To examine any change in the child's play that occurred when mother was participating, an ANOVA was performed on play diversity in each play category. Variables included in the analysis were age (20 and 28 months), play type (exploratory, combinatorial, symbolic, and ambiguous) and condition (mother participating or not participating); all were treated as within-subjects factors.

---

[1]Results of additional analyses are available, upon request, from the senior author.

The child's responses to mother's suggestions as well as imitations of mother's behavior were included in this analysis.

The age main effect did not reach significance, suggesting that play repertoires at each age consisted of about the same number of behaviors. There was a significant effect of play type. The play types were ordered in the following way: ambiguous < symbolic < exploratory < combinatorial, $F(3, 81) = 77.38$. It should be pointed out that, although all differences between the four types were significant, the diversity of combinatorial and exploratory play was much greater, in general, than that of either symbolic or ambiguous play. This point is illustrated in Figure 1.

There was a main effect of condition in this analysis, $F(1, 27) = 16.02$, indicating that play diversity increased when the mother was participating in the child's play.

This analysis also revealed a significant age × play type interaction, $F(3, 81) = 4.83$; 28-month-olds demonstrated a larger symbolic repertoire than did 20-month-olds. There were no differences between the two age groups in the diversity of the other play types.

Finally, the triple interaction of age × play type × condition was significant, $F(3, 81) = 3.67$. This interaction is particularly interesting in that it reveals the selective effect of the mother's influence and guidance. The analysis revealed that 20-month-olds demonstrated an increase in both exploratory and combinatorial play diversity when the mother was playing with the child, whereas 28-month-olds showed an increase only in their symbolic play repertoire when playing with their mothers.

To summarize, we have observed that the diversity of the child's play increased over independent play levels when mother and child played together

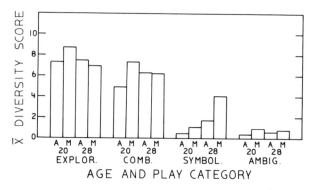

Figure 1. Diversity of activity in each play type. A child playing alone; M mother participating. Ages given in months.

and, further, the play type in which this increase manifested itself appeared to be a function of the child's age.

Maternal Influence

Although we have seen that children playing with their mothers demonstrate increased diversity of some types of play, it is important to assess how much of this increase is due to the mother's explicit guidance (i.e., responses and imitations by the child) and how much of it is due to her more indirect facilitative influence. That is, if the child's responses and imitations were excluded from the analysis, would the effect of mother's participation still be in evidence? The next analysis addresses this issue. The diversity of play was again analyzed by ANOVA with age (20 and 28 months), play type (exploratory, combinatorial, symbolic, and ambiguous), and condition (mother participating or not participating) as within-subjects factors. In this analysis, however, responses and imitations, the indexes of maternal directiveness, were excluded.

The pattern of results involving the main effects of age and play type and their interaction is consistent with that reported for the previous analysis. The variable of interest here was condition. Unlike the results reported above, the main effect of condition did not reach significance, $F(1, 27) < 1$. Further, condition did not interact with any other variables. This analysis lends support to the notion that it is mother's active guidance, and not maternal facilitation or practice effects alone, that account for the observed difference in the child's play behavior.

Assessment of Practice Effects

Although an earlier analysis assessed the effect of session duration on the child's independent play (see "Independent Play"), this does not permit inferences concerning the comparability of those three 5-minute time blocks with the collaborative play session. In an attempt to address the issue of practice more directly, an ANOVA on play diversity was performed using the last 5-minute segment of the independent play session for comparison with the collaborative play session. Because children have had maximum time to investigate the toys and become engaged in some sort of structured play, it was not unreasonable to assume that any improvement resulting from practice with the toys should be obvious by this last 5-minute segment of the independent play session. Furthermore, the independent play session was probably not long enough for fatigue to counteract the effect of practice or increased familiarity with the toys. This analysis treated age (20 and 28 months), play type (exploratory, combinatorial, symbolic, and ambiguous), and condition (mother participating or not participating) as within-subjects factors.

The main effects of age, $F(1, 27) = 9.00$, and play type, $F(3, 81) = 28.90$, were significant and indicated that 28-month-olds engaged in more play overall than did 20-month-olds and, further, that children demonstrated more exploratory and combinatorial play than either of the other two play types, regardless of age or condition. The main effect of condition was significant, $F(1, 27) = 8.84$, and indicated that overall children showed a larger repertoire of play behaviors when playing with mothers than they demonstrated alone. Further, the triple interaction of age × condition × play type reached significance, $F(3,81) = 2.88$, and tests after ANOVA revealed that whereas 20-month-olds showed an increase in diversity of both exploratory and combinatorial play, the 28-month-olds showed an increase only in the diversity of their symbolic play when the mothers were participating. These results are identical to those obtained when the first 5 minutes of the independent play session were compared with the collaborative session. These data suggest that, although longer exposure to the toys may tend to increase the frequency of some codable play behaviors (see analysis in "Independent Play") to the level observed in the collaborative play session, play diversity does not change significantly with increased exposure. It is only during the collaborative play session that play diversity increases, suggesting that the condition effect discussed earlier is not epiphenomenal of increased familiarity with the toys.

Summary

In summary, we have found that children demonstrated greater diversity of play in collaboration with their mothers than they did when playing alone with the same toys. These changes in the child's behavior appear to be the result of the mother's active guidance of the child's play. Furthermore, play behavior is affected differentially by maternal guidance as a function of the child's age; 20-month-olds showed increases in exploratory and combinatorial play diversity whereas 28-month-olds showed an increase only in the diversity of their symbolic play.

FREQUENCY OF MATERNAL SUGGESTIONS

The number of maternal suggestions was analyzed by ANOVA using age (20 and 28 months) and play type (exploratory, combinatorial, and symbolic) as within-subjects factors.

There was a main effect of age, $F(1, 27) = 9.00$, indicating that mothers offered more suggestions to their 20-month-olds than they did to their 28-month-olds. The main effect of play type was significant, $F(2, 54) = 30.54$; tests after ANOVA revealed that mothers gave more combinatorial play suggestions than symbolic play suggestions and the fewest suggestions for exploratory play. The age × play type interaction was not significant, $F(2, 54) = 1.74$; mothers did not differ reliably in the number of suggestions they made in each play category as a function of their child's age.

To summarize, this analysis indicates that although mothers gave different numbers of suggestions in each of the three play categories considered here, there was no interaction with age. The effects of maternal guidance on the child's play discussed in the preceding analyses can not be wholly accounted for by differential behavior on the part of the mothers; mothers do not reliably alter the sorts of suggestions they give their children as a function of the child's age.

MATERNAL SUCCESS RATE

The data on maternal success rate posed some problems. Some mothers gave no suggestions in one or another play category, making the construction of a proportion of the number of suggestions to successful suggestions impossible. Consequently, no quantitative analysis of these data are presented and instead a qualitative analysis is offered to illustrate the findings.

Table 1 presents the maternal success rates by age and play category. These means are based on different numbers of subjects as mothers who did not give any suggestions were excluded (number of cases included in the calculation of each $\overline{X}$ is indicated).

More mothers allowed their children to play without guidance at 28 months than at 20 months of age. Possibly, as children become more capable of playing on their own, their mothers feel less compelled to intervene even though they have been requested to play with the child. The table also indicates that, over all, 28-month-olds responded successfully to suggestions more often than the 20-month-olds. There is an asymmetry in this increase in responsiveness, however. We saw in the preceding analysis that mothers gave different numbers of suggestions in each play category (exploratory < symbolic < combinatorial) but that there was no interaction with age. An angular transformation on the percentage scores revealed that the increase in success rate from 20 to 28 months for exploratory and combinatorial play is rather small (18% in both categories) while the rate of increase for symbolic play from 20 to 28 months is quite dramatic (112%). This could certainly account for the observed increase in symbolic play at 28 months with the mother participating. The 28-month-olds were more likely to follow suggestions for symbolic play than the 20-month-olds, even

Table 1
Mean Maternal Success Rate
in Exploratory, Combinatorial, and Symbolic Play

Play type	Age			
	20 Months		28 Months	
	%	N	%	N
Exploratory	51	16	60	5
Combinatorial	32	27	42	22
Symbolic	10	26	28	21

though the mothers provided both groups with the same number of suggestions for symbolic play.

Although the success rates for exploratory and combinatorial play are higher at 28 months than they are at 20 months, we saw in a previous analysis that, in fact, it was the 20-month-olds who demonstrated an increase in both these play categories when playing with the mothers. A number of facts will aid in the interpretation of these results. First, note that the number of mothers making suggestions in these play categories is less at 28 than at 20 months. That is, although mothers were more successful in getting their 28-month-olds to engage in combinatorial play than they were with their 20-month-olds, fewer of them tried. Further, 28-month-olds tended to initiate less combinatorial play with mothers present than they demonstrated alone when responses to the mothers' suggestions were excluded. The 20-month-olds, on the other hand, showed no difference between mother participating or not participating in combinatorial play when responses were excluded from the analysis. In other words, there is a difference in baseline for combinatorial play in the two age groups when the mother participates—20-month-olds maintain the high level of combinatorial play they demonstrated when playing alone, and 28-month-olds reduce theirs from independent play levels. An analogous argument can be used to interpret the exploratory play results.

It appears that 20-month-olds prefer to use their mothers' assistance for exploratory and combinatorial activities, whereas 28-month-olds take advantage of suggestions by their mothers for symbolic play and devote less attention to the other two play categories when she participates. Seemingly, children are selective in their use of the guidance with which they may be provided.

Figure 2 illustrates data to support this argument. The left panel shows the $\overline{X}$ number of suggestions mothers made in each category at each age. These means are based only on the number of mothers who made suggestions (i.e., the number of cases included in the calculation is the same as that used in the calculation of the success rate). The right panel shows the success rate in each

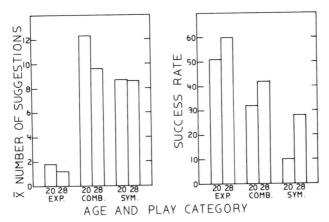

Figure 2.   Number of maternal suggestions and maternal success rate for each play type. Means are based only on the number of mothers who gave suggestions. Ages given in months.

play category. This figure indicates quite well the differential success of mothers as a function of the age of their children. This effect is particularly dramatic for symbolic play; the number of suggestions is nearly identical for the 2 age groups, but the success rates are quite different (10 versus 28%).

These data suggest that mothers *do* actively attempt to guide their children's behavior. Although they suggest more activities to the younger children, the distribution of suggestions across play categories remains fairly constant with age. The differences observed in the child's play in the collaborative session compared to the independent play session appear to stem from the selective use of mothers' guidance by the children; what was useful at 20 months of age became less so at 28 months, and what at 20 months of age was a relatively untapped resource became a highly exploited one by 28 months of age.

VERBAL DIRECTIVES

Although it is not a central issue here, there is an interesting aspect of these data that should be pointed out: the extent to which mothers relied on purely verbal directives to guide their child's play (see Table 2).

At 20 months, 43.3% of all directives were verbal only. If purely verbal directives, as well as verbal directives supplemented by a demonstration or gesture, are considered, this percentage increases to 74.6. At 28 months, 62.1% of all maternal directives used by the children were verbal only whereas 81% were verbal and verbal plus gestural. We think it is noteworthy that even children

Table 2
Mean Percentage of Maternal Directives by Category

Age	Type of directive (%)				
	Verbal (V)	Gestural (G)	Demonstration (D)	V + G	V + D
20 months	43.3	2.7	22.7	16.0	15.3
28 months	62.1	3.0	16.0	13.6	5.3

as young as these are able to make efficient use of purely verbal instruction from their mothers without the help of demonstration.

DISCUSSION

Although it may seem that we have strayed far from the intitial discussion of Piagetian and Vygotskian approaches to the construction of knowledge, we can now retrace our steps and consider these data in that context.

We have seen that the diversity of the child's play increases over independent play levels when the child plays in collaboration with the mother. More importantly, we observed that this increase in diversity was not distributed uniformly across all the play categories used here but rather was localized in only one, and the major determinant of that localization was the child's age. Mothers appeared to directly influence the children's play by providing the child with suggestions for and demonstrations of activities the child could perform, a finding corroborated by other research (e.g., Schaffer & Crook, 1979; Zukow, 1980). Mothers' presence alone did not seem sufficient to effect any change in play behavior.

This capsulized version of the results seems to point to the importance of instruction and collaboration in improving the child's performance, a conclusion with which Vygotsky would readily concur. Yet, there is another component to the story which must be considered. It is the *child* who appears to be determining the effectiveness of mother's instruction; the child allows some of mother's suggestions to pass unheeded while others are attended to and acted upon. This process does not appear to be random; it is as if the children know what they are looking for. Mothers provide their children with far more suggestions than the children ever implement in their play—it is nearly a constant flow of information. The manner in which the children pick over this flow seems to be quite systematic—they look for things that will get them a little bit farther along than they already are. This evidence speaks most directly to the issue of readiness.

SOME POINTS ON INTERPRETATION:
PROBLEMS AND ALTERNATIVES

Before continuing with the discussion, we should spend some time considering a few points regarding the interpretation of these data. It was pointed out in "Procedure" that there was a confound between the order and the location of the experimental sessions. This is problematic, to be sure, and requires that we view these results as preliminary, but analyses were presented that mitigate this problem to some extent. Specifically, the comparison of the first and third 5-minute segments of the independent play session with the collaborative play session revealed identical patterns of results. Further, the observed changes in the child's play behavior when mother participated were found to be the consequence of mother's directive behavior only and there was no general facilitative effect of her presence. Finally, the specific nature of mother's effect on different play types at different ages cannot be wholly accounted for by practice effects.

As always, there are a number of alternative interpretations of these results. For instance, older children may simply be more obedient than younger children or they may be more aware than younger children of the efficacy of instruction in facilitating the execution of tasks. However, if these factors accounted for the results we would expect to find increases of equal magnitude in the three play categories with 28-month-olds deriving more benefit than 20-month-olds (i.e., main effects but no interactions). We have seen that this is certainly not the case; children are not simply getting better as they get older. Another possibility is that some kinds of suggestions are more difficult to comprehend than others and the children followed only those suggestions that they were able to understand. We can probably assume that mothers usually intend that their children understand what they are saying; the mothers' behavior was unconstrained, so they were free to use any method they felt would be successful in assuring their children's comprehension (e.g., Schaffer, Hepburn, & Collis, in press; Wilcox & Palermo, 1982). This comprehension problem may account for some of the observed differences but by itself cannot explain the results, particularly the age × play type × condition interaction.

THE CONCEPT OF READINESS

Let us return to a consideration of the notion of readiness. In the review of the literature presented earlier we found a fairly consistent pattern of emergence and development of play behaviors despite the variation in methodology employed by researchers. Exploratory play is observed at the youngest ages and is followed by a variety of combinatorial activities; finally, children break into the domain of symbolic play. This sequence should lead us to accept the premise that the behaviors defined here as symbolic (whether considered to be truly symbolic or simply appropriate miniature object use) are more complex than exploratory or combinatorial play. The results of this study suggest that children tend to take advantage of mother's suggestions more frequently when the content of these suggestions coincides with tasks the child is currently trying to master than when these suggestions represent domains that the child has already mastered or those beyond the child's capabilities. We found that the younger children made the most extensive use of the mothers' exploratory and combinatorial suggestions and disregarded most of the suggestions for symbolic play; they may be currently mastering the skills necessary to carry out combinatorial activities and, as yet, their competence in the domain of symbolic play is too limited for them to derive any benefit from instruction. The older children, however, have mastered these combinatorial activities and have moved on to more difficult tasks; they find the mothers' guidance in symbolic play most helpful and no longer need that guidance in their combinatorial play activities. It is as if there is some threshold of ability that the child must have reached in order to make use of instructions; below or above this threshold, instruction is either ineffective or unnecessary.

The fact that these children respond differentially to their mothers' suggestions fits quite neatly with the idea that children must have reached some state of readiness in order to incorporate any new, socially constructed knowledge (in Vygotsky's terms) or for children to construct their own knowledge from the information (in Piaget's terms). There is a problem in that the only evidence for the existence of such a state of readiness is the age-dependent difference in the children's play; we are unable to characterize the nature of this state in any detail. However, there is research in other areas that converges on the notion of readiness as an explanatory principle.

A number of studies on language learning have relied on descriptions that attribute a state of readiness to the child (Corrigan, 1980; Moerk, 1980; Nelson, 1977; Nelson, Carskaddon, & Bonvillian, 1973; Slobin, 1973); children tend to imitate those grammatical forms that are just beyond their current level of performance rather than those that are far too difficult or all too familiar. More specifically, a study of language by Retherford, Schwartz, and Chapman (1981) found a pattern that is strikingly similar to the one described in this study. These investigators measured a variety of syntactic and semantic forms longitudinally in six mother–child pairs. Children were seen at $1\frac{1}{2}$ years and again 3–6 months later. The authors found that mothers, rather than matching their speech output to their child's (e.g., Snow & Ferguson, 1977), tended to be consistent over time in the frequency of use of the measured categories. It was the *children* who changed over the course of the study to become more like their mothers; children seemed to select forms from their mother's output that were most useful to them at a particular stage of the language-learning process. It appears that mothers are not necessarily (or always) fine tuning their behavior to be maximally useful to their children but, rather, present their children with a smorgasbord from which the child may select the most delectable items.

Another piece of evidence comes from an analysis of the effect of social inputs on langauge development by Bates, Bretherton, Beeghly-Smith, & McNew (1982), which suggested that a preponderance of motherese may be an indirect measure of the child's failure to comprehend; mothers may respond to cues from the child that signal a failure to comprehend by simplifying their speech to the child. An analogous argument can be made for the present data. Fewer mothers offered play suggestions at 28 months than at 20 months. It was suggested that as the child's proficiency in playing with the toys increased with age, mothers were less inclined to intervene. Mothers who provide their children with a large number of suggestions are responding to their child's limited repertoire of play activities. Support for this claim is provided by Russell (1982) in a study of maternal influence on infant symbolic play. She found, among other things, that maternal directiveness of play content was negatively related to the child's symbolic play. All this information suggests that mothers recognize the efficacy of instruction but are not particularly skilled in determining the best way to present such instruction to make it maximally useful for the child; the child seems to be the member of the dyad who shapes the course of the interaction rather than the mother.

SOME QUALITATIVE CONSIDERATIONS

A number of issues raised earlier can be considered in greater detail here; in addition, we would like to point out some qualities of the child's play that may merit some further research.

It was suggested earlier that the diversity, rather than the frequency, of the child's play may be a better measure of competence or sophistication. A number of children in this study engaged in repetitive behavior that resulted in extremely high frequency scores; their diversity scores, however, were quite low, reflecting a tendency to stick with something that works. Other researchers have made similar observations in the assessment of play skills (Shimada, Kai, & Sano, 1981; Shimada et al., 1979). Jennings, Harmon, Morgan, Gaiter, & Yarrow (1979) found that quality of play was "a better index of underlying mastery motivation" (p. 392) than was play quantity in their study of the relationship between exploratory play and cognitive functioning and persistence. However, rather than using only diversity as a measure of play quality, the best assessment may result from an analysis of play diversity as it relates to total play activity (e.g., a proportion relating diversity to frequency).

It may prove useful to investigate in greater detail the devices mothers employ in instructing their children (e.g., strategy-based versus non-strategy-based referential perspectives, as discussed by Wertsch, in press-a). Wertsch pointed out that adults employ a variety of semiotic devices when assisting children with tasks and emphasized the importance of assessing the extent to which the *child* participates in the activity. For example, two children may successfully insert a triangular block into the shape box when assisted by an adult. However, one child may have received only a verbal instruction ("Put the triangle in the hole") while the other child had the block placed in his or her hand, which was then guided to the correct hole. Clearly, the specificity of instruction required for these two children is radically different. An evaluation of mothers' strategies for instructing and guiding children from this perspective could be informative.

Related to the issue of maternal strategy differences is the apparent variability in maternal "style" during the collaborative play session. Some mothers played a very unobtrusive role during the session, merely approving their childrens' activities and only rarely offering any direction or assistance. Others, in contrast, were very enthusiastic play partners, almost to the point of intrusiveness. They quite actively guided the course of the play session and seemed reluctant to abandon an activity in which the child had clearly lost interest. Children responded differently to this directive behavior—some seemed quite willing to cooperate whereas others simply pursued their own interests and disregarded their mothers' attempts to engage them. Although individual differences of the sort described here must be considered in evaluating the outcome of any study of play, they are interesting in and of themselves because they may provide information about the manner in which the social milieu serves to structure knowledge for the child.

We saw in "Independent Play" that 20-month-olds engage in more ambiguous play than do 28-month-olds. Although 20-month-olds use mothers' instructions and demonstrations to produce what, at least superficially, appears to be symbolic activity, they may not fully understand what it is they are doing. In other words, the children may not be using the symbolic acts productively. An activity highly favored by the children, putting peg people into the toy car, serves as an excellent illustration of this point. At 20 months of age, children inserted the figures into the car without regard for the direction in which the figures were "looking," and often the children did not "drive" the car after filling it. This sort of activity was coded as ambiguous play because the child's intention was uncertain. In contrast, at 28 months most children were extremely careful when placing figures in the car to ensure that they were facing forward. The children often drove the car across the floor with appropriate sound effects. Occasionally, children stopped pushing the car momentarily to adjust a driver whose gaze had strayed from the road ahead. Clearly these older children were treating the figures as "people in a car" and so the activity was coded as symbolic rather than ambiguous. It might be useful to analyze these qualitative aspects of the child's play in order to assess understanding more accurately. It is certainly possible for the child to give the impression that he or she has mastered a skill when, in fact, the analysis and understanding of its meaning is far from complete.

SUMMARY

Vygotsky emphasized the importance of instruction in his theory of development; this study demonstrates that collaborative play in which instruction is provided is effective in altering the kind of play behaviors children will demonstrate. This instruction is not uniformly successful, however; only when it parallels the tasks the child is currently mastering does it appear to have any effect. The abilities that are just beginning to emerge in the child's behavior are the ones Vygotsky suggested were most sensitive to instruction—those in the zone of proximal development. The age-dependent differences in the child's use of maternal instruction observed in this study suggest that children are selecting mothers' insructions that will prove most beneficial in their efforts to master new skills.

There are two points of particular importance that should be emphasized. The first is that mothers *do* instruct their children and suggest a variety of activities to them. Nonetheless, mothers do not seem to be as sensitive to their child's abilities as some investigators would suggest (e.g., Schaffer & Crook, 1979) and are not fine tuning their instruction to match their child's level of skill. Rather, they appear to recognize the value of instruction but leave the selectivity to the child. Secondly, it is the child who is "in charge" in the play setting and mothers appear to accept this arrangement. The child determines which of mother's suggestions will be incorporated into play activity and which will be ignored. To state it strongly, the child seems to have a goal in mind and accepts assistance only in service of this goal.

The results of this study are not incompatible with Piagetian theory, even though we have discussed these data as they support the Vygotskian position. As we pointed out in the Introduction, these two approaches to development share much theoretical ground. Surely some of the skills the child demonstrates are the consequence of the child's own constructive processes rather than a manifestation of internalized, socially constructed knowledge. We have suggested that the child actively selects from the environment the things that are needed rather than internalizing the structure created in the social context;

that is, the process is *child-driven*. The child does not require explicit instruction in order to master all new activities or solve all new problems; he or she is quite a competent hypothesis tester, as the literature on language acquisition makes clear. It is important, nevertheless, to recognize the role that instruction does play in the child's development, a role Piaget did not emphasize in his work. The child is a part of the social world and this context can provide the child with a wealth of information. We are, above all else, social creatures and surely great use has been made of this fact phylogenetically for the cultural transmission of knowledge (Bonner, 1974).

Information in the environment that is relevant to the task the child is mastering will be more closely monitored than irrelevant information. This, of course, implies that the child has some knowledge and/or has made some analysis of the task in question, allowing the recognition of relevant information. It is a process that requires a reciprocity between the child's own constructive processes and information from the social world in the form of instruction or assistance (whether or not it is intended as such). This study illustrates the existence of such a reciprocal process. Mothers are active and willing teachers of their children but their strategy appears to be the provision of wide-ranging guidance rather than tuning in to the level of their child's ability. Children, in the course of mastering any of a variety of activities, rely simultaneously on their own cognitive skills and constructive processes as well as on any assistance that may come their way from the architects in the social world.

ACKNOWLEDGMENTS

We would like to acknowledge the help of Marjorie Beeghly, Andrew Garrison, Sandra McNew, Cecilia Shore, and Carol Williamson, who assisted in the data collection and transcription. We also thank the mothers and children in this study who gave so generously of their time.

A portion of this chapter was submitted by the senior author to the University of Colorado, Boulder, in partial fulfillment of the requirements for the master's degree. She would like to express her gratitude to David Chiszar and to her thesis committee, Elizabeth Bates, Inge Bretherton, and Robert Harmon, for support throughout this enterprise.

REFERENCES

Bates, E. Bretherton, I., Beeghly-Smith, M., & McNew, S. *Social bases of language development: A reassessment.* In H. W. Reese & L. P. Lipsett (Eds.), *Advances in child development and behavior* (Vol. 16). New York: Academic Press, 1982.
Bates, E., Bretherton, I., Shore, C., & McNew, S. Names, gestures and objects: The role of context

in the emergence of symbols. In K. Nelson (Ed.), *Children's Language* (Vol. IV). Hillsdale, NJ: Erlbaum, in press.

Belsky, J., & Hrncir, E. *Assessing performance, competence and motivation in infant play: An exploratory study in construct validation.* Paper presented at the biennial meeting of The Society for Research in Child Development, Boston, April 1981.

Bonner, J. *On development: The biology of form.* Cambridge, MA: Harvard University Press, 1974.

Bretherton, I., McNew, S., Snyder, L., & Bates, E. Individual differences at 20 months: Analytic and holistic strategies in language acquistion. *Journal of Child Language*, 1983, *10*(2). 293-313.

Brown, A. Learning and development: The problems of compatibility, access and induction. *Human Development*, 1982, *25*, 89-115.

Case, R., & Khanna, F. The missing links: Stages in children's progression from sensorimotor to logical thought. In W. Fisher (Ed.), *New directions for child development.* Manuscript in preparation.

Cole, M., Hood, L., & McDermott, R. P. (1979). *Ecological niche picking.* Unpublished manuscript available from the author, Department of Psychology, University of California, San Diego. 1979.

Corrigan, R. Use of repetition to facilitate spontaneous language acquisition. *Journal of Psycholinguistic Research*, 1980, *9*(3), 231-240.

Dunn, J., & Wooding, C. Play in the home and its implications for learning. In B. Tizard & D. Harvey (Eds.), *Biology of play.* Philadelphia: Lippincott, 1977.

Fagen, J. *Animal play behavior.* New York: Oxford University Press, 1981.

Fein, G. A transformational analysis of pretending. *Developmental Psychology*, 1975, *11*(3), 291-296.

Fein, G., & Apfel, N. Some preliminary observations on knowing and pretending. In M. Smith & M. B. Franklin (Eds.), *Symbolic functioning in childhood.* Hillsdale, NJ: Erlbaum, 1979.

Fenson, L., Kagan, J., Kearsley, R., & Zelazo, P. The developmental progression of manipulative play in the first two years. *Child Development*, 1976, *47*, 232-236.

Fenson, L., & Ramsey D. Decentration and integration of the child's play in the second year. *Child Development*, 1980, *51*, 171-178. (Fenson chapter this volume)

Fisher, K. A theory of cognitive development: The control and construction of hierarchies of skills. *Psychological Review*, 1980, *87*(6), 477-531.

Franklin, M. Non-verbal representation in young children: A cognitive perspective. *Young Children*, 1983, *29*, 33-53.

Jeffree, D., & McConkey, R. An observation scheme for recording children's imaginative doll play. *Journal of Child Psychology and Psychiatry*, 1976, *17*, 189-197.

Jennings, K., Harmon, R., Morgan, G., Gaiter, J., & Yarrow, L. Exploratory play as an index of mastery motivation: Relationships to persistance, cognitive functioning and environmental measures. *Developmental Psychology*, 1979, *15*(4), 386-394.

Langer, J. *The origins of logic.* New York: Academic Press, 1980.

Largo, R., & Howard J. Developmental progression in play behavior in children between 9 and 30 months. I: Spontaneous play and imitation. *Developmental Medicine and Child Neurology*, 1979, *21*, 299-310.

Lezine, I. The transition from sensorimotor to earliest symbolic function in early development. In *Early development* (Vol. 51). Research Publication A.R.N.M.D., Baltimore: Williams & Wilkins, 1973.

Lowe, M. Trends in the development of representational play in infants from one to three years—An observational study. *Journal of Child Psychology and Psychiatry*, 16, 1975, 33-47.

Lowe, M., & Costello, A. *Manual for the symbolic play test* (Experimental edition). London: NFER Publishing Co., 1976.

McCune-Nicolich, L. *A manual for analyzing free play.* Unpublished manuscript, available from the author, Department of Education, Douglass College, Rutgers University, 1980.

McCune-Nicolich, L. Toward symbolic functioning: Structure of early pretend games and potential parallels with language. *Child Development*, 1981, *52*, 785-797.

Moerk, E. Relationships between prenatal input frequencies and children's language acquisition: A re-analysis of Brown's data. *Journal of Child Language*, 1980, *7*, 105–118.

Nelson, K. Facilitating children's syntax acquisition. *Developmental Psychology*, 1977, *13*(2), 105–118.

Nelson, K., Carskaddon, G., & Bonvillian, J. Syntax acquisition: Impact of experimental variation in adult verbal interaction with the child. *Child Development*, 1973, *44*, 497–504.

Nicolich, L. Beyond sensorimotor intelligence: Assessment of symbolic maturity through analysis of pretend play. *Merril-Palmer Quarterly*, 1977, *23*(2), 89–101.

Nicolich, L. *Symbolic play: Sequences of development and methods of assessment.* Paper presented at the Southwestern Regional Meeting of The Society for Research in Child Development, Atlanta, 1978.

Overton, W., & Jackson, J. The representation of imagined objects in action sequences: A developmental study. *Child Development*, 1973, *44*, 309–314.

Piaget, J. *Play, dreams and imitation in childhood.* New York: Norton, 1962.

Retherford, K., Schwartz, B., & Chapman, R. Semantic roles and residual grammatical categories in mother and child speech: Who turns into whom? *Journal of Child Language*, 1981, *8*, 583–608.

Russell, C. *Maternal influence on infant symbolic play.* Paper presented at the International Conference on Infant Studies, Austin, March 1982.

Schaffer, H., & Crook, C. Maternal control techniques in a directed play situation. *Child Development* 1979, *50*, 989–996.

Schaffer, H., Hepburn, A., & Collins G. Verbal and non-verbal aspects of mother's directives. *Journal of Child Language*, in press.

Shimada, S., Kai, Y., & Sano, R. *Development of symbolic play in late infancy* (RIEEC Research Bulletin RRB-17). Koganei, Tokyo: Tokyo Gakugei University, 1981.

Shimada, S., Sano, R., & Peng, F. *A longitudinal study of symbolic play in the second year of life* (RIEEC Research Bulletin, RRB-12). Tokyo: Toyko Gakugei University.

Siegel, S. *Non-parametric statistics.* New York: McGraw-Hill, 1956.

Sinclair, H. The transition from sensory motor behavior to symbolic activity. *Interchange*, 1970, *1*, 119–126.

Slobin, D. Studies of imitation and comprehension. In C. A. Ferguson & D. I. Slobin (Eds.), *Studies of child language development.* New York: Holt, Rinehart & Winston, 1973.

Snow, C., & Ferguson, C. *Talking to children.* Cambridge: Cambridge University Press, 1977.

Sugarman, S. *Scheme, order and outcome.* Unpublished doctoral dissertation, University of California, Berkeley, 1979.

Vygotsky, L. S. *Mind in society* (M. Cole, V. John-Steiner, S. Scribner, & E. Souberman, Eds.). Boston: Harvard University Press, 1978.

Vygotsky, L. S. *Thought and language* (E. Hanfmann & C. Vakar, Eds. and trans.). Cambridge, MA: MIT Press, 1962.

Watson, N., & Fischer, K. A developmental sequence of agent use in late infancy. *Child Development*, 1977, *48*, 828–836.

Wertsch, J. Adult- child interaction as a source of self-regulation in children. In S. R. Yussen (Ed.), *The development of reflection.* New York: Academic Press, in press. (a)

Wertsch, J. The role of semiosis in L. S. Vygotsky's theory of human cognition. In B. Bain (Ed.), *The sociogenesis of language and human conduct.* New York: Plenum, 1983.

Wilcox, S., & Palermo, D. Children's use of lexical and non-lexical information in responding to commands. *Journal of Child Language*, 1982, *9*, 139–150.

Zelazo, P., & Kearsley, R. The emergence of functional play in infants: Evidence for a major cognitive transition. *Journal of Applied Developmental Psychology*, 1980, *1*, 95–117.

Zukow, P. *A microanalytic study of the role of caregiver in the relationship between symbolic play and language acquisition during the one-word stage.* Unpublished doctoral dissertation, University of California, Los Angeles, 1980.

Index